YOU GOT TO DO WHAT YOU GOT TO DO

My Experience As A Caregiver Taking Care Of My Parents For Over Twenty Years

By James Colozzo

Table Of Contents

PREFACE-5
Chapter 1-INTRODUCTION-9
Chapter 2-FAMILY-12
Chapter 3-HISTORY-15
Chapter 4-DECISION TO BE A CAREGIVER-17
Chapter 5-BEING A CAREGIVER-20
Chapter 6-WHAT OTHERS DO OR HAVE DONE-26
Chapter 7-RESPONSIBILITY OF BEING A CAREGIVER-30
Chapter 8-LAWS AND BEING A CAREGIVER-35
Chapter 9-MEDICARE AND INSURANCE-41
Chapter 10-GOVERNMENT AND BEING A CAREGIVER-52
Chapter 11-HEALTH CONDITIONS AND BEING A CAREGIVER-56
Chapter 12-MEDICAL PROCEDURES, TESTS AND DIAGNOSIS-72
Chapter 13-FIRST TIME DOING PROCEDURES-80
Chapter 14-CAREGIVING ROUTINES AND PROCEDURES-90
Chapter 15-ADVICE AND BEING A CAREGIVER-96
Chapter 16-RELIGION AND FAITH-105
Chapter 17-ATTITUDES AND BEING A CAREGIVER-108
Chapter 18-HYGIENE AND BEING A CAREGIVER-114
Chapter 19-APPETITE AND FOOD WHILE BEING A CAREGIVER-125
Chapter 20-MEDICATIONS AND BEING A CAREGIVER-131
Chapter 21-BODILY FUNCTIONS AND BEING A CAREGIVER-137
Chapter 22-STAYING FOCUSED AND KEEPING THE MIND SHARP-148
Chapter 23-POSITIVE OUTLOOK AND BEING A CAREGIVER-152
Chapter 24-ACTIVITIES AND BEING A CAREGIVER-157
Chapter 25-CHORES AND BEING A CAREGIVER-167
Chapter 26-THEIR LOSS OF INDEPENDENCE-173
Chapter 27-MENTAL STATE AND BEING A CAREGIVER-182
Chapter 28-EMBARRASSMENT AND BEING A CAREGIVER-198
Chapter 29-SUPPLIES USED WHILE BEING A CAREGIVER-203
Chapter 30-EQUIPMENT USED WHILE BEING A CAREGIVER-207
Chapter 31-TECHNOLOGY AND BEING A CAREGIVER-215
Chapter 32-LIFTING AND BEING A CAREGIVER-220
Chapter 33-TRANSPORTATION AND BEING A CAREGIVER-225
Chapter 34-BEING PREPARED AS A CAREGIVER-238
Chapter 35-HEALTH RISKS AND BEING A CAREGIVER-250
Chapter 36-PRECAUTIONS WHILE BEING A CAREGIVER-255
Chapter 37-YOUR INJURIES WHILE BEING A CAREGIVER-262
Chapter 38-SAFETY AND BEING A CAREGIVER-267
Chapter 39-YOUR HOME AND BEING A CAREGIVER-271

Table Of Contents

Chapter 40-CONCERNS AND BEING A CAREGIVER-279

Chapter 41-WHAT TO WATCH FOR WHILE BEING A CAREGIVER-288

Chapter 42-TAKING RISKS WHILE BEING A CAREGIVER-291

Chapter 43-CHALLENGES AND BEING A CAREGIVER-297

Chapter 44-FAMILY VISITS AND BEING A CAREGIVER-309

Chapter 45-DEALING WITH FAMILY AND FRIENDS WHILE BEING A CAREGIVER-316

Chapter 46-DOCUMENTATION AND BEING A CAREGIVER-334

Chapter 47-ASSISTANCE AND BEING A CAREGIVER-344

Chapter 48-PLANNING AND BEING A CAREGIVER-349

Chapter 49-BURDEN OF BEING A CAREGIVER-359

Chapter 50-YOUR LIFE AND BEING A CAREGIVER-367

Chapter 51-YOUR HABITS AND ROUTINES WHILE BEING A CAREGIVER-378

Chapter 52-NO SUPPORT WHILE BEING A CAREGIVER-391

Chapter 53-FINANCIAL COST OF BEING A CAREGIVER-395

Chapter 54-WHAT YOU LEARN BEING A CAREGIVER-401

Chapter 55-RESPECT AND BEING A CAREGIVER-407

Chapter 56-CRITICISM AND COMPLAINTS-412

Chapter 57-OPINIONS ABOUT THE JOB YOU ARE DOING-424

Chapter 58-ADVICE TO OTHERS-430

Chapter 59-OBSERVING OTHERS AFTER BEING A CAREGIVER-441

Chapter 60-DOCTORS AND BEING A CAREGIVER-449

Chapter 61-HOME HEALTH AND BEING A CAREGIVER-459

Chapter 62-DEALING WITH MEDICAL FACILITIES AND PROFESSIONALS-463

Chapter 63-WOUND CARE AND BEING A CAREGIVER-478

Chapter 64-WHEN THE END COMES-482

Chapter 65-AFTER THE FUNERAL-493

Chapter 66-MY LIFE WAS CHANGED BEING A CAREGIVER-501

Chapter 67-WHAT YOU GIVE UP BEING A CAREGIVER-504

Chapter 68-WHAT YOU LOSE FINANCIALLY BEING A CAREGIVER-525

Chapter 69-PUTTING YOUR LIFE BACK TOGETHER-532

Chapter 70-MOVING ON-548

Chapter 71-THANKLESS BUT REWARDING JOB-554

Chapter 72-KEPT DIGNITY AND PROMISES-562

PREFACE

A lot of people have had to make the decision to take care of one or both parents. I made the decision to take care of my mom and dad. This was a life changing decision and it forced me to do things that I thought I would never or could do. My parents became the child and I became the adult.

My father became ill first with a very aggressive disease. It was a learning and terrifying experience at the same time. His fight for life lasted about two years and he passed away in 1995.

After my father died I lived with my mother because she could not live by herself. She had curvature of the spine and was very unstable on her feet. She needed to use a wheelchair whenever she went out and was on pain medication. I would take her to wherever she wanted to go, take care of the house and make all the meals. Unfortunately in 1999 my mother woke up and said she could not move her legs or stand up. On that day my life changed forever. She could no longer be left alone and needed twenty-four hour care. This lasted until her death in 2013. Eighteen years of my life was spent taking care of my mother and almost fourteen of those years were twenty-four hours a day.

During this time we went through hundreds of doctors visits, multiple medical procedures and hospital stays. We also relocated to another part of the state, switched doctors and medical facilities. There were fun times, bad times and tragedy but we endured through it all. I was the caregiver and she was my mom, therefore she was my responsibility and it was my job to take care of her. We worked together and she trusted me so we were able to work through it all. I believe she had a good quality of life and enjoyed herself until the end. I did the best job I could and I feel that contributed to her long life. It was hard work and was very trying at times but I got through it.

This book is not intended to be a how-to manual. It can't be because everyone's situation is different. It is however the story of how I handled the situation. Some of the so-called experts will say this is all wrong and some will say it is right, it doesn't matter, I did what was best for her health, quality of life and situation. Many people will give advice and say what is best, unfortunately they are not in your shoes. It is always good to listen to what they say but you need to do what is best for your situation. That's what I did and my mom lasted many years when a lot of people thought she was finished. This is my story and I hope it will be useful to you in your own situation.

Just for the record I am not a medical professional or claim to be. I have no formal education on the subject and I am not trying to give any medical advice of any kind. I am an individual who made the decision to take care of my parents. I took care of both my parents for a period of over twenty years and I did so mostly by myself. I was given advice by medical professionals in the way I should care for them and I also learned by trial and error other ways to care for them depending on the situation we faced.

This book is a collection of those situations, procedures and techniques. It is also a narrative of how I handled different situations while I was taking care of my parents. It was a life changing experience that has affected me forever. This is the story of how my life changed and how my future was affected. This book is not meant to be a guide of any kind because every person and situation is different. It is the story of how I handled certain situations during the twenty plus years I took care of my dad and mom.

If you are planning on taking care of a parent get as much professional advice as possible before you take on this responsibly. It is a life changing decision that can last many years. Being a caregiver is an on going learning experience and the education does not stop until you are no longer caring for your parent.

As you read this book you will quickly learn that I am not a professional writer. I'm sure there are a lot of grammar and punctuation mistakes but I have tried to do my best in the writing of this book. I don't have access to editors, literary agents or even proofreaders. I have shown this manuscript to several individuals who gave me their opinions and made corrections. I have done my best to follow their advice and incorporate their corrections to help the book flow more smoothly and make it easier to read.

I was never good in writing or English classes and this is my attempt at being an author. I have written this book in the style of my personal observations and actions. I tell stories of what I have done and what I have seen others do. I give accounts of what people have told me and what suggestions they gave when I was taking care of my parents.

I have included several topics that I had to deal with during the time I took care of my dad and mom. I tried to add as much detail without repeating myself. This is a detailed and comprehensive look at what it took for me to become the caregiver to my dad and mom. It also shows my deficiencies as a writer in the way I describe the story and conditions. I hope you are able to read and understand what I am trying to say and describe.

I didn't start writing this book until 2014. I started taking care of my father in 1993 and he passed away in 1995. I started taking care of my mom part time right after he died. I started taking care of my mom full time in 1999 till she died in 2013.

Over that time there were many situations, conditions, diagnosis and routines that we had to deal with. I have tried to remember as many as I could over that time period. Most of the stories recall what I did in certain situations and how I handled different topics and routines. My memory is still good so I have been able to recall quite a few events and situations.

It might have been better to keep a daily diary of what happened while I was taking care of my parents but I never thought of it and did not have the time. This is the next best thing because it recalls all that was necessary and what needed to be done while I was caring for my parents. I never had any idea how much was involved or how it would take over my entire life.

This is a first hand account on how I took care of my dad and mom. I was involved in everything that was required to care for them. If it needed to be done, I was the one that did it for them. I was their voice and ears in many situations and had to deal with many professionals while I was caring for my parents.

I hope that as you read this book you can get an understanding of what it is like to take care of a parent. Most people only think of the daily routines like bathing and eating. This book recalls that there is a lot more to being a caregiver than just feeding your parent dinner. It also tells the story of how much my life was affected and changed forever after I made the decision to take care of my parents. Most authors don't include the aftermath and what happens to your life after you no longer have to care for your parents. For me it has been extremely difficult and I am still trying to put my life back together.

Chapter 1

INTRODUCTION

In the late nineteen eighties I made the decision to take care of my mom and dad when they got ill. I have two older sisters but they had to deal with their own families and careers. I started a small business in 1984 and that consumed a lot of time and effort therefore I never married. I was still living at home and being my own boss meant I was in a good position to leave work to help my mom and dad. I could go to the supermarket, take them to the doctors and prepare meals. I never thought how this would affect my business. My sisters also helped and sacrificed a lot during those years. I knew they would not be able to help as much when our mom and dad got real sick because they needed to take care of their family's.

My father was diagnosed with asbestosis in 1974. He was a pipe fitter for the Navy at the Long Beach Naval Shipyard. After he was sent to many specialists and expert physicians, the consensus was that he had a diminished lung capacity and he had about five years to live. He listened to his physicians, did the exercises they recommended and refused to let the disease get the best of him. In 1993 he was diagnosed with bladder cancer and that was treated by surgery. Later that same year he was diagnosed with diabetes and required insulin shots. My mom and I learned how to give him insulin shots and how to recognize the effects of high and low sugar. With the family's help he lasted until 1995. During that time he had many stays in the hospital and countless outpatient procedures and exams. He pushed to the end, but in November of 1994 things started to change and he needed oxygen all the time. He started to spit up blood and after many tests he was diagnosed with lung cancer. Forgetfulness and no strength started to become a big issue. In January 1995 he was diagnosed with throat cancer. It was recommended that he start radiation treatments and my dad followed the doctor recommendations. His attitude was always strong. The medical technicians always talked about his good spirits and how he was always concerned with "how they were doing." He continued to get worse and blood work showed there was still a major problem. In March we learned he had a brain tumor. The lung cancer metastasized from the lungs to the throat and then to the brain. This news destroyed his attitude. We tried to keep his spirits up and he would smile, but he knew what was going on and what was happening. In April he said he didn't feel good and couldn't get out of bed. I asked him if he wanted to go to the hospital. He told me he wanted to stay home. My mom started crying and getting nervous. He looked at her and then told me to take him to the hospital. As we entered the ambulance he told me that he would not be coming back. He lasted two weeks in the hospital, in and out of consciousness. He passed away Easter Sunday morning.

After my father died my business was done. I tried to keep it going but too much time was spent taking care of my dad and I closed the business in 1996. After this I tried to do a lot of free lance work to pay the bills.

My mom and dad were close and many thought she would die soon after. Her brother, my uncle, passed away three months after his wife, my aunt. My mom had a strong will to live and she showed it.

My mom had one brother and three sisters. She was the third child and was always considered the weakest because she was diagnosed with a bad heart when she was little. In the late seventies she was diagnosed with scoliosis and severe curvature of the spine, which caused her to be in severe pain. I still blame the City of Anaheim because in 1976 the Freedom Train came to the city stadium for the country's Bicentennial. They forced people to wait in a long line and go through a vendors village before you could get to the Freedom Train exhibit. Once you got to the train, there was no wait and the tour lasted about twenty minutes.The city forced us to stand in the heat for eight hours because there were no benches to sit. After that she was always in pain and could not walk long distances. Whenever we went out she needed a wheelchair to get around. After many visits to doctors and chiropractors, they all gave up and said nothing could be done except pain medication. She went through a list of medications that kept the pain under some control.

In 1993 she found a lump on her breast and after a biopsy is was diagnosed as malignant. She had a mastectomy and the cancer was removed. She had a few reoccurrences in later years but they were treated and she became a breast cancer survivor three times.

Her spinal pain was still a major issue and in 1998 she was prescribed a narcotic pain medication, Hydromorphone. This worked for about two years and then the pain started to increase. Our doctor recommended a pain clinic in the hope that they could control the intensity of the pain. This helped for about two days after the injection and then wore off and she would be in extreme pain once again. These injections could only be performed for a short period of time so my mom was put back on increasing dosages of Hydromorphone to try to control the pain. We stopped the visits to the pain clinic because the injections only controlled the pain for a short time and it was not worth the effort, time or stress that it put on my mom.

We kept moving along and were surviving, then in September 1999 she yelled and told me she could not get out of bed. There was no strength in her legs. She could not lift herself off the bed or put any weight on her feet. On that day my life changed forever.

In the pages that follow I focus more on being the caregiver to my mom because that took the most work and consumed my everyday life. This is the story of how I handled the situation. I did what was best for my mom's health and her quality of life. Many people gave advice and told me what was best for my situation. Unfortunately they were not in my shoes and had no clue what was best for my mom or myself. I always listened to what they had to say, but I did what was best for our situation. That's why, I believe, my mom lasted many years when a lot of people thought she would die. This is my story and I hope it will be useful to you in your own situation.

Chapter 2
FAMILY

I grew up in a close family. We also had cousins that lived about a half hour away and they were like brother and sister. We did the typical things that families have done for years, we had picnics, went to the beach and took drives in the country. The other thing we did as a family a lot, was eat. Hey we were Italian, food was our middle name.

Holidays were always big events and a lot of work. New Year's Day rotated from one relative to another, Easter was at our aunts house in Lynwood, Thanksgiving was at another aunts house in Fullerton and we had Christmas. Mom and dad would prepare for the Christmas dinner weeks in advance. Christmas Eve they would be making ravioli's for the big meal the next day. A lot of food and family arguments meant a good holiday.

We had cousins that lived out of state and they would visit once a year and that always meant another big dinner. That was always a fun time because living in Southern California we were fortunate to be able to go to Disneyland and Knott's Berry Farm. We were also able to go to baseball games. My mom was a real big baseball fan. Being from Rhode Island you would think she was a Boston Red Sox fan but she wasn't. I think she was the only one in her home town that liked the New York Yankees. When the family moved to California she didn't follow much baseball. When the Dodgers came to Los Angeles it didn't mean much. Then the California Angels came into play. She was a Gene Autry fan and she also liked his baseball team. She saw them play at Wrigley Field in Los Angeles and the Colosseum. When they moved to Anaheim we went to the games as often as we could afford the tickets. In fact, the third base coach for the Angels in the 1960s was a high school classmate of my mom and her sisters. He got us tickets for a lot of games. Back then a big crowd was five thousand fans because they didn't win too often. She listened and watched baseball whenever it was on the radio or television. This was something she did quite often in her later years.

Our house was small, it was a little over six hundred square feet and it was too small for a family of five. My folks decided it was time to enlarge the house. My dad worked in construction and maintenance at the Quonset Point Naval Air Station and also in California before the Naval shipyard. His experience made him an owner builder and he taught me how to do construction. He told me that he wanted me to learn how to build a house so in the future I could build my own if I wanted too. When the city building inspector came to the house for one of the inspections he told my dad that he was over building. My dad's response was, "Of course I am, I'm living in it." It was a great experience but it took a toll on my father. It was a long and hard process. He worked five days at the shipyard and evenings we would work on the house. Saturdays and Sundays we were always working on the house and he was exhausted. He was in his fifties and it was hard for him to do what he did when he was young. The entire family helped building the addition to the house. When it was finished we went from a six hundred square foot house with a single car garage to a one thousand three hundred square foot house with an oversize two car garage. It was beautiful.

A few years after the house was finished my sisters got married and moved out. Then the grandchildren came. My oldest sister had a son and my second sister had two daughters and a son. The four grandchildren brought great joy to my parents. They would light up every time they were around and my folks always enjoyed watching them. As time went on they grew up and the two girls got married and the oldest grand daughter had a son and daughter. Now they were born after my father passed away so my mom was the one that knew the great grandchildren. In fact one of the last pictures of my mom shows her with her daughter, grand daughter and great grand daughter, four generations. Along with all this happiness came a great tragedy. My nephew, and my mom's second grandson was diagnosed with PTSD, (Post Traumatic Stress Disorder). He was in the Air Force and served two tours during the second Iraq War and was also a reserve Los Angeles County Deputy Sheriff. He was looking forward to becoming a full time deputy. One night the stress of life got to him and he committed suicide. I got the phone call about three o'clock in the morning from my hysteric sister and then I woke my ninety year old mother and told her that her grandson took his own life. It was devastating for her and all of us.

My family lived in Lynwood house for fifty years. The neighborhood had its ups and downs and we decided to move in 2008. My mom was eighty-eight years old and that was a major step. We both agreed on the move and we decided to move to the mountain community of Tehachapi, California. My oldest sister and her husband bought a house there so they could retire. We bought a house a few blocks away so my sister could help with my mom. It was a good idea and the help was appreciated.

Tehachapi was the location of many fun times especially when the grand children and great grandchildren spent the weekend. My little nephew liked trains and Tehachapi was a train town so he really enjoyed his visits. It was also the location of my mom's 90th birthday party. Her brother and sisters died a few years earlier so she was the last of her family and was also the one that lived the longest. We lived in Tehachapi until my mom passed away in 2013.

After she passed away I had to put the house up for sale because I could no longer afford the monthly payments. It took almost a year to sell because of the housing slump. Fortunately I was able to sell the house and started to try to move on with my life.

Chapter 3
HISTORY

My mother was born in 1920 in Rhode Island. She grew up in the Italian section of Warwick called Natick. All through her life she had medical issues. When she was little she was diagnosed with a bad heart valve. As a sign of the times she was also afraid to go to the doctors. To this day we never knew why, and we never will. Later in life she was diagnosed with high blood pressure.

My father grew up in the same area and they got married in 1948. He worked at the Quonset Point Naval Air Station in Davisville. Her brother and sisters moved to California a few years earlier so she had no immediate family locally. My oldest sister was born in 1951. They moved to Lynwood, California in 1952 so my mother could be close to her family and my other sister was born in 1952. My father had various jobs in those years and finally landed a job at the Long Beach Naval Shipyard in 1961. I showed up a few months later in 1961. We were part of a typical 1950s and 60's family. Dad worked and mom stayed at home. We would walk to the stores and the park because she never learned to drive. The story goes that she quit learning to drive when they put the shift on the steering column. They put us through Catholic school and gave us a very good childhood.

My sisters grew up to have careers and families of their own. I on the other hand decided to start a business after I worked for a major supermarket chain. During these years my mother and father faced many medical obstacles. My father survived ptomaine poisoning, chemicals in his eyes, a slipped back disc and other minor incidents. He also had some hearing loss and diminished shoulder function due to the work at the shipyard. He was diagnosed with fibrosis, mesothelioma, chemical poisoning and asbestosis, which ultimately lead to his death. My mother was also diagnosed with asbestosis in one lung. She was exposed by washing my father's clothes when he came home from work. In fact my sisters and I were also exposed to the asbestos particles on his clothes. My mother later was diagnosed with breast cancer and had a mastectomy. The cancer reoccured twice, she was put on medication and listened to the oncologists orders. All three times she beat it and became a breast cancer survivor.

Here is a list of my mom's medical conditions and procedures. Congestive Heart Failure; Valvular Heart Disease; Borderline Glaucoma; Traces of Asbestosis; Gall Stones and Appendix Removed; Breast Cancer Diagnosed in 1993; Right Mastectomy in 1993; Severe Scoliosis, Curvature of the Spine and Arthritis; Cataract Surgery Both Eyes in 1999; Spinal Decompression of #3 and #5 Vertebrae in 2001; Cancerous Tumor Removed Right Axillary in 2002; Cancer Reoccurred Right Axillary in 2009; Percutaneous Transluminal Angioplasty on lower right leg in 2008; Surgery to remove Colon Obstruction and Scar Tissue in 2008.

Chapter 4
DECISION TO BE A CAREGIVER
Faith And Family

I grew up in a Catholic home and we were involved with our church. My parents put my sisters and I through Catholic school for grades one through twelve. I was always active in church and school activities and continued being involved during adulthood. I was involved in the operation of our parish and also at my former high school. I was the president of the high school alumni association and a member of the school's board of directors. I did this for many years and enjoyed it very much because we did a lot of good for the school. I also made some close friends that are still with me today.

I was always taught that faith and family were the most important parts of life. I truly believe this and that is why I took care of my parents. They gave me life and took care of me all the years that I was growing up and I think they did a very good job. I never had complaints about my life growing up and they did everything that they could in making me a better person. When they needed my help it was my decision and pleasure to take care of them. I did not have a family of my own so it was my duty to care for them. My sisters had families of their own and were doing wonderful jobs in raising their children. They did not have the time or resources to take care of our dad and mom. It was my job and I jumped at the chance.

I was following what I had been taught through my entire life. My parents took care of me, now it was time to take care of my parents. I made the decision and still stand by it today.

Right From Wrong

I was always taught right from wrong and I always did my best to do right. You don't have to be religious to know right from wrong all you need to have is common sense. In the decision to take care of my parents it was more along the line of how I would want to be treated if I was in their position. So for me it was easy to decided because it was the right thing to do.

There is no great theological debate needed if you want to take care of your parents. There is no right religion or faith to help you make that decision. You have to do what is in your heart and you have to feel comfortable with your decision. Some people have a hard time trying to care for themselves and they are actually terrified at the thought of taking care of someone else. Are they wrong for that decision, I say no because they know their limits. Some have trouble taking care of themselves but do wonderful things when they take care of someone else. There are many examples of both sides so it basically comes down to just you.

You need to know what is required to take care of your parents and you have to accept the fact that you are responsible for their care and well being. I made that decision many years ago and never had any regrets. If you are willing to do what is required and make the commitment to care for them, how can you be wrong?

How I Was Raised-Do What Was Right

I was raised and taught to help the family as best as I could. My dad reinforced this issue during his last few days when he told me to watch out for my mother and sisters because they were all I had. He said, "It's up to you now, take care of them." Even though he was old school he meant for us to stick together and help each other. We had talked before about how I would take care of my mom in case anything happened to him. He always thought that he would go first because of his condition and he was right. I told him, "Don't worry, I'll take care of mom," and I did. I tried my best to help my sisters and they did the same for me. They had their own families, which meant their own challenges so I just stayed in the background because I didn't want to interfere. The interesting part was after my mom passed away it was my sisters that came to my aid and helped me get along. He must have had the same talk with them.

18

I did what was right and I never had any regrets. A lot of people criticized me for my decision to care for my parents but I never listened to them. I made a commitment to my folks and followed through with it. Yes, it was stressful and difficult but it was right. I did sacrifice a large part of my life, lost almost everything I had and am still having a difficult time in rebuilding my life but I still say it was right. My mom lived a long time after a lot of people thought she would give up and waste away. She lasted the longest of anyone in her family and went strong all the way to the end. She was an inspiration to the younger generations because of her will and spirit. It was right to help her and keep her going. We had many challenges and for the most part we overcame every one of them. I never could have turned my back on her and left her alone in a care facility. She never would have survived in a facility or under the care of someone else. She wanted to be around her family and I was the part of the family that took care of her. I did what was right and I never had any regrets.

Chapter 5
BEING A CAREGIVER
Not An Expert

Just for the record, I am not an expert in any of the areas that I will talk about in this book. I am not a professional but just a normal person that made the decision to take care of my parents. I asked a lot of questions and received answers from many professionals and I learned from what they told me.

In every situation I learned by watching what the professionals would do in caring for my parents. Sometimes I was taught by nurses, such as in the case of giving my father his insulin shots. I also learned how to change his urostomy pouch and flange with the help of nurses. I learned how to try to lift my mom with a lifting belt according to the physical therapist. I learned what exercises were necessary to keep her legs from stiffening up. I learned from home health on how to change the dressing on a bed sore and how to keep it clean. They also taught me how to change a diaper without lifting my mom. There were so many other procedures I learned by watching the professionals and by asking questions.

I became a sponge and absorbed as much as I could. I knew that this would help with my dad and then with my mom. The more I took care of my parents the more I learned. Sometimes things got easier with what I learned and other times it made no difference. I used what I learned and adapted it to our situation. I learned quite a bit in the over twenty years that I was a caregiver to both my parents. If I was still caring for my mom I would still be learning. The learning process never ends when you are a caregiver. New techniques, procedures and processes are introduced everyday. New medications and treatments are also introduced. You need to learn these as they might help you in the process of caring for your parent. I never stopped learning and I think that helped my mom live as long as she did.

Do What You Got To Do

My attitude has always been, you have to do what you got to do. I couldn't rely on others because they had lives of their own and I felt it would not be fair to interfere with their families. I would have liked some help but I never counted on it.

Whenever the doctor would say we have to change treatment I always knew I was in for more work. They would look at me and say sometimes, "Her condition is worse and so we have to do this treatment." A lot of times that meant more appointments and travel. That also meant more lifting, diaper changing and dress changes. They would tell me and then say, "I wish there was something else we could do." That's when I started telling them, "You got to do what you got to do."

It didn't matter what had to be done, you had to do it because there were never any other options. Whether it was changing a wound dressing or giving an enema, it was what needed to be done. Sure it was embarrassing and sometimes disgusting but it had to be done. If we were rich I guess we could have hired someone to do it but we never had that luxury.

She was my responsibility and it was my duty to do what had to be done. Getting upset about it did absolutely no good because who was going to take my place. I would tell my mom we have to do this procedure and sometimes she would say, "I'm sorry to put you through this." She knew it was difficult for me and I knew it was difficult for her too. We did what had to be done and I believe she lasted a long time because she received the care she needed when she needed it. There was no waiting for someone else and no hesitation in the required treatment.

You Know Your Parent

No one knows your parent better than you and as you start taking care of them you will notice even more. This comes in very handy when you have to tell their condition to a doctor. They forget a lot and it will be up to you to tell the doctors of certain problems and conditions.

21

My problem with both of my parents was that when a doctor would ask them how they felt they would always say, "Fine." They wouldn't say anything else and the doctor would just look at me. I would tell the doctor that they weren't fine and proceeded to tell them about all the problems they were having.

I knew things about them that they didn't know themselves such as sleeping and eating habits. Over the years of taking care of them I knew how certain medications would affect them and how we could counteract it. I knew what they could tolerate and what made them sick. I probably knew them better than I knew myself.

Since I had this knowledge I was able to give the doctors the information needed so they could prescribe the best treatment for the situation or condition. Such information could be that my mom needed antibiotics before dental procedures or my dad was allergic to certain diabetes medication. This was the procedure I followed for the over twenty years I took care of my parents. When a challenge came up I had the information needed so they could try to overcome it.

This knowledge comes from the day to day care of your parent. You will learn all their quirks and mannerisms if you already don't know what they are. You will be able to tell a reaction before there is an action and you will know the result before something starts. All this information will go a long way in helping your doctors diagnose and treat your parent. It will also go a long way in helping you care for your parents.

You Know Their Problems And Their Conditions

Being a caregiver means you have to know your parent's problems. You have to be fully aware of what they can and can't do. You need to know their medical history and their medications. You need to know their allergies and what they dislike. You must know their limitations and basically have to know everything about them.

The reason for this is that you don't want to cause more problems while you are taking care of them. Since you are responsible for their care you don't want to do something that could make them sick, hurt them or even worse.

When you take them to the doctors you will be their eyes and ears and a lot of times have to interpret or repeat what the doctor told them. You are the one in the trenches that has to do all the grunt work so you need to know everything about them. Sometimes doctors forget or don't know certain problems, or they might not read their medical condition and medication list, so you need to remind them of certain problems and condition.

This happens more frequently than it should and I always found myself repeating the medications my parents were taking and information about their condition. One instance was when I would take my mom to the dentist. Due to her heart condition, our family doctor said she needed antibiotics before she ever had any dental work performed. Another point he also made was that the Novocain she received could not have adrenaline because it could cause her heart to speed up. This was noted on the paperwork I gave the dentist and oral surgeon about my mom's medical conditions and medications. Every time we went to the dentist or oral surgeon I had to remind them about the Novocain.

I knew her problems and I made sure I followed through even though others missed it. That was my responsibility because I was her caregiver. By knowing her so well we avoided problems and complications.

Not only do you have to know your parent's problems but a lot of times you also have to relay their condition. For some reason, when they are asked, "How are you feeling?" most of the time they say, "Good." It is almost like they don't want anyone to know they are sick or are in pain.

This happened all the time with my mom, whenever the nurse or doctor would ask her, "How are you feeling today?" she would always say, "Good." They would look at me and I would tell them that she wasn't good and the reason why she wasn't doing good. Most of the times it had to do with the pain in her legs and lower back due to her spinal condition.

This also happened when she was in the hospital and they would ask her, "Are you in any pain?" She would say, "No," as she was grabbing the bed rail or trapeze so hard her knuckles were white. They would look at me and I would say, "She's in a lot of pain." Their response was usually, "It's obvious because of her white knuckles." The other question was, "On a scale of one to ten how do you rate the pain." Sometimes she would yell, "Two!" while she was cringing in pain. One nurse told her one time, "You want to try again?" and my mom's response was, "Twelve!" They would look at me and ask how bad I thought it was and I could tell by how she was squirming in the bed. The pain was severe and was a ten and they would inform the doctor for further instructions. One time the doctor came in when she was in intense pain and he asked her, "How are you feeling?" and she told him while clinching in pain, "I'm fine." She wasn't fine and most of the time everyone new it. I did have a situation once when the nurse asked her to rate her pain and once again my mom said a three or four when it was more severe. The nurse said, "Ok" and wrote it down on the chart. I told her that she was in extreme pain because she was squirming in bed and the nurse told me there was nothing she could do because, "That was the pain number she gave me." I went over and talked to the head nurse who called our doctor and he gave them new instructions for the pain medication dosage.

I was my mom's eyes, ears and mouth. She was confused because of the pain so I had to make sure that the medical staff knew her condition. It's not intruding or telling them what to do it is that you know your parents condition probably better than anyone so you need to relay that information to those that don't know it. Just make sure you do it in a polite way and if you have to call your parent's doctor to relay the information to the staff, then do it.

Unique Position

Being a caregiver to your parent puts you in a unique position as far as their medical condition. You see everything that they do, how they react and how something affects them. When you take them to the doctors or hospital you are their eyes, ears and nose.

You know their conditions like a book and you can relay that information to the doctor. You know how certain treatments affect their condition and how they react. Certain medications might cause an adverse reaction and you are the first one that will notice and you can relay this information to the doctor.

You know everything about them and you can relay this information to any medical professional that needs it. A lot of time the elderly don't understand or hear what they are being told by a doctor and that can cause problems during their treatment. With you being there you hear what has to be done so it can be done properly. It all depends on your parents condition and how much they are still involved in their healthcare but you become their safety net. If they are confused about a treatment or medication you can discuss it with them and call the doctor for verification.

Many times when I was taking care of my dad and mom they would hear something completely different from what the doctor was actually saying. Sometimes they didn't hear or understand the problem or treatment and it was good that I was in the room because I heard everything the doctor said.

I was lucky and my folks rarely second guessed me and were comfortable with what I told them. If they did question me we would call the doctor for verification and then they would be satisfied. I never had a problem with this because it meant they were still interested in their healthcare.

Chapter 6

WHAT OTHERS DO OR HAVE DONE

Every Person Is Different

Just as each situation is different, so is every person. We are all unique and that's what makes our personalities. When you are taking care of your parent you pretty much know their personality, what they can and can't do.

When you are taking care of your parent they still have their personality. One day they are more stubborn and other times they forget things. Unless you're dealing with Alzheimers or serious dementia they act pretty close to the way they always did so you know how they will react to situations.

I knew my parents like a book so it made it easier for me to take care of them. I knew what they liked to eat, what they liked to do and who they liked to visit or wanted to come see us. I knew what doctors they liked and which ones were just tolerated. I knew how they handled different procedures and tests. I knew how they handled good news and bad. I knew how their emotions changed and how to settle them down.

We were close so I did have it much easier than most when it came to know how my parents ticked. I was responsible for their health and welfare and knowing them so well I was able to shield and protect them from as much heart ache as possible. As time when on, I did learn more and I used it to give them the best care I could.

Another Cousin Had Help

A lot of people try to compare what you are doing to what they did in the past as they try to give you advice. Everyone thinks that your situation is the same as theirs was and they know the best way on how to handle it. I had a cousin who took care of my aunt and she always compared our situation to hers. She would always say, "I did that," but what she never said was that she had help. She was able continue with her career, daily routines and even take vacations.

My mom had two sisters that lived together along with my cousins. The oldest had a husband and did not have any children. The youngest was divorced and had two children, a girl and a boy. My uncle passed away and his wife, my mom's sister went into deep depression and never spoke again after his funeral. My cousin and her mother, my aunt, took care of the older sister who was no longer able to care for herself.

My cousin worked for the County in law enforcement and had a very good and well paying job. Her mom was active at their church so both of them had a life away from home. My cousin quickly hired someone to come in and help take care of "auntie." The people she hired were from the church and none of them were professionals and very few of them spoke English. They would take care of "auntie" during the day usually under the supervision of my aunt. At night my cousin and aunt would take over the care duties. They would switch so each one would be able to sleep. I am in no way criticizing the care they gave. They did a fabulous job as well as the people they hired. My aunt lasted for many years in this state and a lot of doctors gave up hope and wanted her put in a convalescent home or hospice. They refused and took care of her at their home.

My interest in this situation is that they had help because of my cousin's job. She could afford to hire people to aid in the situation. She had very little disruption in her career and life. She was able to get away for a week or two at a time. Her mom stayed home with "auntie" while she was on vacation. Her mom could also get away because they would just bring in someone else to watch my aunt.

I'm was never jealous of their situation because they did a lot of work and it did take a toll on both of them. My point is that when she says, "I did that," that is not really accurate. Yes, she might have performed the same procedures as me but the big difference was that she was not alone. There was usually someone around to give her help. If she got hurt someone else was around to help her and my aunt. She never had to sacrifice her career and was able to be promoted almost to the top of her agency. She was able to go on vacation and continue with somewhat of a normal life.

Each Situation Is Different

Just as people are different so are situations. Being a caregiver you have to do what is best for your unique situation. You will receive a lot of good advice but that is usually knowledge that is generally applied to everyone. You need to take this information and adapt it to a way that is useful to you and your parent.

Some caregivers never have to lift their parent or bathe them. My dad was able to walk, even though it was a short distance and he was able to shower himself all the way to the last month of his life. My mom on the other hand could not stand or walk and needed to be lifted for almost everything she did. She needed help with the basics such as taking a shower and dressing herself. This condition lasted for over thirteen years until the time of her death.

When people would tell me to lift her a certain way, like using a lifting belt, it would not work in her situation. She was always afraid of falling and when I tried to lift her using a lifting belt she felt unstable. She would get nervous and start moving her arms which would make me unstable and could have caused both of us to fall. No matter how much the physical therapist tried to get us to use a lifting belt, it would not work. I had to adapt the way I lifted my mom. In the process of lifting my mom I injured a disc in my back. Because of this injury, once again I had to adapt the way I lifted her. I had to always wear a lower back brace and I had to be very cautious every time I picked her up.

When she needed wound care, she needed help moving onto her side while in bed and also needed to be braced so she wouldn't fall back. She didn't have the strength or balance to hold herself on her side. The advisors said she had to hold herself and if we would have listened to them she never would have had wound care. I needed to adapt to her situation using some of the techniques we were taught.

My situation as a caregiver is different from someone else's. My dad's situation was different from my mom's condition. You can take what you learn from others and adapt them to your unique situation.

Chapter 7
RESPONSIBILITY OF BEING A CAREGIVER
Your Responsibility

Just as a child is your responsibility so is your elderly parent. You are their caregiver and as the word implies, give them care. It might be financially if they are not capable of signing treatment documents, their day to day living requirements or both.

Being responsible for them means that any bruises, lapse of medications, confusion or any other condition could be considered your fault. When you take them to the doctor or any healthcare provider they always look at their condition. When you take them to the emergency room or they get admitted to a hospital their entire body is inspected to see if there is any abnormal trauma. Unfortunately elder abuse is a big problem and health providers are required by law to report it to the proper authorities. A lot of times while they are doing their inspection they make you stand outside the room as they look and try to question your parent. In our case my mom wouldn't let them touch her or answer their questions unless I was in the room and it was always a tense time. When they would wheel her to the room I would tell my mom that they were going to examine her but I would be outside the room and they would get me when they were finished. Sure enough when we reached the room they would tell me to wait outside and closed the door. Every time I could hear her yelling at them, "Don't touch me, get my son." This would go on for a while and then they would come out and ask me to talk to my mom. I would calm her down and tell her to let them check her. Being professionals, they were able to check her out while she was being feisty. They sometimes would come out and tell me she was a tough one but that had to do it because of state law. I understood and was never worried because I knew she was taken care of properly.

If they did have a problem I would have been interviewed and her situation would have been reviewed. These healthcare workers deal with these situations everyday and they see some horrendous things. In this day because of some disgusting individuals we have to go through this exercise, it's now part of the healthcare process. Since I was the caregiver I was responsible for my mom's condition and well being. Fortunately I have a conscience and was always concerned about my mom's health, condition and safety.

You Are Responsible For Everything

When you are a caregiver one of the most important things to remember is that you are responsible for everything. You are taking care of your parent and it is your responsibility that they are treated and cared for properly. They are unable to care for themselves so you are helping them to survive. It is a great responsibility.

You have to make sure they are clean, well nourished, safe and that their medications are taken properly. You have to take them to the doctors, to outpatient facilities and possibly to the hospital. All of these locations look at them and check to see if they are cared for properly. You are under a microscope and you must make sure you do things right and legal. This world is a crazy place and there are a lot of elderly people abused and a lot of them are taken advantage of by "so-called loved ones." You need to be at your best so your parent is cared for properly.

I made sure that my dad and mom were taken care of properly. When they went to the doctors they were always clean, well nourished and had a positive attitude. Their attitude would change depending on the diagnosis but I did my best to keep them with a positive outlook. The only time that changed was with my dad and it was about two weeks before he died. He knew what was coming and he finally just gave in and the fight for life left him. My mom's positive attitude lasted till a week before she died and then she became confused, lost her appetite and passed away.

All during their illnesses I took responsibility for their care and well being. I was scrutinized by doctors, hospitals, home health and many other medical professions. I passed the test and inspection every time. I knew these professionals had a job to do to make sure my parents were cared for properly and I never interfered with their inspections. I knew I had done my best and there was nothing else that could be done.

The only time I was a little nervous was when my mom passed away at home. I never was in this type of situation before and I didn't know what to expect. When the paramedics and police came into the house they went right into the bedroom to check on my mom and made me stay in the living room. When they pronounced her deceased the police officer asked me questions, looked at documents and then told the paramedics they could leave. He then told me to relax because he assessed the situation and realized that my mom was well taken care of. He saw no trauma, bruising or sign of malnutrition to her body. He also said the house was well kept and clean. He then called the medical examiner and gave his report and they cleared the situation and told him to call a funeral home.

I knew I was responsible for my mom's condition and situation. I knew I did the best I could in her care but there is always the unknown. I also knew that if a problem was found it would be my responsibility to explain the situation and I would have to accept the consequences. Fortunately for me I did the right thing and there were no problems.

At Your Own Risk

One thing you always have to remember is that you are responsible for the care of your parent. Whatever you do in the process of caring for them and the outcome will be a reflection of the care you are giving them. If you are trying something new and/or different the outcome might not be what you expect. Their might be very little backup and no guarantees so therefore you are doing these procedures at your own risk.

I always did what I had to do when I took care of my parents. A lot of times it was new territory and we both were learning as we were going along. Every time in the back of mind there was always the thought of, "If this didn't work and they got hurt." I knew I would be responsible and be on the hot seat if something happened to them so I made sure that I went through the new procedures several times in my head before I actually tried them. I tried to think of different problems that could affect the way I did things. I would even try dry runs once in a while to see if I could do it and what the possible outcomes would be. Most of the this had to do with lifting or moving them from one item to another.

This "practice" saved me a lot of pain and aggravation. It also saved my parents from being put into dangerous situations where they could possibly get hurt. I was always thinking of the "what if" when I tried a new procedure or technique.

Over the years this exercise saved me from having to explain my actions because I never hurt my parents while I was taking care of them. Yes, we had a few close calls and that was usually because of lifting but we never had an accident. They were never injured and I never had to explain to the authorities why they were hurt.

I Took Responsibility

I took responsibility for all my actions while I was taking care of my parents from the very beginning. I knew from the start it was a great responsibility I was taking and I handled it head on. If there was ever a problem I would be the one to answer for it and would accept whatever the outcome would be. The best way to prevent any problems was to make sure I did the best job possible and give them the best care I could.

When I started taking care of my dad I never knew how I was going to be checked and watched during the time I took care of him. I knew I would be under the microscope from his doctors but I never considered being questioned by different staff in the hospital. I knew they would always check him when he was admitted for problems but I thought they were just for medical issues. I never had a problem and they were more concerned about his medical conditions.

When my mom became sick the situation had changed considerably. On the news you would hear more about elderly abuse and the medical facilities took it very serious. Once again the visits to the doctors office she would always get the once over to make sure that she was taken care of properly. Even though we had gone to these doctors for years they were professionals and had to do their jobs by the book. When I had to take her to the hospital she was always checked and I would be questioned on how I cared for her.

I was never worried because I knew she had the best care and she was happy. But you never knew if somebody would think because I was not a professional they would try to find something to call me on the carpet. It never happened because there was nothing to find and she would be admitted without any problems. If there was a problem I would have been responsible and I would have had to answer for my actions. I was always ready for this possibility because I took responsibility for my actions.

Chapter 8
LAWS AND BEING A CAREGIVER
State Laws Vary

All the years I took care of my parents we lived in California therefore all requirements and laws were based on that state. I am not in law enforcement and I am not an attorney so I have no idea what the laws are regarding being a caregiver. I never had to deal with any enforcement issues or complaints and I was never reported by any medical professional for any reason.

I'm sure there are different laws in each state that deal with being a caregiver and the care of an elderly parent. Most doctors, nurses and medical professionals will tell you what is required and what can get you into trouble. Home health nurses are the best sources for information and they are also the first ones that usually question the care you are giving your parent. If you have a home health situation asking the visiting nurse questions is a great way to learn what you are required to do and what can lead to problems.

I was fortunate to have a home health nurse supervisor come to the house when my mom needed wound care because of the bed sore she received while she was in the hospital. The supervisor taught me a lot as far as what I needed to do to properly care for my mom and her wound. The other nurses were always helpful and gave me a lot of advice during their visits. A lot of it was common sense because it was basically you take care of your parent the way you want to be treated. They also pointed out possible hazards and how to correct them as well as solutions to problems. The one thing they made very clear was that I could not leave her alone in the house. Since she was unable to get herself out of bed and if their was a disaster she had no way to get out of the house. If she was in a wheelchair she might be able to exit the house but why take the chance. This was common sense and simple but because it was so simple it could be something you overlook in the daily routine.

The home health nurse supervisor told me a story of one of her patients that was taking care of his mom and he was an only child. He was a teacher and he worked over forty hours a week and they had home healthcare on the weekends for a condition the lady had. During the week he would change his mom and put a clean diaper on her and made sure she had water, juice and food next to her so she could eat and drink when she wanted. She was unable to walk around so she sat in the recliner the entire day watching television until he came home at night. He had no neighbors or anyone to keep an eye on her. He would come home, clean and change her, then make dinner. He said there was nothing else he could do, had nobody that could help and they never had a problem. The home health nurse had to write him up because he was leaving his mom alone and she was at risk if their was a fire, earthquake, etc. She told me that there was an investigation and in order to keep his mom from being taken away he had to quit his job so he could be with her all the time or hire a full time caregiver. That has stuck with me to this very day because he was in a similar situation like me, except for the fact that he had a job. It made an impression and I didn't leave my mom alone.

Regulations and laws vary by state and county so you need to know what you can and can't do. Once again this is part of your responsibility as a caregiver and you don't want to get in trouble by making mistakes. One thing to remember that if it doesn't seem right, it probably isn't, so don't do it. Laws regarding the elderly are not the same in all states and most are just common sense. It is sad how many abuse cases there are against the elderly and of lot of them are caused by their own children.

The last time my mom was in the hospital it was in Bakersfield, California. The hospital was a satellite location for the local community college nursing program. These students were constantly going into my mom's room and looking her over. One day I stepped out to get some fresh air and when I came back her room was full of nursing students. The supervising instructor came over to me and introduced herself. She knew I was my mom's caregiver and she told me that I had done a wonderful job taking care of my mother. She wanted her students to see how a properly cared for parent looked. I was stunned. I told her it was the normal and right thing to do. She corrected me by telling me it was not the normal situation and most abuse cases were by the children. She when on to say of lot of the so-called cared for parents smelled and were not clean, some even had bruises. She shook my hand and told me I was doing a great job and the students were excited about working with my mom. It was a short hospital stay but we did get to meet a lot of interested nursing students.

Another law in some states is not to leave your parent unattended in the car, especially during the summer. This is a disaster in the making. At their age they can't feel heat very well and they will pass out in no time. They also don't drink as much water so they will dehydrate very fast. Best thing to do is make it a habit to take them with you wherever you go. I know it's a lot more work but it is the safest and smartest thing you can do.

Health Insurance Portability And Accountability Act

Health Insurance Portability and Accountability Act or HIPAA for short was a law that set standards for privacy of health information. I am not quoting the law verse by verse all I know is it made it a lot harder to get information about the care and condition of your parent. It made it harder but not impossible as long as your parent filled out the proper forms.

With my dad I never had an issue with HIPAA because it was not active during his lifetime and illness. When he became ill he told the doctors that they were to talk to me and the healthcare providers followed his wishes. We actually made it easier for them because we wrote a letter that gave me permission to receive all his information. My dad signed it and we had it notarized and had several copies made. If we had an issue I would give the healthcare provider a copy of the letter and it solved any problems we might have had.

With my mom it was a different situation. It first started with Medicare when you called for information they had to speak with her first and then she would give her permission so they could talk to me. They would usually ask her name, date of birth, social security number and then she would tell them, "Talk to my son." Sometimes they would repeat the question or ask her if she was sure and she would say, "Yes." I would then be able to ask questions on her behalf.

In later years, like when we changed family doctors we had to fill out the HIPAA paperwork. The form she signed gave the doctor permission for me to go into the exam room with her and get information on her health. This never was an issue and fortunately she was always able to sign the forms required.

When we went for tests and treatments she had to sign the same forms giving me permission to be involved in her procedures and given information about her condition. The hospital were the same way, I would always have a folder full of papers relating to her condition and after the admission process I always had copies of more forms from the hospital.

It made being a caregiver a little more of a hassle because of the added paperwork but patient privacy is an important personal preference. My mom would get a little annoyed because she had to keep telling people to talk to me or signing forms giving me permission to get her information but she knew it was necessary, In this day and age of everything being public it is still nice that some information is still considered private.

Pre-Admit Hospital Inspections

Being a caregiver also means that you are under a microscope. The care you give your parent is checked every time you go to the doctor or to a medical facility. If you have to have your parent admitted to the hospital they are given a full body inspection when they are admitted. By law, in many states, they have to report any findings of suspected abuse. It is the times we live because there are so many cases of elder abuse and a lot of time the abuse is committed by a child or caregiver.

A pre-inspection is done usually in the emergency room and then a more thorough inspection is done when they are put into a room. You are not allowed to be in the room when the nurse does these inspections because they don't want any interference from family members while they are checking your parent. You have to wait until they are finished and when the job is complete they will come out and allow you to go back into the room.

Another part of this inspection is also to follow the new Medicare rules that regulate bed sores. Many patients were being discharged with bed sores from not being turned enough when they were in the hospital bed. These sores have to be noted on readmission because of Medicare requirements.

When I was taking care of my dad these inspection were not required but he was still checked over by the nurses when he was admitted to the hospital. I was never worried because I knew he was getting proper care. In fact he would come home with more bruises because of the IV's, blood draws and treatments.

While I was taking care of my mom things changed. The inspections started off small and then the last time she was admitted to the hospital in 2013, it was a full body inspection. They wheeled her into a room on a gurney and asked me to stay outside. I knew what was coming and I told them about her condition and that she was afraid of falling and to make sure she had something to grab on. They went in and the nurse asked her questions and also asked if she had any problems with the care I was giving her. I could hear them rolling her from one side to another ands saying , "Arms good, legs good," and "no bruising." After about twenty minutes they came out and allowed me back in the room. I asked how she was and they said, "She's fine." That was a relief, I knew there was nothing to worry about but you never know if you have missed something. I'm sure if I did they would have asked me questions and I would have a chance to explain the situation. Once again my mom came home with more bruises because of all the lab work, diagnostic tests and IV's.

These are not only stressful for you being the caregiver but they also put a lot of stress on your parent. My mom would ask, "Why are you asking me all these questions." They would tell her it was part of the admission process. She would tell them, "Talk to my son, he takes care of me." They would answer, "We will talk to him in a few moments, we just need to finish looking at you." That's how I knew they were stressing my mom out and she was nervous. Every time she got scared she would tell them to talk to me. I would tell her later that they had to do this because of all the people that were hurt. She would look at me and say, "Thank God that's not me."

Chapter 9
MEDICARE AND INSURANCE
Medicare

Everyone knows Medicare is the primary health insurance for senior citizens. Some people purchase supplement insurance through their retirement system, previous employer or associations. Medicare dictates what your supplement insurance pays and what type of care you receive.

When I was taking care of my mom, Medicare was the primary insurance and paid eighty percent of the approved charges. She had a supplement insurance plan through my father's survivor benefits which paid the remaining twenty percent of charges. It was a nice plan because we never had to pay for any hospitalization, doctor or outpatient fees. Now this was before Obamacare so I have no idea how this would be handled today. She died in 2013 and that was before Obamacare was implemented.

The down side of this system was that Medicare also dictated what procedures she would receive because the medical providers would not perform any services that Medicare would not approve. This meant that it was a cookie cutter operation and everyone received the same care and procedures because of the approval and billing process.

As far as hospitalization, doctors and outpatient services we never had a problem with Medicare. Even when my mom needed wound care Medicare covered the supplies, home health and wound center visits. I did find out that home health visits were based on who was caring for the patient. The home health supervisor explained to me that Medicare would only cover a few training visits because I was taking care of my mom. When I asked, "What about people that are squeamish or can't do the job," her response was they have to overcome it or Medicare won't pay for the supplies. She also said in our case because I had already had taken care of my mom,

Medicare would not pay for home health unless their was a new hospital visit. I was saving Medicare money and I had no problem with this arrangement because it was less stress on my mom.

The one thing I could never understand was why Medicare didn't cover incontinence supplies. Medicaid covered diapers, personal pads and bed pads. Medicare covered nothing. These were the most expensive items. Even on sale they were about $15.00 a package and we would use about three to four packages a week. I use to buy them on sale or in bulk to save money but it was still expensive and took a large part of our budget.

I guess the reason Medicare didn't cover incontinence supplies was because they were too expensive and pretty much every elderly person used some type of them. This is one of the major expenses when you are caring for a parent. In order to keep them and your home clean you uses cases of these items.

Supplement Insurance

Supplement insurance covers a percentage of the approved charges that Medicare doesn't pay. Some programs pay 100% of the charges because they have a contract with Medicare and are HMO's. My mom's supplement insurance covered the 20% of charges that Medicare approved but didn't pay. Medicare did pay 80% of the approved charges.

The premium for this insurance was paid for by the survivor benefit my mom was receiving because my dad was a federal worker and was employed at the Long Beach Naval Shipyard. Every year the cost of this supplement insurance would increase and also some years the type of benefits would change. Sometimes covered procedures would be added or dropped. Every year my mom would receive the benefits brochure which would be sent before open season so you could change medical plans. My mom and I would check this brochure for all the changes and to see how much the cost increased. We never changed plans because we felt this was the best option for her situation. A PPO, Medicare was the primary and paid 80%, FEP (Federal Employee Program) was secondary and paid 20%. This supplement also offered prescription coverage which the cost varied year to year and this plan was extremely helpful as far as prescription costs. The cost of the plan at the time of her death was around $180.00 per month and was well worth it just because of the prescription benefit. One of her pain medications was $280.00 per month and her cost was only $28.00. When the Medicare Part D prescription coverage started we received a letter that her plan was equal to or better than the Medicare plans. So we kept her plan and never opted for Medicare Part D.

In our situation, the supplement insurance was necessary. With all the medical procedures, prescriptions and outpatient care my mom needed we never would have been able to afford the 20% co-payment. It was good piece of mind and it allowed us to concentrate on other issues.

Under Obamacare

In 2014 Obamacare became the law of the land and went into effect. This law produced major changes in healthcare and in the way the elderly received care. To this day we are still learning what is in this law and how it affect all of us.

My mom passed away in 2013 and her healthcare was never governed under Obamacare. After the Affordable Care Act was passed and signed into law in 2012 we did start to notice some subtle changes in the way her healthcare was handled. We kept wondering how this law would affect her medical care, prescriptions and life. She was afraid she would not receive proper medical care because this law would ration benefits due to her age.

After she passed away I received some information from her health insurance plan. They kept sending me information for almost a year after she passed away. Just out of curiosity I read how the plan changed because of Obamacare. She was lucky, her plan didn't change very much. It must have been because her supplement was the Federal Employee Program. This is the same program that members of congress and their staff used. My mom had this supplement insurance because she was receiving survivor benefits from my dad's employment at the Long Beach Naval Shipyard.

What Medicare And Insurance Pay

Most people expect Medicare and their supplement insurance will pay for their entire care. While this is true for most medical care it doesn't cover the usual day to day expenses. Some have purchased Long Term Care Insurance to help with the daily expenses of assisted living and once again this usually covers a specific amount per day and not all expenses. A lot of expenses will be paid by your parents or come out of your pocket.

For senior citizens Medicare and if they can afford it supplement insurance, cover most medical expenses. My mom had Medicare, Parts A and B and she paid a monthly premium for it and a supplement insurance. Medicare paid 80% of the approved charges and her supplement paid the remaining 20%. For the most part she never had any out of pocket expenses for doctors, specialist, diagnostic tests, outpatient procedures and hospitalization. Her spine surgery was covered and so was all the tests leading to it and the recovery afterward. It was a good set up and it kept her healthy with preventative care and her supplement insurance also covered prescriptions.

What Medicare and supplement insurance did not pay was for the supplies she needed to survive on a daily basis, such as diapers and incontinence pads. Since she could not care for herself and was not mobile she needed these items for day to day life. I would see commercials on television for these products but when I called they always said they were not approved for Medicare patients. It was usually for MediCal and private insurance. When I gave them her insurance information they said it would not be approved and I would have to pay the retail price for these items. They were expensive and I was doing better purchasing the items on sale at the local stores or ordering online. These items were the majority of our expenses because she used them multiple times a day and everyday. When she was in the hospital I would tell the social worker about the situation and they would say she didn't qualify for these products. Through her entire illness we always had to purchased the diapers and incontinence items.

I had the same problem with my dad when he had to wear a urostomy bag. Medicare and supplement insurance would cover the bags and the flanges but they would not cover the cleaning solution and adhesive. You can't use one without the other. For diabetes they would cover the test meter but not the test strips or lancets. They would cover syringes but not the disposal containers. It made no sense.

Laws and rules constantly change so you have to call Medicare and your supplement insurance constantly to see what is covered and what is not. You get frustrated at the crazy rules and conditions that just don't make sense and realize in the end you will have to foot the bill. You can appeal most decisions but that takes time.

Not Knowing What Insurance Will Pay

Healthcare, Medicare and health insurance have gotten so complicated over the years that it is hard to know what insurance will pay. You are at the mercy of the medical facilities to know what insurance will cover. After the procedures are completed a lot of times you get a Medicare and insurance statement telling you that a certain item or procedure was not covered.

This never made sense to me because you would think that if Medicare and insurance covered a procedure, test or hospitalization because of a certain condition everything needed would be paid. Not so, and you don't know this until you receive the Medicare and insurance statement. They might cover the procedure but they won't cover certain supplies. They cover certain tests but they don't cover certain medications that were used. They might cover this physician but they don't cover that one. The Medicare statements always had a disclaimer that if you didn't know these services weren't covered you are not responsible for the charges. How is the patient to know what is covered and what is not? Patients don't have a Medicare coding book or know what services are paid or denied.

One of my favorites was when my mom was admitted to the hospital and you would receive statements from many different doctors. One doctor was under contract with Medicare and the other was not. They work in the same hospital, don't you think that if it is a Medicare patient, only doctors that have a contract with Medicare should see or work on that patient? It made no sense.

We were fortunate because my mom had great supplement insurance. We never had any great out of pocket expenses for medical procedures. Every time I would go over the Medicare and insurance statement I would always wonder how people could afford their medical care if they had just Medicare. The amounts are staggering and without any reference material it's hard to know how much you will have to pay.

At Their Discretion

When you have Medicare and supplement insurance all services are at the discretion of the plan paying for the services. It all depends on what type of Medicare and insurance plan you have but they make a lot of the decisions on what procedures or type of services you receive. This also applies to equipment or accessories needed to help care for your parent at home. It is all based on age and cost formulas that the average person has no clue what it means.

A lot of times when my mom was in the hospital I would hear that Medicare would not pay for this service or procedure. The one supply that my mom always needed was an air mattress because she was susceptible to bed sores ever since her spine surgery. Every time after that when she was admitted to the hospital it was always the same, "Medicare won't approve an air mattress." They would approve a foam egg crate under the sheets and this would prevent bed sores for about a day. Even though Medicare paid for wound care and supplies for many years they would not authorize an air mattress to prevent them from reoccurring. We would be assigned a hospital liaison and I would tell them of the situation and in about twenty-four hours the hospital would supply an air mattress for my mom. I don't know what they did but they got the unit for her. I'm sure a lot had to do with the new Medicare rules that went into effect a few years ago concerning bed sores and hospital readmits.

When I would receive the Medicare and insurance statements I never saw any billing for the air mattress so I think the hospital ate the cost to prevent any problems or readmit in the future. I will never know but my mom never was readmitted because of bed sores. The sores would show up every time after she was discharged but we were able to care for them with over the counter first aid supplies.

Hospitals and doctors know what Medicare and insurance will cover as far as medical services. Some say their treatments are based in this information because services are paid at Medicare and insurance's discretion and because of this they are in charge of the medical care your parent receives. If you or your parent approve procedures that are not covered by Medicare and insurance you might be responsible for the cost and associated charges. It is hard to know what is covered and what is not so you need to talk to your doctor and the hospital business office.

Medically Necessary

One term you will learn while you are taking care of your parent is "medically necessary." This is the requirement that Medicare and supplement insurance have to see if they will pay for certain services and equipment. If they deem it is not medically necessary then you or your parent will be the one footing the bill.

When my mom required an air mattress after her surgery because she had a bed sore Medicare covered the appliance for a short time. After they deemed she was cured they would no longer pay for the rental of the unit. Her doctor insisted and appealed that she needed it for the rest of her life because she was prone to bed sores but they denied the claim every time. I finally made a deal with the medical supply company to purchase the unit outright and I also became responsible for the maintenance. It was well worth it because that air mattress lasted from 2001 to 2013. I kept cleaning and replacing the air filter and I patched the mattress whenever it tore and we were able to get over twelve years of operation. So I guess I saved Medicare and the supplement insurance a lot of money. That was not the issue, my mom needed the air mattress for her health so I had no choice but to make the purchase.

This is one topic a lot of people don't realize because they think Medicare and supplement insurance pays for everything. When I was taking care of my parents that was not true with the health plans they had.

Now a lot has changed with Medicare and supplement insurance so I have no idea if this type of an appliance would be covered today.

My point is that unless an appliance, such as a bed, lift, shower chair, commode or any other device, is deemed medically necessary by Medicare and insurance it won't be authorized and paid. You might have to pay for these items and go through an appeal process to try to get reimbursed. This could take a long time and in the end you might still have to absorb the cost. You have to make the decision do I pay for the purchase to help my parent or do I wait for the final decision from Medicare and supplement insurance. That is a decision you and your parent have to make.

Cosmetic

Some items are deemed cosmetic by Medicare and supplement insurance and they will not be covered or reimbursed. Sometimes it made no sense what they deemed cosmetic because you needed these items to finish a procedure. You will shake your head in disbelief when you learn what is a covered item and what is considered cosmetic therefore is not medically necessary.

I ran into this situation when I was taking care of my dad and had to change his urostomy bag and flange. He had an adhesive flange attached to his skin that needed to be replaced if it got wet, loose or just wore out. They lasted about three to six days depending on their condition. When you peeled it off the skin it would leave residue from the adhesive and it could cause a rash. Medicare would pay for the flange but they would not cover the alcohol wipes to clean off the old adhesive or the powder necessary to keep the area dry and prevent a rash. It made absolutely no sense because you couldn't put on a new flange until the old one was peeled off and the area was cleaned with no signs of residue. The new unit would not stick.

With my mom they would not cover her air mattress because they said it was a comfort item and it was for cosmetic purposes. The strange thing was they covered it for the first few months of her wound care but the denied coverage as preventative care. The doctor appealed and said it was medically necessary for the rest of her life. They wouldn't budge and it became an item that I needed to purchase. When they listed it for cosmetic purposes I had to laugh because those big red blotches she would get on her backside really didn't do much for her skin condition. Once again it made no sense.

Over the many years I took care of my parents I came across many situations that made absolutely no sense. Most of the time it was with Medicare and supplement insurance and all you could do was appeal and hope for the best. We won some appeals but we lost a lot more and it just added to the expense of caring for my parents.

Saved Medicare Money

Medicare was the primary insurance for my mom and she did have a supplement insurance. Medicare paid 80% of the approved charges and her supplement paid the remaining 20%. This covered hospitalization, doctors, diagnostic tests, procedures and treatments.

We did utilized some Medicare and supplement insurance home healthcare. We used the home health nurse while my mom had bed sores but that was discontinued when Medicare said I could take care of her wounds. They offered a service that would pay for a home health technician to visit once a week to give my mom a bath. We never used this service because she took showers more than once a week and she didn't want a stranger coming in to give her a bath.

Over the years I saved Medicare and the supplement insurance a lot of money because I did a lot of the procedures and treatments they would approve. When she needed wound care after the major incident in 2001 I was the one that cleaned and changed the dressings. We would go to the wound center and they would do the initial assessment and continue to follow up on the care but I was the one that did the cleaning and changing in the interim. They finally told me that Medicare would no longer approve any home care because in their words as Medicare stated, "The son is taking care of his mom." I had no problem with this arrangement because it was easier on my mom. Sure it was more work for me but it made her more comfortable and relaxed.

We only used the emergency room when she was extremely constipated from the pain medication and she needed industrial strength laxatives to clean her out. They also were better at preventing dehydration because they could give her intravenous fluids. This happened only three times during the thirteen years that she was sick. We never went to the emergency room for any other procedures.

We did use facilities for preventative care and for diagnostic tests but that was to keep her healthy. Even with her cancer diagnosis most of it was treated by medication. The only expenses were labs tests and scans. Routine bone scans, cat scans and MRI's were necessary and they were used at a minimum.

The major expense for Medicare and the supplement insurance was for her spine surgery in 2001. That cost a lot of money but the cost of care afterward was minimal to what it could have been. She could have been placed in a rehabilitation center and that would have cost an enormous amount of money. A convalescent facility was mentioned while she was recuperating and that would have cost even more money. We refused because I felt she could get better care at home and would recover faster. My mom and her doctors agreed. Hospice was recommended once and again we refused because that was not the place or position she needed to be in.

Medicare and supplement insurance did supply some durable medical equipment to help with her care. Even that was minimal because instead of waiting for Medicare to approve a piece of equipment I would go out and buy it if the doctor said it was needed and would help my mom. We could have spent a lot more of Medicare's money if I would have submitted some of those claims. Sure I lost money but I didn't have to wait for the bureaucracy to approve the equipment.

I didn't plan on saving Medicare or the supplement insurance money and I figured we would use all that was available but I had to do what was best for my mom. Waiting a few days or weeks for approval could have been detrimental to her care. As far as the home health technicians she didn't feel comfortable with them giving her a bath so I didn't want to put her under any more stress. Many people would tell me that Medicare and insurance would pay for a lot of things and for the most part they were wrong. They do pay for a lot of care and procedures but it is not the magical insurance that everyone thinks it is.

Chapter 10
GOVERNMENT AND BEING A CAREGIVER
Social Security

A lot of people get Social Security and Medicare confused and believe they are the same thing. Social Security is supposed to be a small payment for your work history if you paid into the system. Medicare is a health insurance for older individuals. The way these two services work together is that your Medicare premium is deducted from your Social Security payment.

My mother received a small Social Security benefit. She worked back in the 1940s and paid a little into the system. She received a monthly benefit, just enough to cover the Medicare premium. It was not enough to live on and at that time did not cover prescriptions. She was fortunate to have a supplement plan that covered what Medicare did not pay for medical and for prescriptions.

In her case Social Security paid for her medical coverage and was not a retirement plan. Social Security also does pay a death benefit of $255.00. This is one benefit for some reason I never claimed after she died.

Government Intrusion

When I was taking care of my parents I never had to deal with any government intrusion with their healthcare except the strange Medicare rules and requirements that regulated what was and not covered. Some of these benefit restrictions were just insane but that's the government for you. Under the new rules and regulations of Obamacare I have no idea how this will impact caregiving and the benefits for senior citizens.

With my dad the only government insanity I had to deal with when I was taking care of him was Medicare reimbursements. Once I learned what was covered and what was not it made it a lot easier to deal with.

Unfortunately the only time you knew when something was not covered is when the provider sent you a statement or bill. At that time there was no way to see ahead of time what would be denied or paid. Books were available but they were usually only supplied to medical professionals and staff. Once again it meant opening the wallet and busting the budget every time we found out that Medicare denied a claim.

My mom had the same situation but with the advent of the internet it made it easier to get information on covered procedures and supplies. We were still hit with a lot of items not being covered and it caused a lot of out of pocket expenses but as time went on we learned was covered and what was not.

With both of my parents we never had a situation where treatment was denied because Medicare would not cover the procedure. Every time they went into the hospital, as far as I know, they always received the care and treatment that the doctors prescribed and ordered. Once again they were lucky because their illnesses were not expensive and did not require long hospital stays.

My mom passed away before Obamacare, Healthcare and Medicare reform went into practice, so I never had to deal with any of the new regulations. Seeing what others are going through now it seems like it is a completely different situation. I have noticed this with my uncle, who is now being taken care of by his son, my cousin, part time. They are forced to wait for a lot of doctors visits and procedures. I know it depends on the type of Medicare plan and supplement insurance they have so it might not be an accurate comparison. What I do know is that there is a lot more paperwork and they have to answer a lot more questions than I ever did with my folks. Some of the information required sure sounds like the government wants to know a lot more about the patient and the treatment they are going to receive. Privacy is supposed to be primary but it seems today medical privacy is non existent when it comes to what the government wants to know about you and your health.

New Doctor Rules

With Obamacare and Healthcare Reform a lot of changes seem to be happening in the medical profession. There seems to be a lot more regulations, oversight and lack of privacy. Doctor payments are being reduced while they are being put under a microscope for the care that they give their patients. It almost seems like the federal and some state governments want to put the stand alone general practitioner out of business.

A retired doctor friend of mine was telling me that he had heard from his colleagues that here in California the general practitioners are being questioned for the quality of care they give. They have to report numbers to the state on how much time they spend with a patient and how many patients they see in a day. They are then rated by these numbers and given a quality of care rating. This affects insurance reimbursements and other factors contributing to their practice. It sounds good but the problem is that a stand alone practitioner never see's the amount of patients a doctor at a clinic will see. Clinics are like an assembly line and they see hundreds of patients a day which makes their ratings go up. They spend very little time with these patients but it doesn't matter because it is all about the amount of patients. These clinics get high ratings and a high quality of care score so they receive better reimbursements. The single practitioner is penalized because they spend more time with their patients and therefore see less of them per day which gives them a lower rating and quality of care score. The whole scheme seems ass backwards because you would think the doctor that spends more time with their patient would get a higher score. It almost seems like HMO's, Health Maintenance Organizations, or insurance companies made up these rules to force patients into their plans. So this is forcing a lot of single practitioners out of business because they can't get reimbursed properly. My doctor friend is so happy that he retired because he said he would never be able to make a living anymore seeing patients. I always liked going to his office because I knew he would spend time with us and go over treatments for my dad in great detail. You had to wait in the waiting room or exam room a little longer but it was worth it because he spent time with you when he examined you. He had a sign in his office, "The time you wait is because I am spending time with a patient, Please be sure that I will spend as much time with you as you need." If he was in practice today his waiting room would be empty because he would be out of business.

Another item I was told was that if I was taking care of my parents today in California the doctor could not listen to me for any treatment ideas. I could not make any recommendations because of my parents condition because I am not a qualified medical professional. Yes, this does make sense because I am not a doctor but I can give the doctor information that could help with his diagnosis. Also since I am taking care of my parent twenty-four hours a day I have a keen sense of what they can tolerate and what the possible outcome could be. Today if I gave the doctor this type of information and he agrees he could be investigated for taking advice from a non doctor. What a bunch of crap, only in California can the bureaucrats be so stupid.

I know this is hear say but I include it because I was able to work with our doctors. They listened to what I said and then made their diagnosis after tests and results. They didn't listen to me for medical advice but they listened because I knew what my parents were doing and how their condition was progressing. These new type of rules could cause all kinds of problems for doctors and caregivers. I hope common sense prevails soon.

Chapter 11
HEALTH CONDITIONS AND BEING A CAREGIVER
Arthritis

Arthritis is one of those diseases that can cause a lot of problems. My dad did not have severe arthritis but he did have a little in his hands and knees. It didn't slow him down too much but his other diseases brought him to a halt. My mom on the other hand had severe arthritis all over her body. Her fingers were deformed from the disease making it extremely difficult for her to hold anything in her hands. She had arthritis in her neck and lower back that contributed to her spinal condition and severe pain. Years earlier when she had x-rays of her spine the doctor told her it was a good thing she had arthritis in her lower back because it was preventing her from becoming paralyzed. That seemed strange and when she had her spinal surgery they confirmed that diagnosis. My mom went through hell with arthritis to the point where she would curse the disease every time she couldn't hold something.

I would have her exercise her fingers with a tennis ball so they wouldn't stiffen up and cause pain. She tried and did her best as she went along with her life. Her fingers were so bad that I could not put gloves on her hands when they were cold. Her fingers would stick together and prevent them from going into the gloves. My solution was mittens. Her hands fit very easily in the mittens and kept them warm. It was nice when a family member knitted her a pair that were easy to put on and warm in the winter.

With all the pain medication my mom was taking she didn't complain about the pain from arthritis. She was on enough medication to numb an elephant so it was nice that her hands and neck didn't hurt too much. The problem was that she couldn't move her fingers the way she wanted or move her neck as freely as possible. When she turned her head you could her a crack and it was kind of scary because it sounded like something broke.

She had dealt with arthritis since the 1970s and she somehow grew accustomed to the pain. With the prescription medication the pain was no longer an issue but the loss of use of her hands and fingers was always a problem for her. It was just another challenge we had to deal with and that lasted all the way to the time of her death.

Pain

My mom was always in pain due to her scoliosis and curvature of the spine. As she got older the pain became more intense and took its toll on her way of life. When the pain started to get stronger she would walk with a cane or she would use a wheelchair if we went out. This seemed to keep the pain in check because her body had some sort of support.

As time went on the pain became stronger and intolerable. She was in pain most of the time and it showed on her face and in her attitude. When you're in pain your very uncomfortable and it also makes you irritable. That was when the doctor decided to prescribe the use of pain medication. She started on small dosages of Hydrocodone and this increased over time because the pain kept overcoming the medication. This was about 1990 and increasing dosages of Hydrocodone worked until about 1998. After Hydrocodone became useless the family doctor prescribed Hydromorphone and this once again started to keep the pain in check. As before her body overcame the pain medication and caused the doctor to prescribe and increasing amount of the drug. We even went to a pain clinic for medication to be injected into the spine. This provided some comfort for a day or two but then the pain returned with a vengeance. This lead to her spinal decompression surgery which was to be the cure for the majority of the pain.

Unfortunately the pain became worse after the surgery. In fact pain became so unbearable that it would cause her to hyperventilate and have spasms. The surgeon and the rehabilitation doctor prescribed Fentanyl patches to control the pain. They said they needed to get the pain under control and once it was stabilized they could control it. This was wishful thinking on their part. They would use a scale of one to ten, one being no pain and ten being the worse pain imaginable. At that point when they would ask my mom for a number she would always yell, "Twelve!" They tried a variety of medications to calm her down and subdue the pain. They finally found a dosage of a Fentanyl patch every three days and Hydrocodone every six hours for break out pain on the third day. They also prescribed Morphine tablets for extreme bouts of pain. This was able to control the pain from 2001 until her death. We had to increase the Fentanyl patch strength as time went on and we also had to increase the Hydrocodone dosage to maintain pain control. Every time she went into the hospital they tried to change the pain medication regimen. It never worked and we ended up going back to the old schedule.

During the last month of her life the pain started to subside. She did not complain about pain but she was confused more often . I guess this was mother natures way of getting her ready for the end.

Dehydration

Dehydration is always something you have to be aware of while you are taking care of your parent. As they get older it is harder for them to feel heat so they need to always have water available so they don't dehydrate. This can happen at home or on the road. It can also be a challenge because they sometimes don't want to drink due to the fact they will have to urinate more. They might feel this puts more work on you because you either have to take them to the bathroom more are change their diaper more frequently.

I would always have glass of water in front of or around my mom. I wanted her to drink at least eight 8 ounce glasses of water a day to keep her hydrated. I was told this when my mom was in the hospital after her spine surgery. I learned her urine was cloudy and deep yellow because she was not drinking enough water. I made sure this never happened when she was at home.

Because of severe arthritis in her hands it was difficult for her to hold a glass and my solution was a plastic drinking glass with a cover and an attached straw. This made it easier for her to drink and also easy to keep tabs on how much she was drinking by monitoring how many times a day I refilled the cup. The only problem was these plastic cups, covers and straws were hard to keep clean. Make sure you can disassemble them to clean and/ or replace the straw this way no bacteria can grow in the glass. Sometimes they were hard to find but I would buy new ones every month. This is another expense that many don't know. I would have a couple available and would change them everyday. To wash them I used dish soap and a brush to clean them inside. I would fill them with hot water and drop a denture tablet in them to clean out the inside so the dish soap would not infuse into the plastic. When the denture table stopped fizzing and disintegrated I would rinse them with hot water and they would be ready for the next day. This kept a fresh supply of sippy glasses available at all times.

When we went on the road she was able to drink water out of a plastic bottle. I would place a bottle of water in the cup holder nearest to her and have others available in a portable cooler we took every time we went out. When she finished a bottle she would tell me and I would crack the top open on a new one and give it to her. She was never out of water this way.

She didn't just drink water, she also drank juice, coffee and hot chocolate. The juice would be put into a sippy cup with a straw so it was easier for her to hold. Coffee and hot chocolate were put into a travel mug with a cover and a handle. This way she could sip it without spilling.

We followed this procedure for the entire time I was taking care of her. I probably could have used bottled water or juice boxes at home but to me that was like using paper plates and plastic utensils. That's great for a picnic but it was not something to use in the house. In all the years she never got dehydrated or heat exhaustion. The only times she almost got dehydrated was when she was constipated so much because of the pain medication that nothing would go in or out. Those were the times she had to go to the hospital for an IV and controlled amounts of laxatives and enemas.

Loss Of Appetite

My dad and mom always had good appetites and they enjoyed their food. They were both Italian and liked big meals. They held on to this big appetite almost to the end but when they lost their appetite it happened fast. This was also when I knew it was the beginning of the end.

My dad lost his appetite when he started radiation treatments for his throat cancer. Before that he ate hearty and enjoyed everything he ate. When the cancer treatments started he lost his appetite to the point where it was a chore for him to finish what was on his plate. My dad grew up during the Great Depression and the one thing that made him angry and he wouldn't do was waste food. So when he couldn't finish his meal I knew their was a problem. I didn't want to cut the portions down because the doctors and I felt that he would eat even less because there wasn't as much on his plate. Finally I cut the portions down because he did feel guilty about wasting food and I didn't want to make him upset. As his condition deteriorated so did his appetite and he died within two months of his radiation treatments.

My mom also had a great appetite but the difference between her and my dad was she also liked sweets. My dad would say, "Why have dessert, I would rather have more of the meal." My mom would say, "There's always room for dessert." She ate big meals and enjoyed every one of them. I would always try to make a balanced meal with a meat, vegetable and a starch. She would have a full plate and finish it off. She liked chicken and no matter how I made it she would eat a half a chicken herself. She also would always have room for pie, cake, pastry or ice cream. Even when we went to a restaurant she would clean her plate and amazed waiters and waitresses along the way.

She looked small but she had a large appetite. This lasted until about one month before she died. After her last hospital visit her appetite wasn't as big and she started not eating as much. She tried but it just wouldn't go down but she still did eat her dessert. The last week of her life she was content with soup and she didn't want dessert. That's when I knew the end was near.

Cholesterol

Many people suffer from high cholesterol and it is something that needs to be monitored for good health. My dad had high cholesterol and at first it was treated by medication. As time when on I started working on his diet and we were able to keep it in check by the foods he ate. We had one physician that was always concerned about his cholesterol and wasn't interested in his other conditions. My dad's pulmonary physician, gastrointestinal doctor, cardiologist, urologist and oncologist were more concerned about his asbestosis and other conditions and they were not too interested in his cholesterol levels. That's when we decided to stop going to the general practitioner and stay with the specialists. The general doctor was good but my dad needed more specialized care to deal with his deteriorating condition. As time when on and his diseases progressed his cholesterol levels would be all over the place and became harder to control. This is when all the doctors treating him decided that it was better to let him eat what he wanted because mentally it did more good for him than worrying about his cholesterol levels. We still had to watch his diet because he was diabetic but we were able to control that with insulin and creative cooking.

My mom on the other hand never had a problem with high cholesterol. I learned from taking care of my dad how to control this with proper meals and diet and this also helped me maintain normal cholesterol levels. Once in a while a blood test would show her cholesterol levels were slightly elevated but once again her doctors were not concerned because it wasn't steady. The consensus of her doctors was also the same, at her age let her have what she wants. If the blood tests showed a major change then we would deal with the situation as it came. Her being able to eat what she wanted mentally did more good for her situation than being on a restricted diet. They kept monitoring her results but she never had elevated cholesterol levels on two blood tests in a row, it might have been one out of six and it never became an issue.

I was lucky I didn't have to prepare special meals for her because of her cholesterol or diabetes so our situation was based on my mom's condition. We listened to her doctors and followed their recommendations. Working closely with her physicians went a long way in maintaining her health.

Sugar And Diabetes

High sugar and diabetes are a serious situation and requires special care when you are a caregiver. You might have to prepare special meals and use supplement drinks to make sure your parent is getting proper nutrition. You also might have to learn and be required to give insulin shots to your parent.

My dad had high sugar and for years it was controlled by diet and medication. He wasn't much of a dessert person but did occasionally enjoy a piece of pie. He was a large man and his attitude was why have dessert when you can have a larger meal. This all changed when his sugar levels became harder to control with diet and medication and it was necessary for him to go on insulin.

When his sugar levels started to increase I changed my cooking habits and used no sugar in any of the meals I prepared. The strange thing was he never used sugar in his coffee or other drinks and he didn't eat much pastry. Once I bought what I thought was a treat, a sugarless pie and after tasting it we both agreed no pie tasted better than the sugarless pie.

Everything changed for all of us when it was decided that my dad needed daily insulin shots and that his sugar levels had to be monitored many times a day. A home health nurse came to the house and showed my dad, mom and myself how to give him an insulin shot. It was hard for him to inject himself but he could do it if necessary. My mom learned how to do the injections but she was always afraid of hurting him and she did because she would get nervous when she had to actually make the injection. It fell on me and I was the one that would fill the syringe from the vial of insulin and do the injection. Part of the problem was that it was hard for my mom and dad to read the syringe for the proper dosage. They made magnifiers to attach to the syringes but they were still difficult to read. They could do the blood sticks and operate the testing meter but they also had a hard time figuring out the proper dosage of insulin. At first it was hard for me too but I learned very quickly. Part of the problem is being nervous I could over medicate him with the wrong dosage of insulin. Fortunately this never happened and I was able to dispense his insulin properly until the time of his death.

Dealing with a diabetic and insulin there is so much you have watch. With all his other medical conditions this became quite a chore. The insulin had to be refrigerated and you needed to make sure you always had an ample supply. You also had to take special care and bring a cooler when you went on the road. At that time not all pharmacies carried the specific type he was prescribed so I asked our pharmacy to order it and have it in stock. As time went on he needed protein drinks to supplement his nutrition and you had to purchase the ones that were sugar free. They were more expensive and were not covered by any insurance. The testing meter was covered by insurance but the testing strip were not. The lancets, sugar tablets and alcohol wipes were also another expense that came out of your pocket. The list went on and on.

You had to be aware of low sugar and you had to be ready to give him a sugar tablet so he wouldn't go into a coma. This only happened once and it wasn't noticed by his sugar levels. One morning I took his sugar reading and they were the usual were he needed a small dose of insulin and at noon his levels required that he needed another small dose. Later in the day he became weak, lethargic and out of it. He couldn't walk or stand and get out of bed. I called his doctor and told him of the situation. He started saying that I needed to take him to the emergency room then I asked if it could be low sugar? He told me to check his levels again and sure enough they were extremely low and he advised me to give him a sugar tablet. I did what he said and about a half hour later my dad was a little weak but for the most part back to normal. I called the doctor back and told him about the recovery and he said it was a good call and that low sugar can come fast and out of the blue. Now I found out the hard way the experience of low sugar and I would be able to recognize it in the future. That was the only time I had to deal with a low sugar situation because my father passed away two months later.

My mom on the other hand never had a situation with high sugar. It's a good thing too because she enjoyed her sweets. To the end her sugar levels were never elevated and we never had to due daily, weekly or monthly monitoring. The only time her sugar needed to be checked was with the routine blood tests and it was always normal.

Confusion

As a person gets older they start getting a little more confused and they get overwhelmed by their surroundings and the people around them. Being a caregiver you need to be aware of this situation and be prepared to repeat yourself when you are talking to them. You will be answering questions over and over and repeating yourself several times.

My dad failed rapidly and the confusion started all at once. Sure he would get a little confused but he quickly overcame that confusion and got back to normal. Most of the time the problem would be people talking to fast or too soft so he couldn't understand or hear them.

My mom didn't start getting confused until about the last year of her life. She would forget things once in a while but usually remembered them within a few minutes. She always remembered what happened years before but got confused on current issues. She would think for a while and sooner or later the thought would come back to her.

As time went on the confusion became worse and it got to the point where she would have a blank look on her face and seemed completely out of it. Sometimes she would snap out of it quickly and others she would do this for a few minutes. You could make loud noises and even touch her and she wouldn't acknowledge you. Her doctor said she was having micro strokes and it was normal with her age and situation. This was confirmed during her last hospital visit when they did a scan and it showed scars of several micro and mini strokes. This confusion continued to increase until she passed away.

I was amazed at how fast this happened. It was the same with my dad, it happened quickly and towards the end. They were lucky because this happens to a lot of people early and it progressively gets worse as they get older. I never had to deal with serious confusion, dementia or Alzheimers disease. With all the other ailments and conditions I was thankful this was something I avoided.

Staring Into Space Look

Sometimes when you see an elderly person they have a look on their face like they are staring into space. They have no clue what's around them and it seems like they are not listening or paying attention. I use to see this when I was in junior high school and we would go to the local convalescent hospital to visit the elderly. I made it a point that when I was taking care of my parents they would not be in this type of a situation.

Since I am not a doctor I have absolutely no idea what causes this situation. My only thought was that if I kept my parents busy they would remain engaged. This meant asking them questions about the past and current events. Giving them chores and tasks to do so they kept busy. Playing games or having them do word puzzles to keep their mind sharp. Interacting and playing with the grand and great grandchildren to participate in their lives. All this was to let them know they were still part of our lives and they still had things they could do. They were not useless and they could still bring something to the conversation. Just because they were old did not mean they couldn't still be part of life and be engaged in conversations. Even taking groceries out of the bag gave them something to do and gave them the sense that they were helping.

Watching television can also keep them engaged but you have to talk to them so they know you are around. When I was young people thought of television as a substitute baby sitter and it was to some extent. We didn't watch it all day because we went to school and after we came home we went outside to play. With an elderly person they can watch television but you have to talk to them so they stay engaged with you. My mom liked to watch baseball and she could do this for five to six hours a day. Yes, I let her watch it but I also kept talking to her about the games or teams. I was making her talk about what she was watching. If we had to go out, the television never interrupted our schedule. When people came over it didn't interfere with their visit. It gave her something to watch and learn but it didn't replace the day to day tasks and conversations.

My situation was different because neither of my parents experienced any serious confusion or dementia. That finally took effect in the last stages of their life just before they passed away. During most of the time I was taking care of my parents I kept them busy so they had a purpose and contributed to our day to day routine.

Cancer

I had to deal with cancer many times while I was taking care of my parents. My dad was diagnosed with bladder cancer in 1993. His lung disease, asbestosis, which was diagnosed in 1975 turned to lung cancer in 1994. In late 1994 he was diagnosed with throat cancer and brain cancer was diagnosed in February of 1995 and he died in April of that year. My mom was diagnosed with breast cancer in 1993, again in 2003 and 2007.

My parents were of the generation that when they heard the word cancer it meant a death sentence. Unfortunately for my dad, he survived the bladder cancer but he succumbed to the lung cancer as it metastasized through his body. My mom, on the other hand, beat breast cancer three times, and lived to ninety-three years old.

Both of my parents went to the doctors regularly and followed the physicians instructions. When my dad was diagnosed with bladder cancer, that really through us a curve because we never considered the possibility of cancer to this part of his body. After we learned more about this situation we learned that it was caused by all the chemical exposure he received while being a pipe fitter for the Navy at the local Naval shipyard. We always knew that the asbestosis, which was also contracted from his work at the Naval shipyard, would eventually turn into lung cancer and we just hoped that it would not spread throughout my dad's body. He had constant check ups, x-rays and scans and for years nothing seemed out of the ordinary. He would spit up blood once in a while and he would go to the emergency room and we always thought the worst. After tests and scopes, two of the three times nothing was found. The last time they found a spot and it grew rapidly. He could not have surgery because of his reduced lung capacity so they opted for other treatments. It didn't work and it traveled to his throat, brain and all over his body. It ate away at his body and killed him within six months.

My mom thought she had a death sentence when she was diagnosed with breast cancer in 1993. This occurred a few months before my dad was diagnosed with bladder cancer. I remember when the doctor called me and gave me the news the tumor was malignant I knew I was going to have a hard time controlling my mom from becoming hysterical. I had a signal with my dad, so he knew ahead of time, I sat her down and I told both of them the results. She began to cry and scream and she kept yelling, "No, no." I let her cry for a while then I gave her more bad news that she needed a mastectomy. That started the whole process all over again. We let her cry and my dad consoled her for about an hour and then she calmed down and said, "I going through with it." She went through the surgery and was cancer free for ten years. In 2003 she found another lump and it was malignant. She had the tumor removed and was once again free of cancer. In 2007 she found another lump and it was also malignant and removed. The cancer never returned, and she died in 2013.

My parents had their scares and bouts with the dreaded disease of cancer. My dad won one battle but lost the next. My mom won the battle three times and survived to die of natural causes. She was always afraid of the cancer death sentence but she beat it and went on with her life.

Lifting Legs Up

I was amazed out how fast my mom's legs could swell and change color. Sometimes they would swell after only a few minutes in the wheelchair and other times it would be after a long car ride. They would be cold to the touch and turn dark pink. During our normal daily routine they would swell while she was at the dining room table.

As soon as I put my mom in bed and lifted her feet up the swelling would go down, their temperature would rise and the dark pink color would return to normal. Sometimes they would be fine for the rest of the day and other days the problem would reoccur in the late afternoon when I got my mom up for dinner.

I tried putting a short stool in front of her while she was in her wheelchair and that didn't work because her feet would fall of the stool. She had very little control of her leg movements and sometimes they would spasm. I tried a stool that had sides and that held her feet from falling off but it didn't help with the swelling. The stool was too low and did nothing to help.

This was a battle we had everyday since she had her spine surgery. She went to the doctor and they found out one leg had almost no circulation so she had angioplasty surgery on that leg and it corrected some of the problems. Now both legs were the same because before one leg swelled larger, was colder and was darker.

We finally cured the problem when we bought a reclining wheelchair. This unit was great because it was padded, had large six inch wheels which made it easy to maneuver in the house. It had cup holders and a removable food tray. The best thing about it was it reclined. I could move it into different positions to raise and lower her legs. She was comfortable and her legs no longer swelled when she was in this wheelchair.

The only time now her legs swelled was when she was in the car for a long period of time. I did make some head way with this situation by placing a pillow under her legs after I put her in the car. I didn't prevent the swelling but it did limit it a little. It also kept her legs from getting cold and the color only slightly darkened. It wasn't a complete success but it helped.

Now we had solutions for the wheelchair, car and in bed. It took a lot of trial and error but we found a solution that worked for one issue and one that helped another. Like I have said over and over caregiving is always a learning experience.

Leg Circulation In The Car

The car is one of the hardest things to deal with while caring for a parent. Even if it is a large vehicle, unless you can push the wheelchair right in the car it is always a difficult task. The seats are not the most comfortable and can cause problems with circulation.

When you are driving a lot of times your feet get tired as well as your legs. Pressing the accelerator, brake and if equipped, clutch give you a little exercise for your feet and legs. Now if you're a passenger you are usually cramped in the seat and you don't move around much. Now take someone that can't move around and you could have a serious situation.

My mom couldn't move or feel much on her legs so when she was in the car I had to make sure everything was all right. When I lifted her in I always had to make sure I didn't snag or catch her legs on the car door frame and the same was true for when I lifted her out. We had a Suburban, which has a lot more room in the front seat than most vehicles and her legs still had problems. Her legs and feet would swell, get cold and change color. I had to be careful when I used the air conditioner or heater because for some reason the floor vents were always open a little no matter what the controls were set on. They could cool her legs even more or burn them if the heat was set on high and she wouldn't feel the difference. To be safe I always put a wrap on her legs to prevent the cold or hot air from affecting her legs.

I would stop and get out and rub her legs during long trips to try to help the circulation. I did find out after trial and error that placing a pillow under her feet and legs after I put her in the car helped with the circulation. Her feet and legs didn't swell as much. It also helped maintain the proper color and they were a lighter shade of pink.

This is something you have to be aware of when you take your parent in the car. Their circulation is not as good as it use to be and sitting in a car for period of time can cause problems. Even we have to get out once and awhile to stretch our legs and prevent them from cramping up. Don't forget your parent has the same problems and maybe worse.

No Feeling In Toes

Somedays my mom had feeling in her toes and other days she didn't. It happened to both feet and we never knew why. When we would go to the podiatrist she might feel her trimming her toe nails on one foot and would feel nothing on the other. Even after she had the angioplasty on her leg it never changed. Other times I could touch a toe and she would jump. It was something we dealt with the entire time I was taking care of her full time.

This presented challenges when I would lift her because if I bumped her feet she would not feel it. The problem was also that if they were bleeding she wouldn't feel that either. We had an incident where her toes dragged on the ground while she was being pushed in the wheelchair. She felt nothing all I saw was her toes were bleeding and dirty. This was a challenge that we always had to deal with and try to prevent.

I would put slip-on shoes on her and she couldn't feel them. They would fall off and I would be picking them up and putting them back on her feet. Somebody would bump her toes and she wouldn't feel anything and other times she would stub her toe against the wheelchair footrest and react. It was never the same reaction in the same day or the same foot.

We knew she had poor circulation because her legs would swell when she was seated for an extended amount of time. That was an everyday occurrence and we got it under control by raising her legs up or putting her in bed. Still the feeling in her feet and toes constantly kept changing from none to some. It was a battle we fought until the day she died.

Leg And Feet Skin Dry, Needed Lotion

My mom had poor circulation in her legs and feet and that also led to dry skin. Everyday I would wash her legs and feet with a wash cloth and dry them. Within an hour or two the skin would be dry and have skin flakes. I used moisturizing soap, pure soap and a variety of other types of skin soaps and they all had the same results. I would have to put moisturizing cream on her legs and feet.

When the home health nurse would come to the house she would see the same thing and ask what I was doing to prevent it. When I told her she said that I was doing everything that I could and to keep doing it. When I took her to the wound center they would look at her dry legs and ask questions and I would give them my answers. They would say the same thing keep doing your routine and then they would put moisturizing cream on her legs.

I finally got an answer when we went to the doctor for her poor leg circulation. He said that the skin was drying out because their was not enough blood flow. That would explain the leg with almost no circulation but it didn't explain the other one with reduced circulation. He said that both legs needed more circulation to keep the skin moist and for it to heal. He did the angioplasty on the one leg and that did make a difference to the dryness of that leg. He said to continue using cream to keep the legs and feet moist and it was just going to be the normal routine.

We fought this battle the entire time that she couldn't walk. We never went to a dermatologist because my mom didn't want to go to another doctor. When I asked our general doctor he said that they would run tests and try different creams. He didn't think it was a good idea to put my mom under more stress. She agreed and I just kept trying different lotions and creams. I never found one that eliminated the dry skin but I did find some that worked for a short time. For over thirteen years she had dry skin on her legs and feet. I was never able to get it under control.

Chapter 12

MEDICAL PROCEDURES, TESTS AND DIAGNOSIS

Diagnosis And Problems

When you're a caregiver you need to be ready and prepared for anything. Many times you are hoping for the best and it turns out to be the worst. I always prepared myself for the worst outcome, if the result was positive, I was relieved and then got ready for the next challenge. As time goes on you learn how to get, receive and give bad news. You also have to know how your mom or dad will react. In my case, my mom would get anxious when she got bad news. I found out it was better to tell her straight out and help calm her down as she reacted. This made me ready to handle anything and to say, "You got to do what you got to do."

My dad and I knew my mom did not react well to bad news so when she found a lump on her breast and had a biopsy we made an arrangement with the family physician. This was before the HIPPA (Health Insurance Portability and Accountability Act) so it was just a matter of talking to the doctor privately. I told him to call me and let me know the situation and I would tell my mom the news when I felt she could handle it. He agreed because he also thought this was the best way to handle her situation and he told my mom he was going to call me. She was okay with this because she knew she might pass out if she heard bad news on the phone. A few days after the biopsy the doctor called and gave me the bad news, the tumor was malignant and she needed a mastectomy. This was not going to be easy. She knew the doctor was going to call me in a few days with the results. That day when she was settled down I told her the results of the test. Sure enough, she heard the word cancer and started to cry and scream. My dad and I settled her down and told her that it was treatable but she would have to have a mastectomy. That made her more hysterical. We let her cry for a while and she kept asking questions. I answered what I could and told her I would check with the doctor with her other questions. She was a wreck for about two hours but then told me to call the doctor to tell him she would go through the procedure. That was in 1993. She survived the breast cancer and lived to 2013.

Lab And Test Results

Over the years my folks had many lab tests and that meant a lot of results. Some tests were great and others showed great concern for their condition. I was fortunate that the doctors we had always discussed the results with me and taught me what different tests meant.

When the lab results were normal my folks would always ask me if it was true and I would say, "Yes." If they were not normal they would ask me to explain them. If the doctor explained the results they never understood what they were saying. I made arrangements with our doctors to call and give me the lab results so I was ready to explain them to my parents. If they were abnormal they would fax me a copy of the lab report so I could do research and be prepared for the next step. This was before HIPAA (Health Insurance Portability and Accountability Act) so there was no issue with privacy and my folks had already told all the doctors to give me all the information. They all agreed and it became a great learning experience for me.

My dad had lung cancer and he was having lab work every few days. The cancer moved to his throat and they started radiation therapy. Lab work was required constantly. We lived in Lynwood, California and we would drive down to Long Beach to the oncology center. They would draw the blood and get the results in and hour or so. They would give me the print out and he would ask, "How are the numbers?" I would tell him if they were high or low and he would just smile. The numbers never got better and he died a few months later.

My mom saw how I handled things with my dad so she had a little routine when I would get her lab results. She would say, "Are you sure?" and I would tell her the numbers were okay and I would show her the lab report. I don't think she knew what she was looking at but it made her feel better that I would show them to her.

It was always nice to get normal or close to normal results. When the results were bad and more tests were required it always caused anxiety. Most of the time the numbers were right and I would have to tell her about another problem. Her usual response was, "Oh no." I would tell her we would fight and she usually did. That's how she beat breast cancer three times. Whenever she found a spot we would tell the oncologist and he would schedule tests. They usually came back positive and fortunately for her he was able to maintain her condition with medication. A few times he had to schedule outpatient surgery but after that she was good for a few more years.

One of the last tests she had in 2010 was a cat scan and it showed a mass near her pancreas. The Gastrointestinal Specialist wanted to know what I wanted to do. I asked him what could we do and his response was nothing. I never told my mom about this result and nothing ever showed up on her blood work. In fact her last blood test was almost normal and our family doctor was amazed how good it was for her age.

Her last visit in the hospital never showed any other major abnormalities on most of her other organs but they said her body was weakening. Her heart rate and pressure were low and they said her body was getting tired. They were right and she died two months later.

MRI's

My mom was afraid of almost everything. When we were growing up any loud noise would make her jump. She was afraid of dark places and small areas. I was always concerned that if she ever needed and MRI it would be an extreme challenge.

Open MRI's were something new and were not readily available when my mom was sick. I had an MRI done a few times and it was challenging for me. I have crawled under houses, in attics and have been in dark confined spaces and I never had a problem. For some reason being in an MRI was a little unnerving but I was able to tolerate and get through it. I knew my mom would never be able to handle an MRI because of the closeness and the noise.

Sure enough as her illness progressed the doctors ordered an MRI and I knew I was in for a struggle. They wanted me to take her in so she could see how the machine worked and hopefully that would calm her nerves. Since I knew my mom I knew that wouldn't be a good idea because she would hear the noise and just get terrified. I knew it was better just to have her see it when she was going to have the procedure and there was less chance of her changing her mind.

I prepared her by telling her what she was going to see and hear. I told her what the technicians was going to tell her and what she was going to have to wear. She was concerned but I told her she would be able to do it. I told her the best thing was to close her eyes and think of a nice place she would want to be or think of her family.

We went to the outpatient center, I got her ready, changed her into a hospital gown, went into the room with the machine and then I put her on the platform. The technician told her what she was going to hear and see. He told her that if she had a problem to press the button he was giving her and he would stop the test. She told him, "I'm going to keep my eyes closed." He then said, "If you want to close your eyes, that's fine." We left the room and he started the test. I figured it would be a matter of a few minutes and he would have to stop the test because she would press the button, start getting nervous and begin yelling. He was really good and he was ready for anything if it happened. He went ahead with the test and my mom wasn't pressing the button. On the monitor she had her eyes closed and she looked fine. I was amazed and she went through the entire test without a problem. The technician said, "That's it," and the platform started coming out of the machine. We went into the room and he said, "You did good, Mrs. Colozzo, that wasn't so bad." She looked at him and said, "Yes it was, that's why I kept my eyes closed." We both laughed and I took her out of the room and got her ready to go home.

I told her that I was proud of her and she did really well. She did say that she hoped she didn't have to go through, "One of those" again and I agreed. We were both wrong and she had to have an MRI three more times in her lifetime. The last three were done during a hospital stay and fortunately I was there when they were going to do the test. The last thing I would always tell her was, "Close your eyes," and her response was, "I have them closed." She did fine on all those tests and they never had to stop them because she got nervous or upset.

Diagnostic Results

I had to handle diagnostic results the same as lab results. Once again I had made arrangements with the doctors to give me the information first so I could be prepared when they delivered the news. Whether it was good or bad I always knew ahead of time and I was able to praise or comfort my mom and dad.

This was an easy task if our regular doctors were the ones ordering the diagnostic tests. It became a little more of a challenge when a new doctor or facility was ordering the test. The way I handled this was to have our family doctor call the new physician or facility, request the information and explain our situation. This always worked and I was able to be prepared for whatever the results.

I was able to work with our doctors but it meant a lot of phone calls and conversations. I made it a little easier for them because I was able to give the news in a way that prevented my parents from becoming excited and nervous. I could calm them down so the doctor could explain the treatment and how it would affect them. Whenever we had bad news we always agreed we were going to fight and beat it. Most of the time they did but sooner or later one will get you and it did.

Surgeries

After my mom had her spine surgery the doctors were considering doing another spinal decompression and fusion of the lower back. They were planning on doing this when she had her original surgery but they felt it would have taken too long and it would have been a major stress on her system. After they realized the first surgery was a failure they once again contemplated the spinal decompression and fusion of the lower back. They brought me into the discussion and we all agreed it would be a risky surgery. The surgery could have been as long as seventeen hours and the recovery and rehabilitation could have taken up to six months. Given the fact that she did so poorly during the first surgery and rehabilitation we decided that the risk was too great and that she might not survive. She was 81 years old at the time and we decided a different option needed to be used. When I told my mom she also agreed and did not want to have the surgery.

When we moved to Tehachapi in 2008 she had her first episode with severe constipation. It was in November a few months after we moved to the area. She ended up in a hospital in Bakersfield and after the doctors consulted they said she had a severe blockage and they felt the only option was to perform surgery to remove it. If they were not able to repair the intestine then she would have to wear a colostomy bag for the rest of her life. I was concerned about her age, she was 88 at the time, and how her body would react to major surgery. I talked to my sisters and then I talked to my mom and she wanted to go ahead with the surgery if it would make her better and to prevent these problems in the future. My mom was alert and gave the doctors the permission for the surgery.

We were told the procedure would take four to six hours and then they would let us know. She went into surgery and we waited for the results. About three hours into the surgery the surgeon came out and said she was fine and that they were able to repair the intestine. He said she was so impacted from the pain medication that the feces got stuck on some scar tissue and caused the blockage. He said there was no reason to reroute the colon to a colostomy bag and she would be back to normal in a few days. He said it was touch and go at first but they were able to stabilize her and she came through the rest of the surgery without a hitch.

She recovered within a few days and I took her home in about a week. She bounced back to her normal self in no time as she regained her enormous appetite. We had another bought with severe constipation about a year later. We were taken to the same hospital and the same doctors this time decided on a treatment of mass doses of laxatives and enemas. This worked to clean her out and they prevented her from becoming dehydrated with the use of IV's. In 2013 she had another bought of severe constipation and we were taken to a different hospital. The doctors at that facility also felt that mass doses of laxative and enemas would correct the problem. Once again it did and she was discharged.

She never had another surgery after 2008. I was amazed at how routine it was for the doctors to do major surgery on a person with her condition and at her age. That's why they are the experts and you have to listen to them for their advice and options. My mom made it easy for us because she made the decision to go ahead with the surgery.

Colostomy Bag

When the doctors told us that my mom might have to wear a colostomy bag if they weren't able to remove the blockage and repair her intestine I was very concerned. My dad had survived bladder cancer by having his bladder removed and he had to wear an urostomy bag for the last few years of his life. This thing was a pain because there was always the chance it could leak or fall off. My dad was embarrassed because he had it and was always concerned that it would leak or fail when he went out. For a while he was afraid to go out because of that possibility. Most of the time there were no problems but once in a while we would get a bad bag or a flange that would not attach properly to his skin and leak.

These concerns were going through my head when we were told of this option. I was thinking dealing with urine on pants or a shirts was a problem but not as big of a problem as feces seeping through. I started thinking that my mom would also be embarrassed and stop wanting to go out and therefore reduce her quality of life. I asked to see the products and I was impressed with what I saw. Since the years my dad had to wear a urostomy bag the products had changed and they seemed a little more reliable. I also started to think that if my mom had to wear a colostomy bag we would no longer have to wait for her "to go" and we could leave whenever we wanted. All I would have to make sure was she had a clean and empty bag on and we were good for the day. The doctor also explained that this would also solve some of the problems of the blockages caused by extreme constipation due to the pain medication. I realized that this would mean more work but in the long run it would be better for my mom. I took a deep breath and said to myself, "I have to do what I have to do."

Chapter 13

FIRST TIME DOING PROCEDURES

Not A Medical Professional Or Claim To Be

I am not a medical professional or claim to be. I have absolutely no medical training and have never attended any caregiving classes. The only class I ever attended about caring for someone was CPR training. I was never officially taught by the hospital or any other medical provider.

What I learned was from on the job training and watching the professionals as they took care of my dad and mom. I became a sponge and absorbed as much as I could so I could take care of them properly. Also a lot comes from common sense and the way I would want to be treated.

I cannot give advice or tell anyone what to do because I have no training in this field. All I am doing is telling how I took care of my parents and how I faced obstacles in being their caregiver. I am voicing my experiences whether they were right or wrong and how I handled different situations. I did what I had to do to care for my dad and mom.

If you are going to be a caregiver for your parent get as much training and advice as you can. Every year things change such as procedures and laws so you need to be aware of what is required in your state to be a caregiver. Remember once you make the decision you are responsible for whatever happens to your parent.

Go Where You Never Wanted To Go

When you take care of your parent you're going to have to do things that you never thought you would have to do. Somethings will turn your stomach and others will be downright embarrassing. So when you make the decision to become a caregiver be ready to go where you never wanted to go.

Taking care of my dad was less embarrassing than taking care of my mom. When it was time to take care of my mom there is that initial point that you dread. It is an emotional block you must get through because you keep saying to yourself, "I have to do what?"

My first experience with that was when my mom needed to have a scan of her intestines. This was in the very beginning when she couldn't walk but was still able to clean herself in the bathroom. She needed an enema to clean her out for the test. I was a little hesitant at the doctors office when they told me I would have to give her the enema for the test. I said, "That's going to be a little tough." The nurse said, "No it's not. Just roll her on her side and put it in and squeeze the bottle, nothing to it." Easy for her to say but this was my mom.

Needless to say the evening before the test I went where I never wanted to go. My mom was in bed and I rolled her over on her side. I took a deep breath, found the target, inserted the nozzle and squeezed the bottle, just like the nurse said. I went where I never wanted to go and I did what I had to do.

Coming to find out that was the easy part. The hard part was putting her on the toilet when the enema started working. I was trying to rush so she wouldn't make a mess and we almost had a disaster. She was impatient and I was trying to lift her and put her on the toilet before anything came out and I almost slipped on the floor because my feet weren't planted properly. One leg slipped and I struggled to hold her but I regained control and put her safely on the toilet before she went.

I got over that situation very quickly and it was the start of many more events in the future. The first one was the hardest to deal with because it was something I had never done. These type of procedures are not something you think about while you are growing up and they are definitely not something you plan for. On the other hand it was just as embarrassing for my mom and I know she never thought her son was going to have to give her an enema. Not something she wanted to think about or plan on. When the time comes you don't want to do it but you have to because it is for their health. You overcome your fears or anxiety and you do what you have to do.

Sight Of Your Parent's Body

One of the thoughts that can cause a lot of people to seek therapy is the sight of their parents naked body. I'm sure a lot of people will say that they never want to see it or will do whatever it takes to avoid this situation. Unfortunately when you are a caregiver and taking care of your parent it is unavoidable.

When I was taking care of my dad it was a lot easier to help him dress or take him to the bathroom because we were both male. I never had an issue and it was just a job I had to do to help him. He was a little embarrassed at first and I knew this because every time I had to take him to the bathroom or dress him he would say, "I'm sorry." This stopped after a few times and I would always tell him, "There's nothing to be sorry for, it's my job and I'm glad I can do it." He would smile but I knew he was still a little concerned.

When I started taking care of my mom it was a whole different story, I was embarrassed. When I had to change her diaper the first time I had her put a towel across her front and then I rolled her on her side. I had no problem with seeing her backside but I did with seeing the front. I would place the rolled diaper under her and I would roll her on the other side while she held the towel in place. Once in a while I would get of view of the front and I guess I turned a little red because she would say, "It's okay." I would then roll her on her back and I would reach down and pull the diaper up through her legs. I then turned around and she would pull the diaper up and say, "Okay," and I would turn around and affix the tabs. We did this for a long time, the embarrassment wore off very quickly but we still kept the same routine. I felt it gave her a little bit of privacy. As time went on things became more routine and I never had an issue.

I had to help dress her, give her a bath and clean her up after a bowel movement. I had to insert suppositories, give her enemas and apply ointment everywhere on her body. It all became routine and I did what I had to do. I still remember when a nurse told me how to give her an enema.

She said, "You roll her on her side, find the target, put the nozzle in, squeeze the bottle, let it do it's magic and then get out of the way." This is a round a bout way to say you have to do it because no one else will.

As usual the first time is always the worst and I think fear or apprehension makes it harder. You're embarrassed and so is your parent but it is part of the job of being a caregiver. As time goes on it becomes routine and nothing stands in your way of doing your job.

Sight Of Body Fluids

Another item that can make some people squeamish is the sight of bodily fluids from your parent. One of the things I always remember about going into the hospital to see them was to see the catheter bag on the side of the bed. It was hard to look at but you knew it was necessary.

One of my sisters always had a problem with seeing any type of bodily fluids to the point it would make her ill. She would have to walk out of the room when the nurse would empty the catheter bag and measure the volume. It didn't bother me but it took a few times to get use to it.

I got use to seeing bodily fluids and it became part of our everyday routine. When my dad was sick I would have to look at his mucus to see what color it was so I could tell the doctor and he would know if there was an infection. I would have to look at the color of his urine to make sure he was drinking enough fluids and that his organs were working properly.

When I started taking care of my mom I had to do the same thing. She didn't have lung problems so I didn't have to keep a check on her mucus unless she was congested. I still had to check her urine to make sure there were no problems. When she was constipated I pretty much saw everything as we tried to loosen things up. When the stools would get stuck in her rectum I had to take drastic measures to dislodge it so she would not be in pain. It was not a fun job or sight but it had to be done to prevent her from discomfort and major problems. When she was so clogged that she started to vomit I had to smell it and if it smelled like feces I knew a trip to the emergency room was in order. I came a long way from being turned off by seeing a catheter bag.

When I became a caregiver I ended up seeing and feeling everything. It's like when you are taking care of a baby, you deal with urine, feces and vomit. It's a part of life and it is definitely a part of the caregiving experience.

Sight Of Blood

Another thing you have to get use to is the sight of blood. One of my sisters worked in law enforcement and was not bothered by the sight of blood unless it was someone she knew. She was useless when a family member was bleeding and would have to walk away so she wouldn't pass out. Some people can handle it and others want no part of it.

I never had this problem but once in a while I would have to blink a few times to get use to it. The hardest thing for me was when my dad would spit up blood. For some reason this was difficult for me to see, it didn't make me queasy it was just strange to watch. I guess it was because you didn't know what was causing it or if it was life threatening. When you see a cut on a leg or arm you know where it's coming from and you can deal with it immediately. When it's coming from the mouth you have no idea if it's a scrape, cut or tumor. When that happened there was a call to the doctor and a trip to the emergency room.

My mom didn't hurt herself except for the normal cuts and scrapes usually from paper or broken items. The only time I had to deal with blood was when I had to change her wound dressing on her backside. As it was healing it would bleed when I would clean it. The doctor and nurses told me this was normal and I had to make sure that I removed all the dried blood to prevent further problems. I did what I was told and made sure the wound was always clean. It didn't bother me because I knew I had a job to do.

As with seeing your parents body, dealing with bodily fluids the sight of blood is a normal part of being a caregiver and taking care of your parent. A simple bump or something as serious as a fall can cause them to bleed and you will have to apply first aid. Blood is part of life so put on your gloves and take care of the situation.

Being Squeamish

Being squeamish is a condition that you will have to get over if you want to be a caregiver. You can't get sick over something you see while you are taking care of your parent. You will see all kinds of things and if you get sick there will be no one to take care of the situation.

I was never squeamish but my older sister was and would always leave the room whenever a procedure was done. Some people can handle it and some can't fortunately for my parents my other sister and I could so we never had any problems. My other sister was an LVN, Licensed Vocational Nurse, so she was use to all these situations but unfortunately for me she was only able to visit about once a month because of her job and family. I was on my own for most of the time so I had to deal with all the situations.

I never got sick on anything I saw but once in a while I would look away for a second or two to get use to the situation. I felt that if I got sick I would not be able to properly care for my dad or mom so I made sure I overcame the problem. Most of the time you had no time to think and you just had to deal with the situation. When my dad would spit up blood it was difficult to see but I needed to act quickly so the situation did not get out of control. When my mom would vomit and it would smell of feces I didn't have time to worry about being squeamish I had to deal with the situation immediately to prevent her from becoming dehydrated.

I had to forget about my problems and concentrate on the problems my parents were having. I was responsible for their care which meant I had to deal with all kinds of situations. If I got sick it could lead to problems for them which meant I wasn't doing my job. When things happen you just do what you got to do.

I'm Going In

Many times while you are a caregiver you have to do things that you would rather not do. This could be applying a new procedure you are not familiar with, cleaning a messy diaper, giving a bath, cleaning and replacing bandages on a wound or something else entirely. Times and procedures like this you have to take a deep breath and say to yourself, "I'm going in," and just do it.

I had this happen many times while I was taking care of my parents. One of the first things I remember was when my dad would spit up mucous and the doctor would always ask, "What color was it." The first time I had to look into the tissue almost made me sick, but I had to do it. I was never afraid of blood but when I saw my dad spit up blood on several occasions it did make me a little nervous. The first time I had to give him an insulin shot I think it hurt me more than it hurt him. I had the syringe filled with the proper amount of insulin and I squeezed the skin on his stomach, said to myself, "I'm doing this," and I gave him his injection. We were both still alive so I was successful and I was able to do it over and over. The first time is always the worst because it is something you've never done before.When I had to replace his urostomy bag and flange it was nerve racking because if I did it wrong it could fall off and embarrass him and make a mess. I did it and he did not have a problem. The first time I had to give him a shave in the hospital was terrifying, I wasn't a barber but he wanted me to do it. I let it grow a little because I wasn't sure I could do it and finally he said, "Get the razor and give me a shave." I think we both took a deep breath when I started. It was a safety razor and I didn't draw blood so I considered it a success. The times after were much easier. When I had to wash him up the first time was hard on both of us be we got through it. The first time I had to clean him up after using the bathroom was difficult but I did it. When I cleaned him up after a bowel movement it was extremely difficult and embarrassing for the two of us but we both knew it had to be done. This was followed by the usual, "I'm sorry," like it was his fault for being sick. It was never his fault and I never needed an apology, it was something that had to be done.

With my mom it was the same with every procedure that was new. Whether it was cleaning her up after an "accident" in her diaper to putting her on the toilet. The first time was always difficult. Changing her bed wound dressings was a challenge but it was done. Having to "help her" with a large glob when she was constipated was disgusting but it had to be done. Stuffing an incontinence pad in her diaper was not normal but it was needed and then having to remove it was just as bad. Looking at urine and smelling vomit was all part of the job that might make you sick the first time but you learn fast and get over it.

Over the years I had to do some disgusting things according to some people. This is all part of life and is definitely part of being a caregiver. When the challenge comes all you have to do is take a deep breath and say to yourself, "I'm going in." Remember you have to do what you got to do.

First Time Cleaning Up

The hardest time to do a procedure is usually the first. That is true for the procedures you do as a caregiver. The first time you have to clean up your parent after a bowel movement in a diaper is one you dread and won't forget.

The first time I had to clean my mom up after a diaper "accident" was the day after she came home from the hospital after her spine surgery. Before that I was always able to put her on the toilet so she could do her business. She would call or ring her bell and say, "I gotta go." I usually had enough time to remove her diaper and lift her onto the toilet. The day after her surgery she called I was a little slow and she went in the diaper. When I got into the room it smelled and I knew right away she went and was still going. I told her to finish and she called me when she was done. After she was finished I went into the room and cut the diaper tabs. I rolled her on her side, put on a pair of gloves, took a deep breath and said to myself, "It's now or never," and peeled the diaper off. It was a mess because it was loose stools and it was all over the place. It smelled bad and it looked even worse. She kept saying, "I'm sorry," and I told her not to worry about it. It actually upset my stomach when I first saw it but then I got a hold of myself and realized I had a job to do and this was the way things were going to be from now on. I used a bed under pad and wiped the excess material off her back side. I got the baby wipes and started cleaning her skin. I had to change my gloves a few times while I cleaned her up. I used paper towels to wipe her down so she wouldn't be damp from the baby wipes. It took a while but I got her cleaned up. I had to replace the bed under pad because I got some of the residue on it. I tucked a new bed under pad and diaper under her and rolled her on the other side and pulled the bed under pad and diaper through. I rolled her flat on her back and I had her pull the diaper between her legs so she had a little privacy left. I then peeled the tabs and stuck them to the side of the diaper. I sprayed the room with air freshener and I went outside to dispose of the used diaper, wipes, pads and towels. It was over, she was clean and the diaper was replaced.

We survived her first mess and diaper change. I did it and I didn't get sick. She was a little embarrassed but we both got over it because we had a job to do and this was going to happen again so we had better get use to it. This situation happened many times over the thirteen year period. Things happen so you deal with it, as I say, "You got to do what you got to do."

First Time Wound Care

Just as the first time cleaning your parent from a diaper mess leaves an impression so does the first time you have to do wound care. There is a difference because with wound care there could be blood, puss and a smell that could make some people sick to their stomach. The hardest part is to get started because you don't know what to expect.

The first time I had to change the dressing on my mom's bed wound I was a little apprehensive. I watched the wound doctor open it up and de-breed the wound so the sight of blood didn't bother me. I watched the home health nurses change the dressings many times and I saw the blood, puss and inhaled the stench that came from the wound. I was nervous because I was afraid I was going to make it worse or cause my mom some pain.

When the time came I had my instructions, the saline solution to clean, all the medication and supplies needed to change the dressing. I cut the diaper tabs and rolled my mom on her side. I removed the diaper by tucking it under her. I put a bed under pad on top of the diaper and stared at this bloody dressing on her backside. I put on a pair of gloves, I paused for a while and said to myself, "You can do this." I saw the nurse do it many times before so I knew what to do. I took a deep breath and started peeling the dressing off the wound. It smelt bad and when I removed the dressing it looked bad. I threw away the old dressing and started spraying the wound with saline solution. All kinds of crud, dried blood, old skin and puss dripped out. I wet the gauze with the saline solutions and started cleaning the edges of the wound. More junk came out and the wound started to smell better and clean. All during the cleaning I would ask my mom, "Are you okay?" and she would say, "Yes," or I would say, "does it hurt?" and she would answer, "No." I repeated this process a few times until the wound was clean. I dried the excess saline with dry gauze and applied the medication prescribed for the wound. I then applied a square gauze pad and special adhesive tape to the edges of the pad. I removed the bed under pad because it was wet from flushing the wound and I pulled the diaper out from under her and reattached the tabs. I rolled her onto her back and we were finished. We survived my first wound dressing change.

A few days later we had to go to the wound center for our weekly visit and they inspected my wound dressing change. The nurse said I did a good job and she was surprised that I didn't have to call for instructions.

This was the start of many wound dressing changes. In fact we rarely had a home health nurse come back to the house for a dressing change. They would tell me what to do and I would do it. Once again it was hard to get started but my mom's health was more important than my fears or hesitation. I did what I had to do.

Chapter 14
CAREGIVING ROUTINES AND PROCEDURES
Ways To Call You

Whenever you are taking care of a parent make sure they have ways to call you. I'm not just talking about giving them a phone number where you can be reached when you go out but also in your home. If they need help they need a way to call you so you can assist them.

My parents had several ways to call me and it was not just the usual yelling or calling out my name. I gave them walkie talkies so when I went outside they could summon me immediately. I had old fashioned bells so they could ring and I would her them anywhere in the house. I set up wireless doorbells in the house and garage so they could just press a button and I would know they were done doing what they were doing or if they needed help.

Today this task is much easier with the use of a smart phone because not only can they call you, they can use the picture and video function to show you the problem. The last few years I was taking care of my mom I considered getting her a smart phone. The problem was she never learned how to use a computer. In fact she never would use a calculator because she had to push too many buttons. The learning curve was to high for her and she just wasn't interested. My feeling was if she wasn't interested in learning how to use a smart phone, she wouldn't use it. So she continued using the old fashioned ways to call me.

My folks were never without a way to call me for any reason. The problem I had was a lot of times when they needed me they wouldn't call because they wanted me to rest and didn't want to bother me. That was usually during the night when they needed more water. I still would hear them because I could hear them cough or try to clear their throat and I would get up to see what was wrong. They would say they needed more water because they finished the glass they had and they were still a little dry but they didn't want to bother me because I needed to rest. I always told them to call no matter what but they still waited because they thought they were helping me.

Today with all the new electronics it is much easier for a parent to call you when they need help. This technology also makes it a lot easier for you to keep a check on them and their condition. The good thing, depending on their condition, is that if the technology fails they still can call or yell for you.

Telephone And Items Near The Bed

My mom spent a lot of time in bed and that required that she have necessary items nearby in case she needed them. I was always home with her but I had items near so she could grab them if needed. One item that was always near her was water, so if she got thirsty or had a dry cough she could just grab it and drink when she wanted. I had it in a cup with a lid and an attached straw so she couldn't spill. I would fill that up several times a day because she drank a lot of water. It was nice because instead of calling me each time she wanted a drink she could just grab her cup and take a sip.

The other item I had close by was a telephone with big numbers so she could call for help in case something happened to me. She also had a list of phone numbers printed big nearby so she could call my sisters, neighbor or even 911 if she got no response from me. I had a walkie talkie next to her bed and I would turn it on when I went outside. All she had to do was grab it, press the button and say, "Jim" and I would come right in. I had a bell near her bed in case she couldn't call she could just grab the bell and ring it until I came in the room. She had a flashlight next to her bed in case she needed a little more light during the night. It was one of those small six inch flashlights, all she had to do was turn the front and it would light. This was easier for her than having to push a button or slide switch on the side. I also had a night light in the room so she wouldn't be in the dark during the night and it made her sleep better. A box of baby wipes was close by so she could wash her hands if needed. I also had a few extra incontinence pads on the side of her bed in case she wet during the night so she could change them herself and be dry once again. Because of this possibility there was a plastic kitchen trash can with a lid on the side of the bed so she could throw the used items away. I had removable trash liner and air freshener stuck inside so it wouldn't smell. Her television remote was close by so she could watch TV and she also had a portable radio so she could listen to whatever she wanted.

When she needed something else I would put it by the bed so she could get it and use it. Once again it depends on your situation and what your parent is capable of doing. You will know quickly what they need and want to have nearby. I was lucky because my mom could still use her arms so there was a lot she could do.

Sleeping

After my mom's spine surgery she had to sleep in a hospital bed with the back raised. She had a trapeze so she could lift herself up and reposition herself. She also had to have an air mattress prescribed because she was prone to bed sores because her skin was thin and the hospital did not turn her enough while she was recuperating from spine surgery. Another change to her sleeping habit was she could only sleep on her back because she could not turn herself over.

This sleeping arrangement did not seem to bother her and she got a reasonable amount of sleep. I would put her in bed around 8pm and she would watch television until about 11:45pm and then I would put the lights out and she would fall asleep. She would sleep through the night until about 8:00am, just in time to take her medications. The only difference in this routine would be the third night when we had to change her pain patch. On this night she would not fall asleep until about 2am and it would be because she was exhausted. We would change the patch at 10pm because we found that was the best schedule. It would take from 10pm to about 2am for the pain patch to take effect.

This schedule kept her mind sharp and allowed for a normal routine.

She was never tired and she would not fall asleep during the course of a normal day. She would be up from 8am to 2pm, then she would take a nap until 4pm. I would then get her up and she would stay awake until 11:45pm.

She would get a fair amount of sleep during most nights and she would take a nap in the afternoon. I on the other hand never could sleep through the night. I could hear every sound she made and I could tell when she needed some help. You gain a sense of when they need you. It could be for a glass of water, diaper change or just a bad dream. I was alway able to tell when she needed something.

Sometimes the routine during the day and evening changed depending on the situation. Sometimes we would go out and visit the relatives, go to the store or some other activities. On the days we went out she would fall asleep quicker but the rest of the routine pretty much stayed the same. This procedure went on from 2001 until 2013. It allowed her to have as close a normal life as possible.

Calls To 911

In all the years we lived in our Lynwood home I only had to call 911 for paramedics once. That was the time my dad was spitting up blood and he was too weak for me to bring him to the hospital. That was also the last time he went to the hospital because he died two weeks later.

I was amazed how fast the paramedics came to the house and how efficient they were in their procedures. They were polite and professional and explained everything that they were doing. During the examination they asked me a lot of questions about of my father's condition and asked what I wanted to do. They knew his condition was grave and they worked with me to keep him as comfortable as possible. He was transported to the hospital where his condition worsened by the day until he passed.

My nine year old niece was at our house at the time because her mom, my sister, was there to help me with my dad and mom. When they had my dad on the stretcher to be brought to the ambulance one of the paramedics asked my sister to watch her daughter so she didn't see her grandfather leave on the stretcher. So much was going on at the time neither one of us thought about her being in the living room. My sister shielded her daughter as they wheeled out her grandfather. She was nine years old and she was old enough to know what was happening. Years later she told me that was the saddest day of her life. I always felt bad because I didn't shield her before the paramedics came to the house.

As they were taking my dad out of the house I had to fill out all the forms for the paramedics and ambulance. They asked for any documents pertaining to his Durable Power Of Attorney and DNR paperwork. I had forms that were part of a legal software program that I purchased and my dad had signed them a few months earlier in front of a witness. They accepted this paperwork and after I signed the papers off we went to the hospital.

I never had to call 911 for my mom until the morning she died. I woke up and found her unresponsive in her bed. I called 911 and they came within a few minutes. They came into the house and found her unresponsive and pronounced her deceased. They stayed about a half an hour as the police did their investigation. Once the police were finished asking their questions the paramedics left. While I was on the phone the dispatcher asked if I wanted to start CPR and I told him, "No." I explained that she was stiff, cold and her eyes were rolled back, I also informed him that she had a DNR, Do Not Resuscitate, document. He asked if I was sure and I told him, "Yes, that's my decision." After the paramedics pronounced my mom deceased the police officer immediately asked to see the DNR paperwork. I showed him the document after I got it out of my file cabinet. He read the paperwork and told the paramedics, "We're fine here," and they left.

I signed all the paperwork for the paramedics and police department. I had to supply documents to the police department so they could inform the medical examiner. It paid to have the information in a file so it was readily available. Even though this was a stressful time you need to make sure to have access to documents and information. This is when you become the

responsible party, where your actions are under the microscope and bein
prepared can prevent mishaps and legal situations.

Chapter 15

ADVICE AND BEING A CAREGIVER

Caregiver Advisors Rarely Were Caregivers

Over the years of taking care of my mom we came in contact with many so-called caregiving experts. Every time she was in the hospital someone would visit us and tell us what was best for us or what we needed. The one thing that was common with all these so-called experts was that none of them had ever cared for a parent. The way I found out was I asked them directly if they ever took care of a parent. The answer was always the same, "No."

In the beginning when these experts would visit I would listen to what they said to see if there was anything I could learn for the care of my mom. The other constant thing they would always preach was that I needed a break and I was wrong in not thinking of myself. That would always make me laugh because I was supposed to think of myself over the one that I was taking care of. Sorry, that was not the way I was brought up. It always made me angry when I would hear that what I was taught was wrong and that the new way was better. It was not only in caregiving but life in general. It's just like in religion, you are brought up one way then they change and they tell you that way was wrong and you need to follow the new way.

My mom needed my care to survive, my needs were not important because I could take of myself, she couldn't. In all the visits I never heard anything new so it became a waste of time. They would ask questions and I would answer in a simple yes or no. Sometimes they would say I needed to do something different and from my experience I knew it wouldn't work so I would ask them, "What ifs?" They never had an answer. Lifting was always a point of contention because they would recommend using a lifting belt or lift. These are great tools and work well in many situations but they didn't work in our situation. A lifting belt worked great for lifting my mom out of a wheelchair to a regular chair or from the chair to a bed. It was absolutely useless trying to lift her onto the toilet or into a car. There is no room in cars or some bathrooms for both of you to move together with a lifting belt. You also cannot scoot the patient onto the toilet or into a car. Then there is the patient lift, it was a great tool for lifting my mom off the bed and into the wheelchair. It was useless for anything else. It barely fit into the bedroom and there was very little room for you to move it around. It wouldn't fit into the bathroom because it was too large. Most homes are not caregiving friendly. You couldn't use the lift to put my mom into the front seat of a large vehicle like a Suburban so it would never work with a small car. So it was a limited use tool. Unfortunately the caregiving experts insisted that they worked but had no clue how.

It got to the point that after they realized I had quite a bit of experience with my mom they would just ask if we needed anything. We already had the wheelchairs, walkers, hospital bed, air mattress, commode chair, shower chair, patient lift and a lot of other caregiving accessories. Some purchased by Medicare and a lot purchased by me because according to the insurance they weren't medically necessary.

Now most of these experts learned about caregiving out of a book and in college. Learning from a book is great but in the real world there are a lot of obstacles that force you to modify what is taught in a book. I learned a lot from trial and error. I also had to adapt a lot of proven techniques to fit our situation. As I stated many times, everyone's situation is different and you need to learn and adapt to what is best for you and your parent.

Different When It's Your Parent

Everyone is great at giving you advice or telling you what to do but most of those giving you this advice have never taken care of a parent. Most have never been a caregiver and have no idea how much is involved. Once again it is nice to get free advice but it would be nice if it came from people that actually had the experience.

You are always told that this is the best way to do this or that and when you listen to some of this advice you ask yourself, "Would I want to be treated like that?" Most of the time the answer is, "No," and you realized the advice you have received made no sense. I started asking some people when they gave advice that I thought was ridiculous, "Would you do that to your mom?" Most of the time they would not answer the question and say, "I'm not in that situation," or "I'll deal with it when it happens," or my favorite, "my mom is different."

It is always different when it is your parent and as it should because you should want what is best for them. One piece of advice that comes to mind was to give my parents baby food so it was easier for them to eat. First of all both of my parents had tremendous appetites, could eat on their own and pretty much enjoy whatever they liked. But a nutritionist one time thought they were eating too much and said I should control their food intake by giving them baby food. It was nutritious and easy for them to eat. Needless to say this went nowhere and when I told our doctor he laughed and told me to continue what I was already doing.

Another comment that was often given was to put my mom in a "home" because I had my own life to live and I needed to take care of myself. First of all my mom was in the best "home" she could be in, hers, and second being her son it was my responsibility to take care of her. Once again easy to say when you're not in the position.

Now I know everyones situation is different and people handle them in their own way. The proper way to give this advice is to say, "Have you considered putting her into a home?" Make it question , the answer still would be, "No" but at least you are not telling someone what they should do. Some people are perfectly fine staying in a care facility and it is the only choice for the family but once again it is their choice and their decision. My choice was to take care of my parents, my choice and decision. Neither one is a right or bad choice is what was best for each own's situation.

Some Are Neglected

I was brought up to be responsible and to take care of others. As I grew older I baby sat my nieces and nephews. When I took care of them their safety and care was more important than me. After I decided to take care of my parents they became my responsibility and my life became focused on their needs.

Anybody with a conscience would be shocked to see how many parents are neglected by their children. I was amazed when the community college instructor told me that a lot of elderly patients in the Central Valley of California showed some signs of abuse or neglect. These problems were usually caused by their children or caregivers.

The other thing about these comments are that her nursing students had to see what a properly cared for parent looked like. It's that much of a rarity that the entire class had to come to view my mom. A neglected person was normal but a well cared for person was rare. That's a sad commentary on our society.

Ask For Advice

Everyone's situation is different so there is not a "one size fits all" mentality when it comes to being a caregiver. What works for someone else might not work for you. There are a lot of guides that tell you what is the best technique for many situations. There are also a lot of people that will offer advice on anything that you do.

When I started taking care of my dad I had absolutely no clue what I had to do. I started learning as I took him to the frequent doctor visits he required. I started filling out the forms and listening to the advice and diagnosis of the doctors. I started asking a lot of questions and was amazed of how detailed some of the answers were. As time went on I learned more and more about his diseases and the proper way to care for him. It went so far as I had to learn how to give him insulin shots and change his urostomy bag.

When my mom became ill it was an easy progression to take care of my mom after I had taken care of my dad. The biggest difference was emotionally, it was easier to take care of my dad because he was male than my mother because, well she was my mother. Once that hurdle was overcome, in a few seconds, because there was no time to wait and no one else was there, things moved along.

Over the course of the many years I was a caregiver I received a lot of advice. It came from doctors, registered nurses, licensed vocational nurses, home health nurses, rehabilitation specialists, lab technicians, pulmonary technicians, pharmacists, hospital social workers, dietitians, nutritionist and many others. Advice also came from friends and family. I always listened and asked myself if this advice would work in our situation. A lot of times it didn't, but on the few occasions that it did, it made a difference in the way I was taking care of my mom and dad.

If you read one of many of the books on caregiving these will give ideas and guidelines in the way you take care of your parent. If any healthcare professional gives you advice it is because they have seen numerous incidents of how people take care of a parent. Advice from family and friends is also good because some of this comes from actual experience.

There is no harm in asking for advice because it might help you with your caregiving duties. Any advice that can make things better for your parent and easier for you can go a long way into maintaining the quality of life for both of you. One thing to remember is that because every situation is different, the book is still being written on how to be a caregiver and it will never be finished.

What Works Best For You

Everyone is different and so is everyone's situation. What works best for me and my parents might not work for you and your parents. Being a caregiver is not an exact science because everything has to be adapted to your unique situation.

There are a lot of techniques that can be used in many situations but even these have to be tweaked for you and your parent. For my mom and I lifting was always a sore subject with the caregiving experts and advisors. I would be told, "You have to do it this way," or my favorite was, "this is the right way to do it." When I would ask what was the right way to put her into my car they would never have an acceptable answer. The one that got me was, "You have to buy a different car or leave her at home." Easy said if you have the money to buy a new car or pay someone to watch her. That "answer" was no answer.

I would get this all the time and I would listen but in the end I had to do what was best for our situation. I had to consider what was best for my mom, me and our wallet. If you're limited on funds options are not easy to come by. Medicare and insurance doesn't cover everything and some of the items to make things easier for your parent and you are considered comfort items. They are not medically necessary and therefore you have to pay for them and they are not cheap. Some information you get does help and it makes thing easier for both of you, but once again you might need to adapt this advice to make it work for you.

There are no right answers but there are a lot of wrong answers that can hurt you and your parent. You need to be careful how you use and adapt the advice you receive to your situation because you are responsible for the outcome. If your actions and techniques hurt your parent you're responsible for the consequences. If you hurt yourself, you will be dealing with that the rest of your life.

Ask Questions

One thing that you should always do is ask questions about the care of your mom and dad. It's like the old saying, "The only question I can't answer is the one that is not asked." By asking questions you can learn different ways to help your situation. I even wanted my parents to ask questions because a lot of times they asked things that I never would and the answers were very helpful. Another reason to have them ask questions is that they are participating in their care just as they were when they were younger. It's amazing what you can learn from their questions.

The same is true when they ask you questions. You need to answer them as best as you can with as much detail as possible. You need to make sure they understand the answer and they are satisfied with it. One of the worst responses is, "That's just the way it is." That doesn't answer anything and is just a way of blowing off their question.

I would always explain everything to my folks. They would always ask about what the doctor said and if they missed something. I would repeat whatever I heard and made sure they knew what was discussed. I would explain the questions I asked and the answers I received. I made sure they were part of their healthcare decisions and treatments. If they asked my opinion I would give it and not leave it as, "I don't know."

I learned a lot during the time I was taking care of my parents. All the information I learned has helped me with my life and medical situations. Once again because medicine and treatments change constantly I will always be asking questions about my medical needs and treatments.

Easier To Put Away

Some feel it is easier to put someone in a home than it is to care for them. In some situations that is true because you might not have the proper equipment available to properly care for your parent. Others have no interest or ability to care for a parent and would rather pay someone to do it for them.

It all depends on you and what is best for your unique situation. In my case my parents didn't want to go into a care facility and wanted to stay in their own home. I respected their decision and decided that I would take care of them so they could remain home. I purchased whatever I needed to properly care for them in our own home. I knew it was going to be a lot of work and I prepared myself for the upcoming tasks and commitment.

Even though I prepared myself for the upcoming task I never realized how much work it would entail and how much it would affect my life. During the entire time I would have people tell me that it was time to put my mom in a care facility and move on with my life. I thought that would be selfish on my part and I would be abandoning her after I made a promise to take care of her. I couldn't do it and I continued to care for my mom. Yes, it might have been easier to put her in a home but the promise I made to my dad was more important than what was best for me.

There is no right answer to this question and it all depends on you and what you're capable of doing. I knew it was going to be hard and a lot of work and I accepted that responsibility. Others do not want to take that responsibility and are comfortable in having others take care of their parent. You can't criticize them because you made a different decision, it was what was best for their situation, just as I did what was best for my situation.

Others Wanted To Pay To Put Her Away

I never had to consider putting my dad in a care facility because his condition deteriorated rapidly. From the time I started taking care of him full time to the time he passed away was about six months. My mom on the other hand needed full time care for over thirteen years.

I never considered putting my mom in a home from the time I started caring for her. I made the commitment and I made a promise to my father that I would take care of her. It was a lot of work and I had to do somethings that I never considered doing but it was necessary for her well being.

Once in a while one family member would tell me that I should think of hiring someone to take care of her so I could go back to work. I would always say no because I had the situation under control. Then as time went on they changed their tone to maybe I should put my mom in a home so she could get proper care and I could go on with my life. Once again my answer was no because I remembered my promise to my dad and I was getting along very well taking care of my mom. They upped the ante by saying they would help pay for the facility and hopefully along with Medicare and insurance the entire bill would be covered. I would then be free to get a job and move on with my life. Once again I said, "No," because I knew I was doing the right thing. I appreciated the offer but we were doing okay at the time and I had no problem in taking care of my mom. They thought they were helping by telling me that I needed to put her in a home so I could get my life back. In reality that was what they wanted and what they would have done. It was not what my mom or I wanted. They didn't care that I made my dad a promise when he was dying in the hospital and I was going to keep it.

We had this conversation several times over the course of me taking care of my mom. Even when things started getting difficult and expensive I could not change my mind. I took care of my mom to the end and I kept my promise to my father, what happened after and continues to happen is something I have to deal with.

Never Went To A Support Group

In all the years that I took care of my parents I never went to a support group. In fact I never was even told that support groups existed. The home health nurses and hospital staff in Southern and Central California never told or invited me to any type of support group for caregivers. The only training I received was for the individual procedures that I needed to complete such as my mom's wound care. I'm sure these groups did exist but I also never searched for them. Even if they were recommended I never would have gone to the meeting or seminars.

The reason I would not have gone was that I didn't have the time because I was constantly taking care of my mom. I also would have had to bring her with me because I could not leave her alone. I am also not the type that likes to discuss my needs and situation with others. I prefer to handle things my own way and do what was best for my mom. I did learn when they had training sessions in the hospital, with the home health nurses and home physical therapists. These were specific tasks needed to take care of my mom's condition.

I didn't need a support group because I had the situation under control. Others might need a support group to help guide them during the time they are taking care of their parents. I did what needed to be done the way I was taught and adapted to each situation as it came. I didn't need to talk about it, I just did what I needed to do.

Chapter 16
RELIGION AND FAITH

We were an average family of the time and we followed the Roman Catholic faith. We went to church on Sundays and tried to live a faith based life. My sisters and I went to Catholic school from grades one through twelve. We attended Mass and participated in our parish regularly through our childhood and adult lives.

As my folks became weaker and more ill it was harder for them to go to church. Living in Southern California we were able to find a television channel that broadcast the Sunday Mass. My folks and I were able to watch this together and even though it wasn't the same as being in church it was a good alternative. We did this until my dad passed away.

After my dad died my mom wanted me to take her to church on Sundays. We would go and stay in the back of the church and out of the way of others. She would be in her wheelchair and I would stand behind her. The priests would tell us to go up front but she liked being in the back where we didn't interfere with others. By staying in the back we also kept the aisle open and never restricted regular movement. This also gave us the opportunity to leave if she had a problem without interfering with the service.

As my mom got sicker it was harder for us to go to church. Some of it was because a lot of churches are not wheelchair friendly and they want you to go to the front. My mom never wanted to sit in the front even years before when we were kids, we always sat in the middle or back of the church. My dad use to say, "Only the show off's sit in front because they want everyone to see them." To this day when I go to church I still sit in the middle or back, somethings you never forget.

As time went on it was more difficult to get her ready for church and she didn't feel comfortable anymore. I think she started to get a little self conscience as she started to lose control of some of her bodily functions. She finally decided that she would watch the Mass on television and that's what we did up to the time she passed away. One of the organizations put the Sunday Mass on the internet, "On demand" so it was easy to watch it at the time that was best for her. One of the national television networks would broadcast the Christmas Mass from the Vatican so that was the way she was able to view the Christmas Service.

I was always active and involved in our church and my former high school so we always had nuns and priests visiting. They would come over just to chat or for dinner and spend a few hours with us. She always had the opportunity for spiritual guidance and the sacraments.

Years before she passed away she told me that there was one priest that she really liked and that she wanted him to perform her funeral mass. He was a member of the order that ran my former high school and whenever he would see or talk about her he would always call her "mom." She liked that and always looked forward to seeing and hearing from him. After she died I contacted him and he flew down from Richmond, California to perform the Rosary, Mass and Burial Ceremony. After that he spent hours with the family before I took him to the airport so he could fly back home. We still keep in touch even though he has moved to another location.

Religion was an important part of my parents life and there was no reason why it shouldn't have been part of their later years. It gave them comfort and there was no way I was going to interfere or stand in the way. If they wanted to go to church, I took them. If they wanted to watch it on television, they could. If they wanted to see a priest I called one and gave them the privacy they needed.

Talking about church, a lot of people get support from their church when they are caregivers. My cousin got help from her church when she was taking care of my aunt. She hired several to come and watch my aunt while she worked or went out. None of the churches we belonged to had any services or support groups. Even if they did I probably would never have used them. Both my mom and dad were very uncomfortable with strangers in the house. I don't think they would have liked strangers taking care of them. In fact, when a nurse came to teach us how to give my dad insulin shots he was very uncomfortable when she was around and when it was time for his shot he would tell her that I could do it. My mom was the same way and when home health came in for her wound care she was uncomfortable with a stranger in the house. These woman were professionals and she warmed up to them very fast so it never became an issue.

Churches can be a place to exercise your faith and find comfort. They can also be a place to find help, advice and support. They can be a wonderful resource for you if you can adapt the help to your situation.

Chapter 17

ATTITUDES AND BEING A CAREGIVER

Attitude

An important part of caregiving is keeping your parents attitude positive. Depending on their situation this might not be any easy proposition. As they meditate by themselves they get melancholy or depressed and it make things more difficult for you.

When I was taking care of my dad his attitude was hard to keep positive. Since he had a lung disease sometimes breathing become a chore. It was hard to keep saying everything was all right as he was trying to catch his breath after walking a few steps. One thing that would always keep him positive was when he was around the grandchildren. Some were teenagers and he was always interested in what they were doing. He never felt ill around them. We kept pushing him and he fought as hard as he could until the end. With my mom it was easier to keep her attitude positive. Even though she experienced many hardships and challenges in her elderly years she was always hoping tomorrow would be better.

Many times I would say, "We'll get through this," or "things will get better," and "we'll fight this," Other times it was, "you can beat it," or "you beat it before, you can do it again," and "we'll do it together." I did whatever it took to keep her motivated so she could go on with her life.

One of the best things to perk up her attitude was visits from the grandchildren and great grandchildren. That gave her something to look forward to and enjoy. Talking about her favorite food would also get her excited and she would anticipate the meal when I was cooking. Talking about the advancement in medicine always gave her hope and the will to live on. Any positive news or even just watching a baseball game cheered her up. Phone calls from her daughters and grandchildren were always appreciated and kept her going. Friends calling or sending cards were another way to show she mattered and was just not a relic. Getting out the house to see a nice day would brighten her up. When my oldest sister lived a few blocks away my mom and I would go over for dinner. I would wheel her over and we would be greeted by their dog. He would always come to the door and lead us to the family room. We didn't have pets but my sister always did. My mom would throw his ball or toy and he would bring it back for another round. She would pet the dog and then he would go and lie on his bed. She would enjoy the meal, as would I. She liked it because it was good and I liked it because I didn't have to cook.

All this was a change of pace and it gave her interaction with others. It made her part of life instead of letting it pass her by. This gave her a positive attitude and allowed her to face the challenges that were always coming.

Need Something To Look Forward To

As you get older days and nights seem to blend into one another and time goes by fast. As a caregiver you notice that sometimes your parent gets withdrawn and becomes bored. They have that lost look and they feel that life is passing them by. You have to put yourself in their shoes and see what is wrong.

A major part of the problem is that they have nothing to look forward to. You have to try to keep them busy and involved. Even the smallest task makes them participate and makes them feel important. Going to the grocery store or department store makes their life as normal as possible. Visiting or visits from anyone gives them a change from the normal routine. I would push my mom around the neighborhood in the wheelchair when the weather was nice. It was nice to get her out and to be in the fresh air. We would go to the grocery store and she would want to go down every aisle. Now this was a difficult chore because I was by myself, so pushing a wheelchair with one arm and pulling a shopping cart with the other was like a train going through a tunnel. Sometimes one of the courtesy clerks would offer to push the cart for me and they would always bring the cart to the car for us. Even a drive to get an ice cream cone breaks the monotony of everyday life. In the spring we had a lot of wildflowers growing on the side of the highways. We would take a drive to just see the flowers on the side of the road. In the summer we would go to the local farmers market and I would wheel her around so she could look at all the fresh produce. Then we would stop at a food booth for dinner and get a grilled bratwurst on a bun.

It's a lot of work for you to put them in the car but it gets them out of the house. Any change to the normal routine gives them something to look forward to and it makes their quality of life better because they are not stuck in the house. It also does you a lot of good too because you also get out and can do something different.

Don't Let Them Just Stare Out A Window

When I was in junior high school we had to visit the local old folks home or convalescent hospital as part of our community service. I always remember walking into a big room and you would see a dozen or more individuals in wheelchairs parked at a large window. They would just be staring out the window watching the cars and the world going by. Others would be sitting at tables just looking at each other.

When the youngsters, us, would walk in they would all become animated. They were all trying to get your attention so you would talk with them. I would always go home and tell my folks and say, "What a horrible way to spend your last years." As I got older and realized I would have to take care of my parents I made a vow that they would never be that way.

I made sure that with both my mom and dad somebody was always around and paid attention to them. I kept them engaged and busy until they could no longer function normally. Even when they were slipping away I tried to keep them from just staring out into space. Whether it was talking to them, playing music or pushing them in a wheelchair to get some fresh air, they were not alone and forgotten.

I feel that I accomplished this with both my mom and dad. Unfortunately for me, since I never married and had children I will be the one staring out the window. I have no one to take care of me in my later years, so I will the one watching the cars and the world go by. Kind of ironic.

Will To Live

Most people want to live and have the will to keep going. As we get older many obstacles can be put in our way and make it a challenge. As these bumps in the road take their toll we continue to do our best to keep going.

My folks always had the will to live and the fight to keep going. My dad had so many obstacles thrown in front of him it was amazing that he lasted seventy-four years. When he was diagnosed with asbestosis in 1976 the best estimate they gave him was five years. He was a fighter and had a strong will, so he fought and lasted until 1995. He fought until the last two weeks of his life. The end was near, his body was shutting down and it finally drained the life out of him.

My mom was another one that kept going. When my dad passed away many thought my mom would not last too long. Her brother died a few years earlier, three month after his wife passed away. Her oldest sister, the day after her husbands funeral withdrew so much that she never spoke again and suffered from severe dementia to the point that she could no longer care for herself.

Not my mom, she grieved for a time, they were married forty-six years, but then she started looking to the future. One of the things that kept her going was her grandchildren. She lit up whenever they were around and it helped her make it through the day. I also would not let her stop from doing things. I gave her chores and tasks to do to keep her busy. She had something to do and it made her feel that she was still capable of helping and she wasn't a relic put out to pasture. She would ask, "What are we doing tomorrow?" so I would have to make a schedule to keep her posted on what we were doing. This kept her going even when her health started changing and getting worse. She was always look forward to the next day, week or month.

Her mind was sharp but her spine was a mess and it kept her from walking and being able to take care of herself. When we went to the doctors for routine visits they would say she was doing good and I would tell her that she would outlast me. The doctors would laugh and she would smile and say, "That won't happen but I'm not ready to got go yet."

Stubbornness

My mother and father were old fashioned Italians which meant they were stubborn. Once their mind was made up there was no changing it. If they dug in their heals, the decision was made and it would not change no matter what you said or did. At a certain age everyone gets stubborn. For me it was not difficult to deal with because I was brought up under these conditions.

Taking care of someone that is stubborn is a challenge but you learn how to deal with it. How you phrase procedures and diagnosis goes a long way in avoiding tension. Doctors, nurses and most healthcare providers have the tact of glass. They cut right to the problem regardless of the consequences. That is why you need to work with the doctor and health staff. You need to explain to them that it is easier to have procedures done if a certain tact is used. Some will listen to you and you will be able to work together, If they don't want to listen to you, find another doctor.

When you are the caregiver there is no harm in letting them think they are getting their way. It is a burden on you but in the long term it will make life easier for you. This means no battles and arguments.

Old Stereotypes

As a person gets older a lot of old stereotypes, sayings, gripes, superstitions and language barriers come to the surface. When this happens it can cause you a lot of embarrassment and makes you issue a lot of apologies. Some people are forgiving and some are not. Some pass it off and some will challenge you.

If your parent grew up in the thirties, forties and fifties racism was a common. It can happen at the store, hospital, doctors, anywhere. A common situation is when a health provider is working on your parent they might turn to you and whisper, "Hey, he's black." You look at the health worker and roll your eye's as your face turns a dark shade of red. You tell your parent, "Yes he is and he is here to help you." That usually settles the situation with your parent. You then walk out with the healthcare worker and deeply apologize for the incident. Some say it's no problem, others will tell you it's a problem and they feel uncomfortable. In that situation you tell your parent to keep their comments to themselves. This works for a short time until the next incident.

When this happened with my mom I was able to give her a look and say that the person was there to help her. She would not repeat it and then apologize herself for her comment. After I apologized for the incident I would walk back into the room and she would be mad at herself because of her comments. It only happened the first time she went into the hospital. She would learn from the outburst and realized that her health was in these professionals hands. I only had one lab tech that refused to draw blood because of the outburst. No matter how much I apologized she would not accept it. Not much you can do when they don't accept the apology or understand the situation.

Another problem is language barriers. A lot of hospital technicians speak broken English. An older person that is losing their hearing has a hard time understanding what they are trying to say. Most keep repeating the instructions or start talking louder which makes things worse. Usually the statement, "Why is she yelling at me?" is said. When you are there you have to listen carefully to the instructions and tell your parent what they need to do. This is always a challenge because you're listening to the health technician and your parent at the same time. You have to decipher everything and explain it to your parent so the tests can be completed.

Chapter 18
HYGIENE AND BEING A CAREGIVER
Hygiene

Hygiene is probably one of the most important parts of being a caregiver. Depending on the situation, you might have to clean your parent a little or you might have to clean their entire body.

My situation started off gradually. In the beginning my mom could wash and bathe herself. I could roll her to a table and put a wash basin in front of her and she would clean herself with a wash cloth. Using strategically placed grab bars and a shower chair, I could put her in the tub and she could shower herself. Most of the time she sprayed water all over the bathroom and because of this the bathroom was always clean. I also installed a portable shower head in the bathroom. It was attached to a hose and then to the shower spigot above the tub. I put her on the seat in the tub, closed the door a little to give her privacy and she would wash herself. When she was finished she would put the shower head in the tub so the water would spray down, then call me, and I would go in and shut off the water. I would then giver her a towel and walk out. She would then dry herself , put on a dress and call me.Then I lifted her off the shower chair and put her in the wheelchair or bed. At this time she was able to dress herself so it made things easier.

She was also able to wash herself at the table, brush her teeth and comb her hair. Keeping her nails clean was always interesting. She would scrub but there was always dirt on and under her nails. Scrub brushes were invaluable. She would wash up and I would say, "What about your nails?" She would say she did them, I would look and then get the scrub brush and clean them some more. You always want to make sure the finger nails are clean.

As time went on she was able to do less and I had to do more to keep her clean. She also started to get more stubborn because it was too much work to take a shower. There were many battles, but in the end she always gave in. Usually it took being very blunt, like, "You stink and are getting in the shower." As time went on she lost her privacy because she could not reach most of her body. She could wash her hair and front but the back and below the waist was out of range. That's when she would place a towel over her front and call me. I would go in and wash and dry the places she couldn't reach. Also as time went on she was more unstable in the shower so I bought a new sliding shower chair with a high back and safety belt so she couldn't slip. I could also not close the door and had to be close by in case she needed help. Sponge baths became more frequent because showers were a major undertaking. When my sister would come up to visit she would give my mom a shower. I would put my mom in the shower chair, slide her into the tub and my sister would wash and dry her from head from to toe.

My mom liked to use powder and perfume and when she put it on it was always an experience. She would put on too much powder so when I looked at her and she looked like a ghost. It was also all over and in the air. I would walk in and choke on the powder floating around. I would give her a damp cloth so she could wipe the excess off. My mom also would always carry a bottle of perfume in her purse. When she felt she had an odor, she would take out the small perfume bottle and splash some on. Usually it went on everything and me. When I bought my new Saturn, on the way home from the dealer she decided to put on some perfume. Unfortunately she dropped the bottle. So much for the new car smell.

Washing Up At The Table

Since my mom was in a wheelchair it was difficult for her to wash in the bathroom. Most homes are not wheelchair friendly and that included the new home we purchased in 2008. A simple solution to this problem was to have her wash at the table.

Washing at a table worked out very well because there was a lot of room to put the items she needed to clean herself. I'm not talking about taking a sponge bath but everyday washing, such as her face, arms and hands. She showered regularly and this was to clean her up when she got up and between meals.

I would give her a damp wash cloth and she would wet her face, arms and hands. She would use it a little and then I would rinse it out so she could clean more. I then gave her a wash cloth wet with soap and she would use that. I then gave her a wet wash cloth so she could wash the soap off. This worked well and her skin did not dry out. To give her more independence I would fill a plastic shoebox with warm water and she would use this to rinse. I would empty it out and refill it with clean water so she didn't reuse the dirty water. She would take the wash cloth and put it into the soapy water and then wring it out. When she used the clean wash cloth she did the same thing, she dropped it in the clean water and wrung it out to use it. Because she had arthritis in her hands it was a little hard for her to wring it out completely but she did her best. She was happy to be able to do this herself and it kept her clean.

As time went on it got a little more difficult for her so we started using waterless soap for her to wash. This also worked but she still wanted to rinse it off and she did. She started making more of a mess but it was only soap and water so it was easy to clean up. Even when she splashed water, clean up was a breeze and it gave her some independence and a sense of accomplishment. It was a little more difficult when we had guests because she did not want to wash up in front of them. The solution was to do this same routine while she was sitting up in bed. We had found a way for her to perform her daily routine of washing up.

Plastic Shoe Box

I used plastic shoe boxes to help my mom wash herself. They were inexpensive, easy to clean and reusable. She would use one to spit into when she rinsed her mouth. She used another one to soak her finger nails to make them easier to clean. She had two for daily washing, one for rinse water and one for soapy water.

To keep the plastic shoe boxes clean I would fill them with hot water and throw in two to three denture cleaning tablets. I would let them fizz, sit until the water cooled and then rinse them out. A little soap and water to clean them again to make sure their was no dirt or bacteria. I let them dry out and they were ready for the next use. Another nice feature was that they came with a cover. When they were clean just snap on the cover to keep out dirt and dust. When I used them I would still rinse them out just in case.

I would replace them about every four to six months. These served us well for many years and helped her clean herself during that time. We stopped using them about two weeks before she passed away because she could no longer wash herself.

Soapy Towel

When we were at home I always had a soapy towel nearby so my mom could wash her hands when she wanted. I also had a damp towel so she could rinse off the soap residue. This helped her clean herself and it made it a little easier for me. Especially after a meal she could wash and rinse herself off. I would rinse the towels out several times a day and add just a little soap to one. She never got them confused and she was very comfortable using them. She was very careful when she used the soapy towel and never used it near her eyes.

Little things like this gave her a little independence. She didn't have to rely on me to wash her hands and face plus she thought she was helping me. This came in handy when she would eat candy or something that was sticky. After she finished with the pastry or chocolate she would grab the soapy towel and clean herself off. Sometimes she would hide some candy and I would catch her cleaning off her face. I would ask her, "What did you eat?" She would look at me as she was cleaning her face and say, "Nothing." Yep, just like a little kid.

Dentures

A lot of elderly people have dentures and as a caregiver you might need to assist them when they put them in their mouth. You also might have to help clean and apply the adhesive so they can place them in their mouth. As they get older and lose some functions it can become a chore for them to use them.

My mom had dentures for her upper and lower mouth. Her teeth, because of a fall years before were cracked and they slowly deteriorated. She didn't want to go to the dentist but after a while I convinced her it was a good idea. She went to a dentist and oral surgeon and they removed her few remaining bad teeth. The dentist fitted a nice set of dentures and once again she could smile without being self conscience of her teeth. The one thing the dentist told me was that because she had been without a full mouth of teeth for so long and her age her gums had shrunk and would continue to shrink. He said over time the lower denture would become loose and she it would have to be refitted.

When she first got her dentures she wanted to eat everything that she had trouble with before when her teeth were bad. She wanted to have a steak and I obliged because I also wouldn't eat one before because she had difficulty trying to chew and I didn't want her to feel left out. She caught up on everything she missed and couldn't chew because of her bad teeth.

She had trouble with placing the adhesive on the lower denture. The upper denture would hold to the top of her mouth by suction because it fit very well. The lower denture needed adhesive because her gums shrank over the years The first time she tried to put adhesive on the denture there was more on her and the table than there was on the denture. That's when I came up with a routine. At night I would put the dentures in a container of warm water and let them soak overnight. The dentist recommended using denture tablets only a few times a week because they were abrasive. The next morning during her cleaning routine I would give her a cup of warm water mixed with salt and she would swish it around her mouth several times and spit it into a plastic shoe box. She would do this several times. After this I gave her another cup of warm water and her tooth brush and she would clean and brush her dentures. After they were clean and dry she would put them on a clean paper towel. I would apply the adhesive to the lower denture and she would put both the upper and lower in her mouth.

We did this for years and never had a problem. She never had mouth sores, dirty dentures or bad breath. Over time the dentist was right and the lower denture would loosen and we would have to re-apply the adhesive in the afternoon. Her gums were still shrinking and the denture would fall out. Some of the problem was she didn't press hard enough when she put the denture on her gums and water would seep in and loosen the plate. I wanted to take her back to the dentist to have it realigned but she didn't want to go. She continued to eat steak and other hard foods but it did become more of a chore.

Another thing to remember about dentures is that when you go to the hospital, for tests and procedures they always ask if you have dentures? Sometimes she had to remove them so I always brought a spare denture container with us. When she was in the hospital I would take them with me so she wouldn't drop or lose them. If she was able to eat solid food I would bring them with me so she could eat her meals.

Sometimes she would get frustrated and get mad at me to make sure I went to the dentist. "Take care of your teeth so you don't end up like me," she would say. Good advice because even with new denture technology it is not the same as real teeth.

Finger Nails

Finger nails can become extremely dirty and unsanitary so it is very important to make sure they are always clean. Trimming the finger nails can also be tricky because there is always the possibility of cutting the skin. Keeping the nails clean and trimmed is part of the normal routine of being a caregiver.

I never had to trim my dad's finger nails because he was always capable of doing it himself. Keeping his hands clean was also not a problem because he was always able to stand and wash at the sink. This changed just before he passed away when he was in the hospital. During this time he was washed by the hospital staff because he could no longer do it himself.

My mom on the other hand had a difficult time trying to trim her nails because of arthritis. She also could not get near the sink because she was in a wheelchair and the two houses we lived in were not wheelchair friendly. To solve this problem I would use plastic shoe boxes filled with warm water and soap so my mom could soak her fingers. She would soak them in the soapy solution for a few minutes and then use a finger nail brush to scrub her nails. Then she would rinse them in another plastic shoe box filled with clean warm water. This worked very well for many years.

As she got older it became harder for her to scrub her finger nails so I had to take over this duty. We still used the plastic shoe boxes the only difference was I was the one that would scrub her fingers. I would put on a pair of gloves and scrub her finger nails clean. At this time she was still able to clean herself in the bathroom and after she did her business there were small amounts of residue stuck to her fingers. I would clean them every time she came out of the bathroom to make sure she would have no bacteria on her fingers.

My sister would trim her finger nails during her monthly visit because she did a much better job than me. My hands were to big so it was more difficult for me to use the cuticle scissors and I was afraid I would hurt my mom in the process. My sister was a LVN, Licensed Vocational Nurse, so she had a lot more experience than me. She did a great job and she never nicked a finger.

Finger nails can be the cause of infection or other problems. You have to make sure they are always clean because a lot of time they come in contact with food. We never had a problem with any type of infection in all the years I took care of my mom.

Toe Nails

Trimming toe nails can be challenging because there is always the chance you can trim too much and cause the toe to bleed. The other problem is that if you do trim too much it can be painful and cause discomfort to your parent. If your parent is diabetic it can be dangerous if you do not trim their toe nails properly.

My dad was diabetic so I never attempted to trim his toe nails. He tried himself once and he was scolded by his doctor and was told that he needed to go to a podiatrist for his toe nail care. His illness progressed so fast that he only went to the podiatrist a few times and the rest of the procedures were done when he was in the hospital.

My mom was not diabetic but because of her spinal condition it was well worth the trip to the podiatrist for her toe nail care. Her nails didn't grow fast so we would go about four times a year. These visits were not covered by Medicare or supplement insurance but it was a small cost to pay and it eliminated any problems in the future.

As time went on it seemed that her nails slowed in growing and we cut back on our visits to the podiatrist. I purchased one of those battery operated rotary emery tools for nails to keep the nails trimmed and smooth the rough edges. This kept her toe nails in check for the times in between visits to the podiatrist. Every time she was admitted to the hospital they would trim her nails and this was a plus because it reduced the visits to another doctor.

Some people get squeamish when dealing with toe nails but it was something that you have to take care of. Always wears gloves and be very careful when you trim and file the toe nails. If it is in your budget a trip to the podiatrist is the safest way to handle the trimming of toe nails.

Podiatrist

A podiatrist is well worth the money spent when you are taking care of your parent. Most of the visits to this doctor for routine foot care are not covered by Medicare or insurance unless it is related to a specific condition. Even though most of the visits will be paid by you, the service they perform can keep your parent from having many more problems in the future. If your parent is diabetic it is absolutely essential that you visit a podiatrist for routine foot care.

We had a great podiatrist and my mom really liked her. Because of my mom's spinal condition it was a little difficult for her to stay in one spot while the podiatrist worked on her feet. I would have to reposition my mom several times during the procedure. It was more work for me but it was worth it because the doctor saved us from problems in the long run. My biggest fear was for my mom to have a spasm in her legs while the doctor was working on her feet. I had this vision of her kicking the doctor as soon as she started trimming her nails. We had one close call but the doctor was quick on her feet and was able to move out of the way. It became a running joke every time we went for a visit. I offered to bring her a hockey mask but she said she didn't need it.

These routine visits paid off because my mom never had a serious foot infection or problems with her toes. She did get a toe fungus and that was taken care of with medication. The other reason for these visits was that my mom had poor circulation in her feet because of her spinal condition. Once in a while her feet would get cold and dark pink due to poor circulation and I never wanted to take a chance to trim her nails by myself. The circulation problem was finally corrected when she had an angioplasty in her leg to improve blood flow.

The podiatrist is considered a luxury to some but I felt she was essential to the proper care of my mom. It was another doctor visit every few months which meant a few more lifts but it was worth it. My mom was always willing to go because it meant I would take her to a restaurant for breakfast. She always enjoyed going out for breakfast.

Cleaning Wipes

Baby cleaning wipes are good thing to have around. If they are soft and gentle enough for cleaning a baby then they are definitely good for helping you clean your parent. These are good for cleaning hands and backsides because they don't dry out the skin.

I always had boxes of these wipes on hand. I would buy them on sale and have a box in the bathrooms and in the car. You have to be careful that they don't dry out in the car because of the heat, then they are useless. Keep the seal closed when you're not using them to prevent them from drying out.

I used these wipes to clean my mom when I had to change her diaper. They would remove urine residue and feces. It made the job much easier because you put on your gloves, remove the old diaper and use a few of these wipes to clean up the mess. Then you throw the wipes and your gloves in the trash. She never got a rash and all the residue was always cleaned up.

They are also good for cleaning hands when you don't have soap and water. I use to give one to my mom and she would wash her hands after she used the bathroom and she was good to go. If we were in the car they were always available so she could wash her hands if we stopped to eat. They worked great for me too and I always had clean hands.

If we left the doctors office or other medical facility as soon as we got in the car we washed our hands with the baby wipes. I would also use one to wash the door handle, steering wheel and other items I touched before I washed my hands. This was a way to prevent germs from spreading and putting us at risk.

This was a simple item to have around but they are a little pricey. It's just another added expense but it does make certain jobs easier and it could prevent the spread of germs. The small price you pay could help prevent something major down the road.

Diaper Rash

One of my biggest fears when I was taking care of my mom was a diaper rash. This could have caused a lot of problems because she was always in bed or the wheelchair. It would have been miserable for her and it could have had some dangerous results.

Fortunately for us she never had a diaper rash from any cause. I did my best to keep her clean and free from any urine or feces residue. When she was wet I removed her diaper, cleaned her thoroughly, wiped the area and put on a new clean diaper. When she had a bowel movement I did the same except I used a perianal cream to clean her rectal area of any feces residue. This always made sure there was no debris left that could cause a rash.

This was one of the most important jobs because being technically bed ridden the pain would have been horrible and she would have been so uncomfortable since she had no way to scratch an itch on her backside. The other problem could have been an infection if she did manage to scratch and break the skin this could have caused even more problems.

I always had to be careful because she had a bed wound from when she was in the hospital for her spine surgery. This was always a weak area and it was susceptible to reoccurring wounds. Her skin was thin so I always had to make sure that she was clean so no problems could get infected and cause more wounds. Because of this challenging situation I had to make sure nothing could cause a rash.

I take pride in the fact that she never had a rash. I was complimented by the home health nurses and the various hospitals she was admitted. They were amazed that in her condition she never had a rash or any signs of dirt or debris. That always told me I was doing my best.

Chapter 19

APPETITE AND FOOD WHILE BEING A CAREGIVER

Appetite And Food

My parents loved to eat and enjoyed their food. We were Italian and food was always an important part of our life. Fortunately for them I enjoyed cooking as well as eating so it was a win-win for all.

My dad's diabetes changed how I prepared his food so it wouldn't affect his health. I was surprised at how much food had sugar added. I learned by using different herbs I could retain flavor without using sugar. Somethings did taste different but we all learned to live with it because we were still able to eat most of the foods we liked. My attitude was if my dad couldn't have sugar we did without it also. To this day I use very little sugar when I cook and I don't use it all in coffee and iced tea. We were never large soda drinkers, it was easy to do without so we didn't have a problem and we never switched to sugar free beverages.

After my dad died I didn't change my cooking habits but my mom did make a change to her eating habits, she wanted dessert. My mom always had a huge appetite. We had a small barbecue take out restaurant by our house. She had no problem eating a chicken leg quarter, and four spare ribs. She wore a lot of the sauce but she did enjoy those meals. I would make a 14 inch pizza, she would have three slices. Then have a bowl of ice cream for dessert. She could eat half a chicken with sides of potato, stuffing and corn with no problems. After a meal like that she would say, "There's always room for pie." In fact I knew the end was near when she lost her appetite.

She always liked dessert and with my dad's diabetes she sacrificed by not having any sweets or desserts. Slowly she started craving her sweets and I obliged. I am not a pastry baker so I usually ended up purchasing pies and pastries. I am a bread baker but I was never able to master making pastries. The closest I came was to use a box cake mix and make a sheet cake without frosting. Every time I tried to frost a cake I would make a mess so it was better to leave it unfrosted. My mom didn't mind because she still got cake and she enjoyed it with or without frosting. My mom was lucky because her sugar levels were never elevated. I have to be careful since my dad had diabetes I could be a candidate for the same problem. I don't crave desserts so it is not a problem for me to handle and I have had no problems with my sugar levels so far.

Food was a part of everyday life for my parents and it was something they enjoyed. Both of them had large appetites and enjoyed eating all the way to the end. When they lost their appetite and no longer enjoyed their food I knew the end was near.

Nutrition

Keeping an eye on nutrition for your parent is an important part of being a caregiver. Whenever they are admitted to a hospital their nutrition is always a topic of discussion and advice. Once again you are responsible for their health and therefore you are responsible for what they eat.

When my dad was ill he still had a good appetite and enjoyed his meals. I would make whatever he wanted and tried to keep it as balanced as possible. He was Italian and he loved Italian food so I always tried to make his favorites. When he was diagnosed with diabetes it became a little difficult to cook his favorite meals so it wouldn't affect his sugar levels. I learned by using different herbs I could make the food taste the same and weaned him off sugar. He rarely noticed a difference and the meals were healthier for all of us. When we would go to the doctors or hospital they would always ask about his eating habits and meals. When he explained what he ate they were always pleased with his eating habits. Even when the dietician would come in they would only have a few items to try to make his diet a little better. They were also satisfied with his eating habits.

When he was diagnosed with cancer and the treatments started we had to supplement his diet with protein drinks. We had to use the ones that were for diabetics and they were not cheap. It was for his health so we had to do it and they helped him during his cancer treatments. He didn't like the taste of these drinks but he sacrificed because he knew it was for his well being. It just made dinner more special because that was what he really enjoyed.

When I started taking care of my mom it was a lot easier because she didn't have diabetes. She loved food and she ate very well. I would always make balanced meals such as a meat, a starch and a vegetable. For her part of a balance meal was dessert and she wanted something sweet every night.

Once again when we went to the doctors or hospital they were amazed by her appetite and meals. They would ask her what she ate for breakfast, lunch and dinner and were amazed at her response. She never forgot to tell them about dessert and they would always laugh.

I made balanced meals for both parents and it helped prolong their lives despite their illnesses. I followed the guidelines from the nutritionists and dietitians. My mom and dad also listened and followed the advice they were given. It did help that they both enjoyed food and when they lost their appetites that's how I knew the end was near for both of them. My dad lost his appetite two weeks before he died. He couldn't finish his meal and the next day he ended up in the hospital and passed away two weeks later. My mom lost her appetite about a week before she died. Before she could easily eat two large bowls of soup and at this time she could barely finish a small bowl. She passed away within the week.

Nutrition is an important part of being a caregiver and is your responsibility to make sure your parents are eating properly. I was lucky that both my parents liked to eat and I enjoyed cooking for them. This made a difference in their attitude, quality of life and duration.

Alcoholic Drinks

I never had a problem with serving my parents alcoholic drinks. My mom didn't drink and my dad and I would have a glass of wine with our macaroni (pasta) dinner or a glass of beer with pizza. Once and I while we would have a small glass of brandy in the late evening. That changed when I was diagnosed with iron overload in my blood so I stopped cold turkey having any alcoholic drinks and my dad followed suit in support of me. I didn't even use wine for cooking anymore. My situation came under control and none of us missed the alcoholic drinks. Soon after my dad was diagnosed with lung cancer and so the alcohol meant nothing because we had more important things to deal with. My mom didn't drink so during her entire illness we never drank or cooked with any alcohol. We didn't need or crave it as we went along with our daily routines.

My uncle, on the other hand always drank and still craves it. His son, my cousin, is having a hard time curtailing his drinking. He was a business executive and he lived during that time of cocktails before dinner, wine with dinner and after dinner drinks. My aunt tried to get him to cut down but she never succeeded. After she passed away he began to drink more to deal with her loss. He got to the point where he would be so intoxicated he would lose his balance and fall. He lived alone so he would be passed out on the floor for a few hours. My cousin finally persuaded him to move closer and he purchased a home across the street from my cousin and his wife.

When he moved in he was still drinking heavily and it caused him some problems. One night he was intoxicated and he was watching television. Being in a new home and because of the new surroundings he fell and spent the night on the floor. My cousin went over the next morning and found him on the floor. He was awake and conscience and asked for a blanket because his back was cold. I was staying the night with my cousin to help him repair his car and he called me to come over right away. I rushed over and saw a mess. There was blood on the floor and my uncle had blood on his arms and face. I thought he lost two teeth but I found out he had those pulled years before. I lifted him to a chair and started checking him out. I gave him a wash cloth to wash the blood from his face and I checked for broken bones and asked him to move this and that. Nothing was broken and all the cuts and bruises were superficial. He bit his tongue and that's where the blood on his face came from.

Listening to his story of the cause was almost comical if it wasn't so dangerous. He said he was watching a show on television and they told him to get up and switch chairs, so he did and that's when he fell. My cousin and I didn't know of a television show that played musical chairs and the big problem was that he fell in a different room from where the television was located. This room looked like a crime scene because there was blood on the floor and it was smeared. It looked like he fell and tried to crawl to a chair to sit up where he fell again. He then tried to crawl to a different chair where he gave up and just fell asleep on the floor. He looked horrible because his arms were scarred from skin cancer treatments and he looked like he went through a war. After he cleaned up he did look better but he didn't look well taken care of. I told my cousin that if would have had to take him to the emergency room they would have anticipated the worst and would have asked him a lot of questions about his father's care. He would have been in the hot seat after they did their inspection and he could have had a visit from a social worker because he looked abused. It was all self inflicted but it would have been hard to explain and by law they would have had to investigate the situation. Fortunately that didn't happen.

I told my cousin he would have to cut or stop the drinking and he needed to have a strong talk with his dad. I told him it wasn't going to be easy and he would disagree with him on everything but he needed to curtail it because he would be liable for his dad's condition. I told my uncle of my experiences and how doctors, emergency rooms and hospital inspect elderly patients for abuse. I told him that if he would have gone to the emergency room his son could have been a lot of trouble.

My cousin had a long and heated talk with his dad about the alcohol drinking and told him that they both were at risk. His dad was at risk because he could hurt himself or worse and my cousin was responsible for his actions. After intense conversations his dad agreed because he didn't want to see his son get in trouble and he also realized he had no choice.

They came to an agreement of no more than two half glasses of wine a night at dinner. Before that he was drinking at least a whole bottle of wine along other liquor. Since he has his dinner at my cousin's house he pours his wine before dinner. He has a half a glass before the meal and a half a glass during the meal. He has continued to do this and my cousin hasn't seen any other open bottles of wine at his house across the street. The true test came when his dad had a visitor, a former drinking buddy, and he kept to his promise of two half glasses of wine per day. When his friend wanted him to drink more he said he made a promise and didn't want to hurt his son.

To this day he has kept his promise and in the process his skin has cleared up. He is having better conversations, is up on world events and is sleeping better. He is also enjoying his food more because he can finally taste it. Before the alcohol was destroying his taste and he didn't enjoy his food. In fact since he moved across the street from his son and stopped getting pickled every night he is finally once again enjoying life.

Chapter 20
MEDICATIONS AND BEING A CAREGIVER
Prescriptions

Dispensing prescriptions is a major part of being a caregiver. It is necessary so your parent receives the proper medication and also to make sure they receive the right dosage. A lot of time your parent can't see very good and is unable to read the dosage instruction or understand them.

I always set up the medications for my mom. In the morning I would place the medications in containers with the time written on them. This way there was no confusion or forgetfulness. I would put the bottles on the shelf and give them to her when she needed them. When we went out I would put the bottles in a pouch and take them out when she was supposed to take them. My mom was also alert enough to remember when to take her medications. She would say, "It's four o'clock, I need my pills." She was good about this and when the medication changed she would write down the new schedule. In all the years I took care of my father and mother we never had an issue with medications. No over or under doses. I feel fortunate because that would have been a disaster and it's very easy for it to happen.

Whenever the doctor prescribed a new medication, they would always explain its use and effects to me. After that they would hand me the prescription. My mom would ask questions but she knew it was better for me to handle the prescription. I would go to the same pharmacy and they would fill the new prescription. The pharmacist would always come over and ask if I had any questions. By using the same pharmacy I got to know the pharmacist and staff and they got to know our situation.

Another thing I would do is always give them time to fill renewal prescriptions. I would call for a refill a few days ahead and pick it up a few days after I ordered it. I tried to give them time because I knew they were always extremely busy. This did help because the few times I needed a new prescription, such as after a hospital stay, they would fill it right away.

I'm sure things have changed with the new healthcare system. I still believe, if you can, always talk to the pharmacist and staff because they are a valuable help in your caregiving experience. Be nice to them and they will return the kindness. Too many times I would see people frustrated, be demanding of the pharmacy staff and get absolutely nowhere. I would walk up and they would be nice and accommodating. Then when I would leave I would get dirty looks from the other customers. These people are dealing with multiple bureaucracies on a daily basis. It is frustrating for them as it is for you because most bureaucracies don't listen. They are not trying to hurt you, they are just trying to do their job. Try to deal with your insurance's prescription department, it's a nightmare. I was happy to let them deal with the insurance because it was one less thing I had to worry about. So that's why I gave them time to do their job.

Narcotic Prescriptions

When I started taking care of my mother I thought all prescriptions were the same. As her pain became stronger the doctor prescribed stronger medication to control the pain. I then learned, in the state Of California, there were narcotic prescriptions and they were regulated by the Department Of Justice.

When my mom's pain became so severe that normal pain medication would not help, our family physician prescribed Hydromorphone. This medication was classified as a narcotic in California. The doctor had to issue a different prescription. It was a triplicate form that the doctor and pharmacy kept a copy and the final copy was filed with the California Department of Justice. This prescription could not be refilled and it had a time limit on when it could be filled. The other unique restriction on this prescription was that all the information had to be correct and their could be no crossed out information. Now this was always a chore because we all know how legible physicians write. In the beginning several times I went to the pharmacy and the clerk would refuse the prescription because some information was crossed out, the name was spelled wrong or the birthdate was not legible. I would have to go back to the doctor and he would have to void out the prescription and issue a new one. I learned to have him give me the prescription and read it in his office. If he made a mistake I would have him write another prescription with no mistakes. The other thing that I learned about these prescriptions was that the doctor had to get a book from the state Of California. When he ran out he would have to order another book from the state. He also told me that he only had two patients that used this type of prescription.

We had these prescriptions issued for Hydromorphone, Oxycodone, Morphine Tables and Fentanyl patches. The Fentanyl patches seemed to partially control the pain. These were transdermal patches that were changed every three days. They were prescribed for a thirty day supply, which required ten patches per month. They had different strengths and my mom started on the low strength and worked her way up to the highest strength just before she passed away. They controlled the pain on the first and second day. By the third day she would be in increasing pain and it would crest about the time we had to change the patch. The pain would slowly reduce as the patch took effect. The third day was always a stressful time because she would yell in pain and I could not change the patch too early or she would be over medicated.

Taking Medications

Dispensing medications is an important duty of being a caregiver but it's one you have to be very careful. You are giving them medications that help, prolong and are life saving. You are responsible for giving your parent the right dosage and there are very few if any second chances. You do this wrong and your parent could become sick or worse. Once again you are responsible for their care.

Over time my dad and mom were taking several medications a day. Everyday I would put out the medications for the day. I used one of those weekly medication dispensers and it worked out well for my dad. He was still able to take his medications on his own and we never had any problems.

My mom's situation was different because she had to take her medications several times a day. We had a schedule and followed it like clockwork. She had to take pain medication at 8am, she then took medication with her breakfast, pain medication at noon and 4pm, medication after dinner, pain medication at 8pm and finally at midnight. Every three days at 10pm I changed her transdermal pain patch. Every morning I would fill small bottles with her medication. They were labeled by time and she knew when she had to take them. I also had a schedule by her bed if for some reason I wasn't there. We did this for years and it worked well. She was able to swallow the medication and I never had a problem dispensing it. If the doctor changed her medication I would try to fit it into her normal schedule and place it in the bottle with her other pills. If it needed to be on a different time schedule I would place it in another bottle and label it with the correct time. If we went on the road I had a cosmetic case with all her medications in it. This way I had the actual prescription bottles so there would be no confusion that she was allowed to have those medications. If for some reason we were stopped by the authorities I always had her prescription information available. They might have been concerned because they were in another bottle so we always took the original bottle.

She always remembered to take her medications and was able to take them herself. Near the end she started having trouble swallowing her medications. It took her a little longer and she drank more water but eventually she got them down.

Over the years I never made a mistake with either my mom or dad. They were never over or under dosed and we never had any close calls. I kept a close eye on their medications and the dosages they received.

Side Effects Of Pain Medication

I never knew the side effects of pain medication. When you purchase the prescription the pharmacist always gives you the paperwork with all the warnings and side effects. Not many people read this information because they have confidence in their physician, his diagnosis and treatment.

One of the things about pain medication I never knew was it could cause constipation. When I finally read the disclosure on the medication I was amazed that it could cause constipation. I asked the doctor what to do to prevent constipation and he came up with a treatment that worked very well for many years of using laxatives and stool softeners.

It finally caught up with us in 2008 when my mom didn't have a bowel movement for four days. I tried everything to loosen it up but nothing worked. We finally had to go to the hospital because she couldn't keep anything down and I was afraid of dehydration.

Know what side effects the medication prescribed to your parent can cause. Knowing what can happen can go a long way in being prepared. It might not happen but if it does you will be ready.

Expired Medications

There has always been a discussion about expired medications and if they are safe to use. With the high cost of prescriptions people are always wondering if they can use the expired medications to save money. This is something you need to discuss with your doctor and pharmacist because they are the only ones that would have an answer to this question.

My attitude was it was my parents health and I didn't want to do anything to jeopardize it. Some say they are fine, others say they lose potency overtime and others say they are no good. Just to be safe I always purchased new medications when the old ones expired. Most of the time we used them as they were prescribed and they were depleted way before the expiration date. The only time we had something expire was usually ointments and topical medications. If the doctor prescribed something that we had in our medicine cabinet I would always get a new prescription and have it filled. Once again it was about my dad or mom's health and I didn't want to take any chances. They were also very fortunate to have great health insurance and prescription coverage so the cost was not much of an issue. They had a reasonable co-payment and I always made room in the budget for medications. For their prescriptions I never had to make the decision to save money and use the expired medications. If I was in that situation I would have asked their doctor and pharmacist if that could be an option.

Healthcare and prescriptions have changed so much recently that many people might consider using expired medications. Once again I am not a medical professional and I have absolutely no idea on what to do. What I do know is you need to check with the experts to answer this question.

Chapter 21
BODILY FUNCTIONS AND BEING A CAREGIVER
Smells And Odors

Two things to be considered when being a caregiver is smells and odors. You have to be aware of these situations because if they are around it could make your home seem unsanitary. Another reason you need to be aware of smells and odors is that they can identify certain situations that you need to address.

I did my best to keep a clean house and I was always concerned with odors especially the smell of urine. This is just common sense but it also goes back to the time when I was in junior high we would visit the local convalescent hospital. The first odor that hit you when you walked into the front door was the smell of urine. Most of the patients smelled like they had soiled themselves and were not frequently changed. I made sure that my mother was never in that situation. Now sometimes it was unavoidable for a short time like when your in the car because most vehicles are too small to attempt a diaper change. When she would have an "accident" on the road I would change her immediately when we got home. The same was when she had an "accidental" bowl movement when she passed gas, it was a little potent on the way home but I cleaned her and changed her diaper as soon as we got home.

I kept her bathroom clean and made sure it was sanitary. I changed her sheets daily and made sure her bed and surroundings were always clean. I had a covered trash can on the side of her bed so she could change her incontinence pads during the night and throw the used ones away. Usually she never missed the trash can but if she did the floor would be cleaned and disinfected in the morning.

When we had a visit from our first home health nurse, she was very stern and demanded a clean house. When she first came in our home she literally started sniffing around. When I asked what she was doing she said, "I'm smelling for pee. I can smell the smallest amount of pee. Your house doesn't smell of pee." I told her my story about the convalescent hospital and she laughed. She told me that I was the first home that she had visited that did not smell like pee. A few times she brought in trainees and asked if they smelled anything. They would say no and she would say, "This is not the normal situation, most houses smell of pee."

During these visits from the home health nurse I did learn that some odors did point to situations that needed to be addressed. One was when my mom came home from the hospital after her spine surgery she had a catheter and bag. Once in a while the bag had a strong urine smell when I would empty it. When this happened the urine was also bright yellow. The home health nurse told me that my mom was not drinking enough water. Sure enough my mom started drinking more water and the smell went away and the urine returned to a normal pale yellow.

Another odor I learned was a problem was when my mom was constipated. Because of all the pain medication she was prescribed it was almost like concrete in her intestines. Sometimes the constipation was so bad we had to go to the hospital. The sure sign it was time for a visit to the hospital was when she would vomit. The vomit would smell like feces and I knew none of our usual remedies would work on the constipation. It was time for extreme measures to unclog her and prevent dehydration.

There are many odors and smells that can help identify problems and they are different because of each situation. Also you need to be aware of smells and odors because any visitor could be offended by the stench. A home that smells is considered to be a dirty house and unsanitary. Since you are responsible for the care of someone else that responsibility falls on you and you need to make sure your home is clean and sanitary. Not only does the house have to be clean and sanitary so does your parent. Keeping them clean keeps your home clean and can eliminate a lot of problems.

Feces Smell

One of the most disgusting smells is that of feces. A home that smells of feces is considered unclean and unsanitary. This is also a hard smell to remove because a person lying in bed passes a lot of gas and it smells.

Another item you will be using a lot is disinfectant spray or air freshener. This is to cover the smell of feces in the house as your parent lets out gas. The air freshener just covers over the smell for a short time but after your parent goes to the bathroom all should be well again.

Keeping the bathroom clean and fresh is a must because if it is dirty bacteria can grow and that can be dangerous to you and your parent. Always have disposable gloves available so you can clean the bathroom after each use. Disinfectant spray and cleaning wipes help in this process and they make it easier to clean the toilet seat. Be sure to clean in front of the toilet because a lot of times when they miss it travels under the seat and over the rim to the floor. You will know this has happened when it is yellow in the front where the toilet sits on the floor. If you have a raised toilet seat they get dirty quickly and the plastic gets harder to clean over time because the surface gets dull and stains very easily. These will have to be replaced because after a while no matter how hard you scrub the brown film never comes off. These raised toilet seats also trap feces under the toilet rim, sides and bottom of the raised section. You will have to remove it from the toilet to clean it and make sure there is no residue. This happens when they have a lot of gas and when they go it sprays into the toilet and under onto the raised seat. Not an easy mess to clean.

You also have to be careful and check for feces residue on their body. Even small spots can dry and cause a rash or irritation. When you are changing diapers make sure you clean all areas with a baby cleaning wipe. This includes any folds in the skin and you have to spread the butt cheeks apart to make sure the entire area is clean and free of any residue. I know it sounds disgusting but it is something you have to do to prevent problems in the future. Not only is this to prevent a rash but it also prevents any feces smell coming from the body.

Another time the feces smell can show up is when they vomit. This means their intestines and bowels are clogged and they're not digesting properly. For us this meant a call to the doctor, a trip to the emergency room and a hospital stay. The hospital would have to put my mom on an IV to prevent dehydration and then they would use massive amounts of laxatives and enemas to clean her out in a controlled environment.

Keeping a clean home free of feces smell is a normal daily routine. No one wants to live in a smelly home and it can be detrimental to theirs and your well being. On the other hand a feces smell can be the sign of many things, some can be corrected having a bowel movement, others by cleaning and in rare cases a trip to the hospital. The first two are normal everyday occurrences and can be handled easily. The third is dangerous and can be critical to the health of you parent.

Fluids And Functions

You always have to be aware of bodily fluids and bodily functions. Even though you are taking care of your parent you always need to wear gloves, not only to protect yourself but to prevent them from getting an infection. No matter how you try bodily fluids can get anywhere and functions that are uncontrollable can make a mess.

I got over the embarrassment of bodily fluids and body functions pretty quickly while taking care of both parents. With my dad it was a little easier because I was his son and it seemed more natural to take care of my dad. With my mom it was a different story, somethings you just didn't want to know or see. Being an adult and responsible for her care I got over this embarrassment very quickly, in about two-seconds. One thing I learned was it was also embarrassing for her. I knew this because she kept saying, "I'm sorry." That's when I realized that she was just as uncomfortable as I was and I just needed to do what I had to do.

The urinating, farting and bowl movements are part of everyday life and you need to deal with them. Vomiting is still difficult to see because it is such a violent bodily function but it is part of life so you have to deal with it. I never had a weak stomach so I didn't have a problem cleaning up. As time went on it was just part of the everyday routine. I finally got her to stop saying she was sorry. I told her, "It's part of life and it's my job to take care of it. Don't worry, do what you have to do and I'll clean it up." After a while she became more comfortable with the situation and we never had any problems. Hey when I was a baby she did it for me so it was my turn to return the favor.

By taking care of her, it was my responsibility to see that her body was functioning properly. If there was a problem it was my duty to correct it by normal procedures or if it was something severe by taking her to the doctor or hospital. As far as the fluids are concerned that's what a bucket, mop, soap, wash cloth and disinfectant are for. These functions are something that we all do except for some of us we try to keep them quiet or private. When you are a caregiver nothing is private and everything is out in the open.

Incontinence

As your parent gets older incontinence is a normal part of life. You always need to be aware of this problem because it can cause your parent embarrassment if it happens when you are out. Fortunately today there are a lot of products that can help you with this situation.

While I was taking care of my dad I never had to worry about incontinence because he had an urostomy bag because of bladder cancer. What I had to be concerned with was that the bag would sometimes come loose and leak. No matter how we applied the flange to the skin, once in a while they would leak. We even had some bags that must have been old because urine would seep through. I always brought towels and wipes so I could clean my dad in case there was a problem when we went out. I also made sure to always have a change of clothes on hand and I use to have a light windbreaker always available to cover him in case there was an "accident." This worked well and only once in a while we had a problem when we went out. No matter how I tried to cover him up he was always embarrassed and worried that something worse would happen. Fortunately we never had that catastrophe.

My mom was incontinent for many years and wore the incontinence pads to prevent leakage. She would apply these herself and never had a problem when she went out. When I started taking care of her full time she still applied these pads herself. She had a system where I would put a clean diaper on her and she would place an incontinence pad in the diaper to prevent leakage and to keep the diaper dry while we went out. When the pad was wet she would replace it with a dry one. She would then put the used pad in a plastic trash bag and I would dispose of it when we got home. I always carried disinfectant spray so the car would not smell. I also had a box of baby wipes available so she could wash her hands after she removed the used pad. We did this for many years and almost all the way to the end. I also would use this technique when she had to stay in bed for a while so she would remain dry. She would wet the pad and then remove it and drop it in a trash bin on the side of her bed. She would then replace it with a new dry pad. I had air fresheners in the trash bin so it would not smell and I would empty it very often so her room did not smell.

The only problem with this routine was that we went through a lot of packages of pads and diapers. These items were not covered by Medicare or insurance so it was a great out of pocket expense. It was worth the expense because she kept dry and we never had a problem with a rash or infection. She also never had any "accidents" when we went out and never smelt of urine. She was always clean, dry and odor free.

Constipation

During the entire time I was taking care of my mom she had constipation issues. She was prescribed pain medication for her spinal condition and all the medications she took had constipation listed as a side effect. She was taking so much pain medication it was like concrete blocking her intestines and bowels.

We usually kept the constipation under control with a variety of techniques. One remedy was for her to take stool softeners and Sennosides laxative tablets daily to counteract the clogging power of the pain medication. The stool softeners were easy on the system and so were the laxative tablets. These kept her regular most of the time and she would go daily. Once in a while she wouldn't go for two days and we had to up the ante. A glass of room temperature prune juice would usually do the trick and get her back on schedule. Sometimes she wouldn't go for three days and it was time for extra help. I would warm up the glass of prune juice and in about two to three hours it would unclog her and the system would get back to normal. On these occasions we never went anywhere because you never knew when the remedies would finally work. When they did there was no time to waste and I had to get her on the toilet right away. No diaper would ever be able to hold it.

In rare cases the feces would get stuck in her rectum and I had to use vaseline to loosen it so it could come out. These would be huge hard globs of crap and they would be stuck partly in and out of the rectum. I never knew that thing could stretch so much. She was never in pain because of the medication but it was extremely embarrassing for her. I would put my gloves on and pull Vaseline out of the jar and onto my fingers and wipe it around her rectum while she was still on the toilet. Sometimes the crap would come out all at once and sometimes it took a couple of tries. I had to keep flushing the toilet because I didn't want to clog it and have a bigger mess. This was before California's water shortage so I could flush as many times as I needed. After these ordeals and she was finished I would clean her up and replace her diaper. She would look at me and say, "I'm sorry." I would tell her, "There's nothing to be sorry for," and we would go back to our normal routine.

In extreme case nothing would work and that would mean a trip to the emergency room. I would know when it was time because she would start to vomit after she ate and the vomit would smell like feces. We would go to the hospital and they would confirm that she was extremely constipated with an x-ray or scan. They would start her on an IV so she wouldn't get dehydrated. Then the doctors would discuss what was the best way to treat the situation. One time it was surgery and the others it was with massive dosages of laxatives and enemas. They would work on her for a few days and she would be discharged. Fortunately this only happened three times.

Most of the time we had the situation under control and were able to overcome the problem with our remedies. Once in a while she needed extra help and a hospital visit was necessary. When those times came my biggest fear was dehydration because she couldn't keep anything down. Once the hospital started the IV of fluids she was on her way back to normal and I knew we were good for another year or two.

Diarrhea

Diarrhea didn't happen often while I was taking care of my mom, in fact it was the exact opposite, constipation. Due to all the pain medication it would clog up her intestines on a regular basis. Once in a while she did have loose stools, thanks to the stool softeners, and it did make it easier for her to go. On rare occasions she did get diarrhea and that made for many trips to the toilet. I never wanted to give her something to stop the diarrhea because that would block her up more down the road because of the pain medication. We would let it run its course and I would make her sip water or juice so she wouldn't get dehydrated. On a few occasions I did have to give her the pink stuff to slow things down.

Just because someone wears a diaper it doesn't mean that diarrhea is not a problem. In fact you really don't want them to have diarrhea in a diaper because it is usually acidic and it can cause a rash. The other problem is it makes a mess and it can take you a long time to clean up. It gets everywhere and you have to make sure you clean it all. If my mom had diarrhea I would do my best to get her on the toilet fast and let her sit for a while till she was finished. She would clean herself up and I would put her back in bed and replace the diaper. If she got that feeling again that she had to go I would take the diaper off and put her back on the toilet. We could repeat this process two or three times and it would finally settle down.

It was not something I looked forward to but I would rather lift her many times than have to clean up the mess of diarrhea in a diaper. Fortunately this didn't happen very often but when it did I worked fast. In all the years I took care of my mom she never had an accident where she made a mess on the floor or in the bathroom. She was able to hold it until she was sitting on the toilet. A few times there were some nervous moments and I was always expecting a blowout but it never happened. After these type of situations we both would be exhausted and needed a little rest.

Vomiting

Vomiting is one of the hardest things to watch because it is such a violent bodily function. You see the strain in the throat, face and then the fluid comes out. After that they start to perspire and hyperventilate. It is not something you want to see.

When I was taking care of my dad every so often he would spit up blood and that meant a trip to the emergency room. He didn't vomit blood so it didn't gush out but it was enough to make your heart drop. Due to his lung disease this happened a few of times during his illness. He would be admitted to the hospital and they would do a bronchoscopy and find the cause. Usually is was a popped blood vessel or polyp. They would take a sample and have it analyzed and they would come back benign. The last time he spit up blood was six months before he died and that sample came back malignant.

My mom rarely vomited and when she did there were a few things that decided what was next. I would look at the color to see if it was clear, yellow or brown. If it was clear she was okay and it would pass. If it was yellow I would to see if any food was in it and wait for the bout to pass. If is was brown, I smelled it to see if it had the odor of feces. If she was not constipated I would call the doctor but if she was constipated I knew trouble was coming. It meant she was clogged and no more fluid or food was going down. We would have to go to the hospital and they would have to clean her out in a controlled environment and make sure she didn't get dehydrated. This meant a few days in the hospital. Fortunately this didn't happen too often but it did mean a lot of strain and discomfort for her and a lot of driving for me.

Vomiting is not something you want to take a chance with because of the possibility of dehydration. You also don't want them putting that much strain on their system. It is not something you want to see but it is definitely something you will encounter.

Catheter

Another hard thing to have to deal with while taking care of your parent is a catheter. Sometimes they are sent home from the hospital with this device and it makes caring for them a little more complicated. For some a catheter is actually part of their everyday routine and care.

My mom was sent home with a catheter after her spine surgery and recovery. The first problem I had was when I had to lift her from the wheelchair and into the car the day she was discharged from the hospital. Fortunately for us a staff member from the hospital held it while I lifted her into the car seat. When we got home I had to put it in her lap because she didn't have the strength to hold it. For the next week I had to maneuver around it while I cared for her.

I had to be careful not to bump it and have it come dislodged because then I would have caused her pain, had a leak and a mess. It was difficult at first trying to put on a diaper while the discharge hose came through one of the leg openings. I also had to be careful not to trip on the hose when I moved her because that could cause her a lot of pain as well as dislodge the hose.

Emptying was not a problem because all you had to do was flip over the drain hose and open a valve so the urine would drain into a container. Then I would have to record the amount, color and smell. After the catheter bag was emptied and the info was written down I would empty the container into the toilet and flush. Then the container would be rinsed out for the next use.

We got through the ordeal of the catheter but for me it was a challenge. I never had a problem with the routine of emptying the bag. My problem was I was always afraid I would tug on the tubing and cause my mom pain. With all the lifting and turning to wash her or change her diaper I was always concerned that I would hurt her. Once in a while there was a problem where the tube got caught on the bed rail or something else and she would let me know by saying, "Ow." We never had a catastrophe or major leak and I was always relieved when the catheter was removed. I was lucky some don't have this option.

Chapter 22
STAYING FOCUSED AND KEEPING THE MIND SHARP
Keeping The Mind Sharp

Another thing I tried to do was to keep my mom's mind sharp. I did not want her just to sit around and watch television or stare out the window. I wanted to keep her engaged in conversation and for her to use her motor skills.

This is one of those topics that goes back to my junior high school days when we would visit the elderly in the local convalescent hospital. You would walk in and they would have a line of wheelchairs in front of the window that was facing the street. These poor people were just watching the cars go by. They were waisting their day staring out the window. We would walk in and they would get excited because it was a change to their normal routine.

I was not going to let this happen with my mom. I would get her involved in almost everything in our daily routine. I would make her wash herself as best she could in the morning. When she was able to move her fingers she would do word search and crossword puzzles. She was really good at these puzzles up until the last year of her life. Due to severe arthritis she was unable to hold a pen and write so she scribbled the answers. We would play card and board games. We would discuss baseball, news and politics. We would also talk about the family. I would ask her questions about when she was young and she would tell stories. She would get forgetful but it was not serious, dementia or Alzheimers. I was lucky, her memory was good till about the last six months of her life, then it started to fade.

If I was working in the garage or outside, I would position her so she could watch what I was doing. We had a garden and she enjoyed watching me planting and harvesting the vegetables. She would read recipes and check for something new for dinner. She would watch the food channel and say, "That looks good, we should try it." We did, some was good and some was not. I would ask, "Do you want me to make this again?" If the answer was "no" we looked for something different to try.

I would let her fold clothes and sort out socks. Anything to keep her busy and make her think. I would ask her about certain dates to see if she remembered birthdays and anniversaries. She remembered most of them. The last two years the only birthday she forgot was mine.

When we would take a drive I would make her read road signs. If it was a route we took often I would ask her if she knew where we were? Most of the time she had a good sense of how far we were from the destination. She would look at the cloud formations and weather conditions. At night, I would think she was sleeping because of the monotony of night driving, a car or truck would pass and she would remark, "their going fast." Sometimes it would be, "When we get home I want some ice cream," she was always thinking about food.

All these questions kept her thinking and it made her mind work. She was not staring at the cars going by, she was in one and going somewhere. People were not telling her stories she was talking about her experiences. I made sure she was participating in life.

Talk About Old Times And The Past

I always had my parents talk about old times and the past. I was always fascinated about the times they lived, like the Great Depression and World War II, but it also served a purpose by keeping their minds working. They could remember those times like they were yesterday and they were very vivid in their recollections.

My sisters and I grew up with these stories so we knew them pretty much by heart but the grand children didn't know about their grand parents past. My folks told the grand children about their past and the "old days." They listened and learned a lot from their grand parents.

My dad was very passionate about the Great Depression because his family had a hard time. His stories taught all of us not to waste food and to be thankful for what we had. He always said we needed to be prepared because even though the politicians said it would never happen again, he said there was always a chance and we needed to be ready. Not being able to find a job I feel that I am living through this now.

He was also very strong about World War II and his time in the Marine Corps. My dad would tell stories about when he was in the Marine Corps during World War II. He was in the Pacific and always got upset when most movies and television shows only told stories of the war in Europe. The only time they would mention the war in the Pacific was the dropping of the atomic bomb on Hiroshima. He would say their was a lot more to the war than just that bomb and he was right. His stories were horrific and sad but he did make his points. His oldest granddaughter one time told him that they were learning about World War II in school and they were only teaching about Europe. She told the teacher that the war also happened in the Pacific and her grandfather was there and it was just as bad or worse as in Europe. A few days later the teacher started teaching about the war in the Pacific.

My mom would talk more about her life growing up. They were lucky and her family did not have as bad of a time during the Great Depression. She talked about the war and how the town was empty and all the woman were working to help their families while the men were in the military. Her remembrance of the Great Depression and World War II was so different from my father's. I guess he was living it and she watched it go by.

They would also talk about how they met and their life together. These were topics that were always a hit with the grand children. When they told stories about my sisters and I it would embarrass us and make the kids laugh.

This kept their minds working and kept them a part of the family. They had something to say and they had an audience that was willing to listen. They just didn't sit there and watch the world go by. We were lucky that they kept their memories all the way to the end and kept us terrified and laughing at the same time.

Memories

Memories are important in keeping your parents mind sharp. Some can remember events from years ago but can't remember what happened ten minutes before. There has always been an issue with long and short term memory with the elderly leading to the term, "Senior moment." When dementia and Alzheimers come into the picture it is a whole different story and requires a lot of patience and a different type of care.

I was lucky because both of my parents kept their memory all the way to the end. Yes, they had their "senior moments" but for the most part could remember what they wanted. Sometimes they needed just a little hint and they could remember what they wanted to say or talk about. At the end, about a month before they died, they became confused and started to lose their memory.

Once again having them remember things from their past kept their mind working. They had to think and that was a good thing because it stimulated their brain. I would tell the younger generation to ask them about certain points in my parents past so my dad and mom would have to remember and tell the story. The kids were good at that and always asked to hear the story.

Some memories they might not want to remember because they were tragic or sad but even these can keep their minds working. It can make them emotional and then they can remember the good times to overcome the bad. I'm not a doctor so I have no idea if this is a good thing but it did work for my parents. We learned a lot about their lives and even somethings that were painful for them to talk about.

I was always amazed at the detail they had of the past and how they remembered like it was yesterday. They could look at an old photograph and tell who was in the picture. Once in a while they had trouble identifying someone, most of the time sooner or later the name would come to them. It kept them thinking and they were happy they remembered. Still once in a while they still had their "senior moments."

Chapter 23

POSITIVE OUTLOOK AND BEING A CAREGIVER

Your Attitude

Not only do you have to keep your parents attitude positive you must also do the same with yours. Your attitude affects your parents while you are taking care of them. If you are negative, so are they and that could hurt the way they deal with their illness and situation. It is hard to always be positive but you have to do your best because it will also keep your parents attitude positive.

This was one of the hardest things for me to do because it always seemed like we were getting bad news. You would just get over a hump and then something would come and push you back down. It was hard to stay positive when every diagnosis led to another bad diagnosis.

When my dad was sick I always knew what was going to come. We were told from the day he was diagnosed with asbestosis that eventually it would lead to lung cancer and that could spread throughout his body. When we would go to the doctor and they would find no problems it was always a relief but you alway knew the next time could be the one. When they didn't find any problems it was easy to stay positive and keep my father's spirits up. Then a shock came when he was diagnosed with bladder cancer. That one we never saw coming and it was not something I was ready for so I had a lot of discussions with his doctors. I regrouped immediately and told him all would be well and that he needed the drastic treatment immediately. He had the surgery to remove his bladder and he was able to go on with his life. I pushed him hard so he would not give up and he didn't and was able to beat the bladder cancer scare. When he was finally diagnosed with lung cancer it was extremely difficult to keep a positive attitude because once again you had an idea that something else was coming down the road. I did my best keeping him positive and encouraged my dad to go through all the treatments. He did even though he also knew what was coming. Sure enough within a few weeks we learned that the cancer had spread to his throat, then his brain and all over his body. There was nothing positive about this situation and we both knew the end was near. Everyday when I went to the hospital I put on a good face and told him he was going to beat it and he smiled every time. One day he didn't smile and that was they day he started slipping in and out of consciousness. Two weeks later he passed away. I tried to have a positive attitude to the end but he knew what was happing inside of him and he just went along with me.

With my mom it all started when she had her spine surgery. We had great hopes and for a few hours it looked like it was a success and then it all fell apart. I was telling her she did fine and it went well and then the pain came back and it was more severe than ever. I told her she had to do the rehab exercises so she could move her legs and she refused and she once again was never able to put weight on her legs. I said she was going to be okay and she got an enormous bed sore in the hospital that took six month of wound care to correct. Every time I tried to be positive something else came and knocked her down. To her credit she kept going and fighting so it never brought her down. Same thing with her breast cancer and she beat it by having a mastectomy. I kept telling her she beat it and she was a survivor. It came back and I told her she was going to beat and she did once again. It came back a third time and she had the will and fight to beat it again.

It was easier with my mom to be positive because her illnesses came farther apart. It took over thirteen years for the illnesses to finally take her down. With my dad it was one right after the other over the course of two years. I did my best to keep a positive attitude so they both could fight and beat their illnesses. My dad had a short run but my mom did it for over thirteen years.

Humor

I always tried to use a litter humor with my parents to keep them upbeat.

Sometimes it would make them feel better and smile and sometimes they would push back and turn the tables. It would throw the doctors and nurses a curve and it would make them chuckle at the same time.

With all that we had to deal with it was always nice to have a laugh once in a while. With my dad's illness progressing so fast we never had a time to joke around a lot. I would call him, "Pop" all the time and doctors and nurses would give me a look like, "what." My dad would say, "That's me," and they would just smile. When he was in the hospital I had a routine to tickle his foot to make him laugh and he did every time. This stopped when he became a diabetic and a nurse told me never to tickle his feet so I didn't do it again. I changed to when I left his room I would pat him once on the head and tell him, "See you tomorrow." He would smile and say good bye. When I stayed with him in the hospital when he was in and out of conscience we went through this routine every night for about two weeks. Sometimes he smiled and others he didn't even acknowledge the touch.

With my mom I had a long time to use humor at her expense and make her chuckle. She weighed about 115 pounds and I use to tease her that she was heavy. With all the food she ate you would think she would weigh a lot more. When I picked her up sometimes I would say, "You're putting on weight," and she would tell me, "I'm small." When we would go to the doctors office I would tell them about her appetite and say she was "heavy" and they would look at her and say, "is that true?" and she would say, "no I'm light." My response was, "You lift her twenty times a day and see how heavy she is." They would look at me and say, "That's your job." They were right and they also knew I was joking.

When we had the home health nurses come to change her wound dressings I would draw a sad face on the back of her diaper. When they rolled her on her side they would say, "Oh, what's this?" and chuckle. They would then tell my mom what I did and she would say, "Oh no," and laugh. She would tell them about her nickname and they would laugh and say, "He's wrong, your skinny." They always would say she had a good sense of humor as they went along with the joke. When we would go to the wound center the doctor would tell her, "Your skinny and he's weak." She would tell me in front of them, "See Jim, I'm skinny." They would laugh and she would smile.

Sure it was a warped sense of humor but she retaliated and went along with it. Some of the doctors and nurses looked a little confused at first but then realized what I was doing. I was trying to take her mind off her pain and her condition. In doing so she could tease me and reverse the joke.

Nicknames

During the time I took care of my parents I would always give them nicknames to give them a little chuckle during the day. Some might consider them insulting but I thought of them as a way for them to stay alert and to defend themselves. I didn't have much time with my dad but I did with my mom and she fired back every time. It was a lot a fun and made both of us laugh and smile.

The only nickname I had for my dad was"pop," and it was always interesting to see the faces of nurses or hospital staff when I would say it. Some were confused and some didn't understand. I would walk into the room and say, "Hi pop," and he would light up and smile. When it was time to go home I would say, "See you in the morning pop," and he would say, "you betcha." it was a little routine we had and it went on for years.

I had a lot of nicknames for my mom and they all came from the fact that I had to lift her up. Sometimes when I lifted her after she ate I would tell her that she was gaining weight. I finally gave her the nickname, "Tubby." When I called her that she would laugh and say, "I'm not tubby, I'm skinny." I said it a few times in the hospital and the nurse would give me a dirty look and my mom would say, "He calls me tubby because he thinks I'm fat, but the joke is on him, I'm skinny." The nurse would nervously laugh and I would tell her, "Try lifting her twenty times a day." Then she turned to my mom and say, "I agree with you, your skinny and he's losing his strength." It was all in fun and it put a smile on my mom's face. Later on I came up with another nickname, "lardo." It once again it was based on her having to be lifted all the time. Her response was always the same, "I'm not lardo, I'm skineo." It made us laugh and a lot of times it was when we needed a laugh.

My little nephew gave my mom a nickname and it was one she loved. He was about two years old and he couldn't say great grandma so he called her "gagama." She loved that name and when he learned how to say great grandma she still wanted him to say, "Gagama." He could get away with anything.

Chapter 24

ACTIVITIES AND BEING A CAREGIVER

Entertainment

Entertainment can come in many forms. It can be visits by family and friends, watching television, listening to the radio, playing cards or games. It can also be taking a drive or going to an event. It can be whatever makes you enjoy life.

I was fortunate because my mom liked baseball. When there was no baseball and during the rest of the year we would play card games, checkers and other board games. This kept my mom's mind sharp. She was really good at checkers and Yahtzee. We also would watch old movies on satellite and listen to big band music.

Other times we would drive down from Tehachapi to Chino for the great grandchildren's birthdays or other events. That was a chore because it was a two and half hour drive in each direction. It was well worth it because nothing is better than watching the grandchildren and great grandchildren having fun. This was always a high point and something my mom looked forward to.

Baseball/Sports

Sports is an escape for many individuals. Watching on television or listening on the radio gives people an escape from tasks of everyday life. When they get older and you are caring for them they still enjoy this escape.

During the spring, summer and early fall my mom would watch or listen to baseball. Her favorite team was the Angels and she watched them regularly. My niece, her granddaughter wanted to take her to a game but her husband found out it was not an easy chore. Since she was in a wheelchair, it would have been an ordeal and not very affordable. My mom was happy watching any baseball on television. The Angels, Mets, Dodgers, Red Sox, Cubs, Yankees, it didn't matter, it was a game. When we were in Tehachapi, I purchased the Major League Baseball computer subscription so she could watch her teams. This was an absolute waste of money because the Angels and Dodgers were considered local teams so you could not watch these games live if they were on the local Los Angeles channels. We lived 150 miles away from Dodger stadium and 180 miles away from Angels stadium. It didn't make sense. We had to wait until after the game was over to start watching it. We were too far away for an over the air antenna to get the game and only the cable company could get these stations. We had a satellite system so we could get the games on the sports channels but if it was over the air we were out of luck. Obviously major league baseball was not too fan friendly. I did not renew the service and when games were on the local channels we just skipped those games. We didn't even listen to the radio broadcasts.

My mom was an avid baseball fan and she enjoyed watching it on television and listening to it on the radio. She would watch two or three games a day off our satellite system. It would start in the morning with the Cubs or early east coast games. She would then watch a game from the evening on the East coast or in the central area. When the Angels were on it didn't matter what other team was playing and that included the Dodgers. She use to like the Dodgers but once they traded Mike Piazza she had no use for that team. The satellite package we had included WPIX so she was excited she could watch Mike Piazza when he played for the Mets. She was surprised when one year for her birthday I gave her a Mike Piazza rookie baseball card for a gift. One of the local fast food restaurants had a promotion that if you bought a sundae during baseball season it came in a small plastic helmet. When we went out for errands and passed one of these locations we would stop and I would get her a sundae. She got all the baseball team helmets and ate a lot of ice cream sundaes in the process and she enjoyed every one of them.

Baseball was her escape and she always enjoyed it. When she was a teenager she played on the local softball teams in her town in Rhode Island. She was a pitcher, a south paw and threw a no-hitter once. In fact that's how my dad made his impression. They only had one softball and at one game someone hit a home run and it went over the fence. My dad was on the other side of the fence and picked up the ball. They had to end the game because they had no ball and could not find it. The next day my dad mailed it to her home. They knew each other from church but this made him stand out. He served in the Marine Corps and they got married after World War II ended.

Years ago when she was able to walk we would go to as many games as we could afford, it didn't matter that it was general admission on the upper deck. As she aged and was no longer able to go to a game television was a great substitute. Watching a baseball game kept her attention and it also kept her sharp. She knew the teams, players, positions and announcers. Even though she didn't like the Dodgers she did like to listen to Vin Scully. She would wait for Spring Training and watch all the way through the World Series. Even a few weeks before she died she was watching Spring Training Baseball on television. She was looking forward to the 2013 season and was waiting for the regular games to start. After she passed a way her great grandson started playing baseball. He started t-ball and the next year he started playing the next level. His position was pitcher and he did very well. In the 2015 season he once again was a pitcher and pitched a no-hitter. She would have been proud and would have loved to have been around to see that. I believe she did.

Television-Radio-Music

Watching television, listening to the radio or music is good way to entertain your parents. Years ago they called television a substitute baby sitter for my generation and there is no reason why you can't use this for your parents. If something they enjoy is on there is no reason not to let them watch or hear it. With today's technology there is so much available you can choose whatever they like.

My mom liked baseball and she watched it whenever she could. That was most of spring, summer and early fall. She enjoyed it and it helped her pass the time. She had her favorite team, the Angels, and she watched whenever they were on the television. If we were in the car she listened to them on the radio. She like baseball but I could do without it so I would read or try to work on projects around the house. I could watch for only so long because baseball was a little boring for me.

Other times in the year she would watch old television shows on some of the satellite channels. When I could afford it I would purchase old movies and television shows on DVD so she could watch them whenever she wanted. I set up a television in her room so she could control what she watched or I could transfer programs from the living room.

I could also use this set up for music. She liked big band music from the forties and I would play CD's so she could listen to her favorite band. Once in a while I would hear her singing along with the music and I'm sure it was bringing back lot of memories. Sometimes she would have a tear in her eye for some memory of long ago. I enjoyed that music also because it had character and was relaxing. During the Christmas season I would play Christmas music and that would get her ready for the holiday. She would sing along and enjoy herself while I would be getting the house ready.

When she watched the Sunday Mass on television she would recite the prayers and sing the hymns along with the choir. It made her feel good because she felt she was part of the service. She did that all the way to one week before she died. She forgot almost everything else but she remembered the Mass, her prayers and the hymns.

There was no reason not to let her watch television or listen to music. It gave her something to enjoy and a lot of times it gave me a break to do something else. Sometimes I got absolutely nothing done because I was enjoying it with her.

Clubs

Clubs are another way to keep your parent active. If they were members of a club or organization, as long as they are able there is no reason for them not to continue. It might mean more work for you but it could help keep their mind sharp. If you belonged to a club or organization and you are able to continue being a member make arrangements to bring your parent along and they might enjoy themselves.

For years I was always active in our church and the high school I attended. I was in charge of the alumni association and I was a member of their board of directors. We were always fund raising by having different events. I would bring my mom with me and everyone knew her and always said, "Hi" and visited with her. During the football season I would park my car near the end zone and she could watch the game. Other alumni, parents, teachers and students would go up to the car to say, "Hi" and asked her if she needed anything. Some would bring her hot chocolate and if they really wanted to make her day a piece of cake. We did this for years and she enjoyed every minute of it.

A new administration took over the school and changed everything. All of us "old guys" no longer felt part of the school and decided it was time to part ways. We moved up to Tehachapi a few years later and because of her health never volunteered for another organization.

We still got visits from some of the people we worked with and always talked about old times. When she passed away we held the funeral at the church near the high school. Several teachers, old friends and some prior students came to the service. It was a nice feeling and a sign of support.

Associations

If you have any associations that your parent belong to or you were a part of they can also be a source of help and support. Some offer seminars and online information that could be helpful. Some civic associations have classes that can help your parent adapt to their situation and can also help you understand your role.

We never had access to any associations that would offer any help or services. My dad belonged to a pipe fitters union and nothing was available, they were pretty much a shell because all the ship repair industries had left Southern California. My mom never belonged to any associations and there was nothing in our area that could help our situation. We were on our own and had to find out how to do things by ourselves.

If the resources are available there is no harm in getting more information. It might help you in the care of your parent. The more information you get and you can adapt it to your situation could make things easier for you.

Banquets

Going to a banquet can be quite a challenge when you are taking care of someone. You are risking the unknown because you don't know how your parent is going to react. The only one that can make that decision is you because you know how they handle different situations.

My mom was never interested in going to banquets because she was always afraid she would have an "accident." When we received invitations for weddings in the family we would always decline because of her condition. One wedding we didn't decline was for her youngest grand daughter, my niece. My mom wanted to go so I had to be ready for anything. The wedding was October of 2012 and this was about the time my mom's condition and memory was starting to fade. She was becoming more confused and would forget quite a bit so I didn't know what was going to happen.

The wedding ceremony went on without a problem. My mom was in the church and participated in the Mass. After the ceremony I took her outside and she talked with the family as we waited for the pictures to be taken. We then left for the reception and that's when everything changed. We sat at the family table with my sisters, nephew and cousins. She was always looking around like she didn't recognize anyone. Then she started complaining that she wanted to eat and where was her food? While my niece and her husband were making the toast, my mom said in a loud voice, "Where's my food? What type of a joint is this?" Everyone heard it as well as my niece and her husband. They smiled and my niece said, "My grandma is hungry." It was entertaining but I new something was going on inside because this was a side I had never seen before. When the meal came we got her prepared and she became feisty and combative. She looked at me and said, "Get away from me." I was shocked and continued to get her ready. She devoured dinner and settled down. She had no more outbursts and started talking to everyone like nothing had happened. We left the reception around 8pm because we had an hour and half drive ahead of us. On the way home I was talking to her and asking her if she enjoyed the wedding. She said she did and she commented how beautiful her granddaughter looked. She then said, "The day was great except at the reception this guy kept bothering me. He kept trying to take my food." I looked at her and said, "Mom, that was me." She insisted it wasn't and I told her who was at the table and what she did. She looked at me and said she didn't remember and she was "sorry." My stomach turned and I knew things were changing and we were on a downward slope. When I mentioned it to the doctor the next week he attributed it to a micro stroke and said they might become more frequent. He was also noticing a difference in her and said to be ready for anything.

This was the only banquet we attended and my fears came true. I didn't know what to expect but in my wildest nightmares I never thought that she would not know who I was. This was the beginning of the end and it was only a matter of time.

Outdoor Activities

Just because your parent needs full time care it doesn't mean they can't enjoy outdoor activities. It depends on their condition and how much they can be moved but if it is possible make sure they are properly dressed for the weather and it is just like taking them to a doctor or other appointment. It's more work for you but it might give them some enjoyment or something new to do.

My mom liked to be outside as long as she was dressed for it. Like a lot of elderly people she felt the cool air quicker than me so I had to make sure she always had a sweater and blanket available. In the summer I would put a light colored hat on her head and a thin towel or throw on her lap. If needed I would attach an umbrella to the wheelchair to prevent too much sun from getting to her.

She would watch me mow the lawn or work in the garden while she did her puzzle books. She would watch the children in the neighborhood play and they would wave to her as they rode their bicycles. We would go to picnics at my former high school because I would be in charge of the event. She would be under the trees at a table and my friends would keep an eye on her and bring her things to eat. Some would sit with her and talk baseball or about other topics. Most of the time the conversations were about food and her appetite.

When the family got together for someone's birthday she never had a problem being outside. I was always close by so she felt comfortable and we would have signals if she needed "to go" or had a problem. If the temperature got cold I would bring her a jacket or heavier blanket and she was fine.

She went to see her great grandson play soccer, or at that age, just run around the field. We had to get up early that day because the game was in the morning and we had to make a two and a half hour drive. It was worth it just to see her smile and laugh as he ran back and forth on the field. I just wished she could have seen him play baseball.

I took her to the farmers market in town, to craft festivals nearby and even to restaurants for breakfast and dinner. I took her to the store to buy groceries and regular shopping. She was in a wheelchair and their was no reason why we couldn't go enjoy the events and activities. It made it easier because she had a handicap placard so we always were able to park in front and it was usually a short distance to the event.

As long as I could get the wheelchair to an event or activity their was no reason why she couldn't go. Sometimes it meant more lifting but it was worth it because she enjoyed herself and she was part of the crowd. I didn't want her to ever feel like she was a shut in.

Outdoor Nighttime Activities

Just as outdoor events during the day can be enjoyed so can activities at night. You just have to make sure that your parent is dressed for the weather. Even in the summer months it can be a little drafty in the evening or at night so you have to bring a sweater, jacket and blankets.

My mom's legs would always get cold in the evening so I would put a thicker blanket on her lap and made sure that it covered her legs. I would also put a sweater on her from the front this way if she got too warm she could take it off. Being in the wheelchair it was hard for her to move forward and if the sweater was put on the normal way she would have no way to remove it if it got too warm.

I took my mom to evening high school football games and other evening events at the school I volunteered at. She would enjoy the games sometimes near the end zone or when it was cold in the car parked behind the end zone or the sidelines. She would be wrapped in her jacket and with her blanket and I would bring her hot chocolate. Friends would bring her cake or candy and she would enjoy the game even though she didn't know much about football. She knew what side the home team needed to score on and that was all that was necessary. Even the students knew who she was and would go up to her to say, "Hi." I felt completely comfortable with this environment because she was known by so many and they all knew her condition. If I needed to do something away from her all I had to do was ask a friend and they would sit or stand by her until I returned. This was a Catholic school and the priests and brothers would also bring her hot chocolate, coffee or something to eat. They all checked on her while I was busy handling the event. We always had walkie talkies that covered the entire campus so if she needed me for any reason all she had to do was press the button and say, "Jim."

It was a lot of work for me because I was busy running certain events but it was also an escape because I was doing something different. We did this for many years and she made a lot of friends. Everybody knew "Jim's mom" or Mrs. Colozzo and they would spend time chatting with her. She confused a lot of names, calling Bill, Bob or the other way around but she knew most of them by sight and would wave.

When we moved to Tehachapi we would watch the city's Fourth Of July fireworks from the street. We lived in the middle of the block and we would walk to the end of the street and go through a gate to the main road. We would sit with our neighbors and watch the yearly fireworks show. I would wrap her with a light jacket and a blanket so she could enjoy the show.

If I could enjoy and event or activity I tried everything I could so she could also enjoy them. Once again it was a little more work for me but it helped her get out and do something different. She enjoyed outdoor activities, day and night, until about six months before she died.

Chapter 25
CHORES AND BEING A CAREGIVER
Chores

You never want your parent not to feel useful or lazy. One of the ways to keep them busy, if they can, is to give them chores to do. It can be something simple but it makes them feel like they're helping you and it also helps with their attitude.

My mom always wanted to help with most things that I did around the house. I would let her dust knick knacks. She was of that age that bought all these little items and placed them around the house. I would take them down and give her a wet towel and she would wash these little items. She did the best she could and some of them were hard for her to hold but she only broke a few. When we came home from shopping I would give her a marker so she could place the date of purchase on the cans and packages. This made it easier to rotate what we had in the pantry. I tried to let her sweep the floor in the kitchen but this was a failure. She would push the broom okay but unfortunately she would bump and mark the cabinets with her wheelchair. I stopped this because I had to keep patching the walls and repairing cabinets.

My folks kept everything and a lot of items were in boxes. One of her chores was to go through boxes and see what was in them. She would do this for hours and it forced her to remember a lot of things. A lot of times she knew when she bought or was given an item. It also brought some tears when she would remember my father or other family members that passed on.

All these simple chores kept her arms, hands and mind working. She had a purpose and was helping me in the process. She did these chores for many years but as time went one her arms would get sore or she would get cramps in her hands and fingers. This was due mostly to severe arthritis but also to old age. Most of her chores came to and end in 2013 as it became more difficult for her to think and use her motor skills.

Let Them Help

Most people want to feel like they are helping and it is not different for your parent. As a caregiver you need to recognize that they can help in some ways. It might mean a little more work for you but it goes a long way in helping your parent cope with their situation.

My mom always wanted to help and I saw no reason why she couldn't. Now you have to use common sense, I would never give my mom a knife to cut a piece of meat. She use to cut herself preparing meals before she became disabled, but there were a lot a ways she could help around the house. I know this is old school but using child scissors to cut out grocery store coupons, or even sorting coupons from the Sunday paper. Nowadays with smartphones I know this is ancient so you need to adapt to the new technology.

When I use to do my taxes I would let her sort out the different bills that were paid so we could take the proper deductions. When I was researching stocks to purchase, she would watch the television to get information on those companies and sometimes she even picked a few good ones.

There are a lot of simple tasks that they can do to help you. With a little thought and planning they can to a certain degree help with the daily routine and chores. They will feel much better if they feel they're contributing to the household duties.

Food Preparation

I always tried to have my parents help me when I was taking care of them. One of the ways they helped was with food preparation. I just made sure their hands were washed, clean and that they didn't hurt themselves with the utensils.

I would find simple tasks that would not cause them any stress or harm. I would have them sort potatoes, carrots and other vegetables. Fill up measuring cups with dry product or sort out ingredients on the table. It made them feel good because they were helping with the meals and they always enjoyed taste testing. My dad use to make fried egg sandwiches and he still did as long as he could stand at the stove. My mom liked her sweets so I made her mix the ingredients for a cake and then I would put it in the oven. I would have one piece and she would eat the rest over the course of the week. She would pour the ingredients in a bowl for pudding. Then after I mixed it she would lick the utensils just like a kid.

This was a great way to keep them involved and not to make them feel useless. My folks always liked to cook and I was lucky that they still wanted to try so it made it an easy task for them to complete. I was always watching to make sure they didn't hurt themselves and we never had a cooking accident. I guess it was the Italian in our blood that made food so important to us.

Folding Clothes

Another chore that your parent can help you with if they're capable is folding clothes. This keeps their arms and hands active and it also makes them concentrate on a task. It also allows them to help with the daily routine.

I would wash a load of clothes five days a week. After I took them out of the dryer I would place them on the couch and my mom would do her best to fold them. She had no problem with wash cloths and kitchen towels but the larger items were a little more difficult. She would lay them out on her lap and keep turning them until they were folded. She did this everyday and it kept her hands a little loose. After a while her fingers would get tired or sore and she would take a break and then start over. A few times I told her to quit and she would say, "I'm not finished yet." She wanted to complete her task and do the best she could.

She would also put my shirts and her dresses on hangers and then I would put them in the closet. Socks were a problem but she would pair them up and then I would knot them together. We did this for years and this was her chore. She never complained and was happy to help. As time went on her fingers became more painful and it was more difficult for her to use her fingers and she finally had to stop. She was 92 at the time and did this chore for over twelve years while I was taking care of her.

Doing The Checkbook

Another chore I let my mom do was handle the checkbook. She did this for as long as I could remember with my dad. Once a week they would sit at the table and pay the bills for the month or week. He would keep a budget and tell her the amount of the check to be written. She would write out and sign the check, give it to him, he would verify the amount and then put it in the envelope to mail. She kept the checkbook balanced and this is how they payed the monthly expenses. The interesting part was neither of them ever used an adding machine or later a calculator. They did all their calculations by hand, they checked each other's math and they didn't make mistakes. After I started keeping the budget and paying the bills I kept my mom handling the checkbook. I kept the same routine and this worked well for many years. As time went on when I checked her numbers she was starting to make mistakes. One time we paid the bills for the week and I asked her for the balance remaining in our account. She gave me a total and it was completely different from the balance I kept. It was much larger than it should have been. I checked her numbers and instead of subtracting the checks she wrote she added them to the balance. I subtracted the checks she wrote and her balanced matched mine. She kept insisting she subtracted the amounts but when I showed her the calculations she accepted the fact that she made a mistake. I let her keep writing the checks until she no longer could hold a pen. I kept the running balance of our account and fortunately we never bounced a check. I let her keep doing this chore but I had to be vigilant to make sure she didn't make a mistake. I never got mad at her and she never got defensive as long as I showed her the mistake.

Shredding Papers

One of the chores my mom liked to do was to shred papers. My folks kept every receipt and document from the time they moved to California and since I was their son I did the same. We had boxes and boxes of paperwork from 1952 to the present. Since we were over run with all this paperwork and most of it had personal information on it so it needed to be shredded. That job I entrusted to my mom.

I bought a shredder and made sure it had all the safety features so it would not injure my mom. I went through the paperwork first to see if there was documents that we had to keep and I would set them aside. I would wheel her to the table and put a box of papers on a chair next to her. She would pick out a page and look at it and then place it in the shredder. The paper slot was thin so she couldn't get her fingers caught in the cutter. She looked at every piece of paper and sometime would comment on what the paper meant or how she remembered when they purchased that item. The best part was she was using her mind and it was making her remember the past. I was shocked at how much she remembered. Every box contained many stories and she was pretty much remembering each one.

She started getting better at shredding to where she would check each paper and place about five together and then run them through the shredder. She did this for years and she burnt out five shredders. She finally had to stop when she had trouble with her fingers and she couldn't separate or grab the pages. That was about nine months before she passed away. It was a simple and safe task that kept her using her mind because it was like a trip down memory lane. We had so much paperwork that I still haven't destroyed it all and that is one of my projects for the future.

Want To Do Things Themselves

As people get older they still want to retain their independence and do things for themselves. Being a caregiver you need to be able to recognize what your parent can and can't do. You should allow them to do whatever they can because it will go along way in making them feel that they still can participate in their care. Being able to do things for themselves means they are helping you, which in their mind they are making life easier for you.

I let my parents do as much as they were capable of doing by themselves. My dad was able to do his regular routine all the way until the cancer took control of his body which was about six month before he passed away. During those six months he was able to do less and less and required much more help for his daily routines.

My mom could do a lot as long as it was at a table or counter. She could not stand or walk but if I could maneuver her wheelchair to a suitable locations she was able to do tasks. She bathed and dressed herself for many years as long as I put her in the shower or in the wheelchair. She was able to go to the bathroom and clean herself as long as I could lift her on the toilet. She needed help getting to a location but once there she could do the task herself. She helped sorting out groceries and prepping food. She could even peel potatoes until her fingers finally gave out.

For years she helped with the day to day chores. Slowly this started to diminish as she got older and her body got tired. She kept going till about January of 2013 and then she really started to slow down. She passed away in April of that year.

Chapter 26

THEIR LOSS OF INDEPENDENCE

Loss Of Independence

Most people like their independence and the ability to take care of themselves. Parents are use to taking care of their children and being on their own. When they need help it is hard for them to give up their independence and rely on others.

My mom lost her independence the day she could no longer walk. That day her life change forever and so did mine. She needed help in almost everything she did or would do. She still could make decisions and I let her do whatever she could so she still had control over some parts of her life.

She could clean herself, change her clothes, and eat without help. She could do chores and little tasks if I rolled her to a table or brought things closer to her. She could browse through catalogs and pick out what she wanted to buy. When we went to the store she could pick out whatever she wanted. The only difference with this situation was I had to bring things to her or I had to push her in the wheelchair to see them. It's more work for you but it gives them some sense of independence because they're making decisions.

She never drove so I didn't have the challenge of taking away her drivers license. So waiting for someone to take her to the store never became an issue. She would make out lists and say we needed to go to this store and ask when was a good time to go. I would schedule our trips so we would go to her stores when we had other errands in the area. It worked out well because it got her out of the house and she was able to shop as normal as possible.

After a few hours of pushing her wheelchair in a crowded store I would be exhausted when we came home and she was also tired because of the same reason. We didn't do this everyday so both of us were able to settle down for a few days. We usually went out at least once a week so she was never a shut in. In later years when it was more difficult to get out she did miss going shopping. One of the main problems was as her body became weaker so did her resistance and I didn't want to take a chance of her catching the flu or something else. She understood and had no problem shopping from a catalog.

Privacy

We all take privacy for granted and it is not something you worry about. You take a shower or go to the bathroom, you close the door. You change your clothes, you do it behind closed doors. When you rely on someone to care for you, privacy is no longer taken for granted.

Not only is privacy a concern for your parent it is for you too. One of the hardest things to do is to walk into a room and help your parent get dressed, help them with a bath or lift them off the toilet. It's not just the loss of their privacy it is also hard for you to do because it's your mom and dad and it's embarrassing. Just remember it is more embarrassing to them because like most people they never thought they would ever be in this situation.

With my mom I tried to give her as much privacy as I could. When she changed her clothes I would close the door most of the way but leave it open enough so I could hear her call. The same was when I put her in the tub. I had a shower chair and I would lift her on it and unbutton most of her dress but leave it on her. I would leave the bathroom and close the door part way. She would remove her dress and take her shower, dry herself off and put on another dress. She would call me and I would lift her out of the tub and put her in the wheelchair so she could finish, such as brushing her hair. In later years as she lost motor skills and balance I would have to do more till finally I did everything. I did what had to be done.

The same was when she had to use the toilet. In the early years I would cut the tabs on her diaper, lift her and remove the diaper. I would then place her on the toilet and she would do her business. We had a small half bath in the master bedroom and I took the door off to make it easier for me to place her on the toilet. I gave her a wireless door bell button because I would leave her bedroom. She could clean herself and when she was finished she pressed the doorbell button and I would come into the room to lift her. I would lay her onto the bed and place on a new diaper. Once again as time went on she was not able to do as much so I had to do more and finally I had to clean her up. Once again you do what you have to do.

When she would receive phone calls from my sisters or friends I would leave the room so she could have some privacy. Once again you try to give them as much as a normal life as possible. All it means is stepping away and partially closing doors.

Loss Of Drivers License

Living in Southern California the one thing that allows you independence is a drivers license. When you give up your license you pretty much lose your independence because the public transit system is lousy to non existent. It is hard not being able to go out whenever you want or have to wait for a ride.

When my father became ill I was wondering how I was going to be able to stop him from driving. He drove for over sixty years and it was going to be difficult to take away his drivers license. His license came up for renewal in 1994 and he still wanted to keep it active. Leading up to this point I would be driving him from place to place most of the time so I wasn't too concerned about him retaining his drivers license, at least it was still his identification. He studied the state supplied booklet on renewing his license and after a few days he decided to take the written renewal exam. We went to the Department of Motor Vehicles and he took the exam and failed. He was told he could come back in a few days to retake the exam. We went home and he studied the booklet once again and in a few days we went back to take the test. He passed this time but only passed by one question. When we got into the car to drive home he told me, "It's up to you know, I will never drive again." I was shocked but not surprised because he knew that he was having trouble remembering things and it was best for him not to be behind the wheel. I took him everywhere he needed to go so he never had to drive again.

In our family most of the uncles gave up their licenses without any problems. My mom and two of her sisters never drove. One of her sisters drove but passed away in her seventies and at that time she was still able to drive with no problems. I had one uncle that came home from the store and said he would never drive again. He had no children so his niece and nephew wondered what had happened. Later on we found out that he had a close call and it scared him so he never wanted to drive again. The incident was he went through a stop sign and just missed another car. My other uncle, my mom's brother, had glaucoma so he gave up his license once the ophthalmologist said you can't drive anymore. His wife never drove so there was never an issue.

I have one uncle that is alive and he is still driving. He is the husband of one of my mom's sisters. He moved from out of state to live across the street from my cousin. He is still very independent and stubborn. I don't envy my cousin when the time comes to take away his drivers license. It will be a battle, he is 87 and now living in California. He is going to have to take a behind the wheel driving test so I think the state might have a hand in taking away his drivers license. He probably won't pass the driving test and then the problem of taking away his drivers license won't be an issue. But who knows, this is California and anything can happen.

Vision Loss

Vision loss comes with getting older. I could see very well for years and I could even solder small wires without glasses. After I passed forty I was having trouble seeing small items. I blamed the computer because I was staring at a screen all day and I figured that damaged my eyes. When I went to the eye doctor he said it's not the computer, you're getting old! Nothing like getting hit with a jolt of reality.

We always took care of our eyes and it paid off. I started going to the eye doctor when I was four years old. In fact I am still going to the same family of doctors. I started off with the grandfather, then the son, now the grandson and also the great grandson has started in the practice. This family of eye doctors saw my dad, mom, sister's and myself.

My mom was always concerned about her eyes because her father, my grandfather went blind at an early age. The best information we had was it was due to glaucoma. That was back in the 1930s and very few went to the doctors and no one talked about health issues so we never knew the exact diagnosis. My uncle, my mom's brother was diagnosed with glaucoma in the late 1980s so his doctor assumed it was hereditary. My mom was diagnosed with borderline glaucoma also in the late eighties so we made sure to keep it under control. She went to the eye doctor every six months for tests and exams. It worked because I swear she could see better than me.

In the late 1990s she had cataracts removed and once again her eyesight was good for her age. She could watch television and do crossword puzzles without using glasses. She could read quite a few lines on the eye chart with only a few mistakes. I thought that was pretty good for someone in their eighties and nineties. In 2012 her vision finally started to deteriorate and she could no longer read. On her last eye test in October of 2012 she could only read the large letters on the eye chart. This was when she was starting to get confused so it was a natural progression. She could still watch television so she was happy.

Hearing Loss

Hearing loss is another thing that happens as we get older. The radio and television get louder to the point where you can't hear anything else. We also get use to hearing and saying, "What?"

My dad's hearing loss was substantial mostly because of where he worked. He worked at the Long Beach Naval Shipyard as a pipe fitter and all the loud noises associated with ship repair took its toll on his hearing. Not being supplied with the proper safety equipment was also a major part of the problem. His hearing loss was also magnified because he suffered from tinnitus, ringing in the years. Sometimes it would get so bad that he would shake his head to get it to stop. We would run fans, raise the volume of the television to mute the ringing in his ears. Nothing worked and it was something that he learned to live with. He went to numerous hearing doctors and all of them said there was nothing they could do for him and at that time no hearing aid would work. He suffered with this problem to the day he died.

My mom's hearing was actually pretty good. She could hear whispers and even talk behind her. In order to keep a secret you had to say it in a different room with a closed door. Once again as she got older the radio and television got louder. You also had to raise your voice when you spoke to her. It was also better to stand in front of her and look at her when you talked. We all become lip readers as we start to lose our hearing. She never wanted to go to hearing doctor and never wanted a hearing aid.

The only thing you can do is slightly raise your voice so that they can hear you. Standing in front of them while you talk is also a great help so they can read your lips. As technology improves this might no longer be a problem, if you can afford it. Otherwise this is a glimpse to what is in our future.

Memory Loss

Memory loss is another situation attributed to aging and it affects mostly everyone. I'm in my mid fifties and I'm starting to forget things. Some memory loss is mild and some is severe like dementia and Alzheimer disease.

I was lucky in this situation because my dad and mom just had normal memory loss. As they got older it got worse and when the end was near it was severe. It was the usual confusion and forgetfulness. They never forgot their name or who we were until a few months before they died.

I have a cousin who is helping take care of his mother in law. She is healthy physically but she has Alzheimers. This becomes a practice of patience and understanding. Always answering, "Who are you?" or, "Where am I?" can be a strain on any person. He and his wife take her out as much as they can and try to keep her engaged as much as possible. He is successfully self employed so it makes it a little easier to bear the amount of work caring for someone with Alzheimers. Fortunately he is also able to have a nurse come and stay with his mother in law so he and his wife can continue with their lives and go on vacations. Interesting enough he was the one that would always say that when his folks became old he would put them in a home and let someone else take care of them. His wife put the breaks on that idea and to his credit he his dealing with the situation. My cousin still has some difficulty taking care of his mother in law because it does takes so much of his time and I'm sure he can't wait to get his life back.

It is an enormous amount of work for anyone that takes care of someone with Alzheimers and you rarely hear thank you. When I took care of my mom and dad they would say thank you or I appreciate what you are doing. I never needed to hear that but it made them feel better. Someone with severe dementia or Alzheimers might never say that. I'm sure deep down they want to but they have no way to express it.

Being Independent

Everyone wants to be independent and not rely on anyone for their everyday life. When you start taking care of a parent they feel that they have lost their independence. This reality hits them hard especially if they have to give up their drivers license. In California the drivers license was freedom to go wherever you wanted whenever you wanted to go. They grew up with that feeling and once they no longer have a drivers license the feel that their freedom is gone.

Another situation is they have lived by themselves for a long period of time. They have grown accustom to doing things on their schedule and not someone else's. They have their own routines, ways of doing certain things and no one tells them how to do it differently. When they move in with someone they feel that independence is gone.

The same can happen to you if your parent moves into your home. You have routines that you have followed for years and it feels that they are interfering with your normal life. Their schedule and way of life is different from yours so it can feel like they are intruding.

Once again that is why you have to know what is at stake when you decide to become a caregiver. Everyone thinks that when a parent moves back in it would be just like when you were little and lived with them. Nothing can be farther from the truth because they have gone on with their life and you have gone on with yours. Like the saying, "You can't go back," the same is true with living with a parent. They have gone from being in control of their home and now they are under your control in your home. It is a lot to take in right away and it will take time to get use to this situation. It is an adjustment for you and them.

I didn't have this problem because I was still living with my parents when they got sick. Starting and trying to run a business left very little funds available for rent or the purchase of a home. I paid them rent, kept up the house and helped pay for all expenses so it wasn't like I was free loading. When they became sick it was easy to take care of them and there was no adjustment of having to live together once again. It worked out well for all of us because they received the care and help they needed and there was no adjustment period.

The hard part was when I had to tell them they couldn't do certain things that they had done for years. My dad would like to do the grocery shopping and it would take him hours to go to one store. When he was able to drive that wasn't a problem because he was on his schedule and he would take his time. He couldn't walk very far without getting short of breath so he would get a shopping cart and slowly push it through the store while he shopped, this was before the motorized shopping carts were available. When he no longer drove I would take him to the store and it still would take hours to do the shopping. He was slowing down more and it was more difficult for him to catch his breath. I finally told him that he couldn't do the grocery shopping because he could no longer walk without getting winded. I told him that he could sit in the wheelchair and I would push him around the store so then he still do the shopping. He wanted nothing to do with this idea because he didn't need a wheelchair. We actually had a very strong discussion about it and he finally said, "Fine, you do the shopping." I told him, "Fine," and I did the grocery shopping for about a week. He then decided that he wanted to go to the store with me and that he would use the wheelchair. I once again took him shopping and he pushed himself as best he could and when he got tired I pushed the wheelchair the rest of the way.

We did this for many months until he got to weak to go out. He wanted to keep his independence and any changes would have to be his decision. He finally made the decision and gained back some of his independence.

Chapter 27

MENTAL STATE AND BEING A CAREGIVER

Start As A Baby, End As A Baby

There is an old saying, "You start off as a baby and you end as a baby." That is a very true statement. Taking care of a parent you never saw the baby at the beginning but you definitely see the one at the end.

When my father was near the end the confusion and forgetfulness kept getting worse. As his disease took control over his body he became less aware of his surroundings and those around him. He passed in his sleep on Easter morning. With my mom the progression took many years. She would get slightly confused but was still able to do things. As time went on she would get more confused or forgetful and then became less able to do anything. The last week of her life she knew nothing and could do nothing.

The other part of being an elderly baby is that they get cranky and stubborn. Sometimes they even cry if they don't get their way or if your voice is too loud. I have a loud deep voice and my mom would always tell me to stop yelling or I was too loud. She would get combative if I wouldn't let her do something like try to clean her nails. Sometimes she would get mad when I told her to wash her hands. I would see dirt on her fingers and she would insist that they were clean, just like a little kid.

Eating can be interesting and in the later years I would put a towel on my mom like a bib because she would drop food on herself. I would have to wipe her face because she would be wearing sauce after having macaroni. You knew she enjoyed a fruit or cream pie because a lot of it was on her face. I would give her a napkin and she would smear it from one side to another. After we ate I would clean her and the floor up. About a week before she died I had to feed her. That was difficult because I knew the end was coming and it was hard to see. She was regressing and losing all her faculties.

Going to the bathroom was another issue. She would tell me that she had to go to the bathroom. I would put her on the toilet and she would say I don't have to go. Just like a little kid.

It becomes a challenge because you see them regressing right in front of you. With a baby you see them learn and grow in this situation you see the forgetfulness, confusion and body deteriorate. It also takes a toll on you.

Don't Treat As A Baby

I know the saying goes, "You start as a baby and you end as a baby," but I always felt why rush it. I'm sure because of dementia and Alzheimers some people are in that state but I tried to do everything I could to try to slow this from happening. I was lucky because neither of my parents suffered from dementia and they held their mind all the way to the end. As I have said every situation is different and calls for different reactions.

One of the things that always irritated me was when I would see an elderly person being treated as a baby. I had an aunt, my mom's sister, that went into deep depression and then dementia after her husband passed away. The afternoon after his funeral and burial she was talking to my mom. My cousin had a get together of family and friends at her house after the services were complete. People were talking and eating and my aunt turned to my mom and said, "Look, everyone is having a good time and my husband is in a box." My mom was caught off guard and didn't know how to respond. That was the last time my aunt spoke to my mom and also the last time she was coherent. She fell into deep depression and dementia took over. My aunt, my mom's other sister and her daughter, my cousin, were taking care of her and they started treating her like a baby. They would buy her dolls and talk to her like they were speaking to an infant. They would make baby sounds to get her to respond. When my mom would go and visit she would talk to her normally and she would try to respond to my mom by facial movements. It was so hard to see a strong woman deteriorate into a baby so fast. Now she had excellent care and my aunt and cousin did everything for her and took care of her for a long time. I just felt that she would have been a little more alert if they didn't treat her like a little baby.

But to follow my own advice everyone's situation is different and the way they handled that situation might have been different from what I would have done. My aunt lasted many years in this state because of the wonderful care she received from my aunt and cousin. I never treated my dad or mom as a baby, I treated them like adults all the way to the end. I was fortunate that they were still able to respond normally all the way to last weeks of their lives.

Sitting In A Corner

When my dad was still alive he always tried to go to family functions such as birthdays for the grandchildren. Later holidays were usually at our house because it was easier for my parents to get around. He would always say that he wasn't crazy about the get togethers because all he did was sit in the corner. He would say, "You sit down in the corner and nobody comes to you. Once in a while someone will ask, Do you want a drink? And then they would walk away and leave you alone. I feel like a dummy sitting in a corner." He would tell me and I would tell them that didn't happen until I watched at the next family event. Sure enough he was in the corner just watching the kids and no one went up to him. Once in a while the little ones would go and ask grandpa to watch what they were doing and he obliged immediately. Sure enough someone would ask if he wanted a soda or a glass of water but no one sat and talked to him. I was just as bad as the rest because I was usually watching the kids or talking to cousins and other family members. As time went on he no longer wanted to go to the events and when I told everybody the reason, nobody believed it.

After he passed away and it was just my mom and myself the same thing would happen to her. She was in a wheelchair so she couldn't be missed but once again nobody talked to her. She really didn't care as long as she could watch the grandchildren and great grandchildren. It was amazing, people would say, "Hi" and never talk to her again. I learnt my lesson so I was always near her but very few others would speak to her. There was the usual, "Do you want a glass of water or soda?"

I know this is common because most people don't want to be around an older person. I had just never noticed it and was amazed that it actually happened. Now that I'm in my mid fifties I notice it happens to me too. I sit down at family functions and nobody comes around to talk. I'm sure of lot of it has to do with my abrasive personality. The little one's do come up once in a while and want me to watch what they are doing and I'm happy to oblige. The adults keep their distance so it's just me sitting in a corner. I guess this is payback for the years it happened to my dad.

Ignored

A lot of times people tend to ignore elderly people. I still remember going to the convalescent hospital when I was in junior high school and seeing all those ignored people. They lit up when the saw strangers and all of them had that look that you would stop and talk to them. It was sad to see how these people were spending their final years. We would stay as long as we could and talk to as many as possible before we left. I still remember one lady that started to cry when we left, it left a lasting impression.

Taking care of my parents I tried my best to not make them feel ignored. I asked for their advice and kept them up to date on what I was doing. I had them make decisions and I followed them. I had to make sure they were still participating in life, theirs and mine. I gave them chores to do and had them help me whenever they could.

In the later years I would wheel my mom where ever I had to work so she could watch. She would watch me mow the lawn or pull weeds. I would pick flowers and she would tell me what ones she wanted. When it was time to plant new flowers I would always have her pick the ones she wanted. It was easy because she always wanted me to plant pansies. Her father, my grandfather, use to grow and sell pansies in Rhode Island when she was little. She loved seeing those plants grow and flower.

If I worked in the garage she was there to see what I was doing. Measuring, cutting and assembling she was always supervising. When I built my workshop she had her place on the side to see what I was doing or building. She was a part of everything I did and she enjoyed herself in the process.

We talked about everything and I had her remember things from her past. It kept her alert and it kept her mind working. I made sure she was not ignored and a part of everything we did.

Frustration

One thing you will notice while you are taking care of your parents is that they will become frustrated very fast. It doesn't matter how small or large the task they will get frustrated faster than they did before. This can happen because of their illness, loss of motor skills or memory loss. You will have to deal with this situation and it will get worse as time goes on.

My dad use to tell me that as you get older you have a harder time concentrating and it gets harder for you to learn something new. He said you could read things over and over and they just would not stick. As he aged and his disease progressed this became more true than I ever imagined. It culminated when he had to take a written driving test. He studied the booklet from the Department of Motor Vehicles for weeks until he was ready to take the test. He failed on his first attempt and passed on his second try by just one question. From that day he never drove again because he felt he was not capable of paying attention. At the same time he started to have a shorter fuse and would get upset a lot quicker and more frequent. We later found out that it was the cancer spreading through his body and causing all kinds of problems. He died six months later.

With my mom it was a slower process and she started to get really frustrated about a year before she passed away. She would get mad when she couldn't do something like holding a pen or playing cards. Things would fall out of her hands and she would get upset. This was due to arthritis but she was also starting to lose her motor skills. She also started to disagree more as she forgot things that happened in the past. It was strange she would remember things from the past but forget and get frustrated about things that happened the day before. Other times she couldn't remember the past but knew everything that happened a few days earlier.

It was all part of the age progression and slowly the mind started to get confused. For weeks at a time there would be no problems then for a few days she got frustrated at everything she did or tried. She would get so upset that she would cry. After I kept telling her everything was okay and their were no problems she would be fine and once again be back to her normal self. I never understood it until she had a scan the last time she was in the hospital and they told me she had mini strokes that probably affected her.

It's amazing at what the mind and body does as it ages. She went from being frustrated to being confused in about two months and two weeks later she passed away. It was almost like her mind and body were working together to shut down so she wouldn't know what was happening.

Not Being Aware Of Surroundings

One thing you have to be concerned with while you are taking care of your parents is that they are not aware of their surroundings. They often times don't know where they are or what is around them. If you have them sitting on a park bench or at a table in a restaurant they don't comprehend what is around them. This can make them a target for crime if they have anything of value on their person.

I didn't worry too much about the surroundings around my mom because I was usually with her. She would carry a little bag with her identification and other items but she aways had it hidden and secured to the wheelchair. When we went somewhere she was aways in front of me and I was able to keep and eye on her. The time where she would be vulnerable was when I would park the car and get her wheelchair out of the back so I could lift her into it. That was also a time when I was vulnerable because if I was lifting her I was only concentrating on that task and I couldn't keep my eyes on our surroundings. To try to prevent a problems I always parked in locations where I was able to scout the area as we parked. I also kept her window closed while I retrieved the wheelchair from the back of the car. I would then wheel it to the front of the car, open the door and lift her out. Before I grabbed her I looked around the area to make sure no one was approaching or could be a problem when I lifted her out of the car. This was to be protective but also I didn't want to give anyone a show in case her dress was up and her diaper was showing. We did this the entire time I took care of her and never had a problem.

If your parent carries a purse, this can cause an issue for a lot of reasons. Sometimes they are big and bulky so it makes them hard to carry. Other times they can be dropped, lost or fall off the wheelchair. Laying them in your parents lap can cause them discomfort because of the size, weight or it could cause them to overheat on a hot day. Another problem with a purse is that you could make your parent a target of thieves. They might think they are any easy mark because they don't pay attention and a lot of times this is true. You need to be aware of the surroundings and people when your parent is carrying a purse. If they can walk looping the strap around their arm is an option but it can make them more prone to be pushed on the ground. If they are in a wheelchair they can wrap the strap around the handles but once again if a thief wants it they could knock over the wheelchair.

The purse makes thing easier for your parent and you because it can hold a lot of items that you might have to carry when you go out. Unfortunately it is also a huge target for thieves and they can care less if they injure your parent or you. They will push an elderly person down in a flash in order to grab their purse. If it is wrapped around their arm it means nothing to a criminal to force it off them and possible break an arm or other bone. If they are in a wheelchair they can try to snatch it even if it is attached to the arms of the chair. They can drag your parent down the walk until the straps breaks or the wheelchair turns over. They don't care if your parent falls out and gets hurt.

Everyday there are stories of purse snatching's and how an elderly person was hurt. As their caregiver you need to be aware that this can happen and need to keep a close an eye on the surroundings and who's around you and your parent because once again you are responsible for their care and safety. Even though you are not responsible for the criminal that wants to rob you or your parent it can cause you a lot of problems if they are hurt. If they break a bone it can be a long recovery and a lot more work for you.

A few months ago I went to the store with my cousin and his dad, my uncle. We parked in a lot and my cousin and his wife went into the store to shop. I stayed in the car with my uncle and he was busy organizing his glove box. He was completely unaware of what was around him. He has a smart phone and it is very noticeable in his shirt pocket. There was a row of trees in front of the parking spot and I noticed a young man behind one of the trees. My uncle had his window open and was oblivious to the person in front of him. The man came around the tree and kept watching my uncle and started moving closer. I guess he couldn't see me in the back seat watching him. I leaned forward so he could see me and he immediately stopped in his tracks, turned around and ran across the street. I'm not sure if he was interested in my uncle's smart phone or wallet but it was peculiar that he ran away when he saw me in the back seat. I asked my uncle if he saw the man in front of him and he said, "What man?" He had no clue that someone was watching him. I explained to him the situation and he said, "I had no idea." No matter how many times my cousin and I tell him to be aware of what is around him he still pays no attention. His smart phone makes him vulnerable and him not being aware makes him a target for crime.

Not being aware of their surroundings makes your parent a target for crime or injury. You need to keep an eye on them at all times and keep reminding them that they need to be aware of what is around them. I know it is easy to say but hard to do.

Nightmares

As far as I remember my parents never had nightmares during the course of there illnesses. They never woke up in the middle of the night perspiring, screaming, or yelling about something they dreamed. As the end drew closer both of them had dreams of their parents and siblings that passed away but none of those they never considered those nightmares.

Towards the end my mom started having visions of a lady in her room but she was never scared of her. My parents also weren't prescribed any sleeping medication, muscle relaxers or sedatives. My mom was on strong pain medication but it never caused her to have nightmares.

My uncle is susceptible to nightmares because he his taking sleeping medication. Once in a while when he comes over to my cousin's house for dinner he explains that he had a nightmare the previous night. They usually involve something from his past. He attributes it to the side effects of his prescription medication. He doesn't seem concerned or worried about this situation.

I heard almost everything my parents did when they were sleeping. Anything out of the ordinary that would have caused them trouble while they were sleeping would have drawn my notice. I'm sure as everyone has nightmares once in a while when they are sleeping but it was never brought to my attention or bothered them enough to tell me.

Visions

Towards the end of my dad's life he started having dreams about his deceased parents and relatives. They were not nightmares and he was never afraid. He never had visions of people in his room or if he did he never called out or told any of us.

My mom also started dreaming about her parents a few month before she died. Once again she did not have nightmares or was afraid. She did start having visions of a woman in white that would be standing in her bedroom at night. Several times she called for me and said, "Jim, there's a woman in the corner next to the dresser, she's looking at me." I would go into her room and I wouldn't see anything. She would continue and say, "She's looking right at me and she's smiling." I would tell my mom that I didn't see anything and I would ask, "Is she looking at me?" and my mom would say, "No, she's smiling at me."

This started about six month before she died and it happened infrequently at first. As time went on it would happen a few times a month and about two weeks before she died it happened almost every night. She would call me and I would go into her room and see nothing. My mom would get upset because I didn't see the woman and she would say, "She's right there," as she pointed to the corner. I tried making adjustments to the room lighting in case that was causing a shadow or image but it didn't make a difference.

I never saw anything and she was sure that there was a woman in white in the room. Interestingly my mom wasn't scared of her she just wanted to know who she was and why she was there? I have no idea what she saw or what was going on inside of her head. Maybe it was her guardian angel telling her she was all right. Within one week of these visions happening every night she became really confused and started to forget all of us and her surroundings. She stopped complaining about her leg pain when the Fentanyl patch was about to expire and it was almost like her body was preparing for the end. She passed away within a few days in her sleep.

Nervousness

One thing you will notice when you take care of your parents is that they become nervous and anxious a lot easier than normal. It can happen when they hear loud noises or voices and it makes them jump. This seems to get worse over time and it becomes part of their normal routine. Nothing was ever wrong but they would jump for no reason.

A lot of us jump when we hear a loud noise or pop and we get nervous when we hear people raise their voice because you don't know if that can lead to some sort of conflict. My dad rarely jumped at any noises and he kept his cool throughout most of his illness. Part of the problem was he didn't hear very well and the other one was the he was battle tested in the Marine Corps. As his illness progressed and took its toll on his mind and body he did start to jump when he would hear a pop or loud noise. He would get nervous and excited when he heard loud voices. When you would turn on the television and the volume would pop on he would jump and shake a little. Because of his loss of hearing I had to raise my voice so he could hear me and that never bothered him because he was always looking at me . It was just the unknown and surprise voice and noise that would unsettle him.

My mom always got nervous when she heard a loud pop or noise. She would yell, "What's that," and you could actually see her get nervous and tell that her heart was racing. I always tried to limit any loud noises so it would not frighten her. As time went on I had to raise my voice a little so she could hear me and she would always think something was wrong. I don't know if it was because she was starting to get confused or if something in the past was coming back and made her jump.

She was always a nervous person and thought the worst anytime she was given a choice. Before she heard a diagnosis she would always get nervous and hyperventilate as you were telling her the information. She would get so worked up that she would only hear a few words and never listen to the whole conversation.

I always had to be careful whenever I gave her any kind of news, good or bad. She always thought the worst and would get nervous before I gave her the answer. A lot of the time she was right because the news was not good but once in a while she got worked up for nothing.

Anxious

My dad never got anxious when he had to get a diagnosis and he waited for the doctor to explain the situation and treatment. He never jumped to conclusions and dealt with things as they happened. I think I took after him in the way I handle life.

My mom on the other hand became anxious every time we went to a new doctor or had to go in for a treatment. She jumped to conclusions every time we had to wait for information or a diagnosis. She always thought the worst and most of the time she was right so then she would panic. She never listened about available treatments and outcomes. She was from the generation that all they had to hear was the word "cancer" and it was a death sentence and they would not be around for long. She might have thought that but because of new treatments and medication she survived breast cancer three times. She jumped to conclusions but she also beat it.

I think it goes back to when she was little and when the doctor would visit their house. She would tell stories how the doctor would come to check her father and then something bad would happen. It got to the point that her and her sisters would run and hide every time the doctor came to the house. She never told us what the "bad" thing was but her father did die at an early age. This continued as her mother got older and the doctor came to the house. She and her sisters would hide from the doctor when he came to examine their mom. Her mom, my grandmother, lived into her sixties but something left an impression. My mom would also become anxious about funerals. She never went to her father or mother's wake and funeral. In fact the first funeral she attended as an adult was when my dad died in 1995. She was nervous and anxious during the entire time and it was understandable because she had just lost her husband of over 46 years. She was just apprehensive and nervous but she got through it.

As long as I was around we always knew my mom would get anxious and nervous about different subjects. My dad dealt with as long as I could remember and I had to deal with it after he was gone. It never changed and lasted all the way until her death and I never found out the reason.

Not Listening

I never had a problem with my parents not listening to me when I needed them to follow instructions because of their condition. Both of them knew if was for their health and if they followed the instructions it could make them better. They had faith in what I was doing and in my skills as a caregiver.

I have heard stories that some parent don't listen to their children when they are caregivers and give them a hard time when they are told to do something. I have seen this with my uncle and cousin. My uncle lives across the street from my cousin and still has his independence. He still wants and does a lot of things for himself and is doing very well. Once in a while he needs help and my cousin does it without any questions. The problem happens when my cousin tries to tell his dad how to do something that will make his life easier. Because my uncle has done things a certain way for many years he doesn't want to listen to anything that would make him change his normal routine even if it makes the tasks easier and safer. One item that concerns me is that my uncle looks unstable when he walks. He has a bad Achilles tendon along with a bad knee and when he walks it looks like he is trying to walk on eggs without breaking them. He has a cane and when he uses it he becomes more stable, is able to walk upright and it just looks more normal. He refuses to use the cane even though it is safer for him to walk. His doctor, my cousin and I have all told him it would be safer for him and that he needs it to prevent a fall. He refuses to listen and sooner or later he will fall. His doctor has even told him because of his age, he is 87, a fall could be the end of him. His bones are brittle and if he takes a bad tumble it could be his only one and last. My cousin is having a hard time trying to persuade him to use a cane, I guess it might be vanity because if he uses a cane he thinks he's old.

Hopefully my uncle will learn to use his cane and listen to my cousin for his own care and safety. I was fortunate never have this problem and it made taking care of my parents a lot easier. Like I have said many times, everyone's situation is different and you have to deal with it differently than someone else.

No One Wants To Be Around An Old Person

I guess it's part of human nature that when your young you don't want to be around an old person. Sometimes you see when someone old hold a baby the baby cries and wants to go back to their mother or father. The same happens with a toddler they shy away from an older person and usually have to be pushed toward the elderly.

When I was in junior high school and we had to visit the convalescent hospital, nobody wanted to go and we had to be forced because it was part of a school assignment. The same happened in high school when we would go to a convalescent home for a Christmas party, nobody wanted to go, but we had to because it was part of a class project. The reasons and excuses were always the same, they smell, I can't understand them, they look funny, I might catch something, they might touch me or it's embarrassing. After all the excuses we still had to go and visit them.

After we were there we started talking to the residents and we found out that most of them had some great stories and they were willing to share them with us or anyone that would listen. When I was in school these elderly residents were born from the 1880s to 1900. Their stories were amazing because they went through two World Wars and saw the early days of flight to air travel to space. So much changed during their lifetime and it was amazing to hear of their experiences. After we left we talked about what we learned and to this day I still can remember some of the conversations.

Today the same thing is happening but the big difference is no one wants to learn from an actual person they would rather get the information from the internet. They don't want to physically talk to someone because it is much easier just to point and click. In today's world the elderly have nothing to offer because they are too old and have nothing to show from their lives.

We had to be forced to talk to the elderly and we did it because we didn't have a choice. Today you can't force anyone into doing anything and a vast amount of information is being lost because people don't want to talk to an elderly person. It seems as long as we have the internet we know more than they will ever know, at least that's what we think. We are so far from the truth.

Sitting By Themselves

Whenever you walk into a family function or holiday you will probably notice that the older people are always in the corner or out of the way sitting by themselves. They might be off to the side but they are usually never the center of attention. The younger adults are always in groups talking to one another, the teenagers are with people of the same age or on their smart phones and the younger kids are somewhere playing.

The only time someone goes to the elderly person is to check and see if they need anything. After they get them a drink, snack or what they need that person leaves them to go talk to someone else. They usually just sit there and watch what everyone else is doing.

Last Christmas I spent the day at my cousin's and they invited the entire family. His dad, my uncle, is still alive and is the last survivor of the previous generation. He thought everyone would go over and talk to him and he was disappointed that most just said, "Hi." Some of us did spend a lot of time with him but the younger ones, including his grandson, spent very little time talking to him. The next day he told me that he was amazed that he was, "Just sitting by himself," and nobody came over to talk. He said that when he was young, "I would find the oldest person in the room and go talk to them so I could learn something." I told him things have changed and unfortunately this is the reaction of most younger people. I told him that after I noticed this with my parents I made sure that the younger ones would always talk to my parents and after I "forced" them a few times they never had to be asked again.

He was sad and upset because he wanted to talk and he ended up just watching others. I told him not to feel bad because I'm in my mid fifties and very few of the younger ones talk to me. I'm not sitting in the corner yet but they just walk by and talk to someone else.

They Get Emotional, Hurt Feelings

One thing you will notice when you are taking care of your parent is how emotional they get for the littlest thing. Their feelings also get hurt a lot quicker as well as they have less patience. Once again it depends on their condition and your situation but it is very common.

My dad was not an emotional person except when he got sick. He would get angry quicker and his fuse was a lot shorter. He was always a patient person but that changed as his illness progressed. If you asked questions that he didn't want to answer he would shut you down fast. If he felt that you weren't listening to him he would get emotional and his feelings were hurt. This started about the last year of his life.

My mom on the other hand was always emotional and never had patience. She would always jump to the worse conclusions before she knew what was going on. Fortunately she was usually wrong so she got worked up over nothing. As her illness progresses she would get upset if she thought you were asking the same questions over and over. She would snap back and say, "You heard what I said," "stop repeating what I said." You could be having a simple conversation and then she would just fly off the handle and go into another direction. It didn't last long and then she forgot all about it.

The last six months of her life she did get more emotional and also started to cry. For no reason that I could find she would just tear up. I would ask her what was wrong and she would just say, "Nothing." I would then ask, "Why are you crying?" and she would say, "I'm just thinking." Sometimes she would say she was thinking about my father, her parents, brother, sisters and her grandson. They were all deceased so I don't know if she dreamt about them or that she thought she would be seeing them soon. She never explained the reasons.

It was always a roller coaster ride when my parents would get emotional because I never knew what set them off. It was hard to see them tear up, look confused and sometimes snap back for no reason. I was lucky because it happened towards the end of their lives and I didn't have to deal with it for a long period of time because I'm sure it would have been a stressful time for all of us.

Chapter 28
EMBARRASSMENT AND BEING A CAREGIVER
Awkward Situations

As your parent gets older their mind starts playing tricks on them and sometimes they get confused. This makes them do and say things that they normally would never do or say. Get ready for some laughs, tears and awkward situations for you and others.

Sometimes we would be sitting at the table and my mom would say something that was just unique. I would look at her and say, "What?" and with an innocent face she would look at me and say it again. We could be looking at old photographs and she would say something like, "I didn't like her" or "I never trusted him." It was usually about family members or friends. When I would question her about it she would back track and say, "I don't mean it" or "I didn't say that." That was okay when we were alone. Now when that happened with others in the house or even if those people were visiting it was always an interesting situation. What do you say to them, "I'm sorry she doesn't know what she is saying?" Of course she did, she said it. Some pass is off and some get offended and unfortunately for me this was from events that happened before I was born so I didn't have a solution. Old wounds and grudges that had been forgotten years before come back to the surface and almost always cause an awkward situation. Sometimes she would say things that were funny and all you could do was laugh. She didn't think some of them were funny but others when she repeated them even she had to laugh. Add a table full of people and it made for a good time.

Other awkward situations can arise when your out in public. Old stereotypes can come to the surface and cause problems. My mom grew up in the generation and location where people of different nationalities lived in separate villages in the town. She grew up in the Italian section, but there were French, Polish, Portuguese and Irish sections. A lot of times these groups didn't get along and in the later years that came to the surface. When a nurse tried to take care of her in the hospital that had a French last name she turned to me and said, "Jim, she's French, I don't like her." Of course her whisper was loud enough so the entire floor heard it. The nurse politely asked her, "Why don't you like the French?" My mom told her that they were mean to her in school. The nurse explained that was sometime ago and she had nothing to do with it. My mom apologized and I just turned a deeper shade of red. That nurse handled the situation with class and my mom never had a problem with her care. Some might not be so understanding and it could have caused problems.

I was ready for everything because I never knew what my mom would do or say in public and with others. I knew a lot of my mom's history and background so I was prepared for somethings but others I had absolutely no clue what had happened in the past. Just be ready to explain the situation and also be ready to apologize to many people.

Embarrassment

Taking care of your parent can cause a lot of awkward situations so be ready for some embarrassment. Body noises and functions can come at the wrong time and make for some humorous situations and some not so funny. Just remember they are embarrassed like you, the only difference is they are probably not getting red in the face.

Think of this situation like people crowded in an elevator and someone lets out gas. Everyone looks around and sniffs to see who's guilty. When you have an elderly person in a wheelchair and out in public they are usually considered the one that, "Did it." This also is a great cover for you, if you have to let one go, do it, your parent will get the blame. They will give you a dirty look and might even point you out like, "What did you do?" So do that action at your own risk.

I'm joking but there is really nothing you can do from preventing this from happening. You place a diaper on them, you use powder, deodorant or even perfume to cover any smells. These functions are a natural part of life and it is unnatural if they don't occur. Be prepared to blush and roll your eyes because there is really nothing you can do to stop it or the embarrassment.

Apologizing For Rude Comments

One thing I learned over the years taking care of my dad and mom was to be prepared for anything. As a person gets older they lose some of the tact and courtesy that they learned over their life. They could be walking in a store or you could be pushing them in a wheelchair, they could come at anytime so be ready for whatever they say.

I use to go shopping with my dad and he would get frustrated with other shoppers in the store. The ones that leave their cart in the middle of the aisle so you can't pass while they talk to someone else or are looking at an item on the shelf. He use to push the cart so he had something to lean on so he didn't lose his balance. When someone got in his way he would push his cart into theirs and tell them to, "Move it." Even though a lot of times I agreed with him I would usually go by and tell the other person, "Sorry about that." For those old enough to remember that was a line from the television show, "Get Smart," and I would say that a lot. People would get in his way or bump into him and he would always have something to say and it usually wasn't nice. Most would look at him and then look at me and I would say, "Sorry." It was part of the daily routine and I'm sure most thought he was a crazy old man.

With my mom I would push her in the wheelchair and she always had something to say about someones look or how they were acting. Once again she wasn't too quiet about it and they usually heard her. Her whisper was like someone yelling in a room. I would apologize over and over and once again most of these people thought she was a crazy old lady.

We could be in a waiting room and she would comment on a girls dress or on a guy wearing a tee shirt. If they had a tattoo she made some sort of comment and they usually heard it. They would look at her or me with disgust and all I could do was roll my eyes or say, "I'm sorry."

What else can you do? You can't argue with your mom or dad because it would only make them say it louder. You can't argue with the person they are talking about because that could escalate into a bad situation. All you can do is apologize and hope they understand. I'm sure most of them have an older parent, grandparent, aunt or uncle that does the same thing.

Your Embarrassment

One of the thing that is part of being a caregiver is embarrassment. It could be when your in an elevator and your parent passes gas or while you wheeling them down the street and they make a crude comment. It could be the sight of your parents naked body or you could even get embarrassed by purchasing items at the store.

I got use to being embarrassed real quick when my dad was ill because his cancer spread so fast and he lost control of a lot of functions. He became self conscience real fast so the only time we went out was when he went to the doctors or for a treatment. This situation lasted about six months until he passed away.

With my mom I learned from my dad's situation to expect anything. She was very conscience of what she did and tried her best not to be embarrassed. Sometimes nature has a different plan and things just happen so you just roll with it.

When I would talk to her doctors and they would ask about certain body functions and parts, the first time was embarrassing for me and her but after a while it became normal. You never think you have to answer questions about your mom's anatomy or bodily functions, but when the time comes you just have to deal with it.

Another situation was when I would go to the store and purchase her incontinence supplies. The first time I did this I was a little embarrassed but it wasn't because of what I was purchasing, it was because of the quantity. After a few times I no longer had a concern, it's a part of life. I would have to buy numerous packages of feminine pads and diapers and I would go to the cashier with a cart full of items. The cashiers would ring up the items and then look at me and ask, "Do you want these in a bag?" I would look back and say, "No thank you, the embarrassment wore off years ago." Some would ask if I was taking care of someone and others would smile or laugh.

It was true I bought these items for so long I had no embarrassment purchasing or walking out the store with these items. I'm sure some men would have a problem with this situation and my answer to them would be, "Get over it." That's why I say, "you got to do what you got to do."

Chapter 29
SUPPLIES USED WHILE BEING A CAREGIVER
Supplies

There are all kinds of supplies that you need when you are a caregiver. You need to have a fully stocked first aid station for all types of cuts and bruises. You need to have gauze and bandages for any situation. You have to have cleaning materials for wounds such as saline wash. You have to have ointments and powders to prevent rashes. The list goes on and on.

Just as you have supplies to take care of yourself and your daily needs you need to have the same for your parent. You might actually need more due to the fact that you might need specialty items for their care. Diapers and incontinence pads, if necessary, are just a few of the supplies you will use on a daily basis.

It all depends on your parents situation. In my case I asked my mom what she needed and I had it available for her. I knew what we needed for normal events so I bought it and had it on hand. You have to be prepared for any event and for anytime when you are unable to go out. It also is dependent on what you can afford and what you can store. The more you have available to you the easier it makes the task.

Diapers And Pads

Personal and hygiene supplies are probably one of the biggest expenses that you will have. As their caregiver you are constantly changing your parent because they might be immobile and have no control. There are a lot of products to choose from and some make the chore a lot easier.

I use to purchase supplies at the local chain drug store, supermarket and discount retailer. I would buy them on sale so I could save money. Later on I started to purchase them online because sometimes they had free shipping or two for one sales. Some of the stores the checkers would remember me because of my purchases. When a new cashier checked me out they would always ask, "Do you want me to bag these items?" My response was always the same, "No thank you, the embarrassment wore off years ago." It would either make them laugh or give you a strange look. I would have to purchase diapers, feminine pads and bed under pads. I would buy two package of diapers, four package of feminine pads and one package of bed under pads a week. When there was a sale I would buy a months supply of everything. Many times I would empty out the shelf at the store. These items would average $15.00 a package for the type my mom needed. That was $105.00 a week for incontinence supplies that are one use and will be thrown out. That was a large chunk of the budget and Medicare and supplement insurance did not cover any of it.

My mom needed these items because she had very little control over her bladder. In the beginning she was able to change the pads herself but she was never able to change the diapers. When she urinated the pads and diaper would catch it and then they would have to be changed. Most of the time, up until the last month of her life, she could tell me when she needed to be put in the bathroom for a bowl movement. She would call or yell, "Jim, I got to go!" I would stop whatever I was doing undo the diaper, bring her to the bathroom and lift her onto the toilet. She would do her business, clean up and call, "Ok." I would go in, lift her off the toilet, put her in bed, make sure she was clean and put on a new diaper. She was good to go till the next time.

The diaper was also invaluable if we had to go out. It helped prevent any embarrassments and odors. I alway brought a go-bag with us whenever we went out. I would always have extra feminine pads, bed under pads, diapers, towels, disinfectant spray, soap, cleaning wipes and gloves. I never knew when we would have a situation or "accident" so I had to be prepared for everything.

Perianal Cream

One item that prevented a lot of problems with my mom was an over the counter medication called Balneol. It is a perianal cream that helps clean the rectal area of debris and dried feces. It becomes very useful after bowel movements and diaper changes.

I was told about this cleanser by a rectal surgeon who performed hemorrhoid surgeries. He said it keeps the area clean, prevents friction and irritation when you have hemorrhoids. I figured if it kept the area clean it was a good ointment to clean after bowel movements and diaper changes.

I used this ointment on my mom the entire time I was taking care of her full time. It is hard to find and it usually has to be ordered from the pharmacies. Some retail pharmacy chains sell their own store brand but it is still hard to find and most of the time you will have to order it online. Another problem is that it is expensive, about $20.00 a bottle, but it is worth it because it cleans the rectal area very well and helps prevent and rash.

I told our home healthcare nurse about it and she never heard about this ointment. She did tell me that she wondered why my mom never had a rash because most patients that wear diapers get a rash once and while. She also said she noticed that the rectal area was always clean and free of dried feces or debris. She looked into it and said she was going to start recommending it to her other patients.

It was easy to apply, all I did was put on my gloves, squeeze the bottle and squirt it on some toilet paper and wipe it around the rectal area between the butt cheeks. I would then take a clean piece of toilet paper and wipe it off. It would take the little chunks of feces off and even the small thin residue that remained. If it was really dirty I would do the procedure two or three times until the area was clean.

This ointment did the trick and in the thirteen plus years of taking care of my mom full time she never had a rash. All those years of wearing a diaper she never had an itch or any kind of residue on her backside no matter how bad the bowel movement was or how full the diaper became. Just a little extra care prevented a lot of problems down the road.

Circulation Socks

My mom had circulation problems with her legs after she had her spine surgery. Her legs, calves and feet would swell up every time she sat for an extended period of time. They would also get cold and dark pink but they didn't hurt her. When she was in bed the swelling would go down, they warmed up and the color returned to normal.

I took her to a doctor and he said that her circulation was poor in one leg and almost non existent in the other. He told us that she needed to have angioplasty on the one leg otherwise she was going to lose it. That was a shock and a no brainer and we went ahead with the procedure. The angioplasty worked and brought that leg from almost no circulation to poor almost good. That evened out both legs and she went on with her routines.

Part of her treatment and new routine was for her to wear circulation socks that kept a little pressure on the ankle and foot. These socks are sometime called diabetic socks and are sold at most pharmacies, department stores and medical supply. They did a wonderful job and kept the swelling down while she was in the wheelchair or in the car. I even started to wear them because my legs would also swell when we went on long trips and they kept my legs and feet normal.

They are not that expensive and are definitely worth it because poor circulation can lead to a lot of problems. We were lucky that we caught her circulation problem before it got so bad she could have lost a leg. The doctor was very blunt with his diagnosis and we both took immediate notice.

We never had another major problem with her leg circulation and we kept in check with the circulation socks and lifting her legs as needed. That was another challenge we had to deal with but because I kept on eye on her condition and noticed changes we were able to have the problem corrected. Once again you are their eyes and have to look for any problems that might arise.

Chapter 30

EQUIPMENT USED WHILE BEING A CAREGIVER

Tools And Accessories To Make Things Easier

Over the years there have been major advancement in tools, accessories and supplies to make it easier to take care of someone. Some of these items are covered by Medicare or supplement insurance. Unfortunately some items that are constantly needed are covered only for a short time or not at all. Some items are available for rental or purchase depending on your requirements. Even if some are not covered it might be worth it for you to purchase these items on your own if they can make your job easier and safer.

The first item we needed when I started taking care of my mom was a wheelchair. This was while she was still able to walk. She used a cane around the house or to walk a short distance. Our doctor agreed and wrote a prescription for a wheelchair. Medicare approved the wheelchair rental. When we went on outings or to the store the wheelchair made it easier for her because she was able to get around without the fear of falling. Later on I bought a walker for her to use around the house and yard. This was better than a cane because it gave her more support. I bought the walker myself and never submitted it to Medicare or insurance.

When she lost the use of her legs and was no longer able to stand that's when we started to need more hardware. The first thing we got was a hospital bed with rails and a trapeze so she could try to lift herself up. Medicare agreed with the doctor and approved the rental of the hospital bed. After her surgery we needed an air mattress because she received severe bed sores from her hospital stay. Once again Medicare agreed but it was on a short term basis. The initial rental was for three month with the possibility of three more. Because her skin was thin the bed sores were always a problem and the wound care doctor extended the prescription for three months. Medicare agreed and paid the additional three months. After this period was over the wound doctor said she permanently needed an air mattress. Medicare refused to pay for the air mattress even though it was medically necessary. I ended up purchasing the unit from the medical supply company. They discounted the unit by the amount Medicare paid and I paid the difference. It was about $500.00. I felt it was worth it because it would help prevent bed sores and it did. During the rest of her life the bed sores were kept in check except when she went to the hospital. Whenever she was admitted I would tell the admitting nurse that she needed an air mattress. It was like pulling teeth to have them supply an air mattress in the hospital. Every time she came home I had to deal with bed sores from the hospital. After Medicare modified their rules on hospital bed sores, they finally started to listen to me.

We needed a gel cushion for the wheelchair so the chair seat would not be so hard on her backside. This was considered a comfort item and was not covered by Medicare or insurance. The cost of the gel pad was about $50.00 and was well worth the cost. Another item that was needed was a commode chair. This would make it easier for her to go to the bathroom because we could place it by the side of the bed and I could lift her from the bed to the chair. I received a prescription from the doctor, went to the medical supply and paid for the commode chair. The medical supply company never forwarded the paperwork so I ended up never being reimbursed for this item. It was about $100.00 out of pocket. This was probably the worst item I bought. The first time I placed my mom on it I did not feel comfortable with the unit. I placed it against a wall so she would have some sort of a back rest. The chair had small wheels and they didn't lock very well. The seat was flimsy and the plastic bucket inside was very thin. I placed her on the chair and she did her business. When she tried to clean herself the chair moved away from the wall. When she tried to move herself back it almost fell backward. I was standing on the side and I was able to grab her before she fell back. This would have been a disaster if

I wasn't there. She would have fallen back and she could have hit her head against the wall. We never used this unit again. I thought of it as a death chair and threw it in the trash. I'd rather lift her up and place her on the real toilet instead of taking a chance of her falling off this chair.

After every hospital stay they would always ask if we needed any equipment. Most of the time we had what we needed. One time a physical therapist recommended a patient lift and I asked the doctor if it was a good idea. He did and wrote a prescription for a patient lift. Once again this was a great idea but did not work in normal situations. Medicare approved and paid for the patient lift. The one that was approved was a huge monstrosity and was very difficult to maneuver. It came with the wrong sling so from the beginning it never worked right. It was made to lift her from the bed to the wheelchair or from the wheelchair to the toilet. The frame was so huge you could not maneuver it around the bedroom and forget about even trying to get it into the bathroom. I bought a new sling with a hole in it for the commode but because of the size of the unit it wasn't safe to use to move my mom. I still ended up lifting her myself to the wheelchair or toilet.

Toward the end we needed a more comfortable wheelchair for her because she would tire easily when she was sitting. My sister bought her a reclining padded wheelchair. This was great because I could lift her into it and wheel her to the living room. It had a removable tray so I could serve her meals on it. It also reclined so when her feet swelled or she got tired I could change the seat back to make her more comfortable. This was not covered by Medicare because she already had a wheelchair so my sister ended up paying $600.00 for this chair.

After her last hospital stay the hospital social worker recommended that we get a commode chair. I told her of our previous experience in 1999 and said I didn't want another death chair. She said designs changed and brought one in to show me the difference. She was right, the one she brought had better wheels, locks and a higher back. She submitted the paperwork and Medicare approved this unit. After my mom was discharged and sent home we tried out the new chair. Once again I set it against the wall and locked the wheels. The seat was better and the bowl was bigger and deeper. I lifted my mom onto the commode chair and she did her business. She was able to clean herself without any incident. This unit was stable, safe and didn't move. That was last item we received in 2013. The design of items did change over the course of fourteen years. Now there are so many options and it is a big business to supply items that can help you while you are a caregiver.

Wheelchairs

A wheelchair is one accessory we couldn't do without. I had two wheelchairs, one was purchased by Medicare and was left in the house and the other was a lightweight one that I purchased and left in the car. This made it easier for me to transport my mom around. In the house I lifted her from bed to the wheelchair and rolled her where ever she needed to go. I had a gel pad on the seat so it made it more comfortable for her and didn't cause any wounds on her backside. If we needed to go out I would wheel her to the side of the car and lift her in and then roll the wheelchair back into the house. When we arrived at our destination I would remove the lightweight wheelchair from the car and placed another gel pad on the seat. I would lift my mom out of the car and into the wheelchair. I would then reverse the procedure for the drive home.

This system worked great because I always had a wheelchair with us so there was no place she couldn't go. This also worked in case there was an emergency and we had to leave fast or she had to get out of the car in an unknown location. It was a large expense for the second wheelchair but it was worth it because it was lighter and easier to lift.

As time went on I needed to raise her legs more to prevent swelling. Her sight and strength were starting to get weak so I needed something that was better for her to sit in. The pharmacy had a larger chair that was padded, had six inch wheels, reclined and had a removable tray that I thought would be great for inside the house. I took the measurements and found out it just barely fit through the interior doorway and it would work for my mom. My sister purchased this chair which cost about $600.00 and gave it to my mom. It was great because it was more comfortable than a regular wheelchair and it reclined so it would reduce the swelling on her legs. It had a tray so it was easier for her to eat her meals and I attached a cup holder so her water was always available and within reach. The other nice thing was it had six inch wheels which rolled on the carpet very easily. It was easy to clean and maneuver. This chair worked well and made life a little easier for her and me. I wish I would have seen these chairs earlier because unfortunately she only used it for the four months before she passed away.

Medical Equipment Rental

Over the course of taking care of my parents we required some medical equipment that had to be rented. The doctor would fill out a prescription and we would give it to a medical supply company that would furnish the equipment. Most of the time the rental was covered by Medicare and supplemental insurance. If it wasn't then we would have to purchase the equipment because it was needed.

For my dad's care we needed a wheelchair because he was no longer able to walk without getting dizzy and short of breath. He also required oxygen so that meant that an oxygen generator had to be rented for the house. When the company supplied the oxygen generator they also supplied portable tanks so he could travel back and forth to the doctors or to the medical facility for treatment. A tall oxygen tank was also supplied as a back up in case we lost electricity and the oxygen generator was unable to work.

The medical supply company maintained the equipment and delivered new supplies as needed such as replacement masks, cannulas and tanks. This equipment took up a large area in the house and we had small oxygen tubes running from the front room to the bedroom where my dad slept. The unit made a lot of noise and also generated heat so we didn't want it near where he was sleeping.

After my dad died the medical supply company came and collected the equipment. The only item I kept was the wheelchair because it was a light version that was easy to transport. I ending up purchasing it and I left it in the car so it was always available when I transported my mom.

For my mom we also had a wheelchair but it was heavy and bulky so I left it in the house. When she could no longer stand she needed a hospital bed with a trapeze and bed rails. This was furnished by a medical supply company and they maintained it for many years. She also needed an air mattress which was also supplied but I later had to purchase it because Medicare said it was not medically necessary. The doctor said it was medically necessary for the rest of her life but Medicare still denied the claim anyway. Later she required a Hoyer lift to help me get her out of bed and off a commode chair. She needed a shower chair but that was not covered by Medicare so I had to make the purchase. Later she needed a reclining wheelchair but Medicare also denied the claim and my sister purchased it outright.

Interesting situation occurred with the hospital bed and Medicare. For some reason Medicare rented the hospital bed and after ten years they said they would no longer cover the rental. I had no idea why they rented it because it would have been much cheaper for them to purchase it. The medical supply company called and said they were going to pick it up because Medicare refused to pay the claim. I told them that my mom was still using it and she needed it to survive. They said no and I told them to come and get it. I purchased some hospital bed rails online and I made an angled box to place on a regular bed frame. I bought a thin mattress and placed the air mattress on top so my mom would not be laying flat on her back. The only thing missing was the trapeze so my mom could pull herself up, and I had a plan to make something that would replace it. About a week later the medical equipment supply company called and told me that they would not be picking up the bed because my mom required it to survive. I asked them to send me a letter stating this and they said they would. I told them that if they ever needed to come and pick up the bed they would have to wait while I set up another bed. They agreed and we went on with our lives. They never sent the letter to me stating that we could keep the bed.

After my mom died I called the medical supply company and told them that she had passed away and for them to come and pick up the equipment. They gave me a date and pick up time and they never showed up. I called again and was given another pick up date and time and asked them if they would be showing up this time and they said, "Yes." I waisted another day and they didn't show up to pick up the equipment. I called and I was angered that I wasted two days for them to come and pick up the equipment. I was told this time that they would not pick up the equipment because it was too old and that Medicare paid it off a long time ago. I was free to dispose of the equipment or keep it. I once again asked for a letter stating these facts and once again I never received the letter.

I ended up giving some of the medical equipment to the local hospital guild thrift shop. I sold others at a garage sale and on a local online service. The items that they were going to take back a few years earlier, the hospital bed and trapeze, were paid off by Medicare years before they were going to take them back. If they did come at that time and had taken the bed back I made sure I had another option because my mom needed it.

Durable Medical Equipment

Durable medical equipment are items like a wheelchair, hospital bed, commode, lift or other items that you don't throw out after one use. Oxygen equipment and air mattresses also fall into this category and so do a lot of other items. These are the items that I was familiar with because my parents needed them during the time I was caring for them.

Most of the time these items are covered by Medicare and supplement insurance but it also depends of what type of health insurance plan you have. Your out of pocket can be as little as zero or it could go as high as your coverage allows. You need to check with your insurance plan to see what is covered and what is your out of pocket expense.

Some of these items can help your parent get by with their day to day routines. Others can make the job of caring for them much easier for you. It all depends on your situation and their condition. What might be covered for one person might not be covered for another because of their condition.

If the doctor said certain equipment was required or necessary I would have them order it. If Medicare and insurance approved and paid for it great, if not I would absorb the cost because it would help my parents or me in taking care of them. Some items I was told were not covered and I looked around to purchase them at a reasonable price. This was always an added expense and a shock to the budget but if it was needed I found some way to get and pay for it.

Most people think everything they need is covered by Medicare and insurance when they are taking care of a parent. Things might have changed under the new Medicare and health insurance regulations but I know when I was taking care of my parents a lot was not covered and we had to pay for it. This was one of the big surprises I learned when I stared taking care of my parents.

Chapter 31
TECHNOLOGY AND BEING A CAREGIVER
Smart Phones

With today's technology it's getting a little easier being a caregiver. Emergency alert buttons and smart phones make it easier to be aware of your parents condition. With just a push of a button you can find out if they are okay or need your help. The only problem is they have to be able to operate the device and a lot of our parents were never computer savvy.

My parents were never interested in learning anything about computers. They were old school and still did everything with pencil and paper. In fact neither one of them would use a calculator for any reason. When my dad was sick there were no smart phones and the emergency alert buttons were just starting to appear. We did things the old fashioned way with a bell or walkie talkie. He would call and if I didn't hear him he would ring a bell. If I was outside he would call me on a walkie talkie. This worked well and I was always there when he needed me.

During the time I was taking care of my mom smart phones came on the scene and she wanted no part of them. We still used the bell for calling me and I even rigged up several wireless doorbells in the house so all she had to do was press a button and I would hear that she needed me. We still used walkie talkies if I went outside but that was a little difficult for her to operate because of the arthritis in her fingers. She would press the button to talk and all I would her was a variation of, "Jim." I would come in from outside right away. She could operate a standard phone so I always had a list of phone numbers so she could call family and friends. She also knew to call 911 in case there was a problem with me. Fortunately she never had to call 911 for any reason.

A smart phone might have made things easier for both of us but unfortunately she never wanted to learn how to use one and even if she did she wouldn't have used it because she was afraid of new technology. If your parent is capable of using a smart phone, use them because they can help you in many ways. As time goes on more and more elderly people are more accustomed to smart phones and have no fear of this technology. This can be a help to you in many ways and anything to help you with your task should be welcomed.

Didn't Start Texting Until My Mom's Last Hospital Visit

When I was self employed I was in the video business. I was very involved in technology and new electronics that were coming on the market. I needed to know the newest video and computer technology to design it into my video systems.

When I started taking care of my parents I stayed updated on the newest items and technology so I would be able to get back into my previous profession. As the caregiving became a full time job I continued to try to stay updated on the newest technology but it was moving so fast I got a little left behind. New gadgets and information was constantly available and I was just standing on the sidelines. Smart phones were one of the biggest advancements and could help immensely in being a caregiver. Unfortunately for me I had a cellular phone that only made phone calls and a calling plan that was only good for limited use such as an emergency. The funny part was I was okay with this situation.

I finally upgraded my old phone to one that had a keyboard and could send text messages. Once again unfortunately I never used the text messaging service. I didn't need it because I was busy taking care of my mom and most of the time we were at home. If we were on the road I had no inclination to use the cell phone while I was driving even though I had a hands free set up in my vehicle. Sending text messages was different for me and I felt if I wanted to talk to someone it was easier to call. I also had no interest in social media because one, I didn't care to see or read what other people were doing and two, I felt people didn't care what I was doing. It was all a waste of time or a way to build up your ego and I didn't have time or the need for either.

The last time my mom was in the hospital was in February of 2013 and this was the first time I sent a text message. We were in the hospital room and I didn't want to disturb my mom or the staff by making a cellular call so I sent a text instead. It was to my sisters keeping them up to date on our mom's condition. I found something out that day, it was easy and I was able to get the information out very quickly. Just a few short notes and my sisters were notified of our mom's condition. I finally made it to the 21st century. I used text messaging all through the rest of her illness and after she passed away. I still believe it is still better to make a phone call to explain the situation but sending a text is quick, short and easy. I'm still not interested in social media and I probably never will. Now my nieces and nephews want me to get a smart phone and I'm not ready just yet because of the cost of the data plans. I think I'll wait a few more years before I jump into that field because I have to be able to afford it. So much for Mr. Technology.

Internet

The internet can be a wealth of information and how to be a caregiver. It has replaced going to the library or to your medical provider to get information on the subject. You just need to be aware that just because it is on the internet it might not be correct and beneficial to you in caring for your parent.

You always need to check the sources of information you find on the internet as well as other sources. Some information can be supplied by pharmaceutical companies because they have a new drug for certain situations. Insurance companies publish information on being a caregiver and it might be slanted to what they cover. Care facilities also offer information on different levels of care for assisted living and what is required of you if your parent is in their facility. Universities and colleges have information available if it is part of a study program. You also have various healthcare providers posting information and links to what type of programs and procedures are available. Individuals are constantly posting information on how they handle different situations or a link to where you can get more information on being a caregiver.

The internet is a wonderful resource of information but it does have its challenges. With so much available with a click of a mouse it leaves the process open to misinformation. Be careful with the information you read and check out the sources. Once again read and see if the information provided can be applied to your situation in a safe and proper manner. Just remember as a caregiver you are responsible for what happens to your parent.

Blogs

Today with the internet a quick search brings up numerous articles, pamphlets and books on the subject of being a caregiver. There are also a lot of blogs from many sources on being a caregiver. Some of these are operated by corporations, healthcare providers and individuals.

When I started taking care of my parents the way I received information and advice was from the healthcare providers, pamphlets and books. In later years the internet took hold and it had a lot of information just a few clicks away. Blogs started showing up in the last few years giving advice and telling of different situations. As I have said before there is nothing wrong with getting advice from as many sources as you can but you need to adapt and apply this advice to your unique situation. Everyones situation is different and requires solutions tailored to them. This also is true with information you get from blogs and the internet. You need to be able to check the source of the information and always see if it makes sense and adapt it to your situation. There are many techniques and procedures for different situations and you need to find what is best for you and your parent.

I never used or subscribed to a blog because I was too busy taking care of my mom and I didn't have the time to read what others were doing. You could say the same holds true with this book, this is the description of how I handled situations and took care of my mom and dad. While you are reading this book you need to see what makes sense for your situation and if it might work for you and your parent. If it does, great and if it doesn't, don't try it.

Chapter 32

LIFTING AND BEING A CAREGIVER

Lifting

Lifting was always a challenge because my mom was unable to put any weight on her legs or to help you in any way. So to pick her up you were lifting her entire weight. When I started taking care of her I never wore a back brace. That changed in 2002 when I injured a back disc while I was lifting my mom off the toilet. Since then I always wore a back brace no matter what I did. After she passed away my back sort of healed itself. It was no longer under extreme pressure. To this day I still wear a brace whenever I pick up a large or heavy item. These braces are available online, at department stores, pharmacies and even at home improvement stores. The price is around $25.00 and for that cost it's better to be safe than sorry.

We were never able to get an accurate weight for my mom. During one of her hospital stays they had a scale that weighed the patient and the wheelchair and then you weighed just the wheelchair. That was in 2001 and she weighed at that time 115 pounds. Her weight fluctuated very little so I always used that as the baseline.

Lifting her always depended on the situation and where you were going to put her. Lifting her into a vehicle was always the most challenging because there were so many things in the way. You had to watch out for the roof, the door, if the seat was high or the seat was low. Was the seat too far forward or back? Were her legs straight or bent? Each one of these variables presented unique challenges and you had to plan ahead and compensate for each one. The easiest lift was from the wheelchair to the toilet or the bed. Depending on the bathroom, it could be a straight lift, up and down. For the bed, it was also easy, up off the wheelchair and onto the bed. Then you would spin her on the bed so you could lay her down.

Another thing you had to watch was that the wheelchair was always in the locked position when you lifted her up. My mom had a bad habit of trying to help. I would lock the brake on the wheelchair and then she would unlock it thinking she actually applied the brake. I would start to lift her and the wheelchair would move. I would then have to put her back down, lock the brake and then lift her up again. The solution was when I bent down to lift her I would check the brakes on the wheelchair to make sure they were applied and then I would lift her.

Going to the doctors office was also a unique situation. I use to count how many lifts I would do in a day, especially when we went to the doctors. I think the most lifts I did in a day was twenty-eight. The family doctor was easy. Just roll the wheelchair into the examination room and the doctor would do his job. The eye doctor was more difficult because you had to lift her into special chairs and each change was two lifts. One chair was for the eye pressure and refraction test. After these tests I had to take her off the chair and put her back into the wheelchair. Then I had to lift her into another chair for the actual eye exam by the eye doctor.

Other specialists had other unique challenges. Dentists and oral surgeons were always difficult because I had to lift her into a chair that was surrounded by instruments. One oral surgeon had a machine you had to stand in front off so it could take an X-ray of the entire jaw. This was a challenge because I had to hold my mom up from the back as the machine X-rayed her jaw. They put the shield apron on her but nothing on me. I think over the course of taking care of my mom I had triple the radiation exposure of most people. When we had to go to outpatient facilities for bone scans, MRI's, CAT scans, IVP's and X-rays it was always unique. None of the facilities were the same or had the same equipment. Fortunately most of the time the attendants worked with you. I would tell them what I wanted to do and they would help me with the execution. Most of the time radiation exposure wasn't a problem but sometimes it was more than normal. Before and after her spine surgery, the surgeon wanted X-rays of her back. In order to get her in the proper position I had to lift and hold her for the X-ray. The technician did everything she could think of to shield me from the radiation. She worked as fast as she could so the exposure was minimal. This back X-ray was done four times in the course of two months.

Lifting And The Fear Of Falling

The first time I had to lift my dad off the bed he immediately had a fear of falling. I had him and there was no way he was going to fall but he had that sense. I guess it was because that he was relying on someone else to lift him up and he was not in control of his movements. I would keep telling him that he wasn't going to fall but he still had that sense. I just needed to help him get up off the bed and then I could help him get to the wheelchair. It was an easy lift because he was still able to stand but he just needed a little help to get started. He was unsteady on his feet but once I got him stabilized he was okay. It was just the initial lift that concerned him. Over time and the more we did this procedure that fear finally went away and he no longer had a problem when I helped him up. It finally came to the point when his condition worsened and I had to lift him completely up with no help. He wasn't tall but he was a heavy man and it took all my strength just to get him up. The funny thing was that this should have been the time he should have ben concerned about falling because I had his whole weight on me. Instead he had no problem because he had conditioned himself that I had everything under control. Fortunately we never had an incident where I lost my balance and caused him to fall.

My mom on the other hand never had a fear of falling as long as I was the one doing the helping or lifting. She felt perfectly safe when I would lift her up. In the beginning she was a little unsure as anybody would be when they are lifted completely off the ground. That passed very quickly and she never got scared when I lifted her up. She saw me lifting my dad so I think she figured she was smaller than him so it was easier for me to lift her. The problem came when someone else tried to lift her. We found that out the hard way when she was in the hospital after her spine surgery. Every time the physical therapist would come and try to lift her with a lifting belt she got scared, cried and held on to the bed rail because she said, "I'm going to fall." No matter how they tried she would not let them pick her up because of that fear. If I picked her up she had no problem. I couldn't get the hang of the lifting belt and she didn't cooperate when I tried to use it but when I lifted her straight up she never had a problem.

I did this for over thirteen years and she never fell or was dropped. We had a few close calls but I was always able to recover. As an adult I have never been lifted up so I can only imagine how difficult it must feel the first time. Both of my parents got over this fear because they had faith in my abilities and knew that I would never do anything that would hurt them.

Lifting, Pulling And Helping

The first time I tried to lift my dad he tried to help me by holding and pulling on me. This was the worst thing that he could do because it was putting all the lifting pressure on my back and neck. The force doubled because I was trying to lift and he was trying to pulling himself up on me. I had to stop and put him down and explain that he was causing more harm and was not helping. I explained that it was better for him to just, "Do nothing and let me do the lifting." This is better because I would have control of the way, speed and position of the lift. If he is trying to pull himself up against me he is actually pulling me down and that could cause both of us to fall. After a few times he finally listened and stopped trying to pull himself up. Amazingly it worked and I was able to lift him with no problem. He looked at me and said, "That was easy," and then he looked at me and said, "easy for me but not easy for you." It was a lot of work and strain because of his weight but it wasn't that bad. It was a lot worse when he was trying to pull himself up because the weight seemed like twice as much.

He wanted to help me and in the process he was actually causing more work and possible injury to my neck, spine and back. After the first few times he never did it again and let me do the work. The more I lifted him it seemed the stronger I got and it didn't seem as difficult.

With my mom she did the same thing the first few times I lifted her up. With her she would pull on my neck and try to pull herself up. I would tell her to stop or just go limp. When she did this it was easy to lift her up. Even when I lifted her in the seated position she would pull on my neck and I could really feel it. I would have to keep telling her to let go and then the pressure on my neck would go away. Through the years of lifting her every so often she would forget herself and pull on my neck. She still had some strength and if she did it a certain way it would cause me a problem like a stiff neck or a severe headache. She would look at me and say, "What's wrong?" and I would tell her, "you pulled on my neck." She would say, "I'm sorry, did I hurt you." I would say no but an hour later I would get a headache and she would notice that something was wrong and say, "I did hurt you, I'm sorry." The headache would usually go away during the night. We had these episodes all the way till the end and it was just something I got use to.

I always had stiff necks, sore bones and headaches while I was taking care of my mom. I lifted her so many times in a day that my body never had time to rest from the strain. I did get stronger during this time because it was like lifting weights but the good thing was that it was a natural strength and not forced. After she passed away I stopped lifting and the stiff necks, sore bones and headaches went away. I'm sure I'll get arthritis in my neck because of the strain but at least for now I am pain free.

Chapter 33

TRANSPORTATION AND BEING A CAREGIVER

Transportation Issues

Transporting my mom was always difficult. Since she was unable to stand she had to be lifted into the car and at times this was quite difficult. When the situation started I had a large SUV, a 1990 Chevrolet Suburban. I would wheel her out of the house, down some steps to the side of the car. I'd lift up one of the side arms on the wheelchair, put one my arms behind her back and the other below her knees. I would bend my knees and lift her and put her into the front seat of the Suburban. This worked fine for a few years. Unfortunately, the SUV had over 200,000 miles on it and was getting a little unreliable. To save money I would do my own repairs. The problem with this routine was that if I needed parts or was unable to get the vehicle repaired that day, we had no transportation. This is unacceptable when you're a caregiver.

I started looking for a replacement and a new Suburban was out of the budget, they were about $28,000.00 in 2003. I found the Saturn Vue. It was quite smaller that a Suburban but surprisingly large inside. It was also within budget, around $16,000.00. I bought the Saturn Vue and I immediately was in for a shock. I had a hard time trying to fit my mom into the front seat. The vehicle was lower so I had to bend as I was putting her inside and this put a lot of pressure on my lower back. Fortunately I wore a back brace and this helped. I did find out that the front seat folded flat and forward. I then was able to put my mom into the back passenger seat. This worked out very well because of the folded forward front seat. It gave her a lot of room and she was able to joke that I was her chauffeur. This vehicle would work as long as my back held out.

I kept the Suburban as a spare vehicle and one day we needed to buy some large items at the home improvement store. I put my mom into the Suburban and we went on our way. About three miles from our house I started hearing a loud clicking noise and then a large bang. I felt the vehicle lurch and it started slowing down. The engine was revving up and the speed was receding. I lost the function of the transmission and we coasted to a stop. I called the Auto Club and asked for a tow back to my house, since I did my own auto repairs. About an hour later the tow truck arrived and I informed the driver of my situation. He was very understanding. As he was hooking up the Suburban I was lifting my mom into the cab of the tow truck. When he was finished he drove us and the broken vehicle home. When we got to the house, I got her wheelchair and lifted her out of the truck. The driver lowered the car and went on his way. He definitely deserved and received a tip. Now we were back to one vehicle. Repairs to the old Suburban were too expensive because I needed a rebuilt transmission so I had to sell it to a junk yard.

In 2008, we moved to Tehachapi, California. The house we bought had a slanted driveway. One day I was taking my mom out of the car and I lost my balance. It was an everyday lift but for some reason I lost my footing. She had no idea what was going on but to me it was terrifying. I was trying to figure out how not to lose my balance and drop her. It happened in a few seconds but it seemed like minutes for me. I finally figured that if we went down I would have her land on me. Somehow I stumbled and was able to use the Saturn as a brace. I recovered and did not drop her. I put her into the wheelchair and rolled her into the house. Unfortunately that maneuver hurt my back for a few days. After I explained the situation to my mom we decided we needed to get a higher vehicle so it would put less strain on my back. In 2008 gas prices were rising like crazy but I wanted to get another Suburban because it was higher than the Saturn. I ended up using the leftover money from the house sale and purchased a new Suburban. Because of the high gas prices in 2008 they were about $28,000.00 and I thought I really got a deal until I had to fill it up with gas. A thirty plus gallon tank at $5.00 a gallon made for $150.00 fill up. The good news since everything we did was local I only filled it up once a month.

A few years later, as I was driving on the freeway something punctured one of the rear tires. I exited the freeway and parked. I called the Auto Club and they came out and repaired the tire on the vehicle. I lifted my mom out of the Suburban and put her in the wheelchair. The service attendant raised up the vehicle, put a plug in the tire and got us on our way.

A subscription towing service definitely comes in handy when you are a caregiver. It could be for a tow, jump start a battery or a tire change. It is worth the annual fee.

Being In Public

Being in public is always a challenge when you are a caregiver for your parent. Whether they can walk or in a wheelchair you do your best to make sure they are dressed properly. Unfortunately you have no control of what they say or do and you definitely have no control over what their body does. It can cause some interesting situations.

My mom was in a wheelchair so she and I were always concerned that she was properly covered. She wore a diaper and she didn't want anyone to see it. She would place a small blanket on her lap that would cover her legs. Depending on the weather the blanket would be thick or thin. I had a problem when I would lift her from the car to the wheelchair or vice a versa. I made sure when I lifted her that I slid her dress down in back so she wouldn't moon anyone with her diaper. If someone was standing behind her I would ask them to move so they wouldn't get a show when I lifted her up and they always obliged. I also would stand in front of her after I put her in the wheelchair so both of us could straighten her up.

The uncontrollable part was when she had gas and there really is no way to cover this up. My only solution was let it rip and just smile if someone looked at her. What can you say, "Don't do that." That won't work, it's a part of life and at that age they have very little control of that function.

Spills and messes are all part of the job and they keep you busy while you are out. When they eat they try not to make a mess but it seams they make it worse. It's just like bringing in a little kid into a restaurant so be prepared for a mess. If something is in the way they will knock it over. Even when they drink from a glass be ready for a clean up. You will be spending a lot of time wiping their face and hands. You're just returning the favor from when you were a toddler.

The one thing that can be extremely embarrassing is what they say. They can say anything and you have no way of walking it back or changing it. You will be surprised at what they say and a lot of times the only thing you can do is apologize.

Be prepared for anything and anything will happen. Just make sure you have towels and air freshener handy. Also be ready to apologize many times during the time your in public.

Cover Them While Moving

One thing you always have to be aware of is the appearance of your parent. Sometimes they are not aware of the situation and their body could be exposed to the elements or other people. This could lead to more illness or some embarrassing situations.

When I use to move my mom from the car to the wheelchair I would always make sure she was covered. If the weather was cold I would put a flannel blanket on her to keep her warm. If the weather was warm I would use a beach towel and place it on her so she would not be exposed to others. When you are lifting them from a vehicle to a wheelchair they are sometimes exposed and you don't want to put them or others in an embarrassing situation.

When they are in the wheelchair it is easier for a man because they are wearing pants. In my mom's situation she always had to wear a dress. Most of the dresses buttoned in the front so they were easier to put on. This caused problems because when I placed her in the wheelchair they would stick underneath her and leave her legs and diaper exposed. I would correct this issue by raising her a little and pulling the dress from underneath her. This worked well but even though I wore a back brace it put a lot of pressure on my lower back. I would always place a towel, light or heavy blanket on her lap to cover her whenever she went out. This made her more comfortable when she went out in public.

I tried to make things as normal as possible for her. We had no choice in her condition so I had to adapt routines to allow her to go out in public. I never wanted her to get embarrassed and for her to feel self conscience and I also didn't want others to be embarrassed around her. I think we accomplished this over the many years that I took care of her.

In The Car

Traveling in the car is a great way to get your parent out of the home but it can cause some challenges. Depending on the size of the vehicle there is the concern of getting them in and out of the car safely. Also car seats are not the most comfortable and you need to take special care so that they don't get stiff, sore or bruise while they are riding in the vehicle. You also need to bring items to help you care for them. Just because your in the car their bodily functions continue and it doesn't matter where you are.

When my dad was sick he was still able to get into the car. I had a 1990 Chevrolet Suburban, it was a higher than normal vehicle so I had it equipped with side running boards. This made it easier for my father to get in because he was able to step up into the vehicle. Sometimes he needed a little help such as guiding his hand to the grab handle. As time went on he needed a small stool to stand on so he could step up onto the running board and then into the vehicle. I also would always stand behind him so I could catch him if he fell backward.

This procedure also worked for my mom when she was still able to walk. From the time I started taking care of my mom full time I always had to lift her to get her into the car and this caused certain challenges. The Suburban was high so I started lifting from the seated position in the wheelchair and setting her on the front seat of the vehicle. The side arms of the wheelchair lifted up or could be removed so it made it easier to put one arm behind her back and the other underneath her knees and lift. This put a strain on my back and kept me sore most of the time. Another procedure was to lift her from the front. I would bend down and put my arms around her back and she would put her arms around my shoulders then I would lift her high enough to put her into the seat. I would then put one arm under her knees and the other behind her back and spin her facing forward in the vehicle. I had to watch out and make sure her legs and feet did not catch the front panel of the car. I tried one of those swivel pads and it worked but the major problem was trying to center her on it while I'll lifted her into the seat. Also when I spun her around her feet and legs would spring out and hit the door frame. We made it work and I never dropped or caused any injury to her. My back was always sore and I felt like I was playing Russian roulette every time I picked her up but nothing ever happened with this vehicle.

I had to purchase a smaller car because the 1990 Suburban was no longer reliable and because to limited funds I purchased a 2003 Saturn Vue. This was classified as a small to midsize SUV and it was definitely smaller and lower than my old Suburban. The only way to put my mom into the vehicle was to lift her in the seated position, stand up, then stoop down to lower in the car and then place her in the back seat. The front seat was more difficult to put her in because of the door frame. The rear passenger door opened more, was more square and seemed larger. This worked well because the front seat folded flat and forward so she was able to see out the front. The problem was this put significant stress on my back. In 2002 I hurt my back lifting my mom off the toilet so the only remedy I had available was to wear a lower back brace. This worked wonders and kept my back from giving out and made me feel safer when I had to lift her in and out of the car. I always wore this brace every time I had to lift or move her. I never dropped or injured my mom while we were using this vehicle but I did come close when I lost my balance. That was when we decided to get another Suburban. We had sold our previous home and there was money left over so I was able to purchase with a loan a 2008 Chevrolet Suburban. This vehicle once again made it easier for me to lift my mom in and out as well as being more comfortable for her. We used this vehicle all the way until the time of her death. I would still be driving it today if it hadn't been for a drunk driver who totaled it while it was parked on the street during the night.

Whenever we went for a drive I always made sure I brought plenty of water, change of clothes, extra diapers, pads and towels. I was always prepared to change my mom if I had to either in the car or at our destination. The wheelchair was always in the back as well as extra blankets and cleaning supplies. One time we had a tire failure on the freeway because I ran over something and a nail punctured the tire. I was able to pull off the freeway and then call the Auto Club. They came and were able to repair the tire with no problems. I took my mom out of the car and placed her in the wheelchair. It was September around 9pm and it was a little chilly. I had blankets in the vehicle so I was able to cover her and keep her warm. I had water for her in case she got thirsty. It took about an hour and a half till we got back on our way. She stayed comfortable and safe while the technician fixed the tire.

You have to think of your vehicle as a mobile home and be prepared when you travel. Even if you are going a short distance you have to be ready for anything. The type of vehicle you own also dictates how you are going to be able to transport your parent. We were fortunate to be able to own and purchase vehicles that made it easier for this task.

Mobility

Mobility is one way to maintain a certain quality of life for most of us. Getting around is such a normal routine that we take for granted until we no longer can do it. Being a caregiver and if your parent can move around you need them to maintain as much mobility as possible so they don't feel incapacitated. With todays medical supplies and accessories this has become a lot easier.

I tried to keep my mom as mobile as possible. I could never get her a motorized wheelchair because she would have probably ran over anyone that got in front of her. I was content for her to have a normal wheelchair with the two big wheels and two small wheels. With this she could try to move herself by pushing the wheels with her hands and arms. The wheelchairs with four small wheels wouldn't work because she couldn't pull with her legs and feet. When we went out I would push her from place to place.

I had to be very careful because her feet would fall off the foot rests and drop to the ground. She couldn't feel her feet and she would not know if they were dragging against the ground. The wheelchair foot rests had straps but once in a while she would get a spasm and one of her feet or both would pop out of the straps and go on the ground. As I pushed her I was constantly looking at her feet to make sure they were secure on the wheelchair foot rests. If I wasn't paying attention they could drop on the ground and grind against the concrete, pavement or other surface and she wouldn't feel the pain.

We went out as much as possible when she felt up to it. Most times she wanted to get out and we did except when she was feeling ill or constipated. She would have a good time and when we came home she would rest well for the night. I would be exhausted and sore as usual because of the extra lifts but it was part of our normal routine and it made her feel better.

Water

Whenever you are away from home make sure you bring plenty of water. It's not only for general thirst but you never know when you might be delayed and they will become thirsty. They might also have to take some medication while you are away and they need the water to wash it down. They might get a tickle in their throat or dry cough that they need to wash away. You might even need it to clean a cut or scrape that they might receive. Not only take enough for your parent, make sure you have enough for yourself too.

When we would go out I would always bring a small ice chest of bottled water. I would put one bottle in the cup holder within easy reach of my mother and the cooler would be within easy reach for me. She didn't like ice cold water so the one in the cup holder was always room temperature. If we got stuck in traffic or were delayed in any way she always had water to drink.

If we were not in the car and she was in her wheelchair or other location I always had water available for her. I attached a plastic cup holder to her wheelchair so she always had a water bottle within reach. When we visited someone we always brought her water with us just in case there was none available.

It doesn't have to be just water, it could be juice or some other beverage depending on their condition. My mom liked water because juice and soda would make her more thirsty. All this water could cause more work like more frequent pad and diaper replacement but it is a necessary part of life. This is to prevent dehydration and therefore there is no excuse.

Go-Bag

As we traveled to doctors, hospitals, treatment facilities, shopping and visiting I always brought a go-bag. Sometimes I needed more than one because of all the supplies we needed to take. As time went on it went from a small canvas bag to a large suitcase. It was always stocked and ready to go.

Since my mom was not able to care for herself I had to bring all the supplies necessary to change, wash and dress her while we were away. When she had a wound on her backside I had to bring whatever I needed to change the dressing in case it came off. I would bring paper and cloth towels, cleaning wipes and wash cloths as well as regular and waterless soap. Powder and ointments were part of the kit. Incontinence pads, diapers, bed under pads and toilet paper were stocked in plenty. I had blankets, pillows, extra dresses, socks, sweaters and jackets. When we visited family it was one hundred and fifty miles away so I had to be ready for the road trip. We traveled through the desert to the mountains so I had to be ready for the heat and the cold.

Whenever we went to the doctors or for diagnostic tests I was always ready. If she had an "accident" I was ready to clean and change her. When I took her to the hospital I had whatever I needed for the return trip. I always had a clean change of clothes handy so I could get her dressed when she was discharged and take her home.

Even though I was prepared it seemed like I was always adding something to our go-bag. Whenever she had a new procedure I had to make adjustments to what I needed to bring with us. It might have been a different type of bandage, type of ointment or a different type of pillow or blanket. Our go-bag contents constantly changed for our situation.

Maneuvering The Wheelchair

Everyone thinks that maneuvering a wheelchair is easy and everyone pays attention and gets out of the way. That rarely happens and a wheelchair is a cumbersome item that takes up a lot of space to move around. They come in different sizes and for different conditions but one of the common features makes it hard to maneuver are the foot rests. These things stick out and catch on everything or bump into what ever is around. When you make a sharp turn make sure you have enough room to get by without hitting a wall or a person.

I had to maneuver wheelchairs in all kinds of conditions and spaces. We would have to go across parks to get to some picnic or festival. I had to always make sure my mom's feet never fell off the foot rests because she couldn't feel her feet and wouldn't know if they were dragging on the ground. We had to get in small elevators or go up steps. We were in lines and in crowds. We would go to the grocery store and I would push my mom in the wheelchair with one hand while I dragged the shopping cart behind us with the other. It was like a small train going through the aisles.

My mom would try to push the wheelchair herself because it had the big wheels and sometimes she would get stuck because she couldn't maneuver around something. Years before when she started using a wheelchair because she couldn't stand for a long period of time we went to a local amusement park. We were supposed to meet my sister and her family. We were in the square and I saw my nephew so I assumed they were all there. I told my mom to stay were she was and I would go get my sister and her family. I greeted my sister and I turned around and saw my mom stuck on the trolley car tracks. She moved quite a ways from where I left her and got stuck on the tracks. Sure enough there was the horse drawn trolley car going right toward her. After a "oh sh_t," moment I ran to her and moved her off the tracks. All I could hear was the driver yelling, "Whoa," and I could feel the horse breathing down my neck. When she was out of harms way I asked her, "Why did you move?" She said, "I wanted to save you a trip from coming to get me." After I apologized to the trolley driver they continued on their way.

I never let her push herself again. Where I went she went and that stayed true for the rest of her life. It always brought a laugh when my nephew would repeat the story of how grandma almost got run over by a trolley car horse. We'd laugh but it was a good thing the trolley car horse driver was alert and in control. The horse did look a little confused because something was on the track.

I bring this up because wheelchairs are a wonderful vehicle and make things a lot easier. You can get your parent out so they don't have to stay inside the house. They are great but they do have their downsides. They are difficult to maneuver in close situations and they are on wheels which mean they can roll almost anywhere. All it takes is for someone to loosen the brake and they can roll into harms way. You have to be alert at all times so you don't have a disaster happen. We were lucky and were able to laugh about our situation but it could have been a tragedy.

Doctors Offices

One of the hardest places to maneuver is the doctors office. Not only is being in the office tough but it is also the way to get there. Most of these paths are small and crowded and difficult for a wheelchair to pass. Even with the American With Disabilities Act it seems like a lot of medical facilities are still the most difficult to navigate.

We had a doctor for my dad that the most difficult chore was the elevator to his office. This was the medical building next to the hospital where our doctor was on staff. When I went by myself I would always take the stairs because the elevators were small, crowded and slow. When I was with my dad we had no choice and we always ended up in an elevator with someone coughing severely. I was always afraid my dad was going to catch something. When he was in a wheelchair it was even more difficult to get in the elevator. There was only room for three people and the wheelchair. Most of the time the elevator was full because the handicap parking was on the fourth floor of the parking garage so most people entered from the lower floors. We would have to wait as long as fifteen minutes to get an elevator that had enough room for my dad in the wheelchair and myself. Once we got to the proper floor there was plenty of room to maneuver. Even in the doctors office their was plenty of space to roll the wheelchair to the exam room. Most of the time you were in a waiting room with a lot of sick people and once in a while there was someone who sounded like they were coughing up a lung. I always wondered how many germs were floating around in the doctor's office and which one was going to get one of us. Just another reason for a pneumonia and flu shot.

With my mom we had one doctor that was also on an upstairs floor. This one was a little easier because the parking garage was underground and the handicap parking was on the first floor. We never had to wait for an empty elevator because these were a lot bigger than the other facility. The problem once again was always the sick people that were in the elevator. I was always amazed at how many people coughed or sneezed without covering their mouths. This was especially true with children and most of the time their parents never corrected them. Once again I always wondered what germ was going to get one of us.

This doctors office was small and had very little room to move a wheelchair. In fact people sitting down would have to get up and move to the end of the room when we entered with a wheelchair. If we had to wait no one could enter or leave the office because we were in the way. The solution was that when we entered they would immediately takes us to a room in the back out of the way of the other patients. This worked to our advantage because we weren't waiting in a room full of sick people.

There is no way of knowing if we ever got sick because of a visit to the doctors office. We always took precautions like washing our hands immediately after leaving the office. We also received a flu shot every year and the pneumonia vaccine when it was required. Funny thing is you go to the doctors to get better or maintain your health. You never consider you have to go through a mine field of unhealthy people and get exposed to who knows what before you can see the doctor.

Chapter 34
BEING PREPARED AS A CAREGIVER
Be Prepared For Anything

Being a caregiver also means being prepared for anything. You never know when you have to clean something or someone up. You might have to clean, bandage a cut or wound. You will be changing pads, diapers and other things. You also have to be ready to go to the doctor or hospital at anytime.

I never knew what the day would bring so I basically prepared myself for anything. My mom could be washing herself and drop the water basin on the floor. That meant I had to put her back in bed and change her up. I could be cutting her finger nails and nip a little too much that would cause them to bleed. That meant I had to clean and bandage her finger. She could be sitting at the table and have to "go" and didn't wait till I got her on the toilet. Once again a trip back to the bed and a complete cleaning and changing. Somedays nothing unordinary would happen and others if it could happen, it did.

When we would take a road trip I would always know where the nearest hospital was just in case we had a problem. A cell phone was always available in case I needed the paramedics or just had to call the doctor. I had a cosmetic case with her medications so they were always with us. I made sure the medications were still in their original prescription bottles because some of them could be considered narcotics. I had a go-bag full of supplies for any situation. I had her identification and insurance information always with us.

I was lucky because I never had a situation where she was choking or gasping for air. With my father because of his lung disease breathing was always a problem and in the later years he needed oxygen. He didn't wear it all the time but sometimes he would be short of breath and gasping so much I had to put the mask or cannula on him.

He was also diabetic and if he became confused and lethargic it meant his sugar became too low and he could go into shock so I would have to give him a sugar tablet to bring him back. I always had to be prepared for this situation. If this happened my mom would probably panic so I would also have to be ready to deal with her.

My mom would always panic in stressful situations. My father on the other hand was calm and cool. When we were kids and would get hurt she would get so excited she couldn't do anything. My dad would take charge and straighten things out. He would tell her when you get nervous and excited you can't do anything or help anyone. Fortunately in this trait I took after my father and I never got nervous or excited whenever something happened. I never got upset on what I had to do no matter how disgusting it could be. I did what I had to do.

Have A Plan

When you are a caregiver you are responsible for your parent and yourself. They are relying on you to take care of them and you are always responsible for their condition and welfare. In order to do this you need to have a plan for various situations.

I had plans on how to move my mom around the house and how to transport her by car. I made a plan on how to give her a shower and how to change her clothes. I learned how to properly change her diaper and keep her dry during the night.

I gave her a bell so if she needed me she could ring it and I could hear her anywhere in the house or outside. When she was in the bathroom I gave her a wireless doorbell so when she was finished all she had to do was press the button and I would come to lift her out. I had walkie talkies so when I worked outside she could call me at anytime. It could be to remind me of her medications, if she had "to go" or if something was wrong. I had the phone by her bedside or always near her in case something happened to me so she could dial 911. She had a list of phone numbers of family and friends. I showed her where all the important paperwork was located in case I was incapacitated and she needed important documents. There was a list of doctors as well as a copy of her medical and medications list nearby.

I was young but that meant nothing because I could have fallen and hit my head and she would have been alone. I could have gotten a massive heart attack or stroke and she would have been by herself. I planned for everything I could think of happening. That included natural disasters and riots. We lived in Lynwood, California and we were very near the riots of 1992 so that was always in the back of my mind.

Whenever her condition changed I made a plan to handle the situation. I changed the plans over and over depending on the situation. When we moved a lot of things changed and so did my plans. They were never set in stone and needed to be adapted to her and my conditions and situations.

Medical And Medication Lists

Whenever you go to a new doctor, diagnostic procedures or the hospital they always want information about your medical history and your medications. You can spend fifteen minutes or more filling out these forms and trying to remember dates, procedures and medications. In an emergency situation it is even harder to remember because so much is going on.

I solved this problem years ago after I went through the above when my dad had to be admitted to the hospital. After he came home I made a detailed list with his medical history and his medications listed. When we went to a new doctor, for diagnostic tests or when he was admitted to the hospital I would give them this list and they would photocopy it and put in his chart. Now some providers still wanted me to fill out their form and having this sheet made it much easier. In fact it was more than one sheet it was usually three to four pages. I had his medications listed including dosage and frequency. All of his aliments, diseases and conditions were listed. I also put the history of all his medical procedures and dates. I also included any special conditions and needs that were recommended by his treating physicians. All his doctors and specialists were listed along with their address and phone number. At the bottom I included his insurance information and contact info. The sheet concluded with his contact information which was my name, address and phone number. With all this information available it prevented a lot of mistakes because you could not remember the information. I would update this list whenever there was a change in anything. If his medication changed, we saw a new doctor, a new condition was diagnosed I immediately updated this list.

When my mom became ill I did the same for her. I even made a sheet for my own medical information so it was always available. Whenever I took my mom to the hospital her entire medical condition and medication was readily available to whoever treated her. This saved a lot of time because they knew immediately what her condition was and what type of medications she was taking.

Here is a copy of the last medical and medication list I made for my mom.

Xxxx X. Xxxxxxx

000 Any Lane

Tehachapi, CA 93561

(000) 000-0000

Birthdate: XX-XX-19XX

Age: 92

Medication & Dosage:

Latanoprost 0.005% Solution

1 Drop in Both Eyes At Bedtime

Lisinopril 10mg

1 Tablet Per Day

Children's Aspirin 81mg Tablet

1 Tablet Per Day

Hydrocodone 5/500mg Tablet
1 Tablet Every 4 Hours As Needed For Pain

Fentanyl 75MCG/HR Patch
Apply To Skin Every 3 Days

Sennosides 25mg Laxative Tablet
2 Tablets Per Day

Silver MultiVitamin Tablet
1 Tablet Per Day

Vitamin C 500mg Tablet
1 Tablet Per Day

Allergies: None known at this time.

Blood Type: O Positive

Medication Note:
Per Family Physician Order, Do Not Use Novocaine that contains Adrenalin. Antibiotics Needed Prior And After Any Dental Procedures

Existing Medical Conditions:
Congestive Heart Failure; Valvular Heart Disease; Borderline Glaucoma; Traces of Asbestosis; Gall Stones, Gall Bladder and Appendix Removed in 1982; Breast Cancer Diagnosed in September 1993; Right Mastectomy in October 1993; Severe Scoliosis, Curvature of the Spine and Arthritis; Cataract Surgery Both Eyes in March/April 1999; Spinal Decompression of #3 and #5 Vertebrae in March 2001; Cancerous Tumor Removed Right Axillary in April 2002; Percutaneous Transluminal

Angioplasty on lower right leg in June 2008; Surgery to remove Colon Obstruction and Scar Tissue in October 2008.

*Prone to pressure wounds and bed ulcers. Uses an Air Mattress at home. Requires an Air Mattress when admitted to the Hospital.

Current Medical Equipment At Home:
Hospital Bed With Trapeze, Floating Air Mattress, Wheelchairs, Sliding Shower Chair, Raised Toilet Seat with Arms and Hoyer Lift

Pharmacy:
Our Pharmacy
000 Any Blvd.
Tehachapi, CA 93561
(000) 000-0000

Family Physician (General Practice):
Our Doctor, M.D.
0000 Any Blvd.
Tehachapi, CA 93561
(000) 000-0000

Eye Physician:
Our Eye Doctor, M.D.
0000 Any Avenue
Long Beach, CA 90806
(000) 000-0000

Xxxx X. Xxxxxxx

000 Any Lane

Tehachapi, CA 93561

(000) 000-0000

Page 2: Medical Information (Continued)

Oncologist:

Our Oncologist, M.D.

00000 Any Hwy. Suite 000

La Mirada, CA 90638

(000) 000-0000

Wound Care:

Our Wound Care Physician, M.D.

Wound Healing Center/Any Hospital

00000 Any Blvd.

Whittier, CA 90602

(000) 000-0000, Ext. 0000

Vascular Surgeon:

Our Surgeon, M.D.

00000 Any Blvd., Suite 000

Whittier, CA 90606

(000) 000-0000

Rehabilitation Physician:

Our Rehab Doctor, M.D.

Spine Center/Any Hospital

00000 Any Blvd.

Whittier, CA 90602

(000) 000-0000, Ext. 0000

Health Insurance: Primary

Medicare

Hospital Insurance And Medical Insurance

Parts A and B

Claim Number: 000-00-0000-A

Health Insurance: Secondary

Government-Wide Service Benefit Plan

Blue Cross Blue Shield Federal Employee Program-PPO

Identification Number: R00000000

Enrollment Code: 000

Effective Date of Coverage: 00/00/95

BLUE CROSS AND BLUE SHIELD

FEDERAL EMPLOYEE PROGRAM

FOR HOSPITAL INFO: (000) 000-0000

FOR MEDICAL/DENTAL INFO: (000) 000-0000

FOR PRECERTIFICATION INFO: (000) 000-0000

FOR PRESCRIPTION INFO: (000) 000-0000

Widow of Xxxxxxx X. Xxxxxxx

Emergency Contact:

Xxxxx X. Xxxxxxx (Son)

0000 Any Lane

Tehachapi, CA 93561

(000) 000-0000 Home

(000) 000-0000 Cell

Revised 2-20-13

This information was invaluable every time I took my mom into the hospital or for other procedures. It made the admission or new patient process much easier to maneuver. I have made one of these lists for myself and have told friends and family to do the same.

Accessories, Extra Clothes And Clean Up Bag

Whenever we traveled I always brought accessories and supplies to make sure I was able to properly care for my mom. I could change her in the back of my Suburban if I had to because I had removed the third row seat and had the second seats folded down. I had towels to block the windows and bed under pads to line the bottom. I always had blankets, sheets and pillows to keep her comfortable.

I always brought extra clean clothes because she might soil herself more than once on a trip. Extra diapers, incontinence pads, cleaning wipes, toilet paper and paper towels were always available. If she had a "accident" I wanted to get her back to normal as soon as possible.

I made a clean up bag in case we were at someones house or a different location. I used this to clean the area before I changed my mom. I cleaned up after we were done so there was no residue or problem. This bag had cleaning wipes, alcohol wipes, household cleaning supplies and disinfectant spray. I never wanted to leave a mess anywhere we went.

Another important thing to bring with you is a trash bag. A lot of times there is no place to dispose of this type of waste so you have to take it home with you. That's where the disinfectant spray really comes in handy. It can be a long ride home especially in the summer.

Have A Disaster Plan

Wherever you live there is a chance of some type of natural disaster. We lived in California and that is earthquake country. Everyday there was a chance of a small tremor or the "Big One." One time we had, what I thought was a large earthquake, shake the house. It felt like someone picked up the house and dropped it. I jumped out of bed, ran into my mom's bedroom and started getting her out of bed. It stopped a few seconds later and thanks to computer technology I was able to see that it only registered

2.1 on the Richter Scale. The difference was it was centered about two blocks away and close to the surface. I thought it was the start of the "Big One." Foolish on my part because if it was the "Big One" I would have had a hard time running into my mom's bedroom.

I did have a plan for earthquake, fire and flood or as they say, "Shake, Bake and Surf." In case of possible flood the smartest and easiest thing to do was leave when there was a chance of flooding. We lived near the "concrete river" otherwise known as the Los Angeles River, so if the officials thought it was going to crest its bank we would have left for higher ground. One year this almost happened but it was just below the warning stage so we never had to leave.

A fire on the other hand, one would have little warning. Hopefully the first warning would be one of the many smoke alarms screaming in the house. We had many doors and windows in the house so barring a complete collapse we would be able to escape without any problems. I had a separate wheelchair that I purchased always in the car as well as our "go-bag." I would lift my mom out of bed and place her in the interior wheelchair and wheel her to the side walk while I pulled the car out of the driveway. I would then lift her into the car and we would be far enough away from the burning house and call 911. Hopefully the fire department would be arriving soon to douse the flames. She was the priority and her safety was more important than the house. The 911 would be to save the house because she was already safe.

An earthquake on the other hand happens without any warning. It starts and "bam" it keeps getting worse or it subsides. In this case I would try to get to my mom as fast as possible. Depending on the size of the earthquake the shaking could be so intense that it would be almost impossible to walk. I would get to her any way I could and do my best to cover her and make sure she was safe. When I would be able I would lift her and take her outside away from any falling debris. In this situation your on your own and there is no 911 to call. We always had food stocked away just in case of a disaster so we could survive for many days. That was even true if the house collapsed.

The closet thing we had to a disaster was when the power went out for two days. Lightening struck a power transformer and we lost power during the night. She had an air mattress so the compressor stopped. She rang her bell and yelled, "Jim, I'm going down." I woke up and went into her room and disconnected the bed compressor from the wall outlet and connected it to my battery back up. In a few minutes the bed was back to normal and she went back to sleep. The batteries lasted through the night and she slept without a problem. The next day we learned their was a lot of damage to the power lines so I charged the battery back up with the inverter I installed in my Saturn. The batteries charged in a few hours and we were ready for the next night. I had flashlights and DC lights available and we were able to function with only a little inconvenience. We played cards at night and went about our normal routine. We had natural gas appliances so cooking was never a problem. We didn't open the refrigerator unnecessarily so nothing defrosted. Like my mom said, "It was like the old times."

We had no problems because we were prepared. Granted we were still in the city but unlike the neighbors we didn't have to scramble for flashlights and batteries. We had food and we had back up power. We were good to go and I thought is was a good dry run for a real disaster.

Know What To Do For All Situations

I am not a trained professional but I tried to learn as much as I could about taking care of my parents. I knew their medical history and condition. I knew what they could tolerate and what they could not. Their likes and dislikes were all known to me. Having this information did make it easier to be able to take care of them.

I also had to learn general first aid and in my mom's case wound care. I had to learn how to give insulin shots and supply oxygen. I did learn CPR just in case I needed it. I had to dispense medications and see if there were any side effects. Such as being on a water pill can cause a potassium deficiency so I would give my mom or dad a banana a day to keep this level normal.

Little things like this you learn over time by asking a lot of questions when they go to the doctor or hospital. I would watch how the hospital staff would handle other patients and would learn from what I saw. I would ask the doctor if this procedure would help and they would say yes or no.

You have to be ready at home or on the road. Anything can happen and you need to be prepared. A natural disaster could happen while you are away from home so you might need to be away for a few days. We lived in California, earthquake country, and I always had that in the back of my mind. We could be on the road when an earthquake struck so I needed to be prepared for a few days away from the house. I was prepared for an earthquake, snow and flood.

Caregiving is always a learning experience and you will never know everything. Medicine is changing daily and so is caregiving. New technologies and procedures are making a huge difference in the quality of care. Knowing what to do is the result of learning whatever you can.

Chapter 35

HEALTH RISKS AND BEING A CAREGIVER

Health Exposure Risks

When you are taking care of your parent you always have to be aware of health risks. Someone can visit that is sick and this can cause your parents also to become sick as well as yourself. The same can happen when you go out into crowds or visit family and friends.

I had a strict rule that I followed when I was taking care of my parents. If you felt sick or thought you were becoming ill, do not come over. My parents received their flu shot yearly but I still did not want to take any chances with them getting sick. This caused some problems because the grandchildren were young and in school so catching a cold or flu was pretty normal for them. One of my sisters was also an LVN and she came into contact with a lot people that were sick so she took special care when she came over. She also skipped a lot of visits just to be safe.

The same happened when we went out as I tried to keep them away from people that were coughing and sneezing. The worst place was always going to the doctors office and it seemed that every time you got into the elevator someone was coughing, perspiring or sneezing. I would cringe when we were in a crowded elevator or in one that had a sick child because you never knew what was floating around.

I had the same rule for when we went to visit the family. If anyone was sick or feeling sick let us know so we would not visit. This caused some problems with my mom because she would anticipate seeing her grandchildren and great grandchildren. If they were sick I would cancel the visit until they got better. I needed to be safe because I did not want her to get ill and possibly have some serious problems.

The biggest problem was if I got sick, there was no way for me to avoid my mom. I had to pick her up several times a day and if I had something there was a good chance she was going to catch it. That's why I got the same vaccines as she did so we would be protected together.

This was a constant worry but we survived over all the years I took care of my parents. Being cautious payed off and they never caught the flu or a serious cold. It did cause some disappointments when they couldn't visit the family but they also knew it was for their own good.

Germs

One of the things you always have to be concerned with while you are taking care of a parent is germs. As they get older their resistance is low and they are susceptible to colds and infection. You have to be aware of who is around them and need to stay away from people that are sick. You and them have to wash your hands every time you come in contact with possible forms of germs.

I made sure the house was always clean and the bathroom fixtures were cleaned with disinfectant. If we went out and we had to use the facilities I had a bag with disinfectant and towels so I made sure the fixtures were clean. I had to be prepared for any event and situation.

I had my mom wash her hands all the time. To make it easier I always had baby wipes available and whenever we went out and she touched something she would wash her hands with the baby wipe. I know they weren't disinfectant wipes but I thought those were too harsh for her skin. It worked because she never caught a cold or the flu.

Another form of prevention was her yearly flu vaccine and I would also get one just to be safe. If we were going to a family event I always checked to see if anyone was sick, felt sick or was getting over a cold. If the answer was yes we didn't go to the event. It was better for her to be safe than sick. At her age a simple cold could easily turn into something worse and I didn't want to take a chance.

Another thing to consider was the weather. If it was raining or snowing we didn't go out unless it was absolutely necessary. If I could change the doctors appointment I would so I wouldn't have to take my mom out into the elements. Once again a little precaution went a long way.

I might have been a little over protective or too careful but I was always afraid of more complications for my mom. She had a pneumonia shot and her yearly flu vaccine as protection but they don't cover all influenza. I had to do my best to make sure she didn't get any germs that could cause problems for her in the future.

Contagious Diseases

Keeping your parents away from contagious diseases is a full time job. Most of the time you have no idea where they can be exposed because it can be anywhere. One of the worst places is the doctors office, hospital or any medical facility. Crowded rooms, elevators, halls can all be a problem and they are very few ways to identify a problem.

The same goes for your parent and you have to be sure that they don't have any medical conditions that can affect others. That is why you have to work closely with their doctor and thoroughly understand their condition and limitations. You would not want to have your parent have a condition that could infect everyone that came in contact with them. This is not only serious medically it could also be criminal. Once again it is your responsibility as their caregiver to know their condition and how it has to be handled.

You never know who you might come in contact with that might have a contagious disease. All you can do is be on alert and wash whatever comes in contact with strangers. Those that are close to you, such as family and friends, should have the common sense to stay away if they or sick or contagious. The same goes for you, if there is a problem you need to check with your doctor and if necessary, you need to remove yourself from taking care of your parent until you are cleared. It would be a serious situation and it would definitely makes things harder and more expensive for you.

Elevators And Confined Spaces

One of the worst places to catch germs is in an elevator or a confined space. When you're taking care of a parent you have to take them to the doctors frequently. Doctors offices are usually confined spaces with a lot of sick people. Usually to get to the doctors office you have to use the elevator to get to the proper floor of the medical building.

I would always cringe every time we had to go to the doctors office and ride an elevator. My folks had their flu shots and pneumonia vaccine but you never knew what type of germ was floating around in the elevator or doctors office. People are coughing and there is no place for that spray to go except on the other people in the area. Even if they cover their mouth you always feel like you got hit with a germ or two. A lot of times children cough and sneeze without covering their mouth and that spray just spreads.

You go to the doctor to get better and maintain your health. Unfortunately you have to go through a mine field of germs on the way in and out. The only thing you can do is to take precautions such as a flu shot. Some can take vitamins to help build up their immune system such as Vitamin C and Zinc. I gave my dad and mom Zinc and Vitamin C everyday to help prevent colds and to keep them healthy. Our doctor told us that this was a little prevention and could help prevent serious problems. With my mom the Zinc also helped the wound on her backside heal faster.

Elevators and confined offices are a breeding ground for germs and bacteria. I have said I am no doctor or health professional, but I can say that I followed our doctors orders in taking care of my parents. To prevent possible infections they got the pneumonia shot, yearly flu vaccinations, took Vitamin C and Zinc everyday. I do think it helped because they never caught a serious cold or flu. You must be cautious and careful when you enter an elevator or go into a confined office. If there is someone sneezing or coughing it might be a good idea to wait for the next elevator or stay outside the office until that person leaves. You are responsible for your parent and their condition so you need to be aware of the surroundings

Always Wash Your Hands

To prevent germs and the spread of bacteria you must always wash your hands. Every time you do a procedure, wear gloves and make sure you wash your hands afterwards. Get in a habit of having your parent also always washing their hands. If they can't do it themselves do it for them. If they are not able to get to a sink use baby wipes so they can clean their hands. When you take them out they are exposed to all kinds of bacteria and germs that could cause them harm and a simple solution is just washing their hands.

We did this all the time and I made sure both parents followed the routine. I went to a restaurant supply and bought those aloe cleaning wipes so I could keep them in the car. When we left the doctors office we would wash our hands with these wipes. I also carried a container of baby wipes in the car for the same purpose. This way if we stopped to get something to eat while we were on the road we could wash our hands and eat without contaminating our food. When we left any medical facility we always washed our hands when we got into the car. I would use a moist towelette on the door handles and steering wheel to make sure they were also clean.

We did this for years and we never received any kind of infection. I didn't want anything to happen to cause more problems than we already had and this was a way to prevent things from happening. Bacteria and germs are everywhere you go and in the process of being out you touch many surfaces. It is not being paranoid about germs but it is about being aware. Once again it is about common sense and trying to prevent problems from occurring.

Chapter 36

PRECAUTIONS WHILE BEING A CAREGIVER

Don't Tell You Everything

One thing you have to be careful of when you are taking care of a parent is that they don't tell you everything. A lot of the time they don't want you to worry or they don't want to alarm you so they don't tell you when something is wrong. Another part of this is that they don't want to burden you with more work. Therefore you have to be vigilant about their condition at all times and notice anything that might be different or wrong.

I heard many times from both my dad and mom when I would find something out of the ordinary and I would ask them, "Why didn't you tell me?" The answer was always the same, "I didn't want to worry you." The first time my dad spit up a little blood he didn't tell me for two days. He coughed while he was in bed, grabbed a tissue and I saw a tinge of red in the mucus. When I asked, "When did this start?" thinking he would say just now he said, "A few days ago." I made him get dressed while I was calling the doctor and then we left for the emergency room. That was a false alarm and they didn't find a problem but once again his response was, "I didn't want you to worry."

My mom was pretty good about telling me when she didn't feel good or something was wrong except for the time she felt a spot under her arm. I noticed her checking under her arm for a few days and when I asked her about it she told me, "I think I have a bump." When I looked sure enough there was a little bump on her right side where she had her mastectomy. I called her oncologist and made an appointment. He took a biopsy and sure enough it was cancerous and she had it removed. Fortunately that was the one and only time she kept anything major away from me. Once in a while she still kept little things away like a scratchy throat but she would eventually tell me if I didn't notice.

By being their caregiver you know your parent better than anyone else. You know their moods, behavior and routines. You will know if they are not telling you something just by the way they act and react. That's how I knew if something was wrong because I knew my parents routines like a book. If something was not normal I knew it when they changed their usual habit.

Don't Know What Is Safe

When someone gets older they lose their ability to know what is safe and what is not. They start losing their eyesight, hearing and taste and that can cause problems for them and you. They might not see or hear hazards around the house or might not know if food has gone bad or not.

When my dad starting getting confused it was when he was starting to fail fast so I didn't have much of a problem with him. My mom put herself in situations a lot of times because she was trying to help. Most of the time it would be when she would try to wheel herself with the wheelchair and she would roll into somebody or something. She had a hard time unlocking the brake so she would have to really work at it but when she did she would roll into whatever was in front of her. This would happen when we went out and she would bump into someone in the store or other location. I always joked with her that I was going to get sued because she was going to run over somebody. When she was in the house many times she would get stuck in the hallway because she couldn't make the turn. No matter how many times I told her not to roll herself in the hall she would always get stuck and call out, "Jim, I'm stuck."

This was the only problem I had with her because she was stubborn and wanted to try to do things for herself. Her eyesight was pretty good and her hearing wasn't bad for her age so she didn't get into bad situations because she couldn't see or hear them. One thing I never had to worry about was her sense of taste. She liked food and would definitely know when something was bad.

Once again because everyone and every situation is different we all have things to deal or not deal with. My parents were able to stay out of danger because they were still able to see, hear and taste. Someone else might not be so lucky and have to be watched all the time so they don't hurt them self or those around them.

Don't Scold Them

One thing I never did when I was taking care of my parents was to scold them for something they did. Yes, they made mistakes and messes but that is no reason to scold them and make them feel inferior. People lose patience and snap out when something goes wrong or a problem arises but this can make your parent feel bad or afraid to try to do something.

My parents made a lot of mistakes and messes that caused me a lot more work. They were upset when this happened because they knew it meant more work for me. Things happen and usually happen when you have a ton of other stuff to do but that is still no reason to scold your parent. They're trying and most of the time they are trying to help you. Once again it depends on their condition but no matter what it is it doesn't justify scolding them. You can explain what they did wrong in a calm voice and show them how to do a task so it doesn't happen again but for no reason should you get mad. Lack of patience and frustration do creep into the situation while you are taking care of your parents but you are the adult in the room and you need to act like one. Take a deep breath and correct the situation in a calm and patient manner. You can tell them that they made a mistake and then deal with the consequences and or clean up. You don't want to scold them because they will get upset, cry and even cause more problems because they will get nervous and try to correct the situation. That could lead to even more errors or they could hurt themselves.

Patience and a calm tone is part of being a caregiver. You need to know this from the very beginning because you probably will be challenged with this scenario everyday. If you can't be patient and tolerant then maybe you need to rethink your decision because it could be a long and difficult road ahead.

Don't Put Them Down

Nobody ever wants to be told that they are always doing something wrong and that goes the same for your parent. You can't put them down because they will feel that they have nothing to contribute to their life. Every condition is different but there is nothing that can be gained by constantly putting your parent down. Positive reinforcement can go a long way in helping their attitude toward the future.

I never put my parents down for any reason because I knew that could harm their positive outlook on the future. Sure they made a lot of mistakes and a lot of those caused me a lot more work but I could never put them down no matter what happened. I tried my best to make sure they were always active in their care and putting them down would have allowed them to give up. I didn't want them to give up, I wanted them to fight so they would be around for as long as possible.

I would ask for their advice and a lot of times they had some really good ideas that helped me with their care. If those ideas didn't work out I would tell them, "We tried," and this made them happy because they were participating in their care. They were not completely helpless and they felt they were helping me. I was lucky because they were still attentive and didn't have lapses in memory but even if they did that was no reason to put them down when they made a mistake.

I see how others put down their relatives, even worse, in front of others and it is absolutely disgusting. It is as if everything they do is wrong and they will never do anything right. Overtime this type of attitude will just make it harder on the caregiver because their parent is just going to stop trying. Some get frustrated and start losing their patience because they feel that their parents are not listening to them. They are still your parent and you need to show them respect, even if they don't know what you are doing. Putting them down will only make their condition worse and in the end it will make more work for you.

Defensive When Told What To Do

I never told my parents what to do. When I wanted them to do something I would always ask them. They never refused and by asking it prevented any type of conflict. Most of the time they felt that they were helping me and did the task that I asked. I never wanted to put them on the defensive and feel that I was trying to push them around and giving them orders. They were still my parents and I wanted them to feel like they still had control and know that I still had respect for them.

Now that I am no longer taking care of my parents I am noticing how others are taking care of their parents. Once again I don't know their particular situation so I can't judge what others are doing. I do see a lot of people telling their parent what to do in very strong voices. A lot of times I see the parent dig in their heels, become stubborn and refuse to do the task. I also see the parent talk back and protest when they are given orders.

I do know one situation and that is with my cousin and his father. My uncle is still capable of doing a lot of things for himself and he is still able to drive. My cousin has his own business and takes a lot of time off to help his dad. He tries to help him any way he can and his dad is also very stubborn. He feels that there are a lot of things he can still do for himself and he is going to do them. My cousin gives him his space and lets him do as much as he can by himself. The problem is with my cousin's wife because no matter what my uncle does, in her eyes, he is doing it wrong. She is very vocal about it and my uncle gets very defensive and then he throws his hands up in disgust. I try to tell her to let him do things himself and enjoy the time he is still able to do some tasks. I told her when the time comes when he can no longer do tasks she will look back and wish for earlier times. It falls on deaf ears and I can only see this situation get worse. She gets mad at my cousin because he gives his dad a lot of breathing room and that he needs to reign in his father. She made it clear that he needs to tell his dad what to do and not ask him. People handle situations differently and only time will tell if this is the right approach.

Once in a while my parents would snap at me when I asked them to do a task. It might have been because they were busy, didn't want to be interrupted or just didn't want to do it. Sooner or later they would complete the task and nothing more needed to be said. This asking approach worked very well for me over the twenty years I took care of both of them.

You Can't Be Rigid, You Must Be Flexible

One thing I found out very early when I was taking care of my dad was that I couldn't be rigid with his normal routine. Yes, I did have to be firm so that he took his medications and did what the doctor ordered but I also had to be flexible and do it on his schedule. If I tried to push a little harder my dad would always push back and dig in his heals. He knew that I was only thinking of his well being but he wanted to be in control of his life. I decided to step back and make recommendations and let him decide when he was going to do them. I changed my schedule and routine to make things more pleasant for him. It worked and we never had any problems.

With my mom I started this routine from the very beginning. I was never rigid with her daily routines but I did put time schedules in place for her medications. We talked about the time schedule and she made her points and I made mine and we settled on a schedule that satisfied both of us. Even with tasks that she wanted to perform I showed patience and let her do it at her own pace. This kept stress levels down for both of us and there was never any tension.

Now that I am no longer taking care of my dad and mom I have noticed how others treat their parents while they are caring for them. Some want everything done to their schedule and there are no changes. They force their parent to change and then wonder why they protest or fight back. I see this with almost everyone I see taking care of a parent. They show no patience and don't bend to accommodate their parent. They don't realize that their parent is also not budging because they don't want to be told what to do. When I make a suggestion to be flexible or tell them about the situation the answer is usually the same, "I'm in control and they will do it my way." This type of attitude only leads to stressful situations and could cause problems in the future. Being a caregiver means you have to have patience and be flexible in all of your routines and tasks.

Mental Abuse

One thing you have to be careful is in the way you talk to your parent. Raising your voice constantly, telling them to do things, scolding them, etc., because it can point toward mental abuse. Their minds are not as strong as when they were younger and constantly telling them they're wrong or to stop doing something can play havoc on their mental state. Once again it depends on your situation and their condition.

I tried to never raise my voice to my parents unless it was so they could hear me. I always tried to be positive even when they did something wrong. I never wanted to put them down for any reason so they felt inferior. Sometimes under pressure or exhaustion I would snap and have a short to the point answer. After I caught myself I would apologize for being quick to answer without an explanation. It is very hard to do but you can't let them get upset and start playing mind games because it will always come back to hurt them and you.

I have seen people constantly talking down to their parent or yelling at them in public. Some never have anything positive to say to them and they want them to feel inferior. Once again I didn't know their situations so I can't judge but it just seems strange.

Whenever you take them to a hospital or other medical facility your parents are not only checked for physical abuse but they are also interviewed for mental abuse as well. Any short comings on your part will sooner or later come to light and you will have to explain yourself. The best solution to this possible problem is to avoid it from the start and to show patience and understanding.

I never was concerned about these interviews because I was doing the best I could with my parents situations. I always kept a positive attitude and atmosphere so they would not get confused or upset. It is not just to prevent possible legal problems is also just the right thing to do.

Chapter 37
YOUR INJURIES WHILE BEING A CAREGIVER
Cracked Rib?

I learned the hard way that there are no breaks when you are taking care of your parents. It was when my dad was in the hospital and my mom was having a hard time dealing with his condition because he was just diagnosed with lung cancer. We left the hospital and we stopped at a restaurant for dinner. It was a cold night and it was raining so I had to make sure my mom didn't slip on the wet ground when she got into the car. She could still walk so I stood behind her so she couldn't slip. She stepped onto the running board and fell back a little. Since I was standing behind her I caught her so she didn't fall and I helped her into the car. The next morning when I woke up I had a sharp pain on my right side just under my ribs. It hurt to move and breath and I thought I cracked a rib when I helped my mom get into the car.

We got ready and I took her back to the hospital to stay with my dad. The pain on my side got worse over the next day so I went to see my doctor friend. He poked around and said he didn't think it was a cracked rib. He took a chest x-ray and said I had a partial pneumonia and that was causing the pain. He prescribed medication and said I needed to rest. He said I was okay to take care of my mom because she had a pneumonia shot but I should stay away from dad for a few days. So my two sisters helped by taking our mom to see our dad in the hospital.

This thing hurt like hell and I swore I had a cracked rib. I did what the doctor said and after a few days with the medication the pain started to subside. It was hard because I still tried to protect my mom from falling when she was home or when she got in and out of the car. I also had to stay away from my dad for a while but it was what needed to be done. I was on the telephone constantly with his doctors to check on his condition and find out what the treatment would be. I got through it and after about a week I was back to my normal self when my dad was ready to come home.

I still remember how painful it was and how it hindered my movements. My doctor was spot on with his diagnosis because he was a pulmonary specialist so he knew what the symptoms were for pneumonia. I did what he said and I recovered rapidly because I knew I had some serious tasks and responsibilities up ahead.

Back Problems

I always believed you have to take care of yourself in order to take care of your parent and I always followed this advice. I got flu shots and even the pneumonia vaccine later so I could stay healthy and take care of my mom. I went to the doctors regularly to keep my blood pressure in check and had routine lab work done semi-annually to make sure my body was working properly. I maintained a healthy diet for my mom and myself. All this works well but it can't prevent the unexpected and that happened once when I was lifting my mom.

One day my mom had to go to the bathroom in the afternoon while she was sitting in the wheelchair. We had done this routine many times and there was nothing unusual. I wheeled her into her bedroom, turned on the air mattress, cut the tabs on her diaper and pushed the diaper between her legs to the bottom of the wheelchair. She was in front of the bathroom door as usual and I lifted up. Once in a while the diaper got stuck on her and this was one of those times. As I was holding her in front of the toilet I reached around and grabbed the diaper while she was holding on to me by my neck, As I started lowering her to the toilet I felt something give on the lower left side on my back. I felt something squirt out and then the area got hot along with a tremendous amount of pain. I put her on the toilet and stood straight up and I was in tremendous pain. I tried holding it and it just throbbed and hurt. I tried to lay on the bed and then I couldn't get up and when I finally did it hurt even more. All this time my mom is in the bathroom doing her business and yelling, "What's wrong." I finally told her I hurt my back. I tried everything to settle the pain but nothing worked. This went on for a while and then I started wondering how I was going to get her off the toilet. I couldn't call my sisters because they were working and at this time there were no neighbors available to help. Sure enough a few minutes later she rang her bell and said, "I'm done." I walked into the bathroom and as soon as I bent down the pain became intense. I tried to lift her but I had no strength. I told her she was going to have to wait a few minutes as I tried to settle my back. Her bed was prepped and ready for her so all I had to do was lift her off the toilet and place her on the bed and turn her to lay flat. At this time she could still clean herself so all I would have to do is make sure she was clean and then replace her diaper. I was walking around the house and the pain would not go away and it felt like it was getting worse. An hour went by and my mom was still in the bathroom and the pain was still intense. I tried ice and nothing happened, I tried to sit and couldn't, I tried putting pressure against it and that seemed to help a little. She told me she was getting tired so I had to do something. I got an old wide belt and put it around me and the area were the pain was the worst. I pulled it tight and it seemed to numb the pain. I got in front of her and lifted her up. It hurt a lot but I was able to get her to the bed and put her down. I turned her to lay flat and raised the bed rail. At this point my back hurt like hell, was burning and throbbing. I tried to walk it off and tighten the belt but nothing worked. I finally took a deep breath and gritted my teeth and replace her diaper. She was in bed and safe.

I took some over the counter pain medication to help but it did very little. We had a grab bar in the shower so I got in and pointed the shower head on my back and sprayed the area with hot water. This soothed the pain a little and as long as I was in the shower it was bearable. When I got out of the shower it still hurt but not as much and I was able to make dinner. I kept my mom in bed the rest of the night and hoped she didn't have to have a bowel movement during the night. I gave her dinner in bed and I kept going in and out of the shower to alleviate the pain.

That night I got in bed and the pain once again started to intensify. I took some more medication and laid down. I got into a position that didn't hurt as much but was not comfortable and stayed that way till morning. The next morning it was time to get up and I knew it was going to hurt. I rolled and got to the edge of the bed and dropped my legs. I had put my mom's old walker on the side of the bed in case I needed help getting up. I did, so I pulled it closer to me. Hunched over I grabbed the walker, took a deep breath and stood up. I hurt bad and the pain almost brought me down again. I got a hold of myself and used the walker to hold me while I got to the bathroom and into the shower. I put the hot water on my back and the pain settled down a little.

I remembered that my dad had a back brace in a drawer from when he hurt his back many years before. It was still there so I put it on. It was a little worn and loose but with the help of a belt I was able to draw it tight. This seemed to work and I was able to move a little better. The pain was still there but I could handle it better. The big test would be if I had to lift my mom.

I told her the day before that she might have to stay in bed longer because of the injury to my back. She agreed and did her normal clean up routine in bed. I gave her breakfast and all was going well. I would go in the shower frequently to use the handheld pulsing shower head to heat up my lower back and make it a little more bearable. My mom called and had to go to the bathroom so this was going to be a big test. I put on the back brace, belt and pulled it tight. I cut her diaper tabs and pivoted her to the side of the bed and pushed the diaper all the way through so it wouldn't get stuck on her body. I took a deep breath and lifted her off the bed. It hurt a lot but I could handle the pain and I put her on the toilet so she could do her business. We succeeded in one lift now we had one more to go. When she was finished I tightened the brace and belt more, took a deep breath again and lifted. This time there was more pain but I still could bear it as I lifted her to the bed. Once she was on the bed we were done. I got back in the shower to massage the lower back area and then came out and put her diaper on. We survived two lifts.

I called a doctor I knew that handled back injuries and he made room for me the next day. This was going to be a problem because I had to take my mom to the doctors with me. The next day came and the back was a little better but I still had to go through the same routine of standing up. I got my mom ready the same way with the exception that I put her in a wheelchair instead of the bed when she was finished. I placed a new diaper in the wheelchair and then lifted her on top of it and affixed the tabs. I had my back brace and belt on when I wheeled her to the Suburban and lifted her onto the front seat. It hurt but I was able to do it and then I took off the brace and belt. I was in more pain when I tried to get into the drivers seat because I had to slide behind the steering wheel. We got to the doctors and after I put on my brace and belt I was able to get her out of the car and into the wheelchair.

After x-rays the doctor confirmed that I had an inflamed disc and it needed rest so the inflammation could go down. When he told me I needed rest he started to laugh and said, "Easy for me to say, impossible for you to do." He knew our situation because he was also talking care of my mom. He prescribed medication to get the inflammation down and we went home.

My sister came over the next day and cooked and cleaned the house for us so I could get a little rest. She couldn't come over sooner because she had to work and was unable to get time off. She brought me a new back brace that was taught and it worked great.

It took about two weeks for my back to get somewhat back to normal if it ever did. From that time on I always wore a back brace and had it tight whenever I lifted my mom. We never had a repeat of that situation and I never had another major problem with my back. I still wear a back brace even after she passed away every time I lift something that looks heavy.

This was a serious situation that could have changed everything. It was an accident or fluke event that you could not foresee. Fortunately for both of us we were able to overcome it.

Chapter 38

SAFETY AND BEING A CAREGIVER

Your Safety

Being a caregiver you are responsible not only for yourself but also the person you're taking care of. If you get hurt you are not only impeding yourself but also your parent. That's why you always need to make sure that you practice safety in all the procedures that you do.

Any procedure that you do, such as lifting, must be done in a safe manner. If you hurt yourself, it becomes almost impossible, very painful or both when you try to lift your parent. Applying bandages can also be a problem if you cut yourself with a scissors. It also becomes less sanitary if you have to apply ointment or medicine with a bandaged hand. Gloves prevent this problem but unfortunately gloves are hard to put on when you have bandages on your hand. You have to be careful of sprays and powders so that they do not go into eyes. There are a multitude of hazards that can come into place while you're taking care of someone. Loose carpets and pillows are a disaster waiting to happen. Clothing can snag on items while you're trying to move them around causing you and your parent to fall. Objects sticking out on a table can drop and cause punctures on legs and feet. Something as small as grains of rice on the floor can cause you to slip and fall while your are moving your parent around. Don't forget about spilled water on the floor. Electrical hazards are another concern. Hair dryers, electric tooth brushes, electric shavers, etc., can be the source of shocks and worse. Then you have misplaced electrical cords that could wrap around your feet and cause a fall. There are so many hazards in and outside the house that you need to be aware of.

The best way to be safe is before you attempt a procedure is to stand back and look to see if anything looks out of place. Look at the floor, walls, ceilings, shelves, tables, doorways, etc., to see if all is in its place. Use lifting belts, back and knee braces as needed. Use gloves and protection masks if necessary. Read and follow the instructions on any equipment you purchase or receive. Use the equipment the way it was designed and don't try to make it do something it wasn't designed for. If you do you could not only hurt yourself but you could also injure your parent. You are responsible for their safety and you could get in serious trouble if you put them at risk because you didn't follow directions. Even if you only hurt yourself, you are hurting them because you cannot take care of them until you get better.

Furniture Hazards

Furniture is another hazard in the home. Chairs can move, rugs can curl and floors can be slippery. When a person is not stable on their feet anything can cause them to trip and fall. Furniture needs to be placed so it can't move when someone leans on it. That includes yourself. Many times when I was lifting my mom I braced myself against a chair so I could get some leverage. Tables can cause falls because they are light and move very easily. Picture frames can fall if they are grabbed and mirrors can easily break. Cushions can cause a fall and chairs can tip over when pushed.

Even if they're in a wheelchair a home is hard to maneuver in. My mom would bang into walls and doors with her wheelchair. Furniture had marks where the wheels scraped as she went by. Sometimes she would get stuck between furniture and was unable to back out. I would be amazed how she could get into places that she shouldn't have been because the wheelchair didn't fit. She would get stuck and call for me to help her.

You need to convert your home by moving furniture that could cause problems. This will prevent your parent from tripping, falling and possibly hurting themselves. It also makes it easier on you because you're eliminating possible disasters.

Unstable Walking

Another problem that comes with aging is unstable walking. As we age it is easier for us to lose our balance and fall. Because of this we try to take careful steps and in the process we walk slower and become unstable.

My dad had difficulty walking not because of his loss of balance but due to his diminished lung capacity. He suffered from a lung disease called asbestosis and it played havoc on his everyday life because he was always short of breath. My mom was always unstable when she walked, it was almost to the point of being clumsy. She always said it was because of her arthritis or because she carried too many books when she was a child and it injured her back. We found out later it was because of scoliosis and curvature of the spine. I had it easier with my mom because she knew and felt unstable. She used a cane on her own and used a walker when it was recommended. She also used a wheelchair from her mid sixties when she went out. She was use to it and had no embarrassment from being in a wheelchair.

My uncle who is now experiencing difficulty is very unstable when he walks. He has a bad knee and years ago tore his Achilles tendon. He refuses to use a cane or walker because he has to overcome the pain mentally and work through it. Good idea but unfortunately he is eighty-seven years old and other problems are creeping up. He uses his wheelchair in the house because it is comfortable and it makes it easier for him to get around. I'm sure there is a little embarrassment here because he doesn't want to be seen as old and if he uses a cane, walker or wheelchair in public it just confirms the situation. The reason I say this is because he refuses to use the wheelchair when he goes out because he says he doesn't need it. When he goes to the store he parks near a shopping cart so he can use it as support while he walks. This is a disaster in the making. My cousin has repeatedly told him to use the cane, walker or wheelchair. I have recommended it on several occasions but he is stubborn and refuses to listen. I can make recommendations but since he is not my responsibility I can't make changes to his lifestyle. His doctor has explained to him several times that he needs to have support when he walks. He tells him he has all the necessary tools and he needs to use them. The doctor told him that all it takes is one fall, a break and it is over. If blunt talk from his doctor doesn't change his attitude and he still refuses, he is rolling the dice on when that fall will come.

My cousin is in a tough spot and I continue to advise him on ways to handle this situation. He is a little hesitant to have the father and son talk where he tells his dad, "I am responsible for everything you do and everything you do affects me." Sooner or later he will have to tell his dad the way it is and hopefully it will be soon before the oncoming fall and bone break.

Chapter 39
YOUR HOME AND BEING A CAREGIVER
House Cleaning

Keeping your home clean is a basic requirement for being a caregiver. A clean home prevents bacteria and virus' from infecting your parent and yourself. Dust can collect rapidly and can cause allergic reactions that can mimic a cold or the flu. Also a clean home can prevent falling hazards or items getting in your way while you are trying to move your parent. One of the worse things that can happen as you are lifting or maneuvering your parent is to trip or snag on something that is in the way. This could cause you to stumble or even fall and cause injury to your parent or yourself.

As people get older, for some reason they keep everything and never throw anything out. That is especially true for those that went through the Great Depression of the 1930s. This might lead to a lot of clutter around the house and it also means a lot more dust. My folks kept everything and it lead to a cluttered house. When they became ill I needed more room to maneuver the wheelchair so all the items that cluttered the house ended up in the garage and storage sheds in the backyard. They wouldn't let me throw anything out so I had to store it. After my dad died I started getting rid of some of the items in the garage that were never used, such as cans of used bent nails, I don't know why he kept these. When we moved from Lynwood to Tehachapi I think we filled the local dump with what was in the garage and storage sheds.

The good news when we moved to the new house it was a little larger about 200 more square feet and we did fill it up. The best news was that we no longer had clutter and I was able to maneuver my mom's wheelchair without bumping into things. The other nice thing was that the dust was reduced. The bad news was the house had wall to wall carpeting and it made it a little stuffy and I had to vacuum constantly. I like hardwood floors because it was easy for my mom to roll herself in the wheelchair and it is also easier to dust.

I did my own house cleaning and it was one of the daily chores. I always wish I had some extra money to hire a maid service but that never became an option. I would clean the house when my mom was busy watching a baseball game or doing some task. I admit I am not a very good house cleaner but I kept the home clean as best I could and free of bacteria. Neither one of us ever got sick because of something in the house. I also kept the house free of clutter so I would not snag something and fall while I was lifting my mother.

Most of it is common sense and just a normal routine. No one wants to live in a dirty home and it is also a reflection on you and possibly the care you give your parent. If a nurse comes to your home they might see it is not clean and they might think you don't care and that might have them questioning the care you are giving your parent. I always remember the first time a home health nurse came to our house for the first visit. She actually went around the house sniffing in each room. When I asked her what she was doing she said, "I'm smelling for pee, I can smell pee anywhere, even a little amount" I was surprised and then she stopped and looked at me and said, "I don't smell any pee." I guess I passed the test.

Home Maintenance

Home maintenance can be an expensive part of caring for your parents because you want to make sure your home is safe and working properly. I was lucky because I was able to do all our home maintenance and repairs so we never had to call a repairman or contractor for any reason. This saved us a lot of money because if something had to be repaired all I needed to do was just purchase the parts or supplies.

My dad and I basically rebuilt our Lynwood home so I pretty much new every inch of the house. I use to joke that that house really had my blood, sweat and tears in it. I new every sound, creak and knew what each one meant and how to fix it.

When we moved to Tehachapi we bought a new home so I needed to learn its sounds. There was very little maintenance on this home because it was new but it still needed care as every home requires. I had very little time to personalize this house because caring for my mom took so much time and I never even painted the walls from the original white. When I sold the house in 2014 it still looked as if it was new.

The basics always need to be of concern such as plumbing and electrical. You want to make sure that there is nothing that could cause a shock hazard or plumbing that constantly backs up. Simple walk throughs every few weeks allow you to make sure the house is in good order. If you smell unusual odors such as plastic or any type of burning you need to make sure that you have it checked because you don't want to have any chance of fire. You must be aware of anything that can cause a problem because if something does happen your first concern is to get your parent out of the house and to safety.

A well maintained home is a safe home and it will also give you piece of mind. It can be expensive and put a strain on the budget but it is something that is necessary. A clean, safe and well maintained home is the best way to provide the proper environment to care for your parent.

Clogged Plumbing

My dad was a pipe fitter for the Navy and he taught me a lot about plumbing. He taught me everything he knew about how plumbing works and how to correct problems. This came in very handy when I was taking care of my mom.

Due to the amount of medication my mom was prescribed to reduce her pain it caused a major side effect, constipation and hard stools were the result. This caused a lot of problems for her and the plumbing system in our house. Most of the time her complications were taken care of by laxatives and stool softeners. These medical conditions also caused problems with the plumbing system in the house. In both houses we never had a situation where the toilets backed up and made a mess on the floor. I was always able to catch the problems before it made a mess of the bathroom and house.

When the toilet would back up I would notice it when I lifted my mom off the toilet and lifted her onto the wheelchair. I would see the paper and other stuff didn't flush down the toilet. After I put her in bed or rolled her into the living room I would use a plunger to push the remnants down the toilet. If that didn't work and the problem was still there I would flush the toilet so it would fill with more water. I would drop four to six denture cleaning tablets in the bowel and let is sit for about an hour. Most of the time this would work and break up the hard clumps and with the help of a plunger down everything went. If it was really clogged I would have to use a toilet snake to loosen everything up and once again down everything went. It was funny because every time this happened my mom would say, "I'm sorry." I'd laugh and say, "Yeah, you did this on purpose," and she would say, "yes I did." It was our little joke every time we had a plumbing problem.

I never had to take the toilet bowel off the floor or have a rooter service come and clean the drains at either house. The problem was always at the toilet because it couldn't handle the hard stools. Once again it was one of those things you never wanted to do or think about. Today with the new water saving toilets this might be a bigger problem. It's just another one of those things you just got to do.

Handicap Friendly Home

Most homes were never built handicap friendly which means they weren't designed to handle wheelchairs. Some bedrooms are small and not capable of supporting a hospital bed. Most main and master bathrooms are also small and don't accommodate shower chairs, walkers and lifts. I thought the American With Disabilities Act would change this with new homes. I was wrong and the new home we purchased in 2008 was not handicap friendly except for the fact that the light switches were lower. The interior doorways were only twenty-eight inches wide and the wheelchair barely fit. I was extremely disappointed with these new surroundings but we adapted to them for our situation.

Taking care of my mom in our Lynwood home was challenging because the home was originally built in 1928 and we remolded it in 1973. When we did the renovation we never considered the use of a wheelchair. The hallways were narrow and the half bath in the master bedroom was small. The bedrooms were large and with a hospital bed there was plenty of room in the master bedroom. The living and dining room were big enough so you could use a wheelchair without bumping into any furniture. The kitchen was straight and once again a wheelchair or walker could maneuver. The only problem was going to the bedrooms through a narrow hallway and we had to make a sharp right turn from the dining room into the hall. The only way to do this was to remove the foot rests from the wheelchair and that worked well.

To take my mom to the bathroom I had her hospital bed next to the bathroom and I was able to lift her from the bed to the toilet. To make things easier I removed the bathroom door which gave me more room to maneuver. The bathroom door was only twenty-four inches wide so any extra arm room helped. We did this for years and we never had any problems.

The biggest problem with this house was that it was on a raised foundation which meant three steps. I never had a chance to build a ramp so when we went out it was three steps down and three steps up. The wheelchair had the large wheels so it wasn't that difficult and we got very good at going up and down the stairs.

When we decided to move to Tehachapi I took my mom in the wheelchair when we went and looked at the model homes. The model we looked at was larger and there was no problem moving the wheelchair around the house the only problem was going through the interior doors. They had a smaller house in our price range and one was available so the salesperson met us at the location and let us in. The house was built on a slab so there were no steps but there was about a two inch step up to the floor. The inside of the house was open but once again the interior doors were narrow and I asked the sales person about the American With

Disabilities Act. She told me that they were only required to put the light switches lower and the rest of the ADA did not apply to these homes. I was surprised but we liked the area and I felt I could make the house work for us. We purchased the home and moved in.

Living in the home there was not much difference than our previous home. The hallway was wider but the interior doors were only twenty-eight inches wide and the wheelchair barely fit. In our old home the doors were thirty inches wide and there was no problem pushing a wheelchair through. In fact my mom could wheel herself through the hallway and doors without a problem. In the new house she couldn't do it. Part of the problem was the wall to wall carpeting which caused the wheels to be harder than normal to push. The house had an open floor plan in the living and dining rooms but because of the carpet she could not get around. The kitchen was large and she was able to maneuver her wheelchair once she was pushed onto the linoleum. I was going to replace the carpet with hardwood floors but it was too expensive and we never did. The master bedroom was large and the hospital bed fit with no problems but the Hoyer lift could not maneuver in the bedroom. The master bathroom had a large oval tub and the shower chair just barely fit over the side so it was always a chore to put my mom in the shower. The big problem was where the toilet was located. It was a little room with no window and it was only three feet wide with a twenty-four inch door. To get her from the bed meant I had to lift her from the bed to the wheelchair and from the chair to the toilet. The other option was to carry her from the bed directly to the toilet which was about fifteen feet. Since there were no windows I always had to keep a flashlight handy in case the power went out so my mom wouldn't be left in the dark. This happened quite a few times because the neighborhood lost power two or three times a year.

This house caused more work because of the poor layout but we adapted to make it work for us. Dealing with all the problems I now would be able to design a house that was wheelchair and caregiver friendly. I was amazed that new homes, as of 2008, were not required by the American With

Disabilities Act to be wheelchair and handicap friendly.

Home Retrofits

Smoke detectors are a must in all homes and in some locations they are required by law. Carbon monoxide detectors are needed in homes that have gas appliances and are also required in some areas. If it is in your budget you might consider making some home retrofits that would make some tasks easier and safer for your parent. Something as simple as a grab bar in the tub or shower can go a long way in keeping your parent stable and safe. If you have natural gas or propane appliances an alarm that alerts you to small amounts of gas in the air might be an option to consider. This could alert you if you or your parent left a stove valve in the on position. Some retrofits also benefit the caregiver as well because they can make your routines a little less work.

I had a lot of construction and carpentry experience so I was able to do all the retrofits to our house by myself and that saved us a lot of money. I only had to purchase the parts and I supplied the labor. In fact on some retrofits my mom helped by handing me the parts and tools. By getting her involved this made sure that she would use the item because she "helped."

The simplest retrofit is grab bars next to the toilet and in the tub. These items are available at most home improvement stores, medical equipment supply and some hardware stores. Follow the instructions that come with the unit so you install it correctly. You definitely want to do a good job here because if you don't when your parent reaches and grabs the bar it could come out of the wall. If your skills are not up to the task, don't have time or just don't want to do it, hire a professional to install them. These give a lot of support so you parent can reposition themselves on the toilet and stabilize them while they do their "business." Grab bars in the tub allow them to hold themselves steady why you wash them and also give you something to lean on while you are reaching in. Used with a shower chair or tub stool they give that added support so your parent so they don't fall.

If they're in a wheelchair, a ramp comes in very handy especially if you live in a house with a raised foundation or basement. I never had the time to construct one of these for my mom so I just lifted her up the three steps in the wheelchair. A ramp also comes in handy if your parent uses a walker because they wont have to climb up the steps.

Large faucet and tub handles can help because they are easier to turn. A hand held shower head come in handy because they can wash themselves all over while they are sitting in a shower chair. It also helps you if you're the one giving them the shower because you can spray the water right where it is needed. Be prepared for a little more cleaning if they rinse themselves because from experience my mom washed the entire bathroom when she tried to rinse herself.

There are many items available to make their and your life a lot easier. With the new wireless remotes any item can be turned on and off remotely. Covers for stove knobs are a safety feature that can prevent accidental gas leaks. There are stair lifts to help your parent get upstairs and not to mention the new fancy sit in showers and tubs. There are so many items, accessories and retrofits available that I have no idea what all of them are. I only know of the ones that we needed to keep my mom safe and steady.

Once again every situation is different and so is every medical condition. Whatever your situation, there might be an item, accessory or retrofit that might make it easier and safer. They are not cheap and it also depends on your budget and how much you can afford.

Chapter 40
CONCERNS AND BEING A CAREGIVER
Watch Out For Falls

One of the most dangerous situations for an elderly person is a fall. One of the most dangerous places for a fall is inside the house. As a caregiver you need to be aware of the surroundings and try your best to prevent anything that could cause a fall. With so many items in a home this can be an overwhelming task.

Even when my mom was able to walk she was unstable on her feet. This was due to her scoliosis, curvature of the spine and arthritis. Back in 1997 I was working in the garden, she came outside to see what I was doing and fell. She was using a cane and for some reason instead of planting the cane perpendicular to the ground she placed it at an angle. As she told me, "It just slipped out from under me." After picking her up off the ground I checked her over to see if there were any problems. There was no blood, broken bones, sprains, cuts or bruises. She was okay so I thought. In 2005 when she was getting dentures and the oral surgeon was going to pull a few teeth that were bad he asked if she had ever fallen and hit her mouth. I told him about the incident in 1997 and I told him I never saw her mouth hit the ground and that there was no blood. He said it probably happened fast and it was just enough to crack two teeth. She never complained about teeth or gum pain but I felt horrible.

This fall happened outside but we also had a couple of tumbles inside the house. She slipped on a scatter rug in the bedroom but only fell to her knees. Once again I checked her out and there was no blood or broken bones. She fell once in the living room when she reached for a chair and it moved so she went down again. After this I removed all the scatter rugs and moved the chairs against walls or bookcases. I bought her a walker so she would be more stable in the house. Unfortunately after she got the walker I was the one that got the bruises. She would roll the walker on my feet or place it behind me so I would trip on it. I should have figured this was going to happen because when she used a cane she would always place the cane on my foot when she was near me. Even after she was in a wheelchair my feet weren't safe. She rolled over them anytime I was near. I have large feet so I guess they got in the way.

The house is full of fall hazards. Even the smallest thing could cause a fall. A piece of paper is enough to cause a fall because they could step on it and it could slide on the floor. Towels, wrappers, rugs, yarn, food, anything could be a hazard and cause them to fall. Walk around and check to see if anything is in their path. Tape or attach things that can move or slip. Check to see if any objects could snag them as they go by or wrap around their legs. You have to stay ahead of them and try to prevent a fall. Outdoors is also difficult because it could be anything from a small amount of liquid on the sidewalk that could cause them to fall. It could be a bug or even bird poop that is slippery and causes them to slip and fall. You have to try to anticipate what could make them fall and that's not an easy job.

Bruises

There are a lot of things you have to be aware of while being a caregiver. One of the important ones is to watch out for bruises. As your parent ages their skin is thin and they bruise very easily.

With my mom I was always aware of bruises. After she received the bed sores in the hospital I was told by the wound center that she was susceptible to bruises and sores. This is not something you want to hear with an elderly parent. Just lifting or touching them the wrong way could cause a bruise. In this day of elder abuse just going to a lab or outpatient facility could cause a problem. In most states, the health professionals are required by law to report signs of elder abuse. They are professionals so they have way of spotting abuse versus normal bruising but it is still unnerving when you go into a facility and your parent has a bruise.

Sometimes we would go to a lab and after they drew blood she would have a bruise. It seemed the bruises happened more frequent when we went to outpatient facilities or she had a hospital stay. When we went for scans and x-rays she would bruise because of the movement on the table. She could not turn herself in bed so that is why we had the air mattress at home. When she in the hospital they never turned her enough so she would bruise. The exception was the last time she was in the hospital in 2013. This was after Medicare changed their rules on hospital bed sores. They turned her every few hours so she was never in the same position. Unfortunately because her skin was thin this constant turning caused bruises. In fact when I took her home one side of her body was bruised, I made sure it was documented so I called our doctor to tell him about the situation. I took her in to see him so he knew that the bruises were caused by the hospital stay and not me.

Whenever my mom was admitted into the hospital they would do an inspection of her body and note any abnormalities. I was not allowed to be in the room and would have to stay in the hall. I always knew there wasn't a problem but you're nervous because the nurse could see something that you missed or interpret it differently. Fortunately we never had a problem and they would come out and say she was in good shape. That was always a sign of relief and we could then concentrate on the condition that sent her to the hospital.

In recent years doctors offices, outpatient facilities, labs and other healthcare offices are required to check all patients for abnormal bruising. They also ask the patient questions to see if they are being taken care of properly. This is a sign of the times because there is so much elder abuse and as long as you take care of your parent properly you shouldn't be worried.

Can't Taste And Smell

Some elderly people have a problem with their taste and smell. This can be a problem if they try to feed themselves because they might not be able to taste or smell bad food. Another problem could be that they would not be able to smell a gas leak in the house putting them at risk.

Once again you need to be aware of your parents condition and be able to handle them so they can't harm themselves or possibly even you. You are the best judge of what they can and can't do because you know their condition and routines like no one else. If they have a problem with their taste your smell, you need to be the one preparing their food so you know it always fresh and good.

If they have trouble smelling odors they should not be left alone if you have gas appliances in your home. If they can walk or even maneuver a wheelchair in the house they could accidentally turn on the gas control on the stove. If the burner does not light and they can't smell the gas the kitchen could fill up with gas and it could become an explosion hazard. My cousin had a situation like this with his dad, my uncle, who lives across the street. They were away and my cousin called his dad to check on him. While they were talking you could hear a snapping sound in the background. My cousin had him turn on the camera on his smart phone and he saw that my uncle was in the kitchen. He uses a wheelchair in his house and he was in front of the stove. My cousin told him to turn around and check and see if the stove control was on. Sure enough the wheelchair hit the stove knob and turned it to the ignite position. The burner didn't light but the ignitor kept sparking. My uncle turned the knob to the off position and the sparking sound stopped. My uncle also can't smell very well and had no idea if the kitchen had the odor of natural gas.

When my cousin returned home he purchased a gas monitor and safety knobs for the stove to prevent this situation from happening again. The safety knobs prevent the accidental turning of a stove control and the gas sensor sounds an alarm when it detects a small amount of gas in the air. The devices can help prevent a possible dangerous situation.

Bad Food

Another thing to be aware of is the possibility of your parent eating bad food. Some have trouble with their taste buds, can't smell very well and their eyesight might not be the best. You need to take precautions that there is no spoiled food in the refrigerator or pantry that they could possibly eat and make them sick. If they still can get around they might want to have a snack and grab something that they don't know is old or possibly bad. Everyday go through the refrigerator and pantry to make sure there are no spoiled items.

I know this sounds petty but you are taking care of them. Things that they would never do seem to come out of nowhere and they start doing something different. All you need is for them to get sick on some bad food and have to take them to the hospital. This could put stress on their body and cause other problems. Even if it doesn't send them to the hospital it could cause a big mess in your home that will take you a long time to clean up. Not to mention that you will also have to clean your parent.

Little things and common sense issues can turn into something bigger in no time. Like I have said it is like taking care of a child and you basically have to child proof your home. You know their condition and what they are capable of. It's like the old saying, "Anything can happen," and it usually does. No matter how hard you try there is always something small that gets you and causes a problem. Just a little common sense goes a long way.

Not Aware Of People

Older people tend not to be aware of their surroundings and the people around them. Unless someone is right in front of them they usually don't notice who is around them. Some of it is because of vision loss or tunnel vision but it needs to be a concern. This can cause problems and also make them a target for crime.

My mom only concentrated on people that were about five to ten feet in front of her. Her eye sight was actually pretty good after she had cataract surgery so it wasn't that she didn't see them. It was that she didn't notice them as they blended into the background. Fortunately for her someone was always around and she never had to be concerned with her surroundings. My sisters and their families would always watch to make sure she was okay and not in any danger. Part of my family was in law enforcement and they always drilled it into us to be aware of what was around us so we wouldn't become a crime victim.

Things are difficult today and society has changed. There is no respect for the elderly and some people are always looking for an easy target. You might have something they want or some might think you have money and they will do whatever it takes to get it. They have no problem in injuring you to get what they want and that's why you have to be aware of people around you. I took that very seriously and I always watched people and the surroundings wherever we went. It payed off and we never became a victim of crime or had any problems.

Target For Crime

One thing you have to remember that your parent can become a target and victim of crime because of their condition. A lot of elderly are scammed by personal visits and telephone calls asking for money and help. If they're capable of using email, the internet or a smart phone they can be a victim of a scam. A lot of times they trust people and can be tricked into giving out information they should not release. As a caregiver it is part of your responsibility to watch out for them and not allow them to scammed or tricked.

They can also be a target when you take them out for a doctors appointment, grocery run or just a trip to a park. If they have any type of valuables on them or a purse they can easily become a robbery victim. You can also become a victim because you can be an easy mark because all of your attention is usually on your parent to make sure they are all right. You have to be aware of your surroundings and what is around you so you and your parent can remain safe when you are traveling. All someone has to see is a loose purse or a smart phone in a shirt pocket and they can take it away from you in a flash. They will have no problem knocking your parent or you down in order to get the valuable item. Even worse you could become a victim of an armed attack and could be seriously injured in the process of a robbery. Broken bones could happen if your parent is knocked down or resists a purse snatching. There are so many things that can happen in a flash and could have disastrous results. That why you need to be aware of your surroundings at all times and try to anticipate what could happen. It's not being paranoid it is being safe and responsible.

My dad was always aware of his surroundings and was very careful when he went out. As a former Marine I believe he could have handled anything and I would never have wanted to tangle with him. I had common sense but most criminals do not and we still had to be careful when we went out. I'm sure if something would have happened my dad would have tried to step in to protect me and I would have done the same for him. Fortunately we never had to react to this type of a situation.

My mom was oblivious to what was around her and noticed very little. She saw people she knew and never saw anyone else. I was always on the alert when I took her out because she would have been an easy target by herself. She had a small bag that had her wallet, identification and medications and she held it close to her and hidden. When I would push her in her wheelchair I sometimes felt like a security agent always looking around. Once again we never had a problem and I never had to react to a situation.

Taken Advantage Of

A lot of time the elderly are taken advantage of or scammed. Being a caregiver means that you are there to protect your parent from this happening. The other side of this situation is that if there is ever a problem you are the first one that is suspected and scrutinized.

I never had to deal with this type of a situation because my parents didn't have much as far as assets and that when I was taking care of them we were living month to month. I never realized how much it cost for the care of my dad and mom. It actually cost more to care for my mom than it did for my dad because she needed more of everything. When he passed away her income was reduced because she received a survivor benefit which was 50% of what he received. Her care was much more expensive because of all the supplies she required for day to day living. She was able to pay most of her way but it did not cover all the expenses. That's where I came in and tried to make up the difference. Unfortunately it took everything I had and we basically started living check to check.

Some might have thought I was taking advantage of her because I did not have a job and started living off her. That was nowhere near the truth because of her income she could not afford to hire someone to come in and give her the twenty-four hour care she needed. I sacrificed and did without of lot of things to make sure my mom had what she needed to live the best she could and have the best quality of life I could give her. It took of lot of budgeting, work and sacrifice but it worked and she enjoyed her life to the end.

Cousin Pushed Wheelchair And Ground Toes

People always tried to help and they would get a little upset when I would say, "No thank you." A lot of times they would be in a rush or want us to hurry so we could get to an event on time. Family and friends would try to help especially when I was lifting my mom in or out of the car. I would tell them what they could do so they wouldn't injure my mom or possibly me.

I learned this the hard way because like anyone I am always looking for some help. My mom attended her great grandson's christening and when it was over one of my cousins was pushing her wheelchair out of the church. I went ahead to get the car ready and when I turn around I saw my mom's foot dragging on the ground. She had no feeling in her feet and she didn't know it was on the ground. It had fallen off the wheelchair foot rest and my cousin kept pushing. I stopped her and I checked my mom's feet. Her toes were scuffed up and bleeding so I had to clean and bandage them up. It wasn't as bad as it looked but it could have been a lot worse. I just got my first aid kit out of our supply bag and went to work on her toes. I cleaned the scrapes, put on some antibiotic cream and put on a bandage. I did this in the parking lot and then I lifted her into the car. My cousin felt bad and she kept apologizing. She said she never looked at her feet.

From this time forward I tried to never let anyone else push my mom in the wheelchair. If they did I made sure I told them to watch her feet because they would fall off the wheelchair foot rests. The little straps they had on the foot rests never held my mom's feet. The only way to prevent her feet from falling off was to strap them to the wheelchair. This caused another problem because it put too much pressure on her calves. So the best remedy I had was to constantly watch her feet. This worked and we never had another problem again. You always have to be concerned when others try to help you. They mean well but sometimes it can cause a problem.

Chapter 41
WHAT TO WATCH FOR WHILE BEING A CAREGIVER
Warning Signs And What To Watch For

As you take care of your parent you will learn what to watch out for and certain warning signs that might need your attention. You will gain a keen sense of what your parents usual routines are and how they react to different situations. When you see a change in their normal behavior or mannerisms you will know if something is wrong or not.

It can be the way they blink their eyes or the way they sit in the wheelchair that can alert you if something is wrong. Sure everyone usually waits for someone to say something is wrong but they might not want to alert you or they for some reason can't. You might see them tap their fingers or move their feet in a different way. The way they look at people or how they hear can be a warning sign. They can rub their arm or leg to signify numbness or pain. You will catch on quick to what they are telling you.

Everyone is different and so is they way they react to situations. You are in a unique position because you will know what your parent is trying to tell you with their reactions. I knew my folks like a book and I could always tell when there was a problem. They didn't have to say anything but I knew if they needed help or rest. I spent so much time with them that they didn't even know they were giving me a signal. I watched them so much that I knew when there was a problem.

When we were at the doctors or hospital I could relay their problems to the doctor or staff without them having to say it themselves. They would agree with what I said and then the professionals would make a diagnosis and treatment plan. Most of the time they didn't want to be a bother so they wouldn't say how they really felt. It was a battle I faced the entire time I was taking care of them. I always had my eyes open and watched their reactions and movements. It gave me a lot of information on how they felt and their condition.

Signs Of Trouble

When you know your parent's condition and you take care of them for a period of time you will spot signs of trouble immediately. You will know by the way they act and sound that something is wrong and you will be ready to deal with it. It could be as simple as a cough or they way they hold their arm and you will know that something is not right.

I knew my folks so well that a lot of times they didn't have to say anything to me because I knew that something was wrong. With my dad he would have a look on his face that would alert me to a problem. He was always short of breath so I learned what was a strong event or just a minor wheeze. I could tell when he was getting weak just by the way he walked or talked. I would make him sit down and rest or I would help him to the car. His coughs also alerted me to problems because I could tell if he was having problems by the depth of his cough. Then there was always the color check of his sputum to see if it was white or yellow.

My mom was the same way and I could tell of problems by her reactions and moods. If she was in severe pain I could tell by her eyes and how she would open them all the way. Sometimes she would make a fist and that would alert me to severe pain. If she had "to go" she would lean to one side of the wheelchair and I knew it was time to take her to the bathroom. When she was sleeping I could tell by her breathing or snoring if she was okay or not. As soon as something changed I would get up and check on her. It could be that she needed more water or that she was experiencing more pain than usual. If she had a leg spasm I would know by the sound the trapeze over her bed made and I would go in to help.

When you take care of someone for so long you get to know all their moves and reactions. They "tell" a lot more with their body language than they sometimes say. When you ask them, "Why didn't you call me?" the answer was always the same, "I didn't want to bother you." I learned how to read them so they never had to feel like they were bothering me.

My dad never had a heart attack or stroke so I never had to deal with that type of a situation. The most severe challenge I had with him was when he had low sugar. He was lethargic and slow to respond and that was something anyone could see. I called the doctor and told him of the situation and as we were talking I thought about low sugar and the doctor told me what to do. It worked and we avoided a bigger problem.

With my mom, the last year of her life, she would lapse into times of no response. She would just look at you with a blank look. I would talk to her and there would be no response. I would raise my voice and there would be no change in her gaze. After a few minutes she would come "awake" and say, "Why are you yelling?" I would tell her what had happened and she would say, "I don't remember that." Later we found out that she was having mini strokes and they were affecting her reactions.

Once again I was able to tell immediately that something was wrong because they were not their normal self. I new their mannerisms and routines so well that anything out of the normal was noticeable. This sense helped in preventing more problems over the course of when I was caring for them.

Chapter 42
TAKING RISKS WHILE BEING A CAREGIVER
Self Medication

As I have stated several time before you need to work with their doctor when you are taking care of a parent. That includes asking for their advice on any vitamins or supplements that you may want to give your parent. If they are on prescription medication, the use of supplements and vitamins might conflict with their medications. You need to work with their doctor and pharmacist to make sure there are no problems with their use of vitamins and supplements with their prescriptions.

My parents were on Medicare and had a good supplemental insurance plan so I never had the reason to try self medication. For one I am not a doctor so I have absolutely no business in trying to treat my parents with any medication. The only exception would be if they had a small cut I could clean it out and use antiseptic ointment to bandage it up. Even this could be a problem, as in the case of my dad because he had diabetes and I had to be careful with any type of treatment. When he was diagnosed with lung cancer I read an article where shark cartilage helped control the spread of cancer. I asked his doctor about this and he told me that he wasn't sure of the benefits of shark cartilage but at this stage it couldn't hurt. My dad took shark cartilage tablets and it made no difference. That was the closest I came to self medicating my father.

During my mom's illness we never tried any type of self medication except for the use of prune juice when she was constipated. Once again I asked her doctor if this was okay and he said it was worth a try. This time it worked in most of the constipation episodes we had to deal with. Still once in a while the problem was severe and we needed to make a trip to the hospital for professional help.

Today with the internet there is so much information available at the click of a mouse, some of it is useful and a lot of it is questionable. I would laugh when I would hear from people that would tell me I should do this or that with my mom's care because they read it on the internet. Some of it made sense but before I did anything I would always check with our doctors to make sure it would do no harm to my mom and her condition.

Some people try to self medicate because they cannot afford a visit to the doctor and others do it because they don't trust physicians and pharmaceuticals. That might be fine if your are just taking care of yourself, but you are a caregiver and are taking care of someone else which means you are responsible for their well being. If you are not a physician or pharmacist you should not be dispensing any kind of medication unless you are directed by a medical professional. The result could be tragic medically and legally.

Self Diagnosis

Another situation you need to be aware of is self diagnosis. Over time as a being a caregiver you will notice changes to your parents condition and mental state. Once again you need to work closely with their doctor to get the proper diagnosis. You will be invaluable in helping the doctor with the diagnosis because you can explain the changes better than your parent because you witness the traits and outcome. With the information you provide the doctor can make a more complete diagnosis of the situation or condition.

When I went to the doctors with my dad and mom I would always tell the physician of any changes in habits and condition. I would be as detailed as possible and they would give me advice on what to watch for. If the condition warranted they would order tests to confirm their diagnosis.

One time with my dad he was having a serious problem because he was weak and lethargic. I had no idea what the problem was so I called the doctor. While I was discussing with the doctor the situation a thought came to me that maybe his sugar was low. I told the doctor my idea and he said it was possible and I should check his sugar level and if it was low give my dad a sugar tablet right away and call him back. I did and about an hour later my dad started to get more energy and became more alert. I called the doctor back and told him that my dad was getting better. He also told me to take him in so he could check him out. That was my bought with self diagnosis under the discretion of our physician.

With my mom, my self diagnosis was limited to if I needed to give her a little more medication because of breakthrough pain as per standing doctor advice and if I needed to give her regular or warm prune juice for her constipation. We did this for years and it was part of our normal routine.

Once again I am not a doctor so I have absolutely no business trying to diagnose my parents condition. My job is to care for them under the direction of a medical professional. I am responsible for their care and it would be callous for me to try to diagnosis their condition. Over time you learn of procedures for certain situations but you still need to have those verified by a doctor because not every situation is the same and neither is every treatment. My mom survived a long time because we worked with our doctors and listened to their advice. I didn't play doctor, I did my job as a caregiver by following their diagnosis, treatment and advice.

Today with the internet you can find information on almost every condition and how to diagnose situations. This information can be accurate or it can be wrong and it is hard for you to know what is true or false. That's why you need to listen to the treating physicians because they know fact from fiction. You can do research about conditions and situations and there is no reason not to ask your doctor questions about what you learn. That is why you need to work with your doctor because you are partners in the care of your parent.

Staying In Cars

When you are taking care of someone by yourself you are tempted to leave them alone for a short period of time while you do a quick errand. Other times you might feel you can leave them alone for a longer period of time when you feel that you're in a better environment. No matter which one you choose you will be responsible for your actions if anything ever happens to your parent.

When I would volunteer at my former high school I would always bring my mom with me. I would park under a carport or under some trees and she would be fine for the time I was there. When we would go to Friday night football games I would park my car near the end zone of the football field. It did help that I had complete access to the campus and could basically park wherever I wanted. The key was that I knew she was always safe because it was a controlled environment. Her and I also had walkie talkies so she could call me whenever she needed something. All she had to do was press the button and say, "Jim" and I would stop what I was doing and go to her. The range of the walkie talkies covered the entire campus. The school administration, faculty, religious order and students knew who she was and kept an eye on her. I didn't have to worry about outsiders or intruders trying to harm her. Many would bring her food, snacks, hot chocolate, coffee or many other items and a lot of time it was one right after the other. She enjoyed the attention and also the environment.

As far as leaving her in a car in a parking lot that is a completely different situation. I admit sometime in the spring and fall I would leave her in the car for a few minutes while I went into the bank or store. I would never do this in the winter or summer because of the extreme weather conditions.

Sometimes you don't think of the risk and it was absolutely stupid and irresponsible for me to do this. Looking back now I can see the risk was great for robbery or worse. No matter how safe and responsible you think you are, sometimes you do things that are really dumb and dangerous.

I was lucky that nothing ever happened but if it did I would have been in a great deal of trouble. Since I was responsible for her safety I would have had to accept the consequences of my actions. It would have been a hard lesson but it also would have been my fault.

Use To Leave In Car

One of the dumbest and dangerous things I did with my mom was to leave her in the car when I had to do a quick errand. I never did it in the summer or winter so it was never hot or cold. It was usually no more than ten minutes and she would tell me to leave her because she was, "Ok."

I was lucky nothing ever happened because this made her a target for crime. She always wanted the windows closed except for about two inches from the top so no one could reach inside and grab her. I also never left the keys in the car so someone could break a window and drive away with her or worse, push her out of the car.

It was a lazy and stupid thing to do and even though I thought I was careful in every way, I too did dangerous things. This was not normal for me and in the back of my mind I always had the thought that something could happen. I had this fear that I would walk out of a location and find the police next to my car asking my mom questions. Then I would have to answer a lot of questions and I would be responsible for whatever the outcome would be.

Doing What You're Not Supposed To Do

I was not perfect in the care of my parents and I did make a lot of mistakes. One of the biggest mistakes I made was leaving my mom in the car for a short period of time while I did a quick errand. It was usually when I went into the bank to make a deposit or withdrawal. The last time I did this I got the biggest scare I could and I deserved it.

It was in late spring and we lived in Tehachapi. It was a Friday evening and I went to the bank to withdraw $50.00 for the weekend. I had never used an ATM and I always went to the bank to withdraw enough cash for the week. My mom was in the car and she was doing a word search puzzle. I had the window open about two inches so she got plenty of air and I parked so she was not in the late afternoon sun.

I went into the bank and went right to the teller with my withdrawal slip. While I was standing at the counter something didn't seem right. The banks employees seemed on edge and the teller was not her usual self. The whole task took about five minutes and I walked out of the bank with my $50.00. As I exited the bank I was met by a Tehachapi police officer and he asked me to stand to the side. He had his hand on his weapon and he asked if I had any weapons on me. I told him no and he asked me to lean on his patrol car. As he was searching me all I could think was that this was about leaving my mom in the car. I thought my life was over and I asked if this was about leaving my mom in the car? He said, "No, it's not about your mom," and when he was finished he told me to go to my car but not to leave the parking lot. When I walked to the car I saw police officers everywhere and then all of a sudden they left and one officer told me I could leave. I was still nervous because I never had anything like this happen before. We went home and I had an interesting story to tell.

Needless to say because of my own guilt I never left my mom in the car for any reason. It didn't matter how short my errand was going to be and after this incident I always took her with me. I got a second chance and I wasn't going to try my luck again. The next time I went to the bank I brought my mom inside and I went to the same teller. She told me that they had a threat and they didn't know who or if the culprit was in the bank so the police were suspicious of everyone. She also said after the investigation they determined it was at the other branch in town. From that time forward I used the drive thru teller whenever I had a simple withdrawal.

Chapter 43

CHALLENGES AND BEING A CAREGIVER
Unique Challenges

Being a caregiver means you and your parent are going to face a lot of unique challenges. Both of you will face these situations and will have to overcome them. It is never easy and there is always something over the horizon that will come straight at you and you need to be able to deal with it.

When I was taking care of my dad it seemed that everyday was a unique challenge. I was in uncharted territory and everything was new and a learning experience. My father's situation, when he became seriously ill, proceeded rapidly and he passed away within six months of his worsening condition. I learned a lot such as changing his urostomy bag, putting adhesive on the stoma flange, charting his diabetes, giving him insulin shots, dispensing oxygen, cleaning him up and much more.

With my mom it was over thirteen years of unique challenges and situations. It seemed whenever we went to the doctor or had diagnostic tests there was a new challenge ahead. I learned how to change a bed wound dressing or apply a new kind of wound medication. Some of these medications were applied to the surface and some had to be placed inside the wound, I was learning as I was going along. I did feel better when the staff at the wound center would tell me, "You can do this," or "I have no problem with you doing it," and "you know what you're doing." That was a great vote of confidence.

I had to learn how to apply a transdermal pain patch and see when I had to increase other medication for break through pain without overdosing. That was a lot of responsibility but I did it because I had to.

I had to watch to make sure her legs didn't swell and I had to raise them if they did. In the car I had to be careful about her circulation and if her legs got cold I had to move and massage them. When she was in a wheelchair I had to make sure her feet didn't fall out off the foot rests and drag on the ground. She had very little feeling in her feet so she couldn't feel the ground.

Her ability to feel hot and cold was diminished. She was mostly cold even during the summer so I had to be careful she wouldn't get over heated. In the winter she had to be kept warm and there could be no chance for her to shiver.

She had a pneumonia vaccine and she received a flu shot every year but you always had to careful of getting an infection. Being in a crowd could cause her to get sick or in cold weather could have her get the flu. There is always the chance of getting an influenza that is not covered under the yearly flu vaccine. I made sure I got the pneumonia shot and yearly flu vaccine just to make sure I wouldn't make her sick.

When she had to have special tests it was always necessary to figure out how I could place her on the platform for the scan or x-ray. Sometimes I had to be with her to hold her up in a certain position so I had to wear protective clothing. Sometimes nothing was available so it just had to be done. I tried to limit my radiation exposure but who knows.

When she was admitted to the hospital it was always a challenge because she was not a good patient. I had to make arrangements to be with her to keep her calm so she wouldn't be a bother to the staff or other patients. Some hospitals would sometimes balk at the idea but usually after the first night they would be happy to work with me. She hated being alone, it was just something she did and it had to be addressed.

I always expected a challenge and it usually came. We dealt with various situations and overcame most of them over the many years. That's why I would always say, you got to do what you got to do, and it got us through all of them.

Being Scared

One of the things I will never forget about taking care of my dad was the ambulance ride from our house to the hospital. He was very sick and he was spitting up blood. He was lethargic and pretty much out of it. He knew the end was near and he wanted to stay home. He told me once that he wanted to be at home when the end came. I was always ready for this situation and I expected him to follow through with his plan. My mom knew he was in bad shape and she started to get hysterical which made him upset. He looked at me and said, "Call the doctor I'll go to the hospital." I asked him if he was sure and he said, "Yes I can't put your mother through this." I called the doctor and he told me to call 911 and have him transported to the hospital. I called 911 and the paramedics arrived along with an ambulance.

They surveyed the situation and agreed that he needed to go to the hospital. The problem was our doctor was not on staff at the local hospital but at another hospital in Long Beach, California and that was about fifteen miles away. I informed the ambulance crew and they made the arrangements to transport my dad to the preferred hospital.

They put my dad in the ambulance and during the move he was looking all around. He knew that he was never coming back and he was just looking one last time. They put him in the ambulance and I went with him. They had him on oxygen and I was talking to him. He was telling me to take care of my mom and the family. He told me, "It's up to you know, your the man of the family." I kept talking to him and telling him he would be okay and then he said something to me I will never forget, he said, "Jim, I'm scared." This man was never scared of anything and he was the toughest person I knew. As a Marine he was stationed on the islands in the Pacific and he survived World War II. We never knew what he had to do or what he had seen. He was tough as a rock and he was telling me he was scared. I tried to keep a straight face but no matter how hard I tried, tears started rolling down my face. I caught myself and wiped them away so he wouldn't see but I'm sure he did.

What Do You Say

When you know someone is dying and they tell you they're scared, what do you say? I had absolutely no idea, all I could say was, "It's not your time yet." All those years of going to church, religion classes and practicing my faith came to a scratching halt. I didn't want to say, "You'll be in heaven soon," because I wanted him to hold on and still be with us. I was speechless as I was trying to think of what to say. Finally I said, "When the time comes there will be nothing to be scared of." He looked up at me and said, "I know." I kept one hand on his shoulder and the other held his hand all the way to the hospital. He stayed mostly conscience during the entire trip to the hospital. He kept repeating for me to take care my mom. I told him, "You have nothing to worry about, I'll take care of her." He smiled and said, "I know you will." That was the promise I made and I kept it.

When we got to the hospital he started going in and out of consciousness. They admitted him and from that time on he was never alert again. He was in a daze most of the time and never spoke. He died two weeks later on Easter morning. If he was scared before I'm sure that fear disappeared because he died on Easter morning. In our faith that was the most important day because it was the day Jesus rode from the dead and into Heaven.

Doctors And I Agreed Not To Tell My Dad, Then A Nun Did

When my dad was diagnosed with brain cancer the doctors and I agreed not to tell him right away. They noted on his chart that he was not to be told of the brain cancer as per family and doctor instructions. I knew that if we told him, he would give up and it would be the end of him. I talked to my sisters and mom and they also agreed that this was the best idea. We all felt that he would keep fighting but if he heard the cancer went to his brain he would give up. He was scheduled for treatments and I told him that this was part of his normal cancer treatments. This was one of those "white lies" that I told to keep his spirits up.

He was in a Catholic hospital and they still had some nuns on staff as nurses and aids. I was always there when my dad went in for his cancer treatments so if he had any questions I could ask them for him. One day I got stuck in traffic and I got to the hospital late. I was met at his hospital room door by this nun and she had a long sad look on her face. I thought the worst and she said, "I might have said the wrong thing" She said, "Your dad asked me why he was going to his cancer treatment everyday and I told him that he had brain cancer and this was how they were treating it." She said, "He broke down and started to cry and I didn't know what to do." She continued, "After he went for treatment I noticed on his chart that I wasn't supposed to tell him." Then she added, "I think he should know so I'm glad I told him." I became angry, raised my voice and I gave her an earful. I wanted to know how she didn't read the chart before but was able to read it afterward. How could she dispense medication if she didn't read the chart? I told her that it was not her position and I was the one that was responsible for my dad. The doctor and I agreed that this was the best policy because we wanted him to fight as hard as he could. I finally said, "You just killed him." She started to cry, left and then our doctor got her and he also chastised her for her decision. I could hear what he was telling her and it was basically along the same lines as what I said. He also told her she was not to treat my dad again and to stay away from the family.

About a half hour later they brought my dad from the cancer treatment and I could see that he had tears in his eyes. They wheeled him into the room and he looked at me and asked, "How bad is it?" I told him that the cancer had spread from his lungs to his brain. He said to me, "I'm done, It's over." I tried to explain that he still had a lot of life in him and that he could fight this. I said, "You're not ready to go yet and we can fight this." He said once again, "It's over." One month later he died.

I never saw that nun again and I hoped I never did. She might have thought she did the right thing and in her eyes she did but that was not the point. It was our decision and she had no right to go against the family's wishes and also the doctors. If she didn't read the chart how could she properly care for my dad. We knew my dad's condition and we knew the situation so we did what was best for my dad. That was the first time I got mad at a hospital nurse and I wasn't happy about it. To this day I still say she took the life out of my father.

Moving

Back in 2008 my mom and I decided that we needed to move from our Lynwood, California home. One of my sisters was retiring and they purchased a new home in Tehachapi, California about one hundred and fifty miles away. She convinced us that she would be able to help with our mom's care. My family lived in that house since 1958 and we actually made it bigger because we did a major remodel in 1973. That's when I learned a lot about construction. I really had blood, sweat and tears in that house.

We sold the house in May of 2008 and started moving in July. My folks saved everything and my mom did not want to get rid of anything unless she went through it and she did look at every box and item. Our house wasn't going to close escrow until the end of July so we were going to move our stuff into my sisters house in Tehachapi. She hadn't moved in yet so we were going to use her house for two weeks while we waited for our house to close escrow. It took two weeks to move all of our stuff one hundred and fifty mile aways. We used four twenty-six foot trucks, one seventeen foot truck and one sixteen foot truck. Both sisters and their families helped with the loading of the truck. One sister and her family helped with some of the unloading in Tehachapi.

The interesting part was my mom drove with me in the rental truck every time but one. The only time she drove with my sister was when we had to take my car up to the new location. My sister and mom road in her car, my brother in law drove my car and I drove a seventeen foot rental truck. This was the one time I got stuck as I was driving through the desert. Going up a small incline the truck started to overheat. I pulled into a turnout and let the engine cool down. There was no fluid leaking from the truck and I couldn't hear any hissing sounds. I got back on the highway and a few miles later it started to overheat again. I pulled over and let it cool. I started on the road again and I turned on the heater to make sure the coolant could circulate. This did the trick as I slowly went up the incline. When I reached the summit and started going down hill the temperature gauge of the truck dropped but was still in the high range. It continued to drop a little and never reached the dangerous point again. I still stopped every few miles just to cool the engine a little and check the vehicle. When I got to the house I realized I had a burn on my leg. I drove with the heater on high, through 100 degree plus weather in the Mojave Desert, and it gave me a burn on my leg. The hazards of moving.

The other interesting point was because of my delay my mom was in my sister's car. They got to the house almost two hours before me and she needed to be taken out of the car. My brother in law lifted her out of the car and put her in the wheelchair. This was the first and only time that he ever offered and lifted my mom, When I talked to him later he said it was hard and he was afraid of dropping her. He couldn't believe I did that several times a day. The other interesting thing was my mom let him do it and was not afraid of falling.

On the other trips I would lift my mom into the cab of the rental truck. They were higher than a normal vehicle so I would lift her from the front and she would put her arms around my neck and shoulders. I would raise her to the seat of the truck as I put one foot onto the running board. When I had her backside on the truck seat I would tell her to let go and I would put one arm under legs and the other behind her back. I would then spin her so she would be sitting forward. I then buckled her with the seat and shoulder belt of the truck. She would be in the front seat for the duration of the trip which would be about three hours. When we got to our destination I would reverse the lifting procedure. I had the wheelchair near the cab of the truck and I stood on the running board and spun her toward me. She put her arms around my shoulder and neck and I lifted her as I stepped backward from the running board to the ground. I had to lift her a little higher so she wouldn't catch her feet on the truck step. When we were both on the ground I turned and placed her in the wheelchair. This was probably one of the most difficult lifting procedures because of the chance of falling back. My security was I could hold the grab bar on the side of the truck. If there was trouble my mom could hang from my neck while I grabbed the hold bar and then I could step back. It would put pressure on my neck but at least we wouldn't fall. This was one of those situations that you had to plan the lift and say to yourself, "What if?" All the trips in the truck we never had a problem and she was transported safely.

Those road trips in the rental moving trucks were comical at times. One they are not the most comfortable and they bounce a lot. We would be talking during the drive and our voices would be fluttering because of the road bumps. I wanted to take the shortest routes because of the fuel expense and that took us on the freeways through downtown Los Angeles. Our first trip was on a Friday evening and we were traveling during rush hour traffic. I drove trucks of this size years before so I was comfortable behind the wheel. I made my mom the spotter and she tried to stay aware of any vehicles to the right of us. We traveled mostly in the right lane but when we changed highways or I had to change lanes I would ask her, "Any cars next to us?" She would look into the mirror and look to the right side and usually say, "No, it's clear." I would look into the mirror and see a car or two next to us or sometimes even a large truck. As a spotter she tried but she just would miss cars and trucks. This was going through downtown Los Angles during rush hour on Friday night, I would say, "What about that car?" Her response was classic and usual, "What car?" I didn't change lanes unless I knew it was safe and we had six successful trips. Another time we needed gasoline for the truck and we had to get off the freeway. I was looking for a gas station that was easy to get in and out then back on the highway. We were driving around an area and she would say, "There's one," and of course it was on the other side of the street and I would have had to make a u-turn on a small street. We finally found a safe gas station, filled up the tank and got back on the freeway.

These were adventures and they were fun because she was involved. They were a little stressful at times but looking back they were fun. Every time I drive a truck and I see a car on the right side I think of her saying, "What car?"

Medical Conditions After We Moved

We had some medical situations after we moved from Lynwood to Tehachapi. All three were cause by severe constipation due to the amount of pain medication my mom was prescribed. The first problem occurred about four months after we moved to our new home. We hadn't established ourselves with a new doctor so we went to the emergency room. The local hospital in town treated us very well and stabilized my mom. They then sent her by ambulance to a hospital in Bakersfield that was more equipped to handle her situation.

The same problem happened around a year later and we ended up in the same hospital in Bakersfield. This was around Christmas and the weather was changing and a major snowstorm was predicted. There was only one highway to Tehachapi and the Highway Patrol was telling people that the road was going to be closed because of snow and ice. The doctors were waiting for my mom to have another bowel movement to make sure everything was working so they didn't want to discharge her until she went. Finally the treating doctor saw the news and he came in and said he was going to discharge her so she could get home before the storm. We left the hospital around 3:00pm, it was cold and the snow just started to fall as we were driving up the hill. We got home around 5:00pm and I carried her into the house. Once we got inside she told me she had "to go." I lifted her on the toilet and she went. When she was done I cleaned her up and put on a clean diaper. Everything was working and she was fine. I came out to the living room, looked outside and it was snowing very heavily. I put on the evening news and they said the Highway Patrol had just closed the road to our town. We made it home and were able to have Christmas in our house and my mom didn't have to spend the holiday in the hospital.

This same condition happened four years later and this time the local hospital sent us to a different hospital in Bakersfield. Once again they solved the problem and my mom spent about a week in the hospital. This facility was different because it was a training hospital for the local community college nursing program. I learned quite a bit during this hospital visit about the care of my mom and the job I was doing. They treated us very well.

Handling Bad News

One of the hardest thing to have to do when you are a caregiver is to give bad news to your parent. You might have to explain a diagnosis that might be bad or life threatening or something even worse. I had one of those situations and it was the worst experience of my life.

My mom had her 90th birthday in 2010 and it was a wonderful occasion because she was the oldest left of her generation. We had a big celebration with the whole family and she had a wonderful time. A few weeks later we had a situation that turned out to be the worst time of our lives.

Her second grandson, my nephew, was in the Air Force Reserve and was also a reserve Deputy Sheriff and his goal was to become a full time sheriffs deputy. He served multiple tours in the Middle East and when he came back he was never the same. Unknown to us he was suffering from PTSD, Post Traumatic Stress Disorder and one night the stress grew too much for him to handle and he took his own life.

His mother and father lived a few blocks away from us and I got a call around 3am. My sister was hysterical and I could barely understand what she was saying but I did hear her say her son was dead. My mom was sound asleep so I got dressed and went over to my sisters house. My brother in law met me at the door and told me his son was dead. I thought that he was killed while he was working as a reserve deputy sheriff, when I got inside the house they told me he committed suicide. They also explained his condition and the battles he was having with PTSD. I couldn't stay long because I left my mom alone sleeping so I had to get back to her right away. I left them in a hysterical state and then realized I had to tell my mom the horrific news.

On the way back to the house I knew that there was no way I could try to make this news easier to handle. My main concern was I did not want my mom to get sick and possibly have a heart attack from the bad news. One thought was not to tell her right away but I felt that would be worse. I would have to tell her sooner or later and then the shock could be worse and she would also be extremely angry at me for not telling her right away. It was a little after 4am and I decided I was going to wake her up, give her the bad news so we could console each other because of the extreme tragedy.

I walked into the house and took a deep breath and went into her room. I turned on the light and said, "Mom, mom." I called her a few more times and she finally woke up. She looked at me and knew something was wrong and said, "What happened?" She already had tears in her eyes like she knew what was coming and I told her that her grandson was dead. She immediately started yelling and repeating "oh, no" as she cried. I went up to her and hugged her and then she asked, "How." I told her that he committed suicide and then she became hysterical yelling, "Why, why." I told her I didn't know and we would have to wait for more information. She then started crying more and asked about my poor sister and how she was? I told her I went over and saw her and my brother in law and they were extremely upset and in distraught. My mom wanted me to get her ready so she could go be with her daughter. I told her when it got light outside we would go over. Her and I consoled each other for over an hour.

Around 5:30am I asked her if she wanted to get ready and she said, "Yes," with tears still in her eyes. She kept repeating about my poor sister and why her grandson would do something like this. It took longer than usual to get her ready but we were able to go over my sisters around 7am. I wheeled my mom into the house and she grabbed her daughter, my sister, and they just cried together for a while. She then grabbed her son in law and did the same.

She had to be there to be with her daughter during the aftermath of the one of the most horrific things a parent and grandparent have to go through, the loss of a child and grandchild. It doesn't matter that they were adults it was still their son and grandson and as the old saying goes, "A parent never should have to bury a child," also "a grandparent never should have to bury a grandchild."

We stayed and then my other sister came up with a cousin. Other cousins and friends came up to console the family. It was a horrible day and a horrible experience. That incident lasted almost two weeks because of the investigation and the funeral. He was a veteran of Operation Iraqi Freedom so he was buried with full military honors. He left a hole all our hearts that was never filled.

This was a situation that I had no choice to tell my mom what had happened. There was no easy way to say it or to handle it. If she would have gotten sick, had a heart attack or stroke I would have had no choice but to call 911 and have her taken to the hospital and that could have been the start of a second tragedy. I had a good idea she could handle the bad news as long as I comforted her and showed that I was affected the same way. She needed me to lean on and I needed her. After all she was still a mother and the concern of her daughter was more important than her condition and situation. When she wanted to go and console my sister I knew she was going to be able to handle the situation.

Chapter 44
FAMILY VISITS AND BEING A CAREGIVER
Family Visits

Family visits were the best things that could perk up my mom's attitude. She would look forward to having the family visit especially the great grand children. This would always be a fun time for all and another benefit was I always made a big meal. Just another excuse to eat. I did mention my mom had a big appetite.

The family visits were also good because it gave her a chance to interact with others. She was lucky the grandchildren and great grand children paid attention to her and made her feel special. She had two grandsons and they would drive up for the weekend quite often to see her and she made the most of it. They would spend at least one night with us, so it was a prolonged visit. She would engage in conversation with them about their work and life. If we went out they would keep her talking and entertained. She had two grand daughters one would come up with her husband, son and daughter. They would spend one or two nights with us and the great grand children entertained everybody. We kept a batch of toys for them to play with and they would take them all out and have fun. All you would hear is, "Watch me great grandma, " she did and had a wonderful time.

We would all sit around the table and I would make a big meal for breakfast and dinner. I would make eggs, bacon, potatoes and toast for breakfast and usually macaroni (pasta), meatballs and bread for dinner. Pizzas were also on the menu. I would make enough dough to make four to six, fourteen inch pizzas. Hey, we're Italian, so food was always popular. My mom would keep up with everybody as far as eating, and as usual, according to her, there was always room for dessert. Meals were always fun because everybody talked to her and she was the main part of all the conversations. They kept her busy and I was able to do something else. Sure it was a lot of work but it was something different and I also enjoyed having the younger ones around. It was a break in the routine for both of us.

These were the best times because she forgot about her aches and pains. She interacted with the younger ones and they made her a part of their lives. She was not just a picture or voice in the distance. This kept her going and gave her something to live for because she was not just a relic in a wheelchair.

Grand And Great Grandchildren Visits

It was always nice to have visitors but my mom would get real excited when her grandchildren came to visit. These visits were occasions because the great grandson was three years old and the great granddaughter was a toddler. They would take over the entire house and to my mom they could do no wrong. As they got older you never knew what you were in for or what they would say. In the spring and summer I planted a garden and when they visited they always wanted to pick something. I would put my mom's wheelchair outside and she would watch them pick strawberries. I taught them how to pick, wash and then eat them. They would say, "Here great grandma," and give her a washed strawberry. My mom's face would light up as she said, "Thank you." They were delicious and they would alway pick more than they could eat so they could take some home. After they were done picking strawberries, tomatoes, peppers or beans they would run around the back yard and have a wonderful time. All while my mom would watch them and just enjoy them being around.

Sometime young children don't like to be around elderly people because they are afraid of them. We never had that problem, my niece made sure her children were not afraid of their great grandmother. They would walk into the house and immediately go up to her and say, "Hi great grandma," and then give her a hug. She could hold them, kiss them and talk to them without them trying to run away or cry. It was a wonderful sight to see.

I had a pedal jeep and they would go back and forth on the sidewalk in the front of the house. The neighbors would comment to me that all they could hear was, "Watch great grandma." I would put her on the porch and whatever they were riding, pushing or pulling they always wanted to be watched.

In the winter we would get a little snow so I would clear the porch and bundle my mom up. She would watch the little ones throw snowballs and ride the sled. They never threw anything at her but I was always a target.

Dinners were fun because they would try different foods. I cooked a lot of Italian food and some was different from what they were use to eating. My way to have kids try new foods was I would give them a quarter if they tried something new. I would hear, "Uncle Jim I get a quarter, I tried it." It could get expensive but it was worth it just to see their reactions. If I forgot or was busy my mom would say you owe them a quarter and made sure they got paid.

She would play games with them, watch them play with their toys and just enjoyed being around the great grandchildren. Those nights she would sleep straight through and it made her forget her pain. Those weekends or days in the summer brought great joy to her and let her forget her problems.

After she passed my little nephew told me one day that he missed great grandma. I told him to remember the great times he had and that he brought joy to her every time he came over. She made an impression on him and he didn't forget her.

Get Togethers

Getting together with family and friends always meant for a good time. Most of the time they came to our house so my mom wouldn't have to travel. Staying home meant that I had to cook but I didn't mind because my mom would always enjoy herself.

We lived in the mountains above the Mojave Desert and Bakersfield. It was around a two to three hour drive from Los Angeles and Orange County, California. Our family would come up at least once a month and it always meant a big meal. This could be ten to twenty people at a time. I would make pounds and pounds of macaroni (pasta) and usually enough meatballs to feed an army. Sometimes it was stuffed shells or lasagna.

Sometimes I would make six eighteen inch pizzas at a time. I would make a turkey even though it wasn't Thanksgiving. I always made home baked bread and this was usually gone before we started the meal. The really sad thing was that there were never many left overs. I don't know if everybody just ate a lot or I didn't make enough. I think we just ate a lot because the more I made the more everyone ate. I guess it was the Italian in all of us.

My mom liked her dessert and the family would usually bring a variety of pastry. I wasn't good at making dessert so it was a treat for her. They would bring cakes, pies and other assorted pastry. One of my cousins would always bring an Italian pastry called Pizzelles. They were home made and my mom enjoyed these all the time. For a treat I would put a scoop of ice cream in between two of the Pizzelles and she would eat them before they had a chance to melt.

One of the big get togethers was in 2010 and it was for her ninetieth birthday. She was the oldest, the matriarch, and no one in the family had ever lasted to that age. She was a middle child and lived longer than her father, mother, older brother, older sister, younger sister and youngest sister. It was a surprise for her because the entire family came up. My niece and her family came up on Friday night and surprised my mom. Her great grandson came in and said, "Hi great grandma, were here for your birthday." He almost let the cat out of the bag. My sister lived a couple of blocks away and everyone went to her house. I wheeled my mom over and she couldn't believe all the people and I think it was a little over whelming. They would come over and wish her a Happy Birthday and she would say, "Who's ninety?" When they told her she was ninety she would say, "No, I'm not that old."

I made stuffed shells, gallons of sauce and many loaves of bread. My sister made ham and roast beef and all the sides. It was a feast and celebration. Everyone brought her a gift and if you guessed sweets you would be right. She got candy, chocolate and pastry, she was in heaven. Thank goodness she didn't have a sugar problem because she ended up finishing all the gifts in the following days. Cakes, pies and ice cream was also on the menu and everyone had a great time. After it was over she looked at me and said, "I'm really ninety years old?" I told her yes and her next comment was, "I never thought I would live this long." I told her she had many years left and she agreed.

When friends came to visit it was usually two to four people and they would stay the day. I would make dinner and we would chat about the old days and good times. They all knew my mom liked dessert so they would always bring a cake or a pie. She would light up when she saw the pastry and couldn't wait to have a piece or a slice.

These get togethers brightened my mom's life and gave her something to look forward to. She enjoyed having people over and she really enjoyed seeing everyone having a good time especially the younger ones. The best part was everyone paid attention to her and when she told stories they laughed with her and not at her.

Played Games With Her

My mom always liked to play games and she really enjoyed playing games with her grandchildren and great children. She might have not known the game but she tried just to see the reaction on their faces. I don't know how many times I heard, "Grandma you can't do that," or "Great grandma that's not how we play." It was always good for a laugh and she did it just to make them smile. With the great grandchildren it was fun to watch how they tried to teach her a new game. Most of the time they didn't know how to play so they showed her their way. She would ask, "Are you sure," and they would say, "that's how we play." She would smile and laugh and play the game their way.

Board and card games kept her mind sharp and she also enjoyed them. When her fingers started cramping up or was unable to move them the grand kids stepped up and helped her play her hand. She enjoyed having them around the table and playing the game. We would spend two to three hours playing games when they came to visit. I would make snacks and we just munched our way through the evening. It was especially fun on cold nights because everyone had hot chocolate and marshmallows and the laughter went on for hours.

My sisters and their families were all adults and we just went along with the fun. It brought fun into my mom's life and I believe that kept her going. She would light up when she knew they were coming to visit and be sad when they went home. Living 150 miles away meant they would only come up once a month but it gave my mom something to look forward to and she enjoyed their visits the entire time they were there.

Grandsons Would Come Up Just To Spend Time With Their Grandmother

My mom was very fortunate to have grandchildren that were fabulous. All of them would come up to visit their grandmother and spend time with her. They would ask her questions and want to hear her stories. One grand daughter had a family of her own and it was hard for her to visit because she was working and raising a young family. She did her best and her family made the trip to visit as often as they could. The other grand daughter had a career that took her all over the country and it was hard for her to come up. Once again she did visit whenever she could and tried her best to be over when everyone else came to visit. The two grandsons came up every chance they could. One would come up almost every weekend because his mom and dad, my sister, lived a few blocks away. The other grandson would come up about every three weeks and he always told his friends that he was going to visit his grandmother and he was going to have a lot of good food.

My mom enjoyed these visits and she was the center of their attention. The boys would play games with her or just sit around and ask her questions about her life and their grandfather. I would make dinner or we would go out and they would not leave her alone. She soaked it all in and was so proud of them. She was interested in their lives and jobs and how they were, "Getting along." She always showed encouragement for everything that they were doing and it made them feel good.

After she lost one grandson to PTSD the other one tried to come up more often. He lifted her spirits up every time he visited. He would go out and get her ice cream sundaes or some other sweet treat. She was always happy when he was around and was more appreciative of his visits.

She would tell me it was good to see him and how proud she was of him. She would also tell me sometimes about how much she missed the other grandson with a tear in her eye. I would tell her, "You still have a wonderful grandson and he loves you very much, enjoy him." She would smile and say, "Yes, he is wonderful and I love him."

Chapter 45

DEALING WITH FAMILY AND FRIENDS WHILE BEING A CAREGIVER

Some Family Members

Some family members were not supportive of my decision to take care of my parents, in fact some were hostile. They would say take care of yourself and they can take care of themselves. They also would say hire someone to take care of them and have some self respect and dignity. They will get use to other people taking care of them. I don't want to end up like that. I heard it all and it always had the same message, "That's best for you." They never considered what was best for my mom and dad.

As far as losing self respect and dignity I think it was the exact opposite, I gained self respect and I helped them maintain their dignity. I wasn't anyone else's job, except maybe my sisters, to take care of our parents. I let my sisters take care of their family and I took care of our parents. They didn't lose time from work or their children and our parents were well taken care of. Sure there were some embarrassing situations but we got over it and moved along.

Another one of my favorite lines was, "How can you even do that." That was when I was cleaning and changing my mom's bed wound. How can you do it? Easy, you grow up, show some backbone and do what you have to do. I never let their criticism interfere with the care I gave my parents and it showed when doctors, nurses and other healthcare professionals praised the condition of my parents. They would tell them, "You are very lucky to have this type of care." The response from my dad and mom was always, "I know." They would also say that I spent to much time taking care of them and the doctors would tell them, "He knows what he's doing and he made the decision." They were absolutely right and I never regretted my decision.

A Pariah

After my mom passed away I realized that most of the family only kept in contact with us because of my mom. The visits stopped and phone calls were few and far between. When they did call it was because they needed something or wanted some advice. When I would call them, talking was like pulling teeth and it sounded like they were afraid I was going to ask them for something.

When I sold the house in Tehachapi I received very little help in packing and moving. The town was small and storage facilities were full so I had to wait until one became available. Since it was a cash sale there was a thirty day escrow on the house. One of my sisters moved to Texas and was not available to help with the move. The other sister lived in Southern California and she would come up and help pack and throw items away. My nephew came up to help me move the large items into storage. One cousin and his wife came up and helped me pack and move the other items into storage. The rest of the family that I helped many times move over the years never offered to help. The house was 1500 square feet and I needed four storage units to hold all of my belongings. The last day of the move it was cold and snowing and I ended up loading and unloading four truckloads of stuff from the house to storage. I was exhausted and I had to still return the rental truck. I dropped it off at the rental center and then walked back to my former home where my car was parked, it was about two miles away. I then drove one hundred and fifty miles to my cousin's house where I was going to stay. They were having a family dinner and when I walked in the comments were, "I bet your glad that's over."

That's when I said to myself I was homeless and a pariah to the family. I would never own my own home again and I would never get any family support. I meant nothing to them and the only reason they came to visit was my mom. It was going to be a long road ahead and I was ill prepared for the future. I was right and to this day I am still trying to get back on my feet and I am still a pariah with most of my family.

Old Grudges

One thing that I have found now with my mom gone is that of a lot of old grudges come out of the woodwork. It's almost like since she is no longer around there is no other witness to the past. It's amazing how I saw and experienced things that no one else saw or wants to see now. It all needs to be forgotten because that was in the past and has no bearing now. The only problem with that idea is that it was also my past and I'm still here. It's like people want to erase everything I have done and they have no interests in remembering it.

I'm talking about family and how they are not interested in what I did for my parents. It's like some of them are angry that I took care of them and now I'm fair game because the witnesses are gone. I know it sounds strange but when you talk to some of them they all have convenient memory loss. I was always told by some cousins that I had a great memory and if they wanted to know anything about the family they would come to me. Now that my mom is gone they don't want to know or remember anything. When you tell them about something that happened they always say, "I don't remember that." Even when you have photos or other proof they seem to conveniently forget the past. They couldn't do that before because my mom was around and knew all that happened and heard a lot of what had been said.

I know it sounds petty but I gave up over twenty years of my life taking care of my parents. I saw and heard a lot and was involved in every aspect of their life. Just because the last witness is gone does not mean that I have to be discarded because I still remember things that nobody wants to hear. A lot happened in our family and it is part of our lives and it needs to be remembered.

Siblings

I don't know if it is sibling rivalry or something else but it doesn't matter how close you are there is always a problem with family. I have two older sisters and no matter what I did they would usually criticize me on the task I was doing. If someone disagreed with me or was critical of my procedures they would side with the other people. They would never side with me at all. I always thought it was their way of toughening me up and it did work because I rarely listened and went along with doing what I was going to do. I use to get mad because I felt I was making things easier for them so they didn't have to take care of our parents. They had their own families, careers and responsibilities so they didn't need more work or problems.

Now they always helped when they were around and if they weren't they would come up as soon as possible when I needed them. They would go to the store for us and cook if I wasn't able to do so. If I needed to go to the doctor or for a procedure they would stay with our dad and mom so I could take care of myself. I would try to schedule my appointments to make it less of a hassle as possible for them. When my mom was admitted to the hospital they came as soon as possible and stayed whenever they could. They still had to work and they could not take too much time off. When my oldest sister retired she was around to help whenever she could.

It's probably petty on my part but it just seemed that whenever they had a chance to criticize me or put me down they did. I guess it was because I was their little brother, the youngest and they still wanted to have some control over me. It doesn't matter now and they did help as much as they could so I just will say it was sibling rivalry.

Family Close By

My family has always lived close by, at least by California standards. My oldest sister lived about sixty miles away when we lived in Lynwood and my other sister lived about twenty. It was a short half hour to one hour drive for both of them to come and visit.

When we moved to Tehachapi my oldest sister was about two blocks away and my other sister lived about 150 miles away. One could be over in a matter of minutes and the other had around a three hour drive. When she drove up she would usually stayed a few days so she could spend time with us and help out.

My dad always enjoyed the visits from his daughters and their families.

The grand children always enjoyed being around their grandfather and he loved being around them. He never had the chance to see his grandchildren get married or his great grand children. My mom on the other hand got a chance to see two great grandchildren. She lit up every time they would come to visit and they spent a lot of time with her. Those were good times and with all the problems she had with pain it was nice to see her smile and laugh when they were around.

Having the family close was a great help because I did get help once and while. My sisters, nieces and nephews had lives of their own so I didn't expect help but I did appreciate it when they came over. I never let them do the lifting or the changing but I did let them help with meals and some household chores. It gave me a little break and also allowed me to enjoy their company.

Not every time was great and we were just like any other family, we had our spats. Personalities change and so do our ways of life and sometimes that interferes with family life. Some were short and some lasted a while but in the end we realized that we needed each other.

Family was an important part of taking care of my parents and when they were around we had a good time. When they were not around it was boring and it made you look forward to their visits. It made life much better for my dad, mom and me when we had the family around.

Jealousy

Sometimes jealousy can come into play because some think you have an advantage because you're always with your parent. Some siblings can think of you as the favorite and therefore there is more affection for you. This could eventually cause problems if there is a large estate involved because others think you have a unique advantage.

Fortunately for me I didn't have this problem with my sisters. One, my parents didn't have any estate to talk about and what was in it was used for their care. My sisters would always tease me that I was the favorite because I was the youngest and they would make comments putting me down whenever they could. They would call me a "momma's boy" once in a while but this didn't bother me because I heard that as long as I could remember. Being the youngest and only boy it was expected and I never thought anything of it. I never saw the jealousy monster ever come to the surface to where it caused a problem while I was taking care of my parents. Yes, we did have a lot of disagreements and we rarely saw eye to eye on anything. It was normal for us and we had been doing this for many years because my sisters and I were very different.

After my mom died I did notice that they started to drift away more and keep their distance from me. One sister moved to Texas so that was expected even though we still talked about once a week. My other sister lives about twenty miles away and we have really drifted apart after my mom died. She is a retired LVN and she takes care of her grandchildren four days a week so she is always busy. I don't know if she is jealous of me for some reason, too busy or it's just time for a change. She helped out immensely when my dad and mom were alive and I always did my best to help her with her family. I'm sure when her life settles down things will get back to normal and we will be close as family should be.

Argued With Siblings

I did argue a lot with my sisters when I was taking care of my parents. It was never around my folks so it didn't make our parents upset. Most of the time it wasn't about how I was caring for our dad and mom it was about me giving up my career and ability to earn a living. Both of them were still able to continue with their careers and they both had families. It would have been impossible for either one of them to take care of our dad and mom on a full time basis. This is why I decided to do it so they both could go on with their lives and not be burdened with the care of our dad and mom.

I'm sure they saw something that I missed and had an idea of what was going to happen in the future. I was not focused down the road because I was concentrating on taking care of our parents. Our disagreements were always about my future after I was done taking care of our parents and how I was going to move on with my life.

They brought up some valid points and it helped me make a plan for the future but as always in life not everything goes as planned. When the end finally came the plans I had made were absolutely worthless and I was staring at an unknown future. I still haven't recovered and I am still trying to rebuild my life. Looking back maybe my sisters saw this outcome and that is why they argued with me. I know I did the right thing in caring for my dad and mom. The problem was I didn't consider my future more when I was planning ahead and my only focus was my parents. If I would have concentrated more on what happened after my parents were gone I might have had a better chance at rebuilding my life.

Not A Man's Job

I use to hear a lot of times that it wasn't a man's job to take care of his mother. One of my brothers in law would tell me this once in a while. My response was, "No one else will do it so who's job is it?" His response was always the same, "Hire someone." That is easy to say but hard to do if you do not have the funds to hire a caregiver. I also felt that it was a man's job if no one else would step up to the plate and do it. I never expected or asked my two sisters to take care of my mom. At one point I thought that since I took care of my dad they would pitch in and take care of my mom but that never happened because they were busy raising their own families and did not have the time to take care of my mom. When the time came I just did it and let them go on with their lives.

Years ago people got caught up in "That's a man's job," or "That's woman's work" and today it means absolutely nothing. Some say a "real man" doesn't do this or that and that a "career" woman can't have a job and have a family. Once again that is so far from the truth and it makes no sense. A real man is one that takes responsibility and cares for his family and does whatever it takes. That's what I was doing when I was taking care of my mom. Sure there were things that I never thought I would see or do but you do what you have to do. It doesn't matter if you're a man or woman you suck it up, toughen up and do the job you need to do.

It's easy to say to someone, "Hire somebody," because it's a lot harder to say, "you're doing the right thing." Some people can never see themselves taking care of a parent and doing the necessary jobs it takes. A lot are never put in that situation and are happy they never had to make the decision. For those of us that had to make the decision, it's not, "A man's job," or "a woman's job," it's just a job that needs to be done.

Let The Hospital Staff Do It

It was always a habit that whenever my dad or mom needed something I would immediately do it. If they needed my help I was right there to give them a hand. This would even happen when they were in the hospital. I got so use to taking care of them that I would do something before they even asked. My sister and brother in law would get mad at me and say, "Let the hospital staff do it." My other sister, who was an LVN, said a lot of times the staff was so busy that they couldn't help with the little things that some patients needed and they always appreciated the family's help. One said, "No" and one said, "Yes" but it didn't matter I just did what I needed to do.

I never had any hospital staffer or doctor say that I was in the way or I shouldn't help with my parents care. Most of time, like my sister said, they were so busy with other tasks that they couldn't get to patients as quickly as they would like. As long as I was around this never became a problem and my parents got what they needed. I fed them when they couldn't do it themselves, helped them get dressed and shaved my dad.

The only time I stepped back was when my mom was supposed to have physical therapy. I figured with me around she would try to use me as a crutch and not do the therapy. I was right, even with me not around she wouldn't do the physical therapy. The therapist had to call me in and try to plead with her to do the physical therapy but it fell on deaf years. We ended up paying for that decision the rest of her life.

Every time my folks were in the hospital you always saw the staff busy at work. They put in long stressful days and if I could help in the care of my folks that was not a problem for me. Some say it was a good time to take a break but if they were not in the hospital I still would be doing the work.

Got Upset When She Heard Talk About Putting Her In A Home

During the entire time I was taking care of my mom I never considered putting her into an assisted care facility. Others would mention it to me and sometimes my mom would over hear the conversation. It never caused a problem between my mom and I because she knew that I would not put her in a home.

Most of the time the recommendation to put my mom into a care facility was prefaced by the reason that it was best for me. No one ever said it was what was best for her so I took that as meaning I was taking good care of her. They would tell me that I needed my own life and it wasn't fair that I had to spend my life taking care of her. Some also said that I shouldn't put myself down and show some dignity and have someone else care for my mom. My answer to this line was, I have a great amount of dignity and that's why I was taking care of her.

Most of the time my mom would cast aside these comments but once in a while she would tell people, "I'm fine right here," "I'm not going anywhere," or "Jim has everything under control." On a few occasions she asked me, "Are you okay taking care of me?" My answer was immediate and always the same, "You're staying with me and I'm not going anywhere." She would smile and we went on with our lives.

The interesting thing about the comments about putting my mom in a home was that they were from people that were only thinking of what they would do. They could not see themselves taking care of their mom so they thought that I should do the same. I always told them that I made the decision and I promised my dad I would take care of my mom. That fell on deaf ears because they said he was dead so the promise meant nothing. Talk about loss of dignity.

I knew my mom was upset about these conversations when she would ask me what I wanted to do. She knew the answer but she just wanted a little reassurance. The only time she became nervous and raised her voice that she was fine was when I told her of what might happen if I died. She didn't want to hear of that situation but I had to let her know of the possibility if something happened to me. That made her upset because she knew that if that happened she probably would end up in an assisted care facility. Her final response was, "Be careful and take care of your health, nothing better happen to you."

I did my best to stay healthy and I took care of her to the end. She passed away in her own home and was never admitted to an assisted care facility. I kept my promise to my dad, mom and kept my dignity to the end.

How Different Siblings Can Be

It's amazing on how different siblings can be and how they deal with the same situation. My sisters and I are very different and we have varying opinions on everything. This led to a lot of frustration and heated discussions on how I cared for my dad and mom.

My oldest sister can't handle any type of medical situation and would rather cook and clean than deal with a sick person. She would also rather pay someone to help with the daily medical routines. That would be easy for her because she had a great career and could afford such luxury. When I was taking care of my dad she would never come in the room when I was giving him an insulin shot or helping him up. She would stay in the kitchen and cook dinner. That was well appreciated because it meant that I had one less chore to do. My other sister was an LVN and had no problem diving in and helping with my dad. She was very "matter of fact" and just did the job at hand and did it very well. When I would ask for advice she wouldn't say much except to ask the doctor. I took that as good advice and always asked our doctors whenever I had questions. Her problem was that it was like a chore for her to take care of my dad and I think that was because that was her job and she tried to keep patients at a distance. It was probably hard for her to take care of a family member because she had a good idea of what the end result would be.

When it was time for us to take care of my mom both sisters were extremely busy with their families and careers. I didn't ask them for help and I basically did everything. Once again the oldest wanted to pay for someone to come in and take care of my mom or possibly put her into a care facility. My other sister had no opinion so I was basically on my own. The answer was "no" to a paid caregiver and to the assisted care facility.

They did come visit and helped when they were around. My oldest sister would cook and clean giving me a break from the everyday chores. My other sister would help bathe my mom and help with the chores around the house. I was never angry or mad at them because they were not around as much as I would have liked. I knew they had families of their own and they had to take care of themselves. I knew that when I decided to take care of my mom that I would be on my own.

I also see this with my cousin who is now starting to take care of his dad part time. His father lives across the street from him so it makes it easy for him to check on him daily. He has an older brother that lives about seventy miles away and he rarely comes up to visit his dad. When his father moved in from out of state he told him that he could visit every couple of weeks so his brother could do other things. It hasn't happened and his excuse is that his wife is taking care of her mom so he can't leave her. When they do visit they do bring his mother in law because she still can travel. My cousin has a sister that lives on the East coast so she is not close to help. You would think that she would call often to check on her dad. She has a career and she is too busy to call. When her father calls her to see how's she's doing he usually gets her voice mail. He leaves a message and she calls back in a few days when it is convenient for her. I guess her father is not that important. Once again I know everyone's situation is different so I shouldn't judge but to me this is a little cold and distant.

Siblings are always different and that is what makes people unique. Everyone has their ideas on how to handle situations and has their own way of dealing with them. When you are taking care of a parent this will defiantly make to the surface if you have brothers and/or sisters.

Some Family Members Try To Control Others, Think They're More Important

I come from a traditional strong willed Italian family. In this type of a family some feel that they are more important and try to control others in order to make them feel like they are in charge. Some think they are the patriarch or matriarch of the family and act as if they are responsible for everyone else. What they are trying to do is to control the family so that they are seen as the leader.

My mom was technically the "matriarch" because she was the oldest living family member of that generation. My oldest female cousin would act like she was the oldest in the family and my mom would put her in her place every time she tried to control others. I have an uncle who now is the oldest one of the previous generation so technically he would be the "patriarch." He married into the family so some consider him an outsider and they don't pay attention to him or visit him because they are too busy. Even some of his children and grandchildren don't have time to visit him even though they live about seventy miles away. He is alone except for his youngest son who lives across the street and takes care of him part time. I have an older male cousin who would be the next in line but he is not interested and can care less about being the patriarch in the family. The next in line would be my oldest female cousin and she thinks she runs the family. After her would be my oldest sister and then my next sister. I would be second to last in line for patriarch because there are still a few cousins ahead of me. It all means nothing and nobody cares about it except as a joke and a way to get a rise out of a certain person.

My cousin actually believes that since she is the oldest female of our generation that we should all respect her and that she runs the family. I have a hard time with this situation because she treats the rest of us like we are kids and that she is the smarter than the rest. She retired from one county law enforcement agency and now works for another county law enforcement agency and she acts like she is better than the rest of us. Even her brother and his family think they are more important than the rest of the family. I refuse to put up with this crap and I call her out every chance I can. She told me that I "was nothing and lower than her" which just set me off. I told her that we were equals because we were of the same generation and she told me, "You will never be the same as me." Needless to say we are no longer speaking and I want nothing to do with her. The sad part is that she makes the most mistakes of anyone in the family and is always cheated by outsiders because she listens to everybody except those that have nothing to gain from her. She has been cheated by people from her church, neighbors and contractors of every sort. But she still gives advice even though ninety percent of the time she is wrong.

The problem is that some family members back her up because they have something to gain by siding with her and condemning everyone else. I won't play this game and it has cost me some of my family. I do believe in traditions but I also believe in fairness and that we are all the same. I don't care that she makes more money than anyone else in the family but I do care when she throws it in your face to show off. In one of the dumbest things I did after my mom passed away was I did some work for her around her house. Before I started I made it clear that I would only do the job the right way and that I wouldn't put up with any of her crap. She agreed and I went ahead with the projects. As time went on her old ways started showing up and it became a battle. I finally had enough and when I lost my car to a drunk driver on the side of her house I left. I had enough because she was constantly trying to control me and complaining to other family members. I was done and I moved in with another cousin. One of my sisters warned me that I was making a mistake and to be sure that I know what I was doing. I was desperate because I needed the money so I made a bad decision and my sister was right.

This incident has put me on the "outs" with most of my family because a lot of them have something to gain with this cousin. I don't care and if they want to take sides that is up to them. The interesting thing was that my mom warned me to stay away from this cousin. She said she reminded her of her older sister who tried to control the family and that she didn't trust her. She told me to be careful and that she would try to control my life. As usual my mom was right and it almost happened because I was desperate. Fortunately I woke up and got out of that situation but in the process I lost some of my family.

She still tries to control the family but more and more are getting to know her true motives. Some are starting to walk away from her because they are tired of her control and the way she acts like she is better than everyone else. The biggest problem is that she never listens to anyone and that she thinks only her life is important. Some still side with her because they are beholding to her but I think that will change as the rest of the family keeps walking away from her. She is trying to isolate me from my family and I think in the end she is actually pushing my family closer to me. Sooner or later the truth always comes out and no one wants to be controlled because everybody has to run their own lives. This will be a concept hard for my cousin to accept and eventually she will be alone. When that happens the only one to blame will be herself.

Forgive And Forget

A lot of people tell you that you need to forgive and forget when it comes to things in life. Some say that I am a petty person because I can't forget things that have happened in the past. Interesting enough some in the family say that I have a great memory and I can remember anything that happened years ago. The same family members don't like it when I remember certain things that they want to forget. They usually say, "I don't remember that," and "That didn't happen," or "It didn't happen that way." Most of the time they don't want to remember because the truth is hard to accept when you try to forget it.

I do have a great memory and I can remember almost everything that has happened to me or I have seen since I was about four years old. When I bring up things that have happened in the past, depending on what side you are on, you are either happy or angry. This has caused problems because I can always remember when and who hurt or criticized my parents and tried to make them look bad. My sisters keep telling me to forget what happened years ago because it is no longer important but my attitude is people and history repeat themselves and I want to be ready. Having this attitude has helped very much since my parents have passed away.

I can forgive people for what they have done but I will never forget. People in the family have hurt me over many occasions and years but I am willing to forgive them. I will not forget because it did happen and there will always be a memory. Some of these people also hurt my parents by their words and actions and once again I can forgive them but I won't forget what they did in the past. I'm sure the same will be for me because some will forgive me for what I have done but they will also never forget.

Like in all families my sisters have said and done things that will be forgiven but will not be forgotten. In the same way I have done things to them that they will never forget but they will forgive me. This is all part of life and the way we move on from one challenge to another.

Ok For Others To Back Their Parents, Not Ok For Me To Back Mine

One of the things that has always frustrated me was that I was always criticized for backing up my parents. This criticism was from family and it would drive me nuts. On the other hand it was always okay for others to back their parents which made it so hypocritical.

When my dad was diagnosed with bladder cancer he didn't want anyone to know. He was embarrassed and he didn't want people to know he had a urostomy bag. He told me, my mom and sisters that he didn't want anyone in the family to know or visit him in the hospital after his surgery. My mom and I said okay but this was a hard situation for my sisters to deal with. They didn't understand his reasoning and didn't want to follow his wishes. My mom and I made it clear that it didn't matter what his reasoning was but what did matter was that we comply with his wishes. They went along with it but every chance they had they would criticize us for following my dad's wishes. It was almost like the relatives were more important than their father. The family made a big fuss because they wanted to visit my dad but we told them that he didn't want to have any visitors. For most, that was fine but a few in the family didn't want to hear any of it and caused some problems. My mom and I finally had to put restrictions on who could visit my dad because we didn't want my dad to get upset while he was recuperating. The only ones that were allowed to visit him were my mom, two sisters and their families and myself. I got an earful from both sisters saying this wasn't right and we didn't have the right to shut out the rest of the family. My mom put a stop to this and said, "Yes I do." Years later this subject still came out and my dad finally told both of them that I was acting on his wishes and if they had a problem, it was with him. They later dropped it but even today this subject comes up and I get blamed because I listened to my dad.

The same happened with my mom because when she was in the hospital she would tell me who she wanted to come and visit her. She always wanted my sisters and their families to come and visit. She didn't want the relatives to visit her in the hospital because she was in pain and felt like an invalid. I always followed her wishes and I was always was accused of keeping my mom away from the rest of the family. No one ever would ask her but they would always accuse me. Once again after the hospital visit my mom told my sisters that I was following her wishes and if they had a problem it was with her and not me. They said again they understood but still to this day they side with the relatives instead of with me.

The interesting fact about this was that it was always okay for my cousins to back their parents and we always followed their wishes. When my aunt died my uncle didn't want any of the family to call or visit and we followed his wishes. When others didn't want us to visit we stayed back until they said it was okay. My sisters never had a problem with theses situations but they had a problem when I did it for our parents.

This has been a sore spot in my family relationship for many years and it is still hounding me today. When I was taking care of my parents I always followed their wishes and backed them up on all their decisions. I have paid a price for that loyalty for many years and I will probably continue to pay a price for the rest of my life. The part that makes me angry was that it was okay for others in the family to back their parents and follow their wishes but it was not okay for me to back my parents.

Had Some Good Friends

Over the years I had some very good friends. In fact some friends were more understanding than some family members on why I decided to take care of my parents. Fortunately for me some of these people are still true friends and we keep in touch.

I still have friends that I knew from my old high school because we served on the alumni association. In fact one friend has moved to the East coast and we still keep in touch regularly. He and his wife would visit my mom when we lived in Lynwood and Tehachapi and no matter what we discussed, he would always take my mom's side. We would joke around and he would just make her laugh. Even better his wife would always bring a pie and that would make my mom very happy. I would tell them, "She doesn't need pie," and my friend would say, "of course she needs pie, everything is better with pie." My mom always agreed. He would agree with everything my mom would say and she would always tell him, "I like you." Even though they moved out of state they still kept in touch by phone and they would send my mom birthday and Christmas cards. When they heard my mom passed away they were the only one's that were concerned about me and what was ahead. They were always there for a friendly ear or advice. They still come back to visit California and they always make time so we can get together. They are true friends.

Another friend I had from my old high school still keeps in touch and is always a joy to hear from. He has three children and I saw all of them grow up. In fact his youngest son and daughter also knew my mom and they always interacted with her at our alumni events. His daughter was in high school and she was being taught by my niece, my mom's granddaughter. When my mom passed away they attended the funeral. When her father asked if it was going to be uncomfortable with her teacher being at the service she said, "I knew Jim and Mrs. Colozzo before I knew her." She was a wonderful young lady. I still keep in touch and unfortunately we don't get together as much as we should. He is busy with his career, he's a teacher, and I am still trying to get a job so there is not much time for visiting.

I had another friend who he and his wife also knew my mom. His wife would offer to stay with my mom so her husband and I could get together to talk about old times. She also said it was so I could take a short break. She was wonderful in trying to help even though she was not in the best health. She would tire easily and I never wanted to put her in a situation to where she had to take care of my mom. She needed to take care of herself and not worry about us. We still keep in touch but once again it is hard for us to get together. He is also a teacher and has a very busy schedule. We do keep in touch by phone and email and he is always there when I need to talk.

These friends have always been supportive of me and always offered to help in any way they could. I knew they meant it because they always wanted to help and it wasn't for pity. They were truly concerned for me and my mom. Even some family members just went through the words but they really never wanted to help. These friends supported my decision to take care of my parents and gave me that support all the way to the end and after. Some family members never gave me support but did offer a lot of criticism and after my mom passed away showed no concern for me at all.

Chapter 46
DOCUMENTATION AND BEING A CAREGIVER
Attorney

It is always good to have access to an attorney when you are a caregiver. For one thing they can prepare all the legal forms for your parent such as Durable Power of Attorney for Medical, DNR, Do Not Resuscitate paperwork, Living Trust, Estate Plan, Will and other documents relating to their care, financial matters, disposition and estate. This can prevent a lot of problems so it is good to be prepared.

I had an attorney that I used when I had my business and he quickly became our family lawyer. He use to say that he represented three generations of my family and he did. He represented my mom, one of my sisters and my niece. He prepared my mom's Durable Power Of Attorney For Medical as well as her estate plan. I brought her to his office and he spoke to her alone and they came up with the plan she wanted followed. She made the decisions herself with no influence from me. I never expected any problems when the end came but you never know so this prevented any possible conflict.

These documents were put away in a safe place and were always available when needed. Copies of her Durable Power Of Attorney and DNR order were made every time I had to take my mom to the hospital. When the end finally came, after my mom was pronounced deceased the police officer on scene wanted to see the DNR, Do Not Resuscitate order. It was available and was provided when it was requested.

I had no idea this would happen but it was good that I was prepared and had the documents available. The time and money spent on an attorney and legal documents was invaluable. By being prepared I was able to avoid a possible problem and inquiry because I had the proper documentation. I was my mom's caregiver and I was responsible for her care, well being and her wishes for the end. Part of that responsibility was to have the proper legal documents.

Estate

My mom and dad had a legal plan for their estate and it was basically for the house which they owned outright. My mom legally changed that plan after my father passed away. That plan was once again changed when we moved to our new home in Tehachapi.

My parents estate consisted of the house and their belongings. When my dad passed away the house and all the belongings transferred to my mom. As time went on and my mom's care got more expensive we had to borrow on the house to pay off debts that were incurred for her care. I inquired about a reverse mortgage but was told it was not available for our situation. In the process of obtaining a home loan it was necessary for me to be added to the deed and we were then able to get a home loan. A few years later once again we needed to pay off more debts because of the cost of her care. This time in order to obtain the loan the lender requested that she be removed from the deed and I would be the sole borrower. We complied and the loan was received.

When the house was sold in 2008 I used the remaining proceeds for a down payment on a new home and the remainder went into savings for emergencies. I purchased the new home and the deed was in my name only. During the time we lived in Tehachapi and until my mom died she gave away her belongings to my sisters and the immediate family. She decided that she wanted to give out the items before she passed away so she could see the enjoyment they gave to the family.

After she died the estate had no value because there was no estate left. The emergency money that was in savings was used for her care. When the house was finally sold a year after she died the proceeds were used to pay down the debts incurred during the final years of her life. My sisters never received any proceeds from the sale of the home. As per my mom's wishes and plan the house would be used as necessary for her care so she would not be put in a home or on the street. I complied with her wishes and unfortunately there was no estate left and only debts remained. All the planning she did for years fell apart and now that it is over I still owe debts for her care.

Durable Power Of Attorney For Medical

When you are taking care of your parents it is important to have the proper legal documents. Not only do you need documents that discuss how the finances and property will be handled you also need to have documents that detail how they want their medical conditions handled. The details need to include who will make those decisions if they are unable to do so for themselves and what the decision will be if they need to be resuscitated. In the state Of California, it was called a Durable Power Of Attorney For Medical. You need to sit down with them and discuss how they want the future handled. It is important to do this while they are still mentally in control and are of sound mind. This can alleviate problems down the road when they start to fail. If you wait until they start to fail it can become a problem, time consuming and expensive. One thing to note is that a Durable Power Of Attorney means absolutely nothing after your parent passes away. It is only valid while they are alive.

I'm not an attorney so I do not know what the process is to have this type of a document prepared but for our situation I relied on a lawyer that handled my affairs for many years. In fact I waited a long time before I had my mom prepare these documents and it was finally after her spine surgery in 2001. During her surgery I realized that I did not have the proper paperwork in case something happened. I did have papers with her signature discussing my involvement in her medical conditions but these were copies that I used from a computer legal documents program. Basically all you did was fill in the blanks with your information. It worked and was usable but I didn't feel it was a proper legal document. Back in 2001 the doctors and hospitals were not as stringent as they are today and HIPAA did not exist.

After she recovered from surgery I made an appointment with the attorney. I told her everything was her decision and I would not make any recommendations or demands. I did not want to influence her decisions so I wheeled her into the attorney's office, left her alone with him and closed the door. They were in his closed office for about an hour and then he came out and said he would write out the proper documents. At that time I didn't know what her decisions were and what she said to him. I paid for the services and we left. A week later I took her back to the attorney's office where they once again privately went over the documents, she approved and then signed them in front of the attorney and a witness.

When we got home I learned what her decisions were and what she wanted me to do. She told me to read the documents and that they outlined what she decided. I read the documents and put them in a safe place. It gave me the power to make decisions on her medical care if she was unable to do so and it included a document on her decision for DNR, Do Not Resuscitate.

After this every time we went to the hospital I would bring copies of the Durable Power Of Attorney so they could include it in her chart and file. They would make copies and note it on the admission paperwork. This proved invaluable every time we had to go to the hospital because all the paperwork was already completed and her wishes were documented.

DNR-Do Not Resuscitate

My mom had a DNR, Do Not Resuscitate order, drawn up by the attorney and it was part of her Durable Power Of Attorney For Medical. Every time she was admitted to the hospital I would give them a copy of this document as well as her Durable Power Of Attorney For Medical. During the admission process they would always ask if we had these type of documents and we always were prepared when we went to the hospital.

The DNR order was never used at the hospital for her spine surgery because she never had this document. When she had bowel surgery in 2008 this document was part of her admission package but it wasn't necessary because she came through the surgery without any major complications. It was on file at three hospitals but every time she was admitted they made another copy of the order and paperwork.

The only time it was used was when she passed away. I found her in bed, cold and unresponsive. I called 911 and the operator asked me if I wanted to do CPR. I told him that she had a DNR, Do Not Resuscitate Order, was cold, stiff, her eyes were rolled back and she was lifeless. The paramedics and police arrived very quickly and they went in to check my mom. Within a few minutes they came out and pronounced her deceased and said rigor was setting and she could not be resuscitated. As soon as they made the pronouncement the police officer asked to see the DNR order. I got the order from the file cabinet and he read it in front of me and told the paramedics everything was okay.

I was nervous because I had never been in this type of situation before and I didn't know what to expect. The officer told me that he needed to actually see if I had a written legal order and it wasn't just verbal. That was a very stressful situation but thankfully I had the proper paperwork, if not I could have been in a lot of trouble.

Write Everything Down

I always would carry a pen and pad with me so I could write everything down. When we went to the doctors I could write down information on what I might need to buy. If we were in the hospital I could take notes on procedures or advice from the different doctors. I also used it to write down if there were any problems or incidents that needed to be addressed.

I would write down the name of every doctor or resident that treated my parents. When physical therapy would come in I would take notes on the procedures they did. I would list what diagnostic tests were ordered and what the results were. I learned from these notes and it allowed me to ask questions whenever they were ordered again.

If a nurse did something that I wasn't sure of I would make a note and then ask the doctor the reason for the procedure. I always got an explanation which helped me understand the reasons for the procedures. I would ask about medications and why they were prescribed and what they controlled.

A few times I would question procedures because I felt they would not work with my mom. When they would bring in a wheelchair and asked her to get in so they could take her to x-ray. I would tell them, "She can't walk or stand up," and the response would be, "not at all," and I would say, "no." Little things like that had to be noted on the chart because they could have had bad outcomes.

I even would take notes when my mom was discharged. I would do my own inspections before we left the hospital. I would always have to get her dressed because she couldn't do it herself and while I put on her clothes I would note bruises and marks. I would then point them out to the discharge nurse so it would be documented on the discharge paperwork in case she had to be readmitted. This way when they did the pre-admit inspection it would be noted that the marks and bruises were caused by the hospital.

The hospital had ways to protect themselves and I also had a way to protect me. We never had a readmission to the hospital so I never had to explain any of the marks or bruises caused by the hospital. The only mark I had to always explain was the scar from the bed wound that my mom received years earlier from her spinal surgery. That scar was deep and thank God it was caused by the hospital and it was on her records. It was well documented and never became an issue.

Witnesses

It is always good to have a witness when you're documenting issues about your parents condition. The hospital always has a nurse and an aide when they do the pre-admission inspection. It is a little harder to have a witness when you are the only one taking care of your parent.

I had only one situation in all the years I took care of my parents that I needed a witness. It happened the last time my mom was in the hospital in 2013. She was admitted to the hospital because she was severely constipated because of the side effects of the pain medication she was prescribed. She was vomiting and couldn't keep anything down. In order to prevent dehydration I took her to the hospital for professional help in clearing the constipation. The resulting treatment was mass doses of laxative and enemas. The treatment also required several x-rays and scans. This meant that she was on her side and was rolled back and forth on the cold platforms of the diagnostic machines. Her skin was thin and she was also frail at the time.

When she was discharged everything was normal and I didn't notice any unusual marks or bruises. The only thing visible were the marks from the labs test and IV's. I took her home and the next morning when I was getting her dressed I was shocked. The entire left side of her upper torso was black and blue. It looked like it hurt but she said she had no pain. I called my sister who lived a few blocks away and she came over and saw the enormous bruise. If I had to take her back to the hospital I would have had something serious to explain. I called our family doctor and asked if we could go in right away. They made room for us and I showed his nurse all the bruising. She was also shocked and called the doctor. When the doctor came in he was astonished on how dark her left side was. He explained that it was from all the time she was laying on her side while they gave her enemas and from laying on the platforms for the x-rays and scans. He said her skin was thin and her circulation was poor so she was susceptible to bruising. I asked why it didn't show up sooner and he said it was like a car accident the damage usually shows up days later.

He made notes of the situation and noted it in her chart. He also called the hospital and informed them of the situation. He told them that it was documented and that pictures were taken. This was the one time I was truly scared because I feared I would get the blame for these bruises. They looked hideous. He said I did the right thing by bringing her to him so they could document the situation. He was my witness and I had nothing to worry about.

After a few days the bruises cleared and never came back. She passed away a few months later and never had to return to the hospital. I was glad I had our doctor as a witness but it sure did cause me a lot of worry.

Paperwork

When you are taking care of your parents make sure you have

paperwork relating to their condition readily available. When you go to the doctors, outpatients services or to the hospital make sure you have paperwork that lists their condition, procedures and medications. Make sure you have prescription information when you travel because of lot of times some of the medications could be considered a controlled substance. Have these medication in their original prescription bottles so, if necessary, you can prove that the prescriptions are for your parents. Another important document is to make sure you always have their identification available because every medical facility asks for identification before they perform services. Their Medicare and insurance cards should always be with you in case you need emergency services while you are out.

I always carried a packet or file of papers when I traveled with my dad or mom. It included all the information above as well as contact information in case I was not around for some reason. I had copies of their Durable Power Of Attorney as well as a copy of their DNR, Do Not Resuscitate, document. I never had to use these documents while we were traveling but I always needed them when we went to the hospital, test procedures or a new physician.

At home I would have my mobile file as well as a duplicate in a safe place, usually a file cabinet in my room. I told my sisters where the information was kept in case they needed to use it when I was not there. I updated the information on a bi-monthly basis or whenever a new situation occurred and this kept the files current.

When we went to the hospital we were always prepared and I didn't have to scramble and try to remember information. If I had to call 911 for the paramedics all the information was handy and relative. When I called the morning my mom passed away all the paperwork was available for the paramedics and police officer. It was good to be prepared because you never knew when something was going to happen.

Still Able To Sign Documents

During the entire time I took care of my parents they were still able to sign documents. The only time they were not able to sign for themselves were the last times they were admitted to the hospital. I was lucky because I never became the responsible party for their healthcare expenses until the end.

For all the tests, procedures and hospitalizations my dad had, he always signed the authorization paperwork. Sometimes they would ask me to sign and I would immediately give it to my father and tell them, "He is still able to sign for himself." My dad also knew that before he signed anything that he would always check with me so I could read it and say okay. I'm not a lawyer but I did read everything that he was given and I did tell him what boxes to check and not check. Over his entire illness we never had a major problem with billing and payments. There were the few occasions when someone would not look at the paperwork and bill the wrong insurance or put down the wrong diagnosis or medical code. These were eventually taken care of by phone calls or strongly worded letters. The only time I signed for my dad was the last time he was taken and admitted to the hospital. I signed all the paperwork for him because he was no longer mentally or physically able to sign. He passed away two weeks later.

My mom was also able to sign her own documents for all of her treatments except the last one. She also knew not to sign anything until I read it and gave her the okay. One time the hospital wanted her to sign a form before they would take a CAT scan and she refused until I was there. She told them, "I don't sign anything unless my son reads it." I was stuck in traffic and it took a little longer to get to the hospital. I got to her room, the nurse gave me the form, I read it and told my mom to sign it, which she did. The nurse was amazed at how stubborn my mom was in refusing until I was there and read the form. She said most people never read the forms and sign anything put in front of them. She told me it was good that we were cautious. Once again the only time I signed for my mom was the last time she was admitted to the hospital. At this point she was mentally and physically not able to sign any forms.

This was not done to be stubborn or difficult, it was a way to show that they were still in charge of their healthcare. Yes, I did read and tell them what to sign but they were still the ones giving the authorization. They still had responsibility for themselves. Once again it depends on your unique situation and what is the mental and physical state of your parent. I was lucky because mine were still able to participate in their medical decisions almost all the way to the end.

They Were The Responsible Party

Another reason I let my parents sign all the medical documents was that this made them the responsible party. They were the insured for Medicare and supplement insurance and therefore were authorizing their medical care. If for some reason there was a problem with billing and payment they would be the one's responsible for the bill. It's a technicality and I'm sure some lawyer would have a different opinion but it did make my folks feel better. They felt that by signing the medical paperwork themselves they were saving me from having to be responsible for any bills. I don't know if that would have worked and fortunately we never had to find out. All of their medical bills were always paid and we never had a problem with payment or any type of collection for medical services.

This was before HIPPA and I never had a problem discussing their bills with any medical faculty. Now with the new regulations it is harder to discuss medical billing because they only can speak to the patient. In order for you to discuss the billing situation you have to have permission from your parent before they will talk to you. Once again this depends on your situation and you might have to have legal documents prepared so you can discuss billing issues with Medicare and supplement insurance.

Medical facilities, Medicare and insurance companies have entire legal departments to make sure they get paid for what is billed. One way or another they will always get their money and it doesn't matter who they have to run through the ringer to get it. Make sure you have a plan and the supported legal documents to show who is responsible for what and when. You might never have to use it, as it was with my dad and mom, but if you need to, you have it available. It can save you from a lot of frustration and possibly enormous expenses.

Chapter 47

ASSISTANCE AND BEING A CAREGIVER

Assistance Programs

In some states there are assistance programs for being a caregiver. These could come in handy to cover some of the expenses while taking care of your parent. Your doctor, hospitals and outpatient facilities might have some information available about assistance programs in your area.

During the course of taking care of my dad and mom I was told many times that assistance programs were available. While I was taking care of my dad we were financially stable so I never considered looking into any financial assistance programs. When I was taking care of my mom things started to get expensive and money was going out a lot faster than it was coming in. This was back in 2003, we lived in Los Angeles County and one of our doctors suggested that I call the county to see if we qualified for some sort of financial assistance. They told me that some of their other patients were under the care of their children and they were receiving benefits for being a caregiver. They gave me a phone number to call and told me to give it a try. They said if anyone needed assistance it was me because I couldn't work when I was taking care of my mom full time.

I called the number and after waiting about twenty minutes I spoke to a representative or as they called themselves a "counsellor." I was told some assistance was available but there was certain criteria that needed to be met. The first question she asked was if my mom had any jewelry that was worth over $1,000.00. I told her the only jewelry of value was her wedding ring and she said that would not be counted toward the $1,000.00 jewelry limit. She then asked if she had a life insurance policy. I told her yes and she wanted to know if it was over $1,000.00. I told her it was for $5,000.00, just enough for burial, and she said that could be a disqualification because it was over the limit. She then asked if she had a cemetery plot. When my dad died I purchased a family plot for him and my mom as per his and her wishes. She said this was an automatic disqualification and I would not be able to apply for any benefit. My mom would have to sell the cemetery plot and probably the life insurance before we could be considered for any benefit. She continued to say that most people transfer their assets to someone else so they would be eligible for benefits. I told her thank you for her time and that we would do something else. In order to get assistance you had to cheat so you could get a benefit, definitely not worth the risk.

When I told the doctor he was surprised because none of the other patients told him about these limits. He later told me he asked them for more information and they told him they did change ownership to different names so they could get the benefit. I couldn't lie and do this so we never applied for assistance again. It was our situation, we paid for everything and never cheated to receive assistance from any government agency.

Handicap Parking Placard

An item that can be very helpful when you are taking care of your parent is a handicap placard for parking. Depending on the state and if they qualify it can be very helpful when you have to park at any facility where handicapped parking is available. When space is available it is a much shorter distance for your parent to walk or for you to push the wheelchair. They also make it easier to park at some events because they have special handicap sections set aside.

Both my parents applied for and received a handicap placard in California back in the late 1980s. It came in handy all the time for my dad because he was unable to walk a long distance without getting short of breath. For my mom being in a wheelchair it made things more convenient because we were able to park close to the door of the facilities. This meant less time for her to be out in the elements and less chance for her feet to fall off the wheelchair foot rests.

You have to be careful when you use these placards and they should never be abused. They are a great help when you are taking care of your parent because they make the chore of transportation a little easier. Under no circumstances should you ever use them just for yourself when you do not have your parent with you. After my mom passed away the handicap card was due to expire in two months. I never used the card after she died even though sometimes I caught myself driving toward the row of handicap parking spots. I realized what I was doing and drove away to the first convenient regular parking space. I used the handicap parking spaces legally with my parents for over twenty years and since they have passed away I never used one again.

Financial Assistance

There might be financial assistance programs where you to live to help with the cost of being a caregiver. If these programs are available to you be prepared to do a lot of paperwork and be under the guidance and supervision of the agency that provides the assistance.

One of the reasons I never wanted to apply for any assistance was that they always required visits from various people. It could be social workers, nurses and other individuals to check on the care that my mom was receiving. I never had a problem or worried about these inspections because I was taking good care of my mom but it would place an unnecessary burden on her. She would have to be up and awake when they visited and she would also have to answer a lot of questions. They would address the questions to her while they did an interview and she would get frustrated and upset because they wouldn't talk to me. One time one nurse came to visit and started asking my mom questions about her care and my mom said, "Enough, my son is doing a great job and I am happy with my care. If you don't like it or have more questions, It's time for you to leave." The nurse came to me in the other room and told me, "your mom just threw me out," and I told her it was her decision and she agreed and told me if we needed anything to call. We never called her back.

If you are interested in financial aid and if it's available be prepared to do a lot of paperwork. Another thing is that you will be under a microscope for everything you do and there will also be a lot of strings attached to receiving the benefit. As with life nothing is ever free.

Utility Company Discounts

One thing that might be available is utility company discounts. These can be for various utility services and depends on the type of durable medical equipment required to take care of your parent. Some programs might be available in order to help with heating and cooling expenses. Check with your local utility to see if any of these programs are available for your situation.

My first experience with a utility company discount was when my dad needed an oxygen generator to help him breath at home. This thing was a power hog and the medical equipment company told me to call the power company to see if I could get a larger power allotment at a lower rate. I called and they sent me the form and I quickly filled it out and brought it to our doctor. He filled out the physicians section and I submitted to the form to the electric company. Within a few weeks I received the confirmation that we would receive a higher medical baseline allotment and that would be billed at the lower rate. This was great news because our electric bill tripled with the use of the oxygen generator. The added bonus was that in case of a power failure the electric company would do their best to get our service restored as soon as possible. This was for normal loss of service and did not include storms, earthquake or other disasters. We did have a back up and in case of a power failure, a large oxygen tank in the house along with a couple of portable tanks that could keep the oxygen flowing for my dad. As soon as we got the medical baseline plan our electric bill became manageable again. After my father passed away the program was lifted and we went back to the old way of billing.

With my mom's condition the only item we had that used a lot of electricity was her air mattress. This thing was running anytime she was in bed and it ran almost sixteen hours a day. Once again our electricity bill skyrocketed and busted the monthly budget. I called the power company and they mailed me a form for medical baseline. Once again I filled out the form and had our doctor complete the physician section and submitted it to the electric company. About two weeks later I received a letter saying they denied our application because the unit was for cosmetic purposes and was not medically necessary. For a moment I thought I was dealing with Medicare and the supplement insurance company. When I told our doctor he was dumbfounded and called the electric company. They reaffirmed their decision and I ended paying the electric bill that tripled because of the air mattress.

When we moved to Tehachapi I once again applied for the medical baseline and filled the application the same way I did years before. I brought it to our doctor and he once again filled out the physician statement and submitted it to the power company. Two week later I got a letter saying that the application was approved and we qualified for a larger medical baseline at the lower rate. Our power bill dropped substantially and that definitely helped the monthly budget.

I never knew why it was denied one year and approved a few years later. It was the same unit, working the same amount of hours and it was the same electric company, the only difference was that it was in a different part of California. Once again it made no sense but I did enjoy the savings for the last few years of my mom's illness.

Chapter 48

PLANNING AND BEING A CAREGIVER

Long Term Planning

The only long term planning my folks' generation did, if they could, was to purchase life insurance. Most could only afford policies that paid $1,000.00 to $5,000.00 dollars. They never heard of long term care insurance or it didn't exist. Most of them never gave a thought of who was going to take care of them when they got old. If they had children I guess they hoped that one of their offspring would take care of them. In our case that offspring was "me."

When my folks got sick there was no long term planning. They had life insurance but that wasn't even enough to pay for the funeral. They owned the house and had no mortgage but that was a hard asset that couldn't be sold because we needed a place to live. When my dad was alive we were able to live off what he received from his workers' compensation and what I was able to earn from my business. After he passed away my mom received a monthly survivor benefit that was a portion of what he received. I could still make money doing small jobs but as she became ill trying to do jobs started to become a problem until I finally had to stop. We no longer had extra income and were living just off her survivor benefit.

If there were any long term plans no one ever told me and we were living month to month. I was good at budgeting and I kept us going with the amount we received. As time went on expenses became higher and it grew to the point that we were out of money. I started using our credit cards because my mom needed her supplies and that was the only way to pay for them. As you can see things snowballed from bad to worse.

We finally had to finance the house and to this day I still think that was the biggest mistake I ever made. It solved the current problem and gave us much needed cash for her care but it caused a lot of problems for the future. The borrowing on the house became my long term plan to take care of my mom. It worked but it only lasted a few years. We sold our Lynwood house and moved to a new home in Tehachapi, California. We sold our house for a profit so I decided to keep the profits and use them to take care of my mom. We put twenty percent down on the new home and I got a thirty year mortgage. The extra cash once again helped with her care because I had no worries in buying the supplies and items she needed. I could give her a good quality of life. Her expenses continued to rise as well as all other costs and there was no way to lower our monthly output. So much for long term plans.

When she passed away all the money was gone and I was deeply in debt. The housing market started to improve and I was able to sell the house a year after my mom died. I settled some debts but to this day I am still paying on a lot of others. If I never financed the house it would have been a struggle a few years earlier but I don't think we would have been in the shape we were when she died. It was a mistake.

No Planning

My long term planning was seat of the pants, on the fly which basically equaled no planning. Things became so hectic that I had no time to think of what I had to do for the future. I was thinking of the current time and never thought much about down the road. This caused me to make bad decisions and regret some of those to this day.

My concern was so much for the care of my mom and dad that I never considered what would happen if the money ran out. I tried to keep the bills in check but as time went on they ballooned. Utility costs would skyrocket because you had to keep the house warm in the winter and cool in the summer. I had to keep my mom comfortable so she wouldn't get sick. She had an air mattress that was considered a comfort item even though it was needed so she wouldn't get bed sores. The compressor that kept the mattress working pulled 1000 watts of electricity and it was on sometimes eighteen hours a day. That's 18 kilowatt hours of electricity a day times twelve cents a kilowatt hour that equals $2.16 a day just to run the air mattress. That averages $64.80 a month just so she wouldn't get bed sores. It was well worth it because the alternative would be a nightmare but that is an expense that you can't plan. The cost to run the bed compressor is more than some people pay for electricity for an entire home.

Incontinence supplies were always a major expense and were needed day after day. Prescriptions were another cost even though she had good health insurance. Her transdermal pain patches, Fentanyl, our co-payment was $120.00 a month for the brand name and at that time there was no generic. A few years later when the generic was released the cost went down to $28.00 a month.

There are countless expenses that come up when you are a caregiver and most are not covered by Medicare and insurance. You, your parent or both have to foot the bill for those expenses. Remember, you are responsible for their care and you need to do whatever it takes and can afford in taking care of them. In my case no planning was an expensive option that cost me everything.

Deal With Each Situation As It Happens

One thing I learned over many years was that you had absolutely no control of whatever challenges came your way. Getting upset because something happened or something didn't go as planned did no good and never helped in caring for my parents. I learned to deal with each situation as it happened because somethings you could never plan for and in the long run it made it easier to cope.

It seemed every time we went for a test or diagnostic procedure something would change and it meant more work for both of us. It could be simple like the wound bandage had to be changed every two days instead of every three. It could be more difficult because I would have to take her for more tests or doctors and that would mean lifting and moving her more. Getting my mom ready for an early appointment was not an easy task. Most tests and procedures were always in the morning and that meant an early start for both of us. If we had a procedure at 9am I would have to start getting her ready about 5am. It usually took three hours to get her ready to go out. It also depended on the location of the procedure. If it was a long distance it would be three hours plus driving time. So whenever her doctors would order tests or procedures they would look at me and say, "Sorry." I would look at them and say my usual, "You got to do what you got to do," and then I would deal with it.

If you have no control over a condition you have to deal with it as it happens. You can plan for everything you know but there is always that situation you never saw coming. You don't have time to plan for it so you have to deal with it. Health is one of the things in life that you have no control over. You can do all the preventative care you want and there is always something that sneaks up on you. When you are a caregiver you always have to be prepared for the "unscheduled" or "unplanned" event. They will come and you have to be ready to deal with them as they happen.

Average Person Equals No Future Planning

As with most people we say that we have a plan for the future and when that time comes we realize that we haven't made any plans at all. We or our parents might have planned ahead for their care but none of us have any clue what is coming. Some people can afford long term care insurance but most of us can't because of the cost. Most of us are trying to survive day to day and have no spare money to put away for long term care.

I thought I had made plans for the future and the care of my parents but I had no idea how inadequate that plan was. In fact the plans I made resulted in like I made no plans at all. The amount of money I thought we needed didn't even come close to the actual expenses. Add inflation to that amount and I wasn't even in the ballpark. Things that you give little thought to like diapers take up a large chunk of your budget. Thinking Medicare and insurance are going to cover all the expenses are a dream.

Some people plan to go into assisted living facilities, take a look these locations, they are not cheap. They vary according to the care that you need at the time. They are affordable like an apartment if you don't need any care but once you start needing assistance they get expensive. If you need full time care unless you are wealthy they will drain your savings in less than a year.

In my mom's situation I couldn't afford the daily rate for care. All that she needed and eventually received from me, I could never have afforded from an assisted care facility. She also never would have lasted in one of these locations because she wanted to be with her family and still wanted to have some feel that she had control over her life. With her appetite we could never have afforded the food and she never would have had the ability to enjoy what was left of her life. She would have been in bed most of the time because it would have been hard or too much trouble to lift her out.

The average person with and average pay cannot afford planning for the future. If you were able to put away $500.00 a month for twenty years that would only be $120,000.00 plus accrued interest. Long term care insurance is an option and this is how it was explained to me. If you were able to afford long term care insurance that could cost you at least an extra $300.00 per month. So that's a total of $800.00 a month for long term planning. When the time would come, most long term care insurance pays a certain amount per day, around $200.00 for care. Multiply that by 30 days that equals $6,000.00 per month. That usually covers some assisted care living like the basics, someone coming in two or three times a week and all meals are served in a dining room. If you can't leave your room and you need full time care, the cost per day could be $500.00 per day or more. That means $500.00 a day time 30 days equals $15,000.00 per month minus $6,000.00 per month from the long term care insurance. That means you owe $9,000.00 a month for care. The amount you saved was $120,000.00 divided by $9,000.00 a month equals 13.33 months, just over a year of care. What happens when your parent lives longer than that? All your savings is gone and how are you going to continue to afford this care? To make up the difference where are you going to get the money?

My mom lasted over thirteen years in her condition. In the above scenario that would have cost $9,000.00 a month times twelve months which equals $108,000.00 a year times 13 years that equals $1,404,000.00. Without the long term care insurance the cost would have been $15,000.00 times twelve months which equals $180,000.00 times 13 years which equals $2,340,000.00. We never had that kind of money and did not have any access to it. You need to speak to your insurance agent to get specifics and estimates for your unique situation.

Even though my mom's care was expensive it never reached that high of a figure. I gave her good care and great food for a lot less than an assisted living center. She enjoyed the rest of her life all the way to the end. It was a lot of work for me but I could never have afforded her care any other way.

If You're Rich, Maybe Not

A lot of times you can make things easier by getting help. This is great if you have family members that are close by and willing to help or if you can afford you could hire someone to help you with your tasks. Hiring help is not inexpensive and you need to make sure they are comfortable taking care of an adult. You also need to make sure they have patience and compassion because it is a demanding job.

I never could afford to hire anyone to help take care of my parents and my sisters lived too far away to help with the everyday tasks. So for the entire time it was just me and only me. I had a cousin that took care of her aunt and she was able to afford to hire help to care for her during the day while she was at work. She had interruptions in her life because of the care she gave my aunt but she never had to put her life or career on hold.

When you can hire someone you usually get help and that makes taking care of you parent a little easier because it is not all on just you. With two people things are so much easier because one can be attending to the needs of your parent and the other can be taking care of household chores and tasks. The other nice thing is that in case of emergency there is someone around that can help in the situation. This would be like if you fell or hurt yourself there would be someone else there to give you aid if necessary and your parent still would have proper care.

The only way to have this luxury is to have the funds available to hire someone to help. This could be accomplished by purchasing long term care insurance but this would have to be done prior to your parent's illness. This is an expensive option but if is in your budget it would be something to consider. I never had this option available because it was not affordable for my family.

When you can afford to hire someone you never have to deal with the situation yourself. A lot of people that give advice and had to take care of their parents hired someone to do the day to day routine. Some even could afford assisted care facilities that took care of their parents from the very start of their illness. Some people had the luxury of being able to afford long term care insurance and the majority of their day to day living expenses were covered by this insurance. Others don't have this benefit and the day to day expenses come out of their pocket which means their situation is totally different. If you can afford help your idea of taking care of a parent is talking to them during the day and making sure they are alert and well cared. You don't have to deal with the day to day routine of bathing them or taking them to the bathroom. You don't deal with diaper changes or dressing them for the day. So their situation is nothing like someone that has to do all these tasks by themselves.

I'm not jealous of these people but what always bothered me was that they would tell you what to do. Their situation was nowhere near what I had to deal with and there was no comparison. They were fortunate to have the funds to care for their parent and I had the responsibility to care for my parents by myself.

Plan If I Died, What Would Happen To Her

You are responsible for the person you are caring for and being a good caregiver you need to have a plan in case you can longer care for them. During the course of taking care of my mom I made sure there was a plan in case I got sick or even if I died. I even discussed it with her once in a while so she would know that she would always be taken care of.

If I died the first option would be for one of my sisters to take over her care. My mom received a monthly benefit that would cover some of her care. Her medical was almost completely covered by Medicare and supplemental insurance so that was never an issue. Without the living expenses of a house payment, keeping a roof over her head and the other costs associated with owning a house, she would be able to live in reasonable comfort. The problem with that plan was neither of my sisters would be able to lift her during the normal daily routines. This means they would have to hire help in order to take care of my mom on a full time basis. The solution to this was I had a $100,000.00 life insurance policy that named my sisters as beneficiaries and that would cover the cost to hire someone to help them take care of our mom.

Now another problem could arise if neither sister was able to care for our mom and that became the second option. Her monthly benefit would cover some of the cost of an assisted living facility but there would be a lot more expenses because the detailed care my mom required. To try to solve this problem they would sell the house I purchased and use the proceeds to help with the care of my mom in an assisted living center. This was dependent on the housing market and how much equity was available in the house. If that was not enough, my sisters could use the money received from my life insurance policy.

That money should have lasted for the rest of my mom's life and my sisters might have had something left over for all their work. It was a good plan and kept her mind at ease in case something happened to me. The part she didn't like was if my sisters couldn't take care of her and she had to move into an assisted care facility. That thought was terrifying to my mom and I'm sure it was always in the back of her mind. Fortunately for her that plan was never used and she was able to stay in her own home all the way to the end.

Nothing Goes As Planned

It is always good to be prepared and to make plans but as in life nothing ever goes as planned. There are so many variables being a caregiver that no matter how much you prepare something always happens. So be ready for anything and be ready to deal with it.

Many times we would get ready to go to the store, run some errands or go out for a visit and something would change. We would not go out until my mom was ready and that meant she had to go to the bathroom. We would wait and usually she would go in the morning and then we could leave on our errands. Somedays she didn't go so I would take a chance and we would leave for our errands. It must have been the vibration of the car because after about ten to twenty minutes in the car she would look at me and say, "I gotta go." That meant a u-turn and a trip back home or if we were close, driving to a large parking lot so she could "go." If this happened I would change her in the car and we would continue on our journey. If we were close to home I would drive back because I usually had about another twenty minutes until she "went." We would get back home and I would lift her out of the car and into the wheelchair and wheel her into the house. I would then cut the tabs on her diaper and then lift her onto the toilet. She would go and when she was finished she would ring her bell. I would lift her of the toilet back on the wheelchair and then lift her onto the bed. I would make sure she was clean and then I would put a new diaper on her. If we still had time I then lifted her off the bed into the wheelchair and wheeled her to the car. I lifted her in the car and away we went. That was a total of six lifts in less than an hour and that was just to go to the bathroom.

Most of the time when this happened we would cancel our errands and try to do them the next day. That was a lot of extra lifting for me and it was also tiring for her. The time it was frustrating was when we would be going out for an appointment and I would have to call to tell them we would be late, postpone or cancel. They were always accommodating and we never had problems. If it was for a family get together and we had to cancel it was disappointing but we had no choice.

These were all non serious events and fortunately for us we never had to deal with an emergency. Some events were a little more hectic like when the transmission failed and we had to be towed home or when we had a tire blow while on the freeway. We dealt with then as they happened and moved on to the next day.

Chapter 49

BURDEN OF BEING A CAREGIVER

Burden

Some people see taking care of their parents as a burden and that shows in the care they give. They are short tempered and usually snap at their parent when they don't cooperate. This can take a toll on the caregiver and the quality of life of the parent.

From the time I started taking care of my dad I was always tired. After he passed away the same was for when I was taking care of my mom. It seemed like the days and nights were one and they never stopped. The constant lifting, cleaning and maintaining the house was a never ending chore. It was like being a mother taking care of her children, the work never ends. The only difference was my mom was larger than the average child and she wasn't going to grow out of it she was heading deeper into it. Taking care of her put a lot of stress on my body to the point that I was always sore and had more than the usual muscle pains. As far as the mind, it was constant job twenty-four hours a day. Even when she was sleeping I was sill checking on her and I always had a sense of how she was doing. I was always on alert. Yes, it was a burden to take care of my folks but I thought of it more as a challenge. I made the decision so I had to follow through with the best job I could do. They were relying on me to survive and I had to make sure that I didn't let them down.

With my dad he felt bad that I was always taking him to the doctors, to diagnostic tests and procedures. He told me a few times that he was a burden on my life and I would tell him he was wrong because, "I want to do it." He would ask, "Are you sure?" and I always would answer, "Yes." I had no problem going with him because I was learning what to look out for and how to handle different situations. As his condition got worse I was able to use the knowledge I learned to care for him and try to make his life a little easier. It was no burden because, "I wanted to do it."

During my mom's illness it was the same way, I wanted to do it. I wasn't forced and I made the choice to take care of her. Yes, it did happen quicker than I had hoped but you have to work with the cards you are dealt. I jumped in and took care of her immediately. Once again I learned from watching the nurses, doctors and others on how they cared for her. I used this knowledge to give her the best care I possibly could. Once again she was not a burden because I made the decision to take care of her.

I was never forced to take care of my parents, I just did it because I felt it was my responsibility. I never thought of their care as a burden to me because it was a job I needed to do. Yes, it took over my entire life but that's what it takes to take proper care of your dad and mom.

Not Going To Change

A lot of parents are never going to change and it doesn't matter how hard you try. They have been set in their ways for many years and change is not in their vocabulary. As far as control that is another issue that they will not give up easily because that also means they are losing their independence. My parents didn't change and I didn't try to make them. They went on with their normal routine as long as they could and then when they were ready they told me when it was time to take control. In both cases this was close to the end so they controlled, for the most part, their entire life.

Being a caregiver means doing what is best to provide the best possible care You know your parents better than anyone and you will know if they are willing to change or give up control. It does depend on the situation and you or they might not have any choice in the matter due to a medical condition.

From my experience things worked out a lot easier when we worked together. I didn't try to force them to change so they didn't push back. We had a great understanding and working relationship which led to them having a better quality of life. I accepted the fact that they were not going to change and I worked around that idea to give them the best care possible. Once again it was more work for me but in the end it was worth it.

At That Age, Let Them Have What They Want

I was always under the impression that at my parents age, let them have what they want. As long as it didn't interfere with their health, let them enjoy what they wanted. That was my attitude towards activities, food and life. Our doctors agreed and they said, "At this stage let them have what they want."

When my dad's cancer was diagnosed we still had to be concerned with his sugar levels but under the doctors advice we let the cholesterol levels slide. They told me to make him whatever he wanted and he could have as much as he wanted. My dad obliged and I was cooking some pretty big meals. As the cancer spread his appetite diminished and finally it disappeared. That's when the cancer spread to his throat, brain and other areas. He died within a month of when we learned the cancer spread to his brain.

The doctors told me to give my mom whatever she wanted to eat because she didn't have sugar or cholesterol problems. She obliged and enjoyed every meal she ate and every dessert that was put in front of her. She also went every place she wanted to go as long as I could lift her and wheel her around in a wheelchair. My feeling was that as long as it didn't affect her health or hurt her in any way let her do what she wanted to do. If it made her happy and enjoy life, what was wrong with it. Her doctors felt the same way and they always complimented her on her attitude and her look on life.

Once again it all depends on your situation and the health of your parent. As always work with your doctors to see what your parent can and can't do. What is allowed for their condition and what other restrictions might be necessary for their condition. I was lucky to be able to let my parents enjoy what they wanted because it made them happy even though they had some serious health conditions.

Don't Affect Health

Our doctors told me that my parents basically could have anything they wanted as long as it didn't affect their health. I agreed with this idea because I felt that what they had been through and that they were going through so many health issues that they should enjoy whatever they could. This attitude was mostly for food and it did give my parents something to enjoy. My dad had diabetes so I had to be careful with his sugar intake but anything else was never a problem.

It was amazing how just being able to eat the food they enjoyed helped my parents. They would smile when I would make one of their favorite meals and enjoy it to the last bite. I guess when you have so much wrong with you having something you enjoy can make the day just a little better.

The same is true for activities and as long as it didn't affect their health there was no problem allowing them to do something they enjoyed. Of course one of the things they enjoyed the most was being around their grandchildren and being a part of their lives. My mom was fortunate to be around her great grandchildren and that gave her great enjoyment all the way to the time of her death. If I could get my parents to a function I would do whatever I could to let them enjoy the activity. If they couldn't get to the function I would have someone videotape it so they could view it later. Even though they watched the event on video is still gave them enjoyment in seeing what had happened in the life of the family.

Once again it was more work for me in the process but it was worth it just to give them a little enjoyment. Too many times when people are considered "sick" or elderly they are left alone and not allowed to enjoy the rest of their life. I wanted to do whatever it took to make sure that didn't happen to my parents.

Don't Try To Limit Them

Another thing some people try to do is limit their parents activity and what they can eat. Once again this depends on their situation and what their doctors tell you they can and can't do or have. You never want them to overdo an activity or to over indulge to where it can make them sick.

I never tried to limit my parents on what they did or ate. Yes, I had to control sugar for my dad because he had diabetes and he had no problem with that because he knew it was for his health. As long as I was able to make what they wanted there was no reason to limit how much they ate or received. They knew it was bad to over eat and the never ate too much and got sick. I would ask them what and how much they wanted on their plate and I would give it to them. They both grew up during the Great Depression and hated the idea of wasting food. They both believed in the saying, "Take what you want and eat what you take." If they wanted a second helping that was no problem and it made me feel good because they were enjoying my cooking.

The same went with activities if they wanted to try to do something and I felt they wouldn't hurt themselves there was no reason not to let them try. Sure you had to watch what they were doing but it also gave them the satisfaction of helping you and contributing to the household. They didn't feel useless and felt if they could help in any way that would help me in the process of taking care of them. Yes, once again it was more work for set up and to watch them but it did give them something to do and it also kept them busy so they were not just staring at walls.

I have come across some that are taking care of a parent and they limit their activities and meals not because it is bad for their parent but because it is inconvenient for them. They have not checked with their doctor, they just don't want to do it because it is too much work or they want to control their parent and train them so they conform to their own schedules and personalities. Once again I don't know their unique situation so I can't be critical because I don't know their medical condition and restrictions.

They Earned It

I believe when someone gets to a certain age they have earned enough respect to do what they want. Once again it depends on their physical, mental and medical condition but they should be allowed to enjoy themselves. It also means that whatever they do has to be safe and cannot cause harm to themselves or anyone else.

When I was taking care of my parents this topic was usually more aimed at food. If my dad wanted a second or third helping of ravioli's, I had no problem with that, it was what he wanted and I wasn't going to stop him. If my mom wanted a donut are another piece of cake, why not it made her happy and she enjoyed it. Once again neither of these affected their health, hurt themselves or others. They wanted it and they had sacrificed enough during their life that I wasn't going to stop them from a little enjoyment.

Same went with activities, even though it was usually more work for me, it was not a problem to take my mom out to visit or go on an errand. It was something she wanted to do and she earned the right to tell me what she wanted. She wanted to take a drive to see the great grandchildren, I loaded up the car and we drove to see them. The little ones came to visit and wanted to play in the snow I bundled her up so she could watch them make snowballs.

Little things like this went a long way in making them happy and allowed them to enjoy their life. Once again it might mean a little extra work on your part but it can go a long way in giving them a better quality of life. They took care of you growing up and now you are returning the favor, they earned it.

Takes Over Entire Life

I knew that when I decided to take care of my parents it was going to be a lot of work. What I didn't know was that it was going to take over my entire life. I did get a break for a few years after my dad died because I was only taking care of my mom part time. When that finally became a full time job there was very little room for anything else.

It is just like taking care of a baby because my mom was so reliant on me. She could do very little for herself unless I helped her. Once she was at a table she could help with a lot of tasks but it was getting to the table that took all of the work. She had to be lifted in and out of bed. She had to placed into a wheelchair or lifted out. She had to be lifted on and off the toilet. She had to be slid onto a shower chair and into the tub. During all these task I was right there with her because I was the one doing the lifting and moving. I had to keep an eye on her so she didn't fall, slide down or lean out of the wheelchair or other apparatus. I had to change her diaper, clean her up and get her ready every morning. I had to get her prepped and ready for bed every night.

I made all the meals and did all the clean up. I kept the house in order by keeping it clean and neat. I did the shopping and all the errands and I took her with me when no one was available to sit with her which was most of the time. She was part of my entire life because she could not be left alone.

Most people think of caregiving as making meals and sitting down to chat. That might be true in some cases but it definitely wasn't true for me when I took care of my dad and mom. Yes, making meals and chatting was part of the daily routine but there was a lot more work involved in making sure they were taken care of properly and had a decent quality of life. When I started I had no clue how much it would take over my entire life but I sure learned fast.

White Lies

I never lied to my parents but once in a while I didn't tell them the whole truth. I didn't want them to worry and I wanted them to have a positive attitude so I would tell them they were all right even though I knew that wasn't completely true. I didn't want to upset the progress they were making when a little bump came in their recovery.

I was always in contact with the doctors during my dad's illness. As his condition got worse I talked to his doctors two or three times a week. They would inform me of lab results and different tests and I would relay the information to my dad. Toward the end there was never any good news and all the tests were bad. I would tell him he was doing fine just to keep his spirits up and try to keep him from quitting. It worked for a few months and then finally he succumbed. I think he knew I wasn't telling him everything and he knew I was doing it so he would fight and stay around a little longer.

I did the same with my mom when I would get her test results. Most of the time her labs results were very good and I would tell her that she was doing fine and to her credit she would ask me, "Are you sure?" I would tell her yes and show her the lab results. She didn't understand what she was reading but there was nothing on the paperwork that would cause her to be alarmed. The problem with her was when she had diagnostic tests. I don't know how many times I heard a doctor say, "I've never seen anything like it." That was the response I would hear when they would look at her bone scans and x-rays. Her spine and neck were a mess and that explained why she was always in so much pain. When she would ask me about the results I would tell her she was, "Unique." I would eventually explain her condition to her and she tried her best to understand. I left out a lot of the big words so she wouldn't get scared and she was always satisfied with the explanation. Once in a while she would still ask me, "Are you sure?" and I would still always say, "Yes, I'm sure."

Chapter 50
YOUR LIFE AND BEING A CAREGIVER
Your Health

Being a caregiver you are responsible for the health of your parent, but you also cannot neglect your health. If you're not healthy you can't take care of your mom or dad. As you stay focused on their health and well being you need to do the same for yourself.

While taking care of your parent you frequently become exhausted. In my case it was constant work and I had to make sure that I didn't burn out. If I did there would be no one to take care of my mom or myself. I always made sure that my mom ate well so I also was able to keep well nourished. I always prepared balanced meals so both of us were able to eat healthy. We always kept washing our hands whenever we touched something that could carry bacteria. I always wore gloves whenever I had to do a procedure that was dirty and messy. I tried to get enough sleep so I wouldn't become so exhausted that I could drop. I kept the house at a reasonable temperature so we wouldn't be cold or too hot. Both of us would get yearly flu shots and we also got the pneumonia vaccine. I made sure I got lab work and diagnostic tests as the doctor suggested so nothing unexpected could creep up. I do have high blood pressure and am currently on medication so I followed the doctors orders. Regular doctors visits for maintenance and routine eye exams to make sure I could see properly. All of this was to make sure I was healthy so I could take care of my mom. Most of the time she would see the doctor first and we would go over her condition and diagnosis, then I would wheel her into another office and the doctor and I would discuss my condition. Going to the eye doctor was an event because we would always go out for breakfast afterwards. We would go to the same restaurant and usually have the same waitress who would always ask if it was a good day at the doctors.

I would joke with the doctors that my mom was in better health and she would outlast me. It was always good for a laugh, especially when my mom would say she wanted to live to be one hundred. She didn't get that chance.

Stress

I was diagnosed with high blood pressure and was prescribed medication in 1987 when I was twenty-six years old. I was running my own business and the challenges put me through a lot of stress. That was nothing compared to being a caregiver.

Over the years I kept my blood pressure under control until I became a full time caregiver. The doctor increased my blood pressure medication from one prescription to two and that just barely kept my pressure under control. We would go to the doctors and my mom's blood pressure would be low to normal. They would check mine and it would be sky high. If it went down the doctor would joke that something was wrong. I always donated blood and never had a problem with the pre-screening tests except for my blood pressure. That was the wild card, most of the time it was just below the limit they allowed for blood donation. A few times it was too high and they would tell me to come back another time.

So what causes all this stress? It could be the lack of sleep, the never ending lifting, diaper changes, clean ups, doctor visits, diagnostic tests, outpatient procedures or any of the other daily life procedures that you have to do for someone else. There is no stop, no waiting for someone else to do it and no shift change. You don't go home to escape because you are home and there is no escape. No matter how calm you are it affects you. That is why you need to make sure that you see a doctor regularly so they can monitor your condition. Your doctor is your partner and needs to work with you so you can do what is best for yourself and your parent. I was lucky I had many doctors that worked with me every step of the way. Only one would be a thorn in my side and unfortunately it was the one my mom liked. After a few strong chats he decided it was best to work with me instead of putting up road blocks. I never thought it was him but his office.

His wife ran his office and basically controlled his practice. I would talk to him and we would agree and then I would leave the exam room and his wife would change everything because she would say we don't do that. Talk about increasing my stress. I went to the doctor for help and not to increase my risks.

The situation came to head when my dad was dying in 1995. I was at his bedside and I needed my blood pressure medication refilled. I called the pharmacy to refill the prescription and they said the doctor refused to refill the prescription because he wanted to see me. My last visit was three month prior. I called the doctors office and spoke to his wife and explained the situation about my father being on his deathbed. She wouldn't budge. I asked for the doctor to call me back and to my surprise he did. I exploded on the phone and he agreed to refill the prescription. He wanted me to keep him informed of the situation and to go in for a visit when things settled down. We had this doctor for twenty-five years and I was disappointed at the way I was treated. We came to an understanding and after my father passed away I went in and saw the doctor. As usual my blood pressure was high but under control and he was surprised that I went back to him. We never had a problem again and I stayed with him until we moved in 2008.

Break Time

When you are a caregiver there is rarely break time because even when things have settled down you are always aware of what your parent is doing. It's a seven day week twenty-four hour a day job and there are not many breaks in between. You can catch some down time when they are resting that is if there is any day or night left.

I would get my break time usually when I put my mom to bed at night. I would start a load of clothes in the washing machine and then try to relax for a while. She would be set for the night and be watching television and I would sit in my rocking chair or lay on the sofa and also watch television. We had satellite with two receivers so she could watch baseball, when in season, and I could watch something else. Sometimes I would read a book, article or surf the internet. I had a DVD collection of old movies and television shows and they were a great escape to relax.

I also liked to work in the garage and tinker. We had an attached garage so I could leave the door open so I could hear my mom call. She also had a walkie talkie radio so she could call if she needed me. She had a bell to ring in case she couldn't operate the radio because of stiffness in her severely arthritic fingers. I would also come in and check on her about every twenty minutes.

This was my break time and it was my sort of escape. I had to make sure all my work was done for the day and if it was completed it was nice to unwind. One or two hours at night went a long way in giving me a break from the normal day.

Your Hobbies

Just because you are taking care of your parent full time doesn't mean you don't have time for some hobbies. You are at home so you can do something you enjoy and it doesn't take much time to unwind. I found this kept me going over the years in giving me a small escape from the everyday routine.

I had a few hobbies that I liked to do when I had some down time. My dad was into woodworking and he had purchased a lot of tools over the years. In my old profession I use to design custom film and video editing systems so I was familiar with woodworking for consoles and work stations and I ended up also purchasing a lot of tools for work. I had a small workshop in the garage so I could do some woodworking projects and repairs. During the day I would wheel my mom to the interior garage door so she could watch me do my woodworking projects. Safety was the name of the game because if I got careless and got hurt no one would be around to take care of my mom. I made sure I always had the proper safety equipment and especially safety glasses.

When I was young my dad built me a model railroad and over the years it became neglected and when we moved from Lynwood to Tehachapi it was damaged. My little nephew like model trains so I wanted to repair this layout for his use when he came to visit. This required a lot of time and patience but it was also something I could do at night. I also use to do electronics with my business so I mixed this with the woodworking and model railroading so I could make something nice. Well, the project took a long time and unfortunately it was never finished because my mom's health started to deteriorate. I no longer had the time to work on it and when she passed away I had to sell the house. The layout is in storage and I hope someday I can finish it and give it to my little nephew.

These hobbies were an escape from the everyday routine and even kept my mom engaged. She would make suggestions or ask a lot of questions on what I was doing. It was a good way to clear my head so I could continue to do my job taking care of my mom.

Time Off And Time To Relax

When you are taking care of a parent there is very little time off or time to relax. Unless you have someone than can fill in for you, it is all you all the time. You have to try to find some ways to unwind and relax.

I rarely got any time off and even those times when one of my sisters would watch my mom I was still technically working. They would come over and watch her so I could go to the store, buy groceries or other supplies. Yes, it was time out of the house but it was still doing the house chores. So I had other ways for me to unwind and relax.

I had a garden in the back yard and I would work in it during the spring and summer. I would wheel my mom to the door so she could see me working in the garden and ask me questions. I could relax and work in the garden while at the same time keep an eye on her. The good thing about this was the fresh vegetables and fruits in the summer. It was well worth the work because there is nothing better than fresh vegetables and fruit. In fact when the grandchildren and great grandchildren would come up they would always enjoy picking strawberries and vegetables. We always had a lot so they were able to bring some home. It was nice to let the city kids taste home grown veggies and fruits. My little niece and nephew still remember about picking items from the garden and ask me when I'm going to make another one. The little girl misses picking strawberries and eating them fresh.

Another way I relaxed was doing woodworking in the garage. I would do small projects like bulletin boards and quilt racks. I made other items for my nieces and nephews and I even made a pink wooden train for the youngest niece. The garage got too small so I built a workshop and a separate greenhouse in the backyard. My mom supervised all the construction from her spot in the back doorway. It took a while because I did it in my spare time but I finally got them finished after I built them from the ground up.

These were things that allowed me to unwind and take care of my mom at the same time. At night after I put her in bed I would lie on the sofa or sit in a rocking chair just to relax. Sometimes I would watch television, listen to music or even read a book. It was the only way I could relax and settle down. True I was still watching my mom but it wasn't hectic and I was able to put my feet up for a while and relax. This went a long way in keeping me sane and calm. I never knew when something would happen so I had to catch a break whenever I could. I did this for many years and in fact today I still try to keep the same routine. I don't have to watch my mom but I still have the stress of trying to find a job and go on with my life. I still need to catch a break whenever I can.

Getting Normal Sleep

From the time I started to take care of my dad I never got normal sleep again. Because of his condition he would wake up all hours of the night and I would hear him. I would listen to hear what he was doing, if he was coughing I would hear him take a drink. I could hear his breathing and I knew if he was having a good or bad night.

My mom was the same way and just by the sound of her breathing I could tell if it was going to be a good or bad night. When her pain would flare up I knew she would have a difficult night and I would check on her to see if I needed to give her more medication. If she coughed a certain way or if the bed made a certain noise I could tell what was wrong.

In the process of knowing all these sounds I never was able to get normal sleep. It's like having a baby or toddler in the house, the parents always listen and know what's wrong. When you have children it is rare for you to have normal sleep and the same holds true when you are the caregiver to a parent. You learn to catch sleep when you can and you always want to be on the alert because you are responsible for their care.

I took care of my parents for so many years I am still not able to get normal sleep. It has been over two years since my mom passed away and I am still not able to sleep through the night. I hear every noise in the house and outside. I'm hoping that over the next few years I will learn once again what it's like to get a normal nights sleep.

Naps

My dad would take naps in the afternoon because he would get winded and short of breath. He would lay on his bed and because the bed was at an angle, headboard lifted about six inches, he was able to relax and calm down. He would rest for about two hours and he would be ready for the evening and then he would go to bed around midnight.

I would get my mom up in the morning and keep her up till about 2pm. I would then put her back in bed until about 4pm so she could rest for a while. Sometimes, if I was caught up with my work, I would also use this time to rest on the sofa. It helped both of us unwind for an hour or two. Around 4pm I would give my mom her medication and then I would get her out of bed. She would watch television and I would start preparing dinner.

When we were on the road and if it was a long trip she would take a nap while I was driving to our destination. The same would happen when we would be driving back in the evening or during the night she would take a nap while we were traveling. She would wake up about every twenty minutes and ask, "We're are we?" I would tell her and she would slowly doze off again. When we would get home we would get back into our normal routine.

These naps never upset her sleep patterns and most of the time she got right back to her normal sleep routine. Once in a while her spinal pain would act up and that would cause discomfort so I would have to adjust her pain medication. She would then get back to her normal sleep pattern and we were back to our routine.

I would try to catch a nap whenever I could. Sometimes it was hard to keep the eyes open and I would doze off in a chair for a few minutes. She would make a noise or sound and I would immediately get up. She knew I was tired and she never did it on purpose it was just that sense I had when I heard her make a noise. She would say, "I'm fine, go back to your nap," I would try but most of the time I couldn't and I would get up and go back to my chores.

High Blood Pressure

I was diagnosed with high blood pressure back in the late 1980s. I have been dealing with this condition and it has always been controlled by medication. My doctors always tell me that when I reduce the stress in my life my blood pressure will get back to normal. They would say it with a smirk when I was taking care of my dad and mom because they knew the stress was only going to increase and my blood pressure wouldn't be going down anytime soon.

Sure enough my blood pressure was always high when I started taking care of my dad and grew higher as his condition worsened. After he passed away and the tension subsided my pressure went down but was still a little elevated. When I started taking care of my mom it started to climb and then it rose way up when I started taking care of her full time. It stayed at the high level almost the entire time I took care of her because the stress of the job never stopped. When she passed away it dropped a little and came almost close to normal.

A few months after she died it started climbing again because the after effects of her death. Being broke, unemployed and facing an unknown future put a lot of stress on the body. It has remained elevated and I don't think it is going to go down anytime soon. My doctor is concerned and he tells me to slow down and not to worry because things will get better but he is keeping a close eye on me. The medication is still working and keeping my blood pressure under control but my doctor wants to take me off the medication. He believes the best medication is no medication and I am trying to control the blood pressure myself. My doctor will tell me when that time comes and I need to follow his orders to keep my health in check. One of the things I learned over all the years I took care of my parents is to listen to the doctors advice.

Your Medical Procedures

Taking care of your parents also means you have to take more care of yourself. If you become sick you can pass that sickness to them and cause more problems for them. Flu shots are good preventative medicine as well as a pneumonia vaccine. More demanding procedures such as lab work or other diagnostic test can help prevent a major medical incident for you. Just remember that if you get sick their might not be anyone that could fill in and take care of your parent,

Two such medical procedure are a colonoscopy and endoscopy. I have always suffered from stomach problems and I have always had tests and procedures on my intestines. My dad would have polyps in his colon so his doctor said that I should be checked every five years. I've had gastritis and severe acid reflux so I would alway get an endoscopy as well.

To have these procedures they usually put you under an anesthetic so you do not feel any discomfort. My doctor would tell me that I would be out of for a while and I would definitely sleep well that night. I also could not drive and I needed transportation to get home. Well, this could cause a problem because if I was out of it I would not be able to properly care for my mom. Also if I was going to sleep soundly that night I would not be able to hear her if she had a problem. My doctor agreed and said since that I had no one that could stay with her I couldn't chance it and I would have to have the procedures without anesthetic. He said the good news was I would still be able to drive because I wouldn't have any drugs in my system. He said it would be a little uncomfortable but I could handle it.

The first time I had the procedure I had a niece drop me off and she was going to pick me up when I was finished. My doctor and I became friends over the years because he took such great care of my father. When the time came they wheeled me on the gurney into the procedure room. For years I worked on cables and camera systems that did this type of a procedure but I never saw or felt how they worked. That changed pretty quickly and I found out how they worked and felt. The colonoscopy was uncomfortable but tolerable and I was able to see on the screen what the doctor was doing. I would ask questions and he would answer them. Once and awhile I would make a crude joke and he would laugh and tell me what to expect next. After this procedure was over I felt a little drained but I was alert.

The next procedure was the endoscopy and that was hell. The hardest part was trying to swallow the probe because I kept trying to cough it out. It felt like I was choking but I finally was able to swallow it. Once it was in it was uncomfortable and it did cause a little stress on the system. My eyes were watering and I was hot but this procedure didn't take too long. When it was over it was so great to get that tube out of my throat. He took a couple of samples that came back benign. I was good for a few more years

My niece came back, picked me up and drove me home. Her mom, my sister stayed with my mom while I was having the procedure but she couldn't stay the night. I felt a little drained but I was able to take care of my mom the rest of the night. I was able to sleep but I was still able to sense and hear what she was doing and that she was okay.

A few years later I had to have both procedures again and had to go through the same situation. This time my other sister stayed with my mom and her husband drove me to the outpatient facility for the procedure. He went out and had breakfast while I was having my innards checked. Before the procedure, while I was getting ready one of the nurses was concerned that I wasn't going to have anesthesia. I overheard her talking to my doctor and she voiced her concern to him. He said he wasn't worried because I had the procedure before and tolerated well. Her concern then went to the idea of what if I saw that there was a problem. My doctor told her, "I'm not worried, this guy has seen a lot and all the years I've known him he has never got excited at problems." He continued to say, "If he sees a problem and he asks me about I won't lie to him I will tell him the truth that we'll have it checked and wait for the lab results." She dropped the issue and never made more about it. I was pleased with his answer and it made me feel good. This time the procedures were just as uncomfortable but at least I knew what to expect and how to handle it. My doctor once again described what he was doing, answered my questions and laughed at my corny jokes. During the procedure I saw something that looked unusual and I asked, "What's that" True to his word he answered truthfully, he said, "a piece of crap." Being completely embarrassed I said, "Sorry," and he went along with the procedure. Both procedures went well and once again a few samples were taken but everything was benign. My brother in law took me home and I was able to continue taking care of my mom as usual. A little sore after the tests but I was able to respond to all her needs.

By taking care of my health I was making sure that I could take care of my mom. It's coming up time for another round of these tests and this time I think I will have the anesthesia because I am no longer taking care of anybody. I know what is going to happen and I know what they need to do so I am completely comfortable with the procedure. The only difference is that I will have to find a different doctor because my friend passed away a few years ago. I miss him because he enjoyed his work, listened to you, laughed at my corny jokes, showed concern and was a joy to visit.

Chapter 51
YOUR HABITS AND ROUTINES WHILE BEING A CAREGIVER
Daily Routines

One of the best ways to keep your parent busy, alert and engaged is to have daily routines. These could part of their daily hygiene or helping with tasks around the house. These help them retain whatever motor skills they have and keep their mind alert because they have to think.

My mom would have a daily routine, she would wake up about 8:00am just in time to take her morning medications. I would raise the bed and prop her up so she would be comfortable. After this I would give her a cup of coffee, in a spill proof container, and turn on the television so she cold watch the morning news. She would drink her coffee in about a half an hour. I would open the drapes or shades to let light into her room. About 9:30am I would get her ready for the bathroom. I would have her roll to the side and I would remove her diaper and then I would spin her to sit sideways on the bed. I would then lift her up and put her onto the wheelchair that had a new disposable bed under pad on the seat. I would then wheel her into the bathroom and lift her off the wheelchair and onto the toilet. We had a raised toilet seat with side rails so she was stable. I rolled in a small cart that had a wet wash cloth, soap, powder and deodorant. I also put a clean dress on the cart. This was what was called a Duster, it had snap buttons on the front so it was easy for her to put on. I would leave her so she could do her business. She would do what she had to do and then clean up. She would then call me or ring a bell. I put a wireless doorbell button in the cart so if she needed me she could press the button so I could always hear her when she needed me. After a while I felt like Pavlov's dog, always responding to a bell. While she was doing her thing I was cleaning up and prepping the bed. I would strip the bed, wash the air mattress, change the sheets and put down a clean disposable bed under pad. When she called I would remove the cart, change the bed under pad on the wheelchair, lift her up, put her in the wheelchair, roll her to the bed, lift her again and put her sideways on the bed. Then I would spin her so she could lay flat on her back. I raised the bed rail and had her with my help roll on her side. Then I would check her backside to make sure it was clean and look for any sores. After the morning inspection I would put on a clean diaper. She was good to go.

I would remove the bed under pad from the wheelchair seat, lift her off the bed, put her into the wheelchair and roll her to the table in the dining room. I would then bring out her toothbrush, false teeth, a plastic cup with warm salt water, nail brush, hair brush, a wet wash cloth and towel. I would fill a plastic shoe box with warm water and soap so she could soak her fingernails. She would let them soak for a while and use the nail brush to clean her fingernails. She dried her hands and then went to clean her false teeth. After this I gave her a cup with warm salt water and she swished it around to clean the inside of her mouth. She spit it out into another plastic shoe box. I then put the adhesive on her dentures and she put them into her mouth. It was time for her to wash her face with the wash cloth and dry herself off. Then she would brush her hair and she was ready for the day.

We then had a breakfast lunch combination. It would be ham and eggs, pancakes, waffles or sandwiches. After "brunch" I would work around the house and she would watch television, shred some papers, do crosswords or whatever she felt like doing. Around 1pm I would give her a snack and about 2pm I would put her back into bed so she could take a nap. I would change her diaper so she was comfortable. Sometimes I would rest but mostly I would catch up with the house chores. Around 4pm I would get her out of bed and then I would start prepping dinner. She would watch the news or a baseball game while I made dinner. I would give her the plates, silverware and napkins and she would push them or place them where they needed to go. We would eat around 6pm. After dinner she would pile everything up and I would take them to the sink to wash. I would clean up the kitchen and she tried to clean the table with a wash cloth. After this she would have a bowl of ice cream or other dessert. Around 8pm I would put her back into bed. I would change her diaper and she was ready for the night. She would watch television till about 11:45pm and then I would turn off the lights. I had a nightlight in her room so she wasn't completely in the dark.

She would fall asleep in about a half an hour. I would also settle down for the night and get some rest. This was our daily routine, it would change a little if we had to go to the doctors, store or other errands. It worked for many years and in fact did not change until about two months before she died.

Weather Conditions

Being a caregiver you always have to be aware of the weather conditions. Elderly people feel hot and cold weather differently and it affects them more. They usually feel colder and don't feel heat as much so it can cause problems when they are out and about.

When we would go outside, a lot of times my mom would be cold and I would be perspiring. It was in the mid seventies to eighties and she would be cold. My solution was a light sweater put on from the front. This was in case she got warm she could easily take it off while she was in the wheelchair or car. I would always keep her legs covered when she was in the wheelchair because the dresses she wore would show her diaper. A light beach towel, blanket or wrap would do the trick. As the weather became cooler I would use a heavier blanket or wrap to keep her warm.

In the car there was always a difference because I would be hot and she would be cold. Driving at night I liked it a little cool to keep me alert, if the car was warm I would get drowsy. I usually had the air conditioning on low and she would be cold. I would close the vents on the dash on her side so the air wouldn't be on her and point the other vents toward me. If she got too cold she would put on her sweater or jacket from the front. If she was still cold I always had a fleece blanket available in the car and she would cover herself with it. Another thing to watch is most vehicle air conditioning systems let air out onto the floor. This is one area my mom could not feel. Even though the air was set to the vent position some cold air came out of the floor vent. I always made sure that she had a wrap covering her legs in the car preventing her legs from getting the cold air. If I or she put a blanket on we made sure it covered her legs.

If it was going to rain or snow and we had to go out I made sure she was dressed appropriately. She had severe arthritis in her hands and it was difficult to put on gloves so we solved this problem by using mittens. They kept her hands warm and were easy to put on. Scarfs kept her warm as well as a hat to keep her head dry. Lifting her into the car was a problem when it rained because I couldn't lift her and hold an umbrella at the same time. The Suburban didn't fit in the garage because it was full of stuff and there was not enough room to open the door fully and lift her into the vehicle. My solution was to wheel her out while she held the umbrella. I would put a light towel on her head then put the umbrella in the car and lift her into the vehicle. She kept dry and then used a brush or comb to fix her hair. Usually we did not go out in the rain and snow but if we had to, for a doctors appointment, this worked well.

Weather conditions is another time you plan ahead and plot your moves. We were able to travel in sunshine, rain, ice and snow. I made sure we had extra blankets, gloves, scarfs and mittens in the winter in case there was a problem. I also made sure our vehicle was ready for all kinds of road conditions.

Snow And Ice

When we moved to Tehachapi, California I had to learn how to deal with snow and ice while I was moving my mom. When we lived in Southern California the only thing I had to be concerned with was a little rain so it was easy to maneuver my mom in this kind of weather. If we had to travel I would wait until the rain stopped or I would cover her with a light rain coat and lift her into the car. We never had a car port or had the car inside the attached garage so she did get a little damp when I had to lift her into the car. The only time we went out in rainy weather was when we had a doctors appointment or some other diagnostic test that we couldn't or want to cancel. Most of the time I was able to put other errands off until the weather cleared up.

When we moved to the mountains the snow amounts were very small but it still could cause some problems. Once again the only time we went out was doctors appointments or diagnostic tests. Our doctor was very understanding and I could change our appointment if the weather was bad and I didn't want to chance taking my mom out into the cold. I had to be careful of the cold weather and I had to be very concerned with possibly slipping on the ice when I lifted her.

Our attached garage at this house was too full so I was not able to put our car into the garage. I tried to clean it out but never was able to make enough room for our Suburban. Whenever we had a snow storm I would clear our driveway right away so I always had clear access to the road. One of our neighbors was a highway patrolman and he would stop when I was clearing the driveway and ask if I needed any help. I always said no because I needed the exercise and he would tell me every time that if I needed help getting my mom out and to the hospital to let him know and he would help. I was very appreciative of our neighbors because they all watched out for us. Our driveway was always the first cleared so if I needed to leave to take my mom to the hospital, I could.

The problem I would have was if the ground was icy. I could wheel her out of the house and she could wear a thick coat to prevent the cold air from getting to her. The problem was when I had to lift her into the car if the driveway was icy. My solution was to always clear a spot on the grass next to the driveway so I had a place to stand on. Yes, it would be soft and muddy but it was better than possibly slipping on ice on the driveway. It worked and I never had problem lifting her into the car when it was icy.

The difficulty in taking my mom out into the winter weather was as soon as I opened the door, no matter how much she was bundled up she would say, "It's cold." I would tease her and say, "No it's not," and she would tell me, "your crazy, It's cold." I would then ask her if she was ready and out we went. I would roll her to the car, open the door, step on the grass and lift her from the wheelchair and into the front seat of the Suburban. I would have the car running with the heater on so it was warm when she got into the car. When I would get in after I put the wheelchair back into the house she would say, "Now that's better."

She would enjoy our drives through the snow and take in the beauty of it. When we got to the doctors I would park right near the door so it was easy to lift her out of the car and into the wheelchair and roll her right into the office. Many times we didn't cancel our appointment because there was not that much snow or it wasn't that cold. We would go into an empty waiting room because a lot of other patients had cancelled. It was good for us because we would have extended chats with our doctor because we were the only patients in the office. We also discussed and settled all the worlds problems in that time.

We would leave and if she felt like it we would get something to eat so I didn't have to cook. We would get home and I would back the car in the driveway, get her wheelchair from inside the house and lift her out of the car and into the chair. Once again she would say, "It's cold," as I was wheeling her into the heated house.

After we ate and settled down I would make her some hot chocolate so she could "warm up" some more. We did this routine for the five years we lived in Tehachapi and we never had a problem. Once again it all depends on your situation and your parents condition how you handle the weather. Fortunately for me it was not a major chore.

Hot And Cold-Heating And Cooling

Taking care of your parents means you have to be aware of many different variables and one of those is hot and cold. As a person get older it's harder for them to feel heat than it is for them to be cold. They can be cold in the middle of summer and be freezing in early fall or late spring. It becomes a roller coaster ride to try to keep them comfortable and safe from the hot and cold weather.

My mom would be cold in the summer and I would be sweating as soon as the temperature hit eighty degrees. In the house I would open windows and she would ask for a sweater. When we finally had an air conditioned home as soon as I turned it on to cool the house she wanted her sweater put on.

When we were driving in the car we had the same situation. She was always cold and I was always hot. When I turned on the air conditioning she would put on her sweater or raise up a blanket. It was never blowing on her but it did cool the car down. In the winter I thought the car was just right and she would be freezing so I always had a fleece blanket available so she could cover up.

It's just one of those things you have to deal with and be prepared to handle. It could be going into a store and it's cold to them so you have to make adjustments to make them comfortable. Even going to the doctors office or other medical facility, they can be overwhelmed by the air conditioning.

It is a lot easier to carry extra sweaters, jackets and blankets to keep them warm that it is to try to stay cool. In all the years I took care of my mom she was always cold and I had to remain aware of the situation. I also had to be aware that her legs would sometimes get cold while we were in the car or while she was in the wheelchair. I always had to make sure they were covered so she didn't have problems. She couldn't feel the cold in her legs so it was something I always had to check by feeling her lower legs.

These are things that I learned over the course of taking care of my mom. I made myself aware of her comfort level and made sure that we maintained it wherever we went. It took extra time but it made sure that she didn't suffer from heat exhaustion or frost bite.

If They Can Be Left Alone

When I was taking care of my parents part time I was able to leave them alone. When my dad was ill, my mom was still capable of watching him so I was able to go shopping and do odd jobs to try to make ends meet. After my father passed away my mom was still able to care for herself but that all changed the morning she woke up and was unable to stand. From that point forward she needed full time care.

When you are able to leave them alone for a while you still can carry on with somewhat of a normal life. You do have to check on them frequently but they do not rely on you for everything they need. You still might be able to hold a steady job and you are definitely able to go to the store and carry on with most day to day routines.

If they are able to walk or even if they are wheelchair bound, as long as they can push themselves, they can leave the house in case of emergency. If they are bed bound and there is an emergency situation and you're not around that can lead to a tragedy. You would be responsible because you left them alone.

Enjoy the time that your parents are still able to get around or can be left alone for a short period of time. As their illness progresses it will be harder for them to care for themselves and then you will need to spend more time with them. Eventually they will need full time care and you will not be able to leave them alone. You will either have to take them with you when you go out or have someone stay with them while you do your errands. It will be a life changing experience.

Explain Using Examples

Whenever I had to explain something to my parents I tried to use examples to make it easier for them to understand what we were talking about. If I had to use props or drawings I did to help them understand. They always wanted to know what was happening so it was my job to make sure they understood.

I would use pens, pencils, paper clips or whatever I could find to explain how something worked. My drawing abilities are atrocious so I had to make stick figures to get some points across. Trying to explain certain conditions was hard at times but we were able to get through it.

One of the things I tried to explain to my mom was why she was in so much pain after her spine surgery. She didn't understand what a spinal decompression was so I had to make her understand what this meant. I used the example of a stream that had a bunch of branches in it and the branches had to be removed so the water could move freely. The river was her spine and the water flow was her nerves. When they removed the branches the water flowed freely but unfortunately because the stream became small and caused reduced water flow the water rushed in and went over the edge and raged toward the lake. The lake was her brain and it received a huge amount of water. The water flow was the pain signals in her nerves and they raged toward her brain and caused a huge amount of pain. The stream was restricted as was the pain and when the restrictions were removed the water plowed through just like the pain signal did to her brain. She understood everything and it helped her realize why she was in so much pain. Our rehab doctor was listening when I was explaining the situation to her and later told me, "I never heard it explained like that." It worked and she knew about her condition. I could have used all the terms the doctors used and it never would have set in.

With my dad I had a similar discussion about his lung volume. His lung capacity was diminished because of asbestosis. Both of his lungs did not equal the breathing volume of one lung. He did understand volume and flow rates when it was involved in plumbing so I used that as an example. Two tanks can hold 60 gallons a piece which gives you a total of 120 gallons. Your right tank, lung, holds 35 gallons and your left tank, lung, holds 20 gallons for a total of 55 gallons. He then understood his breathing situation.

Both of them didn't understand big words and definitely didn't know some of the medical terms. I had to make it simple so they could understand their condition. It was their life and they had the right to understand what was happening.

Pets

Pets can also be part of the caregiving experience because if your parent has a pet you might also have to take care of it. This can lead to more work and responsibility so it is something you have to consider. A pet can also keep your parent occupied while you are doing some of the other tasks around the house. Depending on their medical condition a pet can be helpful to your parent or it can be a liability. Talk to your doctor to make sure if your parent is able to be around a pet.

The last time we had a pet in the family was back in 1980 and after that dog died she was never replaced. All during the time I took care of my parents I never had a pet to worry about. I had my hands full just taking care of my dad and mom.

My oldest sister always had dogs and when we would visit her dogs were always around my mom. One of her dogs had this thing about balls and as soon as he saw my mom he would grab a ball or two and bring them to her. He would place it in her lap while she was sitting in the wheelchair and she would toss it behind him. He scrambled and got the ball right away and brought it back to her. He would play with her the entire time she was at the house.

My sister had another dog that was a little shy and always stayed in the background. When we would be at the door he would be behind my sister or brother in law and he would start to bark. Once he saw my mom in the wheelchair he would come right over and put his head on her lap. She would pet him on the head and he would then lead us toward the family room. This would happen every time we went over. When it was time for us to leave he would follow us to the door and put his head next to my mom. She would once again pat him on the head and then he would walk away from the door.

My nephew had a large dog and he looked ferocious but he was as gentle as a lamb. After my nephew died my sister and brother in law took the dog and cared for him. That dog was a big brute and was also a little clumsy. Their house had a long hall that went from the front door to the family room. When that dog heard a knock at the door or the doorbell he would run to the front door. He had a loud bark and he made sure you heard it. When we visited I would knock on the front door and you could hear the dog run to the door. He made his loud bark and then my mom would call his name. He would calm down and stop barking. The door would open and he would be right in front wagging his tail. He would put his head on my mom's lap and she would say his name as she patted him on the head. He would turn around and lead us to the family room. Once again when we left he would lead us to the door, put his head next to my mom, she touched his head and he would watch us go on our way.

One time my sister and brother in law went away for a few days and we watched their dog. He was a big baby and cried most of the time but he was always next to my mom. When it was time to go to bed I didn't want him in the bedroom because I was afraid his fur might cause my mom to cough or sneeze. During the night he just whimpered while he stayed in the living room. I finally brought him in the hall and he went right into my mom's bedroom and laid at the foot of the bed touching the bed post. My mom said his name and he stopped crying and stayed there all night. We never heard him cry again and we did this for three nights. During the day he was always at my mom's side and he was fine. When my sister and brother in law came home and picked him up he was very excited. He did go up to my mom and she touched his head before he left.

After my mom died a few month later I had a garage sale and I had my mom's wheelchair out front. My sister and brother in law walked over and they had their dog with them. He went right over to the wheelchair and started sniffing around. He then sat down and started to cry. I was amazed he knew what had happened. He liked her and she liked him so they had some sort of a bond.

Common Sense

Taking care of your parent relies on a lot of common sense. First of all you need to treat them the way you would want to be treated. The other thing is whatever procedure you have to do, such as lifting, is done in a safe manner so you don't injure them or yourself.

You have to be sure that items are not in place that can cause your parent to slip or fall. Items need to be put away so they can't injure them when they pass by. If they are still able to walk, loose rugs can cause serious injury. Even if they are in a wheelchair the wheel can get stuck on the loose rugs and cause a problem for them to move around.

You need to stand back and look around and see if anything is a problem in your home and could cause injury to your parent. Just like when you child proof your home when you have a toddler, you have to try to anticipate what might happen. All it takes is a little time and common sense.

If they are sitting in a wheelchair for a long period of time they need softer pads so it doesn't cause a wound on their backside. If they are sitting in a regular chair you might need to put a pillow behind their back to give them a little more support. You might have to do the same when they are sitting in the car.

If you have to lift them from the bed to a wheelchair always make sure there are no objects in the way that could interfere with the lift and the brakes are applied on the wheelchair. Also make sure there is nothing on the floor or any loose carpeting that could cause you to trip and fall while you are lifting your parent.

I would walk around the house everyday to make sure nothing was in the way that could injure my mom or myself. If she got hurt because of something careless that would make me irresponsible. If I got hurt because of something out of place no one would be able to take care of her.

All the years that I took care of my dad and mom they never got hurt on loose items that were in the house. I just used a little common sense and tried to anticipate if there were any problems. I also always treated them the way I would wanted to be treated if I was in their situation.

Many More Situations

I have only touched the surface with the situations I had to deal with during the time I was a caregiver. As I have said before every situation is different and there are many ways to deal with those situations. My solutions were what I did to deal with the problems we faced in our everyday life. Your problems will be different and you will have to adapt to your own unique situation.

So many people are taking care of a parent which means there are many ways to handle different situations. Some learn from books, some from the internet, some learn from medical providers and others learn while they are doing the caregiving.

You will get a lot of advice from many different sources and that's good because it will give you many options to choose. Listen and see what is best for you and your parent and try to adapt them to your unique situation. Some might work, some might not and others might work in a combination with something else. You just have to remember that you are responsible for the care of your parent and whatever procedure you use must be done in a safe and effective manner. You do not want to do anything that can jeopardize your parent or yourself.

Chapter 52

NO SUPPORT WHILE BEING A CAREGIVER
Plan On No Help

When I started taking care of my dad and mom I knew that I was pretty much on my own. My two sisters both had families and careers of their own and were very busy which meant they didn't have much time to help. I did hope that when their children grew up and they retired, if my mom was still around, I would get some sort of extra help. I didn't plan on it so I was not surprised when it didn't happen.

When my dad was sick I did everything to help him such as taking him to the doctors, dispensing medication and insulin shots, driving him to tests and procedures. As his health failed I helped him with cleaning, shaving and getting dressed. He failed quick and when everything gave out he was bed ridden and the hospital staff took care of most of his needs.

With my mom there was a completely different situation. She was in good health except for the fact that she couldn't walk and therefore couldn't do the basics of life. She lasted a long time and needed day to day care. I hoped that my sisters would help and they did when they visited like help with a bath or make dinner but this was usually for two to four hours a week. Even when my back went out they only came one Saturday and Sunday to help with the care of my mom. With an inflamed disc I was still doing the everyday duties of taking care of my mom and that included lifting her to the toilet.

One sister was retiring and she and her husband bought a new home in Tehachapi, California. They said we should buy a home nearby so when she retired she could help with the care of my mom. We purchased a home about two blocks away with the hope that I would get some help. When my sister retired they moved into their house in Tehachapi and she did help with somethings. She would buy some groceries for us and she would make us dinner once or twice a week. This did help because I didn't have to make dinner once in a while and she would buy items at a box store which saved us money. The problem was that every time she helped it was on her schedule and not my mom's. If somedays my mom didn't feel well she wouldn't help. They would buy what they wanted, not what we needed. It was always, "This is best for mom," never asking mom or me what was best. I never got help with lifting or changing my mom because my sister just, "Couldn't do that." When I needed her to stay with my mom she was always doing something else. When I had a doctors or other appointment I would have to take my mom with me. I appreciated the help we received because any help is great I just wish it was a little more useful.

My other sister lived one hundred and fifty miles away and she would come up for the weekend when she was not working. She would help give my mom a shower, help with the laundry and dinner. She would sit with her, play cards or board games with my mom so I could go shopping. This helped immensely but it was usually once a month.

Most of the time we were on our own and I took care of her day to day needs. I don't want to seem ungrateful but I was hoping for a little more help to make things easier. I never planned on it and it really never happened.

No Support, Just Criticism

One thing I learned over the years of taking care of my parents was that you will get very little support and a lot of criticism. Most people like to tell you what you are doing wrong but never offer or have a solution to help. These people always knew someone that took care of somebody but never had to do the work themselves.

I got very little support from family. I never specifically asked for support or expected it but it would have been nice to hear once in a while that I was doing a decent job. Most of the time all I heard was, "Let someone else do it," "hire somebody," "let Medicare and insurance take care of it," "they should have planned better," "I don't want to live like that," "have some self respect," "go out and get a job" and many more. It was more that they wanted to tear me down than give support for what I was doing. My attitude was they should have been happy because I took the responsibility so they could go on with their lives. I never waited for it and it never came.

I would listen to all this and just go on with our daily routines. It meant nothing to me because I always felt and knew I made the right decision. It got to the point that it would go in one ear and out the other because it was always the same tune and if it meant nothing before it wasn't going to mean anything when I heard it again.

Still Criticized Today

After all the years of taking care of my dad and mom I am still criticized today for the decisions I made. Some of the criticism is because they think I waisted my life and some is because they feel I spent too much money in taking care of my parents. It really doesn't matter because for one, I can't go back and change things and two, I probably would still make the same decisions.

It is easy to criticize others when you are not in their shoes and do not know what they do on a day to day basis. When I made the decision to take care of my parents I knew that I was giving up a lot in order to help them. I figured I would take on the burden so others could go on with their lives and take care of their families. When the time came that I no longer had to take care of my parents I could move on with my life. It was a good decision and I am happy that I made it. The thing that has surprised me was how difficult it is to find a job when you have been out of the workforce for so many years. How being a caregiver means absolutely nothing on a resume and to some it can be detrimental because it shows you put family ahead of work. I never thought that two years after my mom passed away that I would still be looking for employment.

Along with this I never thought I would have to defend my decision over and over. Yes, I took care of my parents and it took a lot of time and effort. Yes, it was expensive and since I did all the work mostly by myself I was unable to get a job while I was a caregiver. I did what was right and now I am paying the price for making the right decision.

Chapter 53

FINANCIAL COST OF BEING A CAREGIVER

Costs

Being a caregiver is expensive and a lot is not covered by Medicare and insurance. There are always supplies and accessories that you need to help you take care of your parent and most are necessary. These costs can add up and break most household budgets.

My mom could not take care of herself which meant she could not use the toilet, shower or dress without help. For not being able to use the toilet there are a variety of incontinence supplies and diapers available to help with this function. Unfortunately they are not cheap and were not covered by Medicare and her insurance. The incontinence supplies or pads would be used to keep her dry because she had little control over her bladder. This also helped in the amount of diaper changes. She would place a pad in her diaper and when she urinated the pad would absorb the fluid. When she was finished she would remove the pad and throw it in the covered container on the side of the bed. She would then replace it with a new pad for the next event. When the diaper became wet it was replaced. She would go through a package of pads every two days. These had forty pads per package and they were $15.00 a package. I would replace her diaper three times a day or more and there were twenty in a package and it also cost $15.00 a package. So pads would be thirty days divided by two which equals fifteen times $15.00 equals $225.00 for incontinence pads. Diapers would be thirty divided by six equals five times $15.00 equals $180.00. Add this to the pads that equals $405.00 just for diapers and incontinence pads. That doesn't included the under pads for the bed, powder, baby wipes and other skin products.

All this adds up and takes an extreme toll on the monthly budget. You can save money by purchasing these items on sale or by buying bulk quantities online. There is no easy way to get around this subject, they are necessary items and you have to buy them to take proper care of your parent.

Expenses

There are a lot expenses associated with being a caregiver. Some are covered by Medicare and insurance, unfortunately a lot are not. These expenses are needed usually monthly and can put a strain on any budget.

One expense that is often overlooked is the cost of transportation. Going to many doctors or just one monthly visit can add to your vehicle expense. Gasoline is not cheap and neither is vehicle maintenance. You have to have reliable transportation because you never know when you have to go to a medical provider or facility. In some situations, like an emergency you can call an ambulance but for most non life threatening issues it is your responsibility to get your parent to the healthcare facility.

Another expense is any special food that your parent might need. You might have to purchase soft foods which are more expensive, a blender or food processor if you want to prepare your own. Protein drinks are often necessary to help maintain their nutrition when they don't have a strong appetite or eat properly.

If they are diabetic there are several foods that can make life easier for them such as the diabetic protein drinks or special items for when their sugar levels are too low. Some diabetic supplies are not covered such as alcohol wipes and lancets.

If they have a urostomy or colostomy bag there are a lot of items that are not covered and are a huge expense such as adhesive and water barrier cream. Belts that hold the bag to the body are usually not covered and neither are the hoses and the container for overnight care. Powder to keep the flange area dry and free from a rash is necessary but is also not covered because it is considered a comfort item.

Special pillows and cushions are needed to keep them comfortable and free of bed sores. Bedding supplies need to be changed often and replaced because you can only wash them so many time before they fall apart. Socks to help with circulation might be required to keep their legs and feet from swelling.

This is only a sampling of what might be required expenses for you to take care of your parent. In our situation it seemed that every time we went to a specialist or came home from a hospital stay our expenses went up between fifty and one hundred dollars a month. True some items were no longer needed but the expenses never seemed to go down. Price increases were always a problem and it seemed every time oil went up so did the cost of the supplies. Most were made of some sort of plastic and that is made from oil. Now when I say Medicare or insurance didn't cover certain items that was in our situation and was a few years ago. Medicare and insurance rules and covered items are constantly changing. You need to check with Medicare and your insurance to see what items are covered and which are not. All I know is be ready for a lot expenses as time goes by and how much will be spent in taking care of your parent.

Utility Usage

I found out the hard and expensive way how much utility usage increases when you are taking care of a parent. Heating expenses go up dramatically because it seems that they are always cold. Electricity usage goes up because they need brightly lit rooms because it is hard for them to see in dim light. Televisions are on a lot more as well as other electric appliances. If they need special equipment this can use substantially more electricity but it is required to keep your parent healthy.

I found out how expensive electric costs were when my dad needed an oxygen generator to breath. Even though we got a medical baseline discount from the electric company our bill still went up dramatically. This item was on most of the day and it used an enormous amount of electricity. Not to mention that it also dissipated a lot of heat that caused the house to warm up.

My mom needed an air mattress and this unit was on all the time while she was in bed. That averaged about eighteen hours a day. It was a compressor that used a lot of electricity and also generated a lot of heat. Once again when we finally got the medical baseline our electric cost went down but it was still substantially higher than the average bill.

My mom also was always cold and therefore our heating expenses were high. I had to keep the house at 72 degrees otherwise she would complain she was cold. I would put a sweater on her and even extra blankets but she always said she was cold in the winter. I, on the other hand, was always sweating and I had to go outside to cool down. We had natural gas and in the winter time that was expensive to heat the house. It's not as expensive as propane, fuel oil or electricity but it still takes a chunk out of the monthly budget.

Even water usage goes up because it takes them longer to take a shower and they do waste more while they are bathing. We never had to worry about a water shortage but I can see how this would affect areas that do. They also require more warm water because once again they are always cold. You have to be careful to make sure the water does not come out too hot from the shower because they can scald easily. Warm water requires more energy and also means more of an expense.

These might seem like small or insignificant items but when you are living month to month they can cause some serious budget problems. I never considered energy usage and costs until I started taking care of my parents and started paying the bills. It is often taken for granted or just another normal everyday expenses but it will go up a lot when you start taking care of a parent.

Paying For Your Own Supplies

We never had the luxury of having Medicare or insurance pay for the necessary supplies for the everyday care of my mom. Over the years I was told that some insurance and government programs pay for supplies, such as diapers and incontinence pads. I made the decision to keep Medicare and our supplement insurance because it offered less out of pocket expense for medical care and hospitalization. I never knew how much of an expense the day to day supplies would become.

I did my best to save money on the supplies my mom needed for everyday life, such as diapers, incontinence pads, bed under pads, powders, ointments, etc. I bought these items when they were on sale and if I could afford to buy a bulk quantity I would. Sometimes you could order these items online at a good price and they included free shipping. Other times you could go to different retail stores and buy them on sale. I would try to buy a weeks supply at once so I always had enough on hand in case we couldn't go out and get to the store.

I'm sure I overpaid a lot of times but I needed to have them on hand at all times because my mom couldn't do without them. I would see advertising on television for the supplies but when I inquired my mom's Medicare plan and supplement insurance was not eligible. That was before 2013 so I have no idea if the rules and restrictions have changed. Check with Medicare and your supplement insurance to see if these items are covered. If not be prepared for a large expense that will last the entire time you are taking care of your parent. This was one of our biggest expenses and they were items she absolutely needed everyday to maintain a good quality of life.

People Have No Clue How Much This Costs

Over the years taking care of my parents I learned most people have no idea how much it costs. There are physical costs as well as financial costs and both take an extreme toll. The physical costs put a lot of wear and tear on your body as well as on the mind. The financial costs put a burden on your budget because you are going to have to purchase a lot of items and accessories that are not covered by Medicare and supplement insurance.

The financial costs were massive and it broke our budget in the very first year. The expenses kept going up as she needed more supplies, accessories, clothes, special foods and medications. Medicare and supplement insurance paid for a lot but they didn't pay for everything and that came out of our pockets. In fact after my mom passed away in 2013 I realized I was broke and still owed a lot of money. As of 2015 I am still in the process of trying to get back on my feet and paying off the bills. I had to sell our house to get a little extra cash to cover the debts for the cost of taking care of her.

The physical, mental and financial costs are immense and are never talked about or considered. Most people think everything is covered by Medicare, supplement insurance and long term care insurance. They are wrong because they have never had to deal with this type of a situation and have absolutely no clue what it costs. I thought I had everything under control and I was wrong. The physical and mental costs I had no problem dealing with and overcoming, the financial cost hit me like a ton of bricks and knocked me down to the point of not being able to recover. It has taken a serious toll on my life and future.

What You Can Afford

As you take care of your parent you will find that there are a lot of accessories and tools that can help make being a caregiver a little easier. Some of these items are covered by Medicare and supplement insurance but a lot more are not. Your out of pocket expenses can take a huge toll on your budget and wallet.

While I was taking care of my parents I tried my best to purchase items that they needed and Medicare and insurance would not reimburse. I tried to stay on budget and only purchase items we could afford. Easy to say but hard to do because I was talking about my parents health. If they needed something and I had the cash available I would buy it and if the cash wasn't available I used a credit card. My justification was they needed it so I had to get it. We didn't go overboard and it wasn't for items that we wanted but it was for items we needed. I would ask myself do we want it or do we need it. If it was needed, it was purchased and if it was wanted, I passed.

I did my best to purchase only what we could afford, unfortunately it didn't work. It has been over two years after my mom passed away and I am still paying off the debt of the necessary items for her care. Hopefully in your situation you will be better at budgeting or have better resources for purchasing the necessary items.

Chapter 54

WHAT YOU LEARN BEING A CAREGIVER
A Learning Experience For Both

When you become a caregiver it immediately turns into a learning experience. No matter what you have been taught or what you have read you will always be learning when you are taking care of your parent. Not only is it a learning experience for you but it is also a learning experience for your parent.

New procedures, techniques and medications are constantly being introduced in the medical field. Depending on your parents condition and diagnosis these new procedure might be able to help you. What you do today might not be what you do tomorrow. The same goes with your daily routines, what you have done for many months might change because you learn to do something different that makes it easier and/or better for your parent. Anything that can help you with your daily tasks should always be welcomed.

Your parent is also learning because probably this is the first time someone has had to take care of them since they were a child. Things that they did for themselves for years now have to be handled by someone else. Routines that were normal and they took for granted have to be carried out by someone else so they can go on with their daily life. That might be hard to get use to so they are learning how to cope with the situation. That is another reason why you need to put yourself in their shoes because it would probably be hard for you if you were in the same situation.

I started learning from the time I started taking care of my dad part time in 1992. I continued to learn until my mom died in 2013. Everyday was a learning experience and most of the time we learned together. We worked in unison and it helped me take better care of both of them. You have to have an open mind and be willing to learn new tasks and procedures so you can give your parent the best quality of life possible. Sure you can continue to do things as you did before but it might mean more work. If something can save you time, energy and strain on your body you should consider trying it because it can make things better for you and your parent in the long run.

Things Change As You Learn And Adapt

As things change while you are a caregiver the more you learn, the more you can adapt means the more you can do. Caregiving is not an exact profession because it is different for each person that you are caring for. It is also a job that you never stop learning from because it is a constantly revolving process.

Medical conditions change and you need to learn new techniques on how to handle those situations. With my dad his condition changed very rapidly and I needed to adapt very quickly. Learning how to change an urostomy bag and flange was something that had to be learned immediately because he needed that for his everyday life. Checking his sugar levels, reading the results, measuring the insulin and giving him the injections was something that had to be done right away and I had to learn fast and deal with it. I had to be aware of low sugar situations and what to do if they occurred. When his breathing was deteriorating I had to learn how to dispense oxygen at the right levels and be able to change tanks at a moments notice. His condition was constantly changing and I had to learn and adapt to each change.

With my mom's spinal condition, after the initial shock from the surgery her condition was the same for many years. Granted it was a lot of work because I had to lift her or maneuver her for everything she did. Even during this time I would notice little changes that would make me make adjustments in the way I moved her or in her daily routine. Sometimes I would have to lift her differently because she was sore on one side or had a pain here or there. Major changes had to be made in her lifting procedure when I changed vehicles. As her condition changed and as time went on I had to make changes to our normal routine. I had to make sure that she was always on a gel cushion when she was sitting in a wheelchair so it didn't cause a sore on her backside. I had to make sure her legs never dropped off the wheelchair leg rests when she was being transported. Things like that changed because of her condition and I had to be able to recognized it and deal with situation immediately.

Being a caregiver you will be constantly changing the way you care for your parents. You will know them so well that you will be able to notice every little change and you will adapt your care to deal with it. It is a continuing learning experience that will last as long as you are caring for them.

Sleeping With One Ear Open

Over the years of taking care of my parents I developed a sense that I could always hear them. Even when I was sleeping I could always sense or tell when everything was ok or if there was a problem. I always told people that I would sleep with one ear open so I could hear what was happening.

When my dad was sick I could always hear if he was having a bad night. He slept in the room next to me and I could hear him, cough, gag, wheeze or spit up. Even when I thought I was asleep I would get up every time he had a problem. I always felt somewhat rested but I would get up every time he needed something without him having to call me.

The same thing would happen when I started taking care of my mom. She slept in the next room and I could always tell if she was having a good or bad night. It's hard to explain but I just knew when she needed me or was having difficulty. I knew when her pain was elevated or when her legs were swollen and I could never figure out how I knew what her condition was at that time. I knew her sleeping habits and patterns so well that I could immediately tell when there was a change and if she needed help. She rarely called except when she had to "go" during the night. That was the one instance I didn't pick up on right away and she would have to call. All she had to say was "Jim" and I would get up immediately. She didn't have to yell or raise her voice, I would hear the first time and every time.

In all the years I took care of her I always knew when she needed me and was there to help her. The only time this didn't happen was the night she died. That was the one and only night I slept straight through without hearing anything. I knew she was ill and I said to myself that I wasn't going to sleep but just take short naps so I could keep an eye on her. It didn't happen and I fell into a deep sleep. I woke up the next morning and found her unresponsive and lifeless. I called 911 but it was too late and she was gone. I have no idea why that happened except that was her way of moving on without any fuss or worry for me. I'll never know but it was strange and when I told the paramedics and police of that occurrence their response was that they see that all the time. Things happen and there is just no explanation. I believe it was God's way of peacefully taking her and saying it was time for her to be with him.

Till this day it still bothers me that I heard nothing or knew there was a problem. All the years of taking care of my dad and mom and hearing every sound so I could take care of the situation and this night I heard nothing. I developed a sense to hear them over the years I also guess that sense was also developed so they could go in peace.

Easier For A Son To Take Care Of His Father

Some say it is easier for a son to take care of his father than it is for him to take care of his mother. I never heard that it was harder for a daughter taking care of her father than her mother. I do know that it was a lot easier for me to take care of my father. I don't know if it was because we were both male or it was just something that had to be done. You are a little apprehensive at first but after a deep breath you just do what you have to do. After the first time I never had a problem washing or shaving him. The first time I had to clean him up after a bowel movement was difficult but I was able to get through it. I think it was more difficult for my dad because he was embarrassed that he ended up in that kind of situation. He would apologize and I would tell him that I was part of life and my job. I also told him that if I would have needed that type of care he would have done it. He would smile and then I would keep going with the task.

I had to help and lift him into bed every night when he was starting to fail. It all became routine and I never had a problem. I would change his urostomy bag and flange and it never caused a reaction. I had to give him insulin shots several times a day and it didn't make me squeamish. I did what I had to do when he needed it done.

One of my sisters could have done the same because she was an LVN and did it for strangers. Some say it is different when it is your own family but I know she would never would have had a problem. She did fill in for me when I had to do a job or go see the doctor. My other sister would have had a problem because she could never handle these type of situations. She would rather cook and clean than take care of the medical situations.

It worked out well because we all did what we had and could do. My dad was happy that he was being well taken care of and that the three of us were working together. This was the first time the three of us ever had to take care of a sick family member for a prolonged period of time.

Son Taking Care Of His Mother Is Different

Some say a son taking care of his mother is different and I admit I thought that way. I figured when my mom got sick my sisters would take care of her because I took care of my dad. When the time came that was nowhere near reality. Both of my sisters worked and had families of their own, it would have been extremely selfish of me to expect them to take care of my mom. I had no family or relationships so I took control and decided to take care of our mom.

Yes, it was difficult in the beginning but the first time you do anything is always the hardest. I just took a deep breath and did what I had to do. After I was finished with the task I would say to myself, "That wasn't so bad," or "I did it." After a while I just did whatever I had to do without even taking a deep breath.

Once again I learned it was probably more embarrassing for my mom than it was for me because she never thought she would be in this type of a position. Yes, at times it was embarrassing for me but I am an adult and I got over it very quickly because I had a job to do. Turning red in embarrassment is not a way to handle a difficult task. You just do what you got to do and move on to the next task or challenge.

I never had another thought about it being harder for a son to take care of his mother. That phrase doesn't mean anything because it is not true. What about an only child, a son or daughter, that has to take care of both mother and father? They do it because they have to and there is no one else. I was lucky I had sisters that could help once in a while. An only child doesn't get help from any siblings, they are on their own. It doesn't matter if it is a daughter taking care of her father or a son taking care of his mother.

Chapter 55

RESPECT AND BEING A CAREGIVER

Respect

I believe that you always have to show respect for your parent. Even when they seem like they are not there you still need to show you care and respect them. They have put their lives in your hands so they trust you and you need to show that you are worthy of that trust by showing respect, after all they're the ones that gave you life.

Of all the things I had to do for my parents I never lost respect for them. I had to bathe them, change them, clean up after them and a whole lot more because they couldn't do it themselves. After all those unpleasant jobs I still had great respect for my mom and dad. I made sure they never lost their dignity and that was accomplished by always showing them respect. I was in my thirties, forties and fifties and I would still listen to their advice and wisdom. Sometimes I disagreed and we would discuss it and most of the time, after some thought, they were right on most issues. I was an adult but was still their son and treasured their advice.

Some people lose respect for their parents when they're old because they are no longer relevant because times change and have passed them by. They feel they are a burden and show no respect for their opinions or comments. This can play on their mind and cause problems in the future because they feel they're not welcome or needed. Others think that because they need care in their elderly years they didn't plan their life properly and therefore are getting what they deserve or the results of their inactions. No one knows what the future holds and it is almost impossible to plan for everything. Just look at your future, do you know what is going to happen or what you are going to be like in thirty years?

It is so easy to show respect because it is the right thing to do. Once again put yourself in their shoes and see how if you were in their position how would you want to be treated? I'm sure, like most people, you would want your caregiver to treat you properly and to show you respect.

Neighbor Would Bring Over Cake And Candy

When we lived in Lynwood we had some great next door neighbors. They moved into the house next door where an older woman lived since the middle 1960s. This lady and my mom were friends and she passed away in 1999. The house was sold and the new people that moved in were not very friendly, had frequent visits from the sheriffs department and finally moved out a few years later. The family that moved in after was fantastic and quickly became friends. It was a husband, wife and teenage daughter and we got along from the day they arrived.

Almost every night after dinner my mom would be watching baseball or something else on television and the neighbor would come over. I would go out on the front porch or yard and we would just talk. We would talk about the area, politics, family religion, anything that interested us. He quickly learned of our situation and a few times a month he would bring over a dinner plate for my mom and I. His wife was an excellent cook and she made traditional Mexican food. She also made cakes and he would bring over a few slices of cake once in a while and that really made my mom light up because she enjoyed her sweets. Even his daughter would bring over cup cakes or a candy bar for my mom when she came home from school. They were just wonderful people and my mom enjoyed their company. One of the nice things about our nightly chats was that it gave me a break and I could go outside for a few minutes to relax. My mom was fine in the house because she was in her wheelchair and I could always hear what she was doing so she was never in any danger.

When we moved they helped us pack up and load the moving trucks. They came several times to visit when we lived in Tehachapi and their visits were always enjoyed. I missed our daily chats and my mom missed the cakes and pastry but most of all I missed their friendship. When my mom passed away one of the calls I made was to them. He knew as soon as he heard my voice that she was gone and as a good friend he shared his genuine sympathy. He had to take a day off from work, and they paid their respects and attended the funeral. He said he would always remember my mom's smile when he brought over anything sweet.

Other Neighbors Walking By Showed Respect

My parents lived in Lynwood, California for fifty years and they saw the area change dramatically over that time. After my dad died it was just my mom and myself living in the house my parents bought in the 1960s. Some called the area depressed and its crime rate was higher than a lot of the cities in Los Angeles County but we called it home for many years.

As time went on the neighborhood changed and it wasn't as safe as it use to be. We had some neighbors that were great and we watched out for one another and other neighbors that were always suspicious and had a lot of visits from the sheriffs department. When I would work in the front yard I would wheel my mom out on the front porch so she could watch me mow the lawn, pull weeds or some other yard work. She would work on her puzzle book and enjoy the day. Once in a while people would walk by and they would always say, "Hi," "good morning," or some other greeting. The interesting thing was that they were always addressing my mom on the porch first and then they would say the same to me in the yard. We always responded and returned the greeting. Sometimes these individuals looked a little intimidating but they always were polite and sociable. I remember one day I was trimming the flowers in the front and my mom was on the porch in her usual spot and this young man walked by. He looked at my mom and said from the sidewalk, "Hello ma'am, you have a blessed day." She thanked him and told him to have the same. If you were to see this guy in an alley you would run the other way. He then walked by me and told me, "Have a nice day sir." I also thanked him and returned the compliment.

This happened quite a bit and it was amazing how a lot of these people had respect for an older person. You hear stories about how some take advantage of the elderly so a lot of times you are cautious. It was nice to see some young people showing respect to an older person.

I'm Old Fashioned And Kids Need To Show Respect

My parents were old fashioned and so am I so there are certain things that are expected. One of those items is respect and that is something the younger generation should show to the older one. My parents believed that everyone in the family of their generation were equal and that the younger generation should show respect to them. My parents would never say hello to any of us that were younger unless we said it first. It was a matter of respect and all of us knew it.

I believe in the same attitude and I never say hello to the younger generation unless they address me first. When the kids were young I had no problem saying, "Hi" to them first but soon they learned that it was their position to address me first. Now that they are older they follow through with this attitude.

As time has gone by and the younger generation is getting older they are forgetting this attitude so they expect the older generation, me, to forget the past and traditions. I am hard headed so I refuse and I still follow with the attitude that I was brought up with. If the younger generation doesn't address me first I say nothing to them. I act as if they are not around and most of the time they just walk by me. This is part of the "sit in the corner and don't disturb us" attitude This has caused some problems with some family members because they feel that I should show respect to the younger generation. They forget that respect is earned and it is not just given because they are standing in front of you. This has happened with cousins and their families and I am glad to say it hasn't happened with my nieces and nephews. They always showed respect to my mom and dad because they were their grandparents. They also showed respect to me because I was their uncle and they continue to do this today. In fact my little nephew and niece are practicing this attitude. They are still young but their mother taught them that they always address the adults first. They practiced this with my mom and they continue to practice this with me. I am very proud of them and their parents.

In this day and age respect is one of those traits that is disappearing.

Like I said I'm old fashioned and I believe in the attitude and customs I was taught. The younger generation showed my mom respect because she was the oldest left in the family. Now that she is gone there are still older ones still left in the family. We showed respect to our parents, uncle's, aunt's and other adults. Is it a crime to ask that the younger generation show us respect now that we are older? I don't think so.

Chapter 56
CRITICISM AND COMPLAINTS
Some Will Say This Is Wrong

When you're a caregiver be ready for a lot of advice and criticism. Everybody has an opinion on how you should take care of someone. It can come from family members, friends and medical professionals.

I would always listen to advice and criticism and then review it according to our situation. Some family members would say I should not take care of my mom and I should hire someone to do it for me. I should have some dignity, be a man and pass the responsibility to an agency or nurse. Some friends said I should worry about myself and let others handle the task. Some of the medical professionals would say I was going about the whole caregiving experience wrong.

I'm sure some will read this book and say he knows nothing and he did everything wrong, the proper way to take care of someone is this way. A lot of the so-called experts learned the information in a classroom or from a textbook. Some of these teachers and authors did not have real world experience. Even some of the hospital staff were unaware of certain situations and would not take this into consideration when they would work out a caregiving plan. People and situations are different in life and that doesn't change when they get old or need help. Caregiving is not an exact science and is an ongoing process, everyone's situation is different and so is every patient. Some patients can walk, some have memory loss and some are combative. You have to work with what you have been dealt. Don't be so sure what Medicare and insurance will pay for caregiving. You might be in for a surprise to learn how little they allow. If you can afford it, hire someone to help with the daily routines. If you have siblings, maybe they will help, but once again don't be so sure. Some people can handle this situation and others want to be nowhere near it. It never hurts to listen to what others are saying, you might learn something and that could be beneficial to your situation.

My mom was stubborn and would not listen to some of the recommendations and procedures. So what was I supposed to do, say, "Do it this way or I won't take care of you." I don't think so. I took care of my mom the way that was least intrusive to her and my life. She got the care she needed, was well nourished and enjoyed her life to the end. I'm happy with that result.

Nursing Students Wanted To See How A Proper Cared Parent Looked

The last time my mom was in the hospital was February of 2013. The hospital was in Bakersfield, California and was a teaching hospital for the local community college. During the day there was always a large number of nursing students going from room to room for training.

As with all the visits to the hospital while we lived in Tehachapi my mom was severely constipated. This was the side effects of the pain medication and it plugged her up. We kept it in line with stool softeners, laxatives and warm prune juice. Most of the time this worked but once in a while everything would be blocked and we needed to go to the hospital for professional help. The first sign of problems was my mom would vomit. I had to be careful of dehydration so I gave her fluids to stay hydrated. This also would come up and the vomit would have the smell of feces. This was when it was time to go to the hospital. We would go to the local Tehachapi hospital and they would give her intervenes fluids to prevent dehydration. They would stabilize her and send her to a full service hospital in Bakersfield, California, about an hour away by ambulance. Sometimes I would follow the ambulance by car but this time I was able to ride in the cab of the ambulance on the trip. My sister was in town, so I had a ride home.

We got to the hospital, after admitting, body inspections and tons of paperworks my mom was stable and they planned for the next days diagnostic tests. As usual they did x-rays and scans and found out she had a severe blockage and it needed to come out. The treatment was enemas and laxatives.

Now that was the job of the nursing students under the supervision of the Registered Nurse that was running the school program along with the hospital staff. I'm sure this procedure was not on the school's brochure trying to attract new students. They would come in and say it was time for her treatment and I knew it was my time to leave. I would go out, get a cup a coffee and some fresh air.

When I would come back to the room, everything would be aired out and my mom would be sitting in bed and one or two nursing students would be talking to her. During the day other students would come in to check on her and they would actually spend a lot of time with her. One time I went out to get a snack and I when came back there were about twelve nursing student in and around the room. First thought in my mind was that something had happened. I picked up the pace and I was met by the instructor of the class. She stopped me, asked me if I was Mrs. Colozzo's son, and told me everything was fine. She told me that I was doing a fine job and that she wanted all her students to see how a well taken care of parent looked. She complimented me on my mom's condition and care. She said the students liked working with her and were learning a lot. I made a joke about the job they had to do but she said that's all part of the career. She told me that most of the elderly parents they saw were neglected. Some were abused and a lot were malnourished. She said that for my mom's age and condition she was in great shape and had a great attitude. The students looked forward to taking care of her and meeting me. That explained a lot because whenever I was in the room the students would ask me a lot of questions about my mom and her care. I never knew how bad it was for some people.

To this day I still can't understand how children can treat their parents in that way. Talking to the college instructor it made me feel good, reinforced what I was doing was the right thing and I made the right decision. Unfortunately it also taught me how cruel some people are to their parents.

Nobody Else Cares What You Do

One thing you will learn over time is that nobody cares what you do. It doesn't matter how difficult the situation or how much work it is most people are oblivious to what you have to do. Family will tell you they will help but for the most part that doesn't happen because it is too inconvenient for them.

I found this out the hard way when I started taking care of my mom. I have two sisters and I always thought that they would help in the care of my mom. I took care of my father and I thought that when my mom got sick they would do the same for her. I lived with my mom so I would take care of the day to day chores and tasks. I didn't want them to cook and clean but I did think that they would help her with a bath or shower. They both had families of their own so I didn't want to interrupt their lifestyle but I was hoping for a little help. I was wrong, the only time they would offer help was on their schedule and they expected my mom to adapt to them. That was not something she could do because of her condition. One came over once a month and the other was too busy with work and her family. When one sister came over it was such a chore for her to help my mom with a shower that I finally said enough and I started doing it. When I told her that I was going to help my mom in the shower she said, "Ok." After that she didn't visit as much and did very little to help except to buy supplies once in a while.

It was more work for me and it didn't matter to anyone else. It was like they expected me to do it and they were glad they didn't have to help. That's when I learned not to rely on anyone and that I was going to have to take care of my mom all by myself. I never faulted them for their actions because I knew that their family came first but don't say you're going to help and then walk away.

Not Their Concern

Most people have no concern for what you do as being a caregiver. They are not interested in how much work it is, how much it costs or how it affects your life. They see what you are doing and are just happy that they're not you. This not only applies to outsiders but it also includes family and friends.

They see how much work it is and yes they might open a door for you or carry a bag but other than that they want very little to do with you. They see the end result, as in our case, my mom was happy, clean and enjoying life, and they think all is well. They didn't realize that it was a twenty-four hour a day job for no pay. There was no way to go out and get a regular job. They would look at me like I was waisting my life or was just too lazy to get a job. They felt I was mooching off my mom and did nothing to help her.

That was the attitude of some friends and family and I didn't care. I did my job and that was to take care of my mom and dad. I didn't do it for pay, I did it because it was the right thing to do. I didn't need their approval or blessing and I didn't care that they were not concerned with the situation. Even to this day I am still defending myself for the decision I made. I'm finally at the point where I did my best and they are the ones that need to do some soul searching.

People Praise You Because They Are Glad It's Not Them

When you are taking care of your parent be prepared to get praise from some people and pity from others. I call it false praise because they are too complimentary and it just sounds and feels fake. In my experiences, when someone continues to praise you for what you are doing they are just showing pity for you.

One thing that I would hear and it would get to the point that, one I didn't believe it, and two, it irritated me, was when people would say, "You must love your mother very much to be taking care of her." What? Yes, love had something to do with it but more importantly it was the right thing to do. The more I heard this type of a statement I started to realize they didn't mean it and it was a way to deflect the situation. Most of those that said this never took care of their parents and if they had children they did very little in their upbringing. They hired someone to take care of their children or did as little as possible because they interfered with their way of life. Others that would make that comment also had that look on their face like, "Thank God I don't have to do that." This would happen over and over and it got to the point where I would get irritated and respond, "It's the right thing to do." Some would get caught off guard and then regroup and say, "Yes," and others would get defensive and say, "I couldn't do it." My favorite response was, "I don't have time."

Some people actually meant what they were saying and you will know this from the start but the others are just irritating. I didn't need pity, what I needed were people to say once in a while, "Good job." That's it, I didn't need the flowery words and all the smoke they would try to blow up my behind.

Those That Mean It Are The Ones That Offer To Help

Over the years of taking care of my mom I would get praise from some family and friends. Most of the time it was just words and it really didn't mean anything to us because there was no belief in what they said. My mom would tell me after, "I don't believe them," or "they don't mean it." Once in a while someone would say something that we both believed and interesting it was usually the person that offered to help.

I never wanted help when I was lifting my mom because we had a system and it worked very well. If someone tried to help I was afraid it would cause a problem because they were not use to our procedure. Another problem was when I lifted her sometimes her diaper would be exposed and I didn't want to give them "a show" or have them see something that might make them uncomfortable.

Some family and friends would offer to carry bags or clothes while I put my mom in the car. Some would offer to push the wheelchair so I could get a short break. Others would sometimes load the car and even put the wheelchair in the back of the car after I lifted her into the car. This doesn't seem like much but it was very important to us. They would say my mom looked good and healthy and then they would say, "I'm so glad I saw you," and then walk away. Some relatives and friends would just walk away as were leaving and never offered to help. It's being petty but she was the only one left of her family and she was the oldest.

We did have some family and friends that always offered to help when they saw her. When we visited them they would help unload and load the car. They would comment on how she looked and how well she was taken care of and she would reply, "I know, I'm lucky."

My mom and I were never a fan of just words and we could tell who meant it and who didn't. Unfortunately there were a lot in the family that didn't mean it and were just happy they were not in my situation. Through the years we knew who was sincere and who was blowing a lot of smoke.

Momma's Boy

Of all the years I took care of my mom the one thing that always made me laugh was when someone called me a "momma's boy." I was the youngest and my sisters always told me I was the favorite. That was never true because my parents never had a favorite. Out of the three of us I was the one that always got in trouble, was not the smartest and I caused more headaches for my mom and dad while I was growing up. I think the reason they thought this was because there was ten years difference from my oldest sister and nine years difference from my second sister. When I was little they helped take care and watch me so they always felt because I was the youngest I was the favorite. My parents made it clear that they had no favorites and that we were all treated the same and they were right.

I never considered myself a "momma's boy" because I always thought they were spoiled and selfish. I don't think a "momma's boy" would have done some of the things I had to do. I don't think they would have changed her diapers, cleaned her up, dressed her, lifted her on the toilet and the numerous other things that were part of caring for my mom. It was a job that needed to be done and there was no glamour or benefits from doing these tasks.

For some it was just a way to ding me or make fun of the decision I made to take care of my mom. It was also a way to poke fun at me because of what I had to do. Like I said it would always make me laugh whenever I heard that term. If what I had to do was the real definition of a "momma's boy" then I had no problem with it. I guess it might have also been a compliment because I was doing what a lot of others could never do.

Everyone Knows Better

As in life everyone knows better than you on how to be a caregiver. They always know someone that did this or that and that this what you should be doing. Mind you, they've never been a caregiver but they do know what's best for you. I would get sick and tired of always being told what was best for us. I finally got to the point of listening and just saying, "Thanks." It didn't matter what you were doing, "You're lifting wrong," "let her do it herself," "hire someone," or one of my favorites, "I would never do that." That was pretty obvious because they also never wanted to help but they always knew better than me. Most of time this came from family members and it would just drive my mom and me nuts. She would tell me, "If there so smart how come they never helped their parents," and she was right. Most of them never had to care for their parents because they got sick, went to the hospital and died. There was no prolonged illness or condition, but they knew what was best for my mom.

When outsiders would give advice I would listen because I might learn something new and occasionally that did happen. I would learn of a new technique and apply it to our situation, if it worked, great, if it didn't we would go back to our old ways. You can't close the door on advice because you never know if it can help you in the care of your parent.

It would just get old and frustrating when everyone would tell you what to do or what someone else did with no regard that everyones situation is different. Sometimes they would actually argue with me because they said I was wrong and their friends were right. When I would explain that my mom's doctors were pleased with the care she was receiving, it didn't matter because they knew someone that did it right because it was different from what we were doing. I felt vindicated when I was complimented every time we saw a new doctor or when my mom was admitted to the hospital. They were always amazed at the care she was receiving and that was all I needed to hear.

You Become The Villain For Doing What Is Right

To many people I became a villain because of the decision to take care of my parents. Some thought I was taking advantage of the situation because I no longer wanted to work and pay my own way. They thought I had become lazy and was comfortable living off my parents and could not support myself.

These people also had no idea how much work was required to take care of my mom and dad. They also didn't know how much stress it caused and how it affected my health. True it made life a little easier because I didn't have a full time paying job and I was able to focus solely on the care of my parents. The other thing was that my dad and mom had no problem with this arrangement because they were being cared for in their own home. They didn't have to rely on strangers and their care was personal. They felt they were getting better care from me than they would get from someone else or a care facility and they were right.

I took care of my dad and mom the best possible way I could. I was always more concerned about their health and their quality of life. In the process I gave up a lot and had to rely on them for day to day expenses when I could not do odd jobs. It was not something I was proud of because I always tried and wanted to pay my own way. I never felt comfortable living off of them but it also never interfered with their care. I worked full time in caring for them and if that made me a villain for doing right I really didn't care.

Damned If You Do, Damned If You Don't

No matter what you do whenever you are a caregiver someone will always complain or criticize you for what you are doing. They have a better way to do this, they know someone that did that or have no concern in anything you do. Most of the time this comes from people that have never been a caregiver and would never want to be one.

In my situation I never got any credit from family while I was taking care of my parents. No matter what I did I was always told I should have done something else. If I wanted to discuss care and diagnosis with the doctor I was wrong if I questioned him. If I didn't ask questions I was wrong or we had the wrong physician. I was damned if I did and damned if I didn't. It was frustrating and came to the point where I finally told them to mind their own business because I had the situation under control. Then they told me I shouldn't be taking care of my parents and I should hire someone to do it or put them in a care facility. I don't know if they were trying to shame me so I would walk away and move on with my life. On the other hand they never offered to help and always would have something else to do when I needed a little extra help. I finally got to the point where I didn't ask for any help and didn't expect it either. They would get defensive and tried to put me down whenever a friend or other family member would praise me for the work I was doing. The only time they would be put in their place was when a doctor or other medical professional would praise the care that my dad and mom received. After the doctor left they would be back to their old ways of criticizing.

I ended up with a thick skin because I just got tired of hearing about how wrong I was for the decision to take care of my parents. Instead of thanking me for the decision to care for my dad and mom they would just say I should have done something else. I finally stopped listening and went on with giving my parents the best care they could receive.

Always Criticized

It doesn't matter what you do or how much work it takes you will always be criticized by someone. You are doing things wrong or someone else had the same situation and they did it this way. Or my favorite was, "Why should you do this, let someone else do it."

Most of the time these statements came from people that never had to take care of anyone. They were making these comments for the way they handled their situation. Taking care of a parent is a personal decision and people handle it in different ways.

What made me upset was when these comments came from family members. They could see how I was taking care of my parents and to criticize me for the decision I made was ridiculous. They should have been happy that they didn't have to sacrifice their lives to do the same. Instead of criticism they should have been giving support. I wasn't looking for financial support but moral support would have gone a long way. I didn't need to hear it but it would have been nice if once in a while they would say, "Thanks." It never happened, all I would hear is you need to do something else.

I would be told it wasn't fair to me to spend time taking care of my mom and it wasn't fair to her. They would never ask my mom what she wanted and didn't care that her answer was, "I'm happy the way things are." They would just ignore what she wanted and insist they knew best. As usual they were wrong.

Later on I did start asking people, "If I made the wrong decision what should I have done?" Most of the time the answer was, "I don't know," or "it should have been something else." Never any specifics just more criticism, I finally just ignored what they said and we went along with our lives. My mom was never concerned about what they said and her comments were, "If they're so smart let them come and take care of me." They never took her up on that offer.

From the time I started taking care of my dad to the day my mom passed away I was always criticized for my decision. I never got support but just comments like, "You waisted your life," or "you have no future" and "you should have gotten a job and paid someone to take care of them." There might be some reasoning with these statements but I made the decision that I thought was best for the care of my parents and myself. I can't go back and change what I did so I have to live with the decisions that I made. I still know I made the right decision.

Use As What Not To Do, Or As To Do

As I have stated before you will get a lot of advice from many sources. There are also several books and workshops available on the subject of being a caregiver. You have to make up your own mind what advice best suits your situation.

I did not write this book as a "how to" guide. I wrote it to document what I went through as I took care of my dad and mom. All the advice I received was from people that never cared for anyone, had help or put their parent in a senior care facility. I took care of my parents, for the most part, by myself. I had very little help and I was the one that was with them twenty-four hours a day. There were very few breaks and definitely no vacations. I was the only help they had during the day and night. My sisters came when they did not have to work and when they were able to get away from taking care of their own families. I had no family and I was self employed so I was able to change my schedule as needed.

As you read this book you can see if any situations are similar to what is happening in your life. You can consider what I did or you can dismiss my situations completely. You have to do what is best for your situation and your parent.

Chapter 57

OPINIONS ABOUT THE JOB YOU ARE DOING

Making It Harder Than It Should Be

Sometimes when you have a routine it is hard for you to make a change. In the process of your normal duties you might be making things harder than it should be. Once in a while you should step back and re-evaluate your procedures to see if you are doing more work than needed. I made a lot of changes over the years while I was taking care of my parents. Most of it was necessary because of the change of their conditions but some of it was because it made things a little easier for me.

Taking care of my dad was pretty straight forward and their was not any time to make changes. With my mom because I took care of her for so many years I did make changes to make taking care of her a little easier. Some of the changes were because instead of doing individual tasks I would group things together. This took place with my mom washing herself up at the table. I would bring the items she needed one at a time so she could do a specific task at a time. This meant a lot of trips to the bathroom and the sink for me and it took time. I figured if I gave her only one item she would complete that task fully and not try to skip something. An example would be washing her face and rinsing out her mouth. I would bring her a wash cloth and she would wash her face and then I would return to the sink to rinse it out and she would do it again. This took time but one day I realized if I placed a plastic show box in front of her with soapy water and one with clean water she could wash her face and rinse out the wash cloth and clean off the soap residue. It took the same amount of time to set up the little "cleaning station" but I wasn't constantly going back and forth to the sink to rinse out the wash cloth. The same went for when she cleaned her dentures and rinsed out her mouth. Instead of her doing one task at a time with the items I gave her, I would put all of them out at the same time and she went from one task to another. It saved me time and it let her take care of herself.

Another task that I made harder than it should have been was lifting her from anything. I was taught how to use a lifting belt when she was in the rehabilitation hospital after her spine surgery. I never could get it quite right and she also didn't cooperate. I started just lifting her straight up and putting her where she needed to be. This was a lot more work, caused a great deal of strain on my neck and back. I'm sure there were a lot of easier ways but this worked and I never tried anything different.

When you talk to some professionals they have advice on how to make your life a little easier while you are taking care of you parent. It is always good to listen and hopefully you can use these techniques to help your tasks become a little easier. Once again you have to adapt this advice to your unique situation and make sure it is a viable alternative. Over time you will learn "tricks" and shortcuts to help you with your task of being a caregiver. I did because I never stopped learning during the entire time I cared for my parents.

Like Usual, No One Wants To Listen

It seems that whenever you want to explain yourself or a situation no one ever wants to listen. A lot of the times they think they know more than you or they are not interested in what you have to say. Most of the time this happens when you try to explain why you're taking care of your parent or how you are doing the job. Their response is usually part of the "as long as it's not me" attitude.

Most of the time when people would give me advice they would shut me down when I tried to explain my situation. Sometimes they would just say, "Your wrong," or "I don't want to hear it." It was okay for them to give their opinion or advice but it was not okay for me to defend myself.

This would come from some family members or acquaintances that had no idea of what I had to do. They basically would just say, "Get somebody else to do it." Once in a while it would come from a so-called expert at the hospital but they would usually change their mind when they saw how much I did and how my mom was treated. Her health and condition was the best defense that I had when these professionals questioned my work.

Now that I am no longer a caregiver I notice what other people are doing when they're taking care of a parent. I try not to give advice unless they ask me and I also don't want to come across as a know it all. I am noticing that even when they ask me questions they never listen to my answers. They know what is best and they're not interested in what I have to say. I have a cousin that asks me questions about taking care of his dad because of my experience but he rarely listens and his wife prefers to get all the information from the internet. That's fine, because their situation is different and they are handling it their way. If they ask me I will tell them, if they want to listen that's up to them.

Your Frustration

Not only does your parent get frustrated so do you. The only difference it is not good for you to show your frustration. It can make your parent anxious or nervous and can cause problems for you.

You will need a lot of patience while you are taking care of your parent because you will be doing the same task over and over. They will be set in their ways so if they make a mistake, they will be making the same mistake over and over. It's just like when they have hearing loss you repeat yourself constantly, the same goes for tasks. Depending on their condition, this can happen many times a day, day after day. You just have to grin and bear it and just be patient because the worse thing you can do is lose it and snap at them. This can scare your parent and even make them cry. It is not worth the stress on their system just because you have become frustrated. Step back, take a deep breath and then continue with the task, even though you probably have done it a few times before.

Another cause of frustration for you is when other people constantly tell you what to do when they have no clue or experience. It's like the saying, "Everyone can spend your money better than you," because everybody can take care of your parent better than you. I have no problem with someone giving me advice when they have actually had the experience of taking care of a parent. I would get advice from some that never had to do anything for their parents because they were still healthy and able to take care of themselves. Does it make them feel good to give someone advice of which they know nothing about or is it they just want to sound important?

This would always frustrate me and my mom would notice because I probably made a funny face or rolled my eyes. She would tell me, "What do they know, you're doing fine," or "don't listen to them, you know what you are doing." She was right, she had complete faith in my ability and her life depended on it. She had a way to say the right things to make me forget what others were saying.

Some Never Have To Go Through This

A lot of people never have to take care of their parents because somethings else has made that decision for them. Their parent could have passed away suddenly or at an earlier time. Another reason is that their parents put enough money away so they could be cared for in an assisted living facility or some just might not have any intentions of caring for their elderly parents. Once again it depends on the individual circumstances and what they can handle.

My parents were around when they became elderly and sick. They didn't have the luxury of being able to put money away for their future care. Like most people they were living paycheck to paycheck and month to month. Raising a family there was never anything left for assisted living when they became old. Even with their insurance and monthly benefit there was never enough to put into savings for the future. That's where I came in and decided that I would care for my parents. It was something I had to do and there was no hesitation. I could not let them fend for themselves because that is not the way they raised me.

I have lived pretty much my entire life month to month. I know how hard t is to try to put money away when you are just trying to survive. My family never had the luxury of not worrying about tomorrow because we were just trying to survive. In my parents later years I did my best so they wouldn't worry about the future or their care. Yes, it was a lot of stress and a lot of work. I made many sacrifices and put my life on hold but it was the only way I could care for my parents. Looking back I know I succeeded in this task.

Unless You've Done It, You Have No Idea

Unless you have cared for someone you have no idea how much work it is. It is a never ending job because you are always needed. Even the simplest task can become a lot of work because your parent is relying on you for everything. It is easy to say what to do but it is a lot harder to actually do it.

With my mom I had to pretty much do everything for her. It was not just the lifting and changing but it was simple things too. If she wanted to work on a puzzle book I had to bring it to her. If she wanted a snack I had to get it or if she wanted another cup of coffee it was up to me to pour her another cup and bring it to her.

If she couldn't reach the tissue I had to bring it closer or if she spilled something I was the one that had to clean it up. The simple tasks that we take for granted she needed help for everyone one of them. I use to joke that she knew just when my backside was just about to sit on a chair because she would call me. I would just be sitting down and I would hear, "Jim" and I would get up right away. The same happened when she rang her bell, as soon as I started something or was going to take a short break she would ring the bell and I would go to her.

It was exhausting and it happened everyday for over thirteen years. No one has a clue how much work taking care of an elderly woman requires. The only way you would know the amount of work required to take of her was to have done it yourself. That why I would always ask the staff member from the hospital that would give advice on being a caregiver if they had actually done the job. Everyone I came across had the same answer, "No."

I'm Done

One thing that has happened after my mom passed away is that I'm done dealing with people that always thought that they knew best. For years I had to deal with family telling me that I had to do this or that and what I was doing was wrong. A lot are still trying to tell me how I should run my life and what changes I need to make. I'm finally at the point where I don't care or listen to what they say.

I am still being criticized for the decision to take care of my dad and mom. I have been told many times that I ruined my life and have no future because of my decision. I have no career or job and it doesn't look like I will attain anything in the near future. I am trying to gain employment but do to lack of a recent and verifiable job history no one seems to want to take a chance on an interview. There are plenty of people looking for employment so why should they take a chance on someone who has been out of the workforce for over twenty years.

True it was my decision to take care of my parents and put my career on hold. Their care became a full time job and there was nobody there to do it but me. When I made the decision I never thought the job market would change and everything would have to be online. In fact when I made my decision the internet was just starting. I always thought when it was time for me to get a job, I would apply, hopefully get an interview and then I could sell my skills. This doesn't happen anymore because you can't sell your skills online with a brief application or resume.

I know my life is a mess and the future doesn't look too bright but I have to deal with this situation. Constantly beating a dead horse by telling me I was wrong over the last twenty years is not going to change anything now or help me get a job. Instead of being positive all I hear is that I made a mistake and caused all these problems myself. I'm done listening to all the criticism of the past and I have no interest in their opinions on my future. Telling me I was wrong over and over does not help with the future. I need to concentrate on finding employment so I can get my life back on track.

Chapter 58

ADVICE TO OTHERS

Family Has No Clue What's Coming

Most people have no clue what is involved in being a caregiver to a parent. It consumes your life by taking over your day to day duties. Even if you can afford to hire someone to help, unless it is twenty-four hours a day, your life will be substantially interrupted.

I have a cousin who is now taking care of his father, my uncle. He is in his late eighties and is still able to do quite a lot for himself. He moved from out of state and bought a house across the street from his son, my cousin. This works out very well because he is still independent but has the comfort of knowing his son is across the street in case something is needed or happens.

This was almost not the case. My uncle is a retired corporate executive and is of that generation that liked their alcohol. After his wife, my aunt passed away he started drinking a lot more than usual. When she was alive she kept him in check and now with her gone he was trying to drink away the pain of her loss. Many times in his home that was out of state he would stumble, fall and get hurt. Sometimes he would fall asleep on the floor where he fell and once he sobered up he would get up. The problem was made even worse when he had friends visit and he would drink even more. That was one of the main reasons for having him move closer to my cousin. Fortunately he was able to purchase another home.

After he moved into his new home he continued his old ways. I came to visit, this was after my mom passed away, and the next morning my cousin came and got me because his dad had fallen on the floor. I went over and he was flat on his back. I helped him get up and checked him over. He was bleeding on the arms and face. When I looked at him I thought he went through a war. His skin was all bruised, he was missing teeth and he looked a mess. Coming to find out the missing teeth were not an issue because he had them pulled sometime earlier. The bruises on his arm were from skin cancer treatments that he had over the years. I cleaned him up and saw that there was only minor scratches from the fall. The problem was he had too much to drink, was in unfamiliar surroundings and started to hallucinate because of the alcohol.

My cousin asked me for help and I showed him how to lift his dad so both would not get injured. I gave him other advice, from my experience with my mom on lifting, walkers, wheelchairs, grab bars, etc. My cousin and I went to the store to get some supplies, gloves, urinal bottle and a raised toilet seat to make things easier for his dad. We also purchased a back brace to support his back while he lifted his dad. As we were driving I told my cousin that this was just the beginning and he had absolutely no idea what was coming. He told me he knew this was going to happen but he just never realized how fast it would come. I also told him he needed to have a heart to heart talk with his dad. If my cousin would have taken my uncle to the hospital they would have separated them and probably would have called social services because of his condition. They would have seen the same bruises that I saw and would have jumped to the conclusion he was abused. I told my cousin that he needed to explain to his dad that because of the alcohol, the falls and the bruises, he could have been taken away and his son could be put in jail for abuse. He agreed and had a long talk with his dad. His father was stunned that all this could happen because, in his words, "Stumbling." He agreed that he would cut back on the alcohol but my cousin set a limit. No more than two half glasses of wine per day. Before this he would drink a bottle of wine a day and sometimes have other liquor as well. This was a hard limit to swallow, but as my cousin told him, "It's either this or I could go to jail if something was to happen." This worked and to this day he only has two half glasses of wine a day at dinner. The bruising cleared up and he has not fallen or stumbled since.

My cousin got a second chance because his dad recovered. His father is able to still get around and care for himself. On the other hand, all it would have taken was an alcohol induced stumble and he could have been bed ridden or worse. My cousin and uncle got a reprieve until the next hurdle comes into play.

Talk To Your Spouse Or Significant Other

I never married because when I was young I started a business. I felt the business would take all my time and energy and it wouldn't be fair to start a relationship because I was too busy. The business took a lot of work and caused a lot of stress. When my dad got sick I made the choice to take care of him and try to run the business. This choice caused my business to fail because taking care of my dad was a lot of work and took all my time. When my mom became ill, I moved from taking care of my dad to taking care of her part time while I still did odd jobs. When she could no longer walk her care became a full time job.

I never had to discuss any of this with a spouse because I never had time for a relationship. My sisters on the other hand were married and had families of their own. I felt it wasn't fair to burden them with the responsibility of taking care of our dad and mom. They needed to be there for their children and didn't need the worry of being a caregiver.

The decision was easy for me because basically I had no one to answer to and tell me, "No." Other people don't have this luxury because they are married and or have families of their own. Being a caregiver and taking care of a parent is one of the hardest and most demanding things you might ever have to do. Make sure you talk to your spouse or significant other and both of you understand how much work it is and how much time it will take. I see this with my cousin who is just starting to take care of his dad, my uncle. It is starting to take more time because he his taking his father to many doctors. His life is starting to change and his wife isn't use to the situation yet. She still feels their life is normal and that nothing will change. My advice to both of them was, "You have no idea what might be coming." They are lucky because my uncle can still do a lot of things for himself and he is actually living in his own home. As time goes on that might change and they need to be prepared for becoming full time caregivers. I keep telling them that they need to discuss how they will handle that situation if it ever happens.

My cousin has sometime to think about what might be coming down the road. Some people don't have that luxury and have to make the decision right away. My mom was walking one day and the next she couldn't stand up and never walked again. I made the decision in an instant that I would take care of her. If I had a spouse I would have discussed it before I made that decision.

Stress On Relationships

Being a caregiver can put serious stress on relationships. If you're taking care of a parent full time that is a twenty-four hour a day job. It takes a special person to accept the competition of a parent needing care all the time.

My mom needed me to help her with almost everything that she did. Yes, she could do simple tasks but I would have to set them up for her. If she needed to go to the bathroom I had to stop whatever I was doing and put her on the toilet. That day to day demand can put a large amount of stress on a single person and it could put even more stress on a relationship. I could just see this scenario of having someone over for dinner and my mom would ring her bell and say, "Jim, I gotta go." I would then have to leave and put my mom on the toilet and when she was finished, clean her up. Then come back out and continue making dinner. Not something you want to have to deal with or explain when you are trying to start a relationship.

If you are in a relationship or married it might be a little easier because your friend or spouse already knows what you are dealing with on a day to day basis. Unfortunately the stress of being a caregiver could interfere with your relationship because you have very little down time. There is not much time to go out or go on vacation. I never had a chance to start any relationship while I was taking care of my mom, so the only stress I had was from the day to day routine of being a caregiver. Even if I did have a relationship I couldn't afford to have someone stay with my mom but if it is in your budget, have someone stay with your parent so you can get away. It will go a long way in relieving the stress of the day to day routine.

No Idea How Much Work It Is

The amount of work involved in being a caregiver is enormous. You figure that everything you do for yourself you have to at least multiply it by two. That is in its simplest form. Add to that if you have to lift them, bathe them, change them or even possibly feed them. Once again it is like having a baby or small child in the house with the exception that they are much larger. They are just as demanding as an infant and maybe even more because they are set in their ways. An infant is learning about life, the person you're taking care of has lived life and wants to continue doing what they have done for many years. The difference is the mind and/or body is no longer cooperating.

Not only is it an enormous task it is also and great responsibility. Now that you're taking care of them your are not only responsible for their care but you are also responsible for their condition and what they do. Many times over the course of the time you are caring for them you will be tested and judged on the quality of care and their condition. Every time you go to the doctor, medical facility or hospital you will be under the microscope for the care you are giving.

This adds more stress to the job because you don't want to make any mistakes that can cause complications or something even worse. Dispensing medications properly is all part of the job and needs to be done accurately so it doesn't cause them any harm. Even how your home looks and how it's kept is going to be reviewed and questioned. There is so much work involved that it seams like a never ending job. For the most part the job doesn't end because your are living with it twenty-four hours a day, seven days a week. That's why I came up with the saying, "You Got To Do What You Got To Do," You just have to deal with it and move on to the next day.

How Much Time It Takes

People tell you that you are spending too much time taking care of your parent have no idea how much time it really takes. They think all you have to do is fix them some breakfast, put them in front of the television and you can go on with your life. That might be true in some situations but most of the time it is a lot more work than that.

I tell my cousin and his wife, they are just starting to take care of my uncle part time, that they have no idea what they are in for. I tell them as time goes on the work is going to get harder and more involved. I keep telling them to enjoy these days when he still can do a lot for himself because when the time comes for them to take care of him full time they will no longer have any time to themselves. They say they understand but I don't see them heeding the warning. Right now their inconvenience is taking him to the doctor appointments and diagnostic tests. He still can take care of his own personal needs so they haven't had to adjust to that situation. They did have a scare a few month ago when he fell and couldn't get himself up. That was a stressful time for my cousin because he was thrown right into caring for his dad. He had to help his dad to the bathroom and help him wash. He did it but he was sure happy when his dad recovered and was able to take care of himself once again. I told him that was a preview of what's coming and his answer was, "I hope not." He was amazed at how much time and work it was just to take care of his dad for a few days. He told me, "How did you did this so long with your mom and dad?"

How I did it was that I had to give up a lot and sacrifice my career in order to take care of my parents. There was no way I could work a full or part time job and give my parent the care they required. It took all my time and energy to care for them.

No One Wants Advice

I learned very quickly after my mom passed away that no one wants your advice when they are taking care of someone. I have a cousin who's wife is taking care of her mother who has Alzheimers disease and she has to do pretty much everything for her. She can still walk with the aid of a walker but has to be taken to the bathroom, needs help getting dressed and ready for bed. She can feed herself and do other tasks but she has to be watched all the time. One time we were together at another cousin's house for dinner and they asked me questions on how I use to take care of my mom. They asked questions about lifting, putting on diapers and other tasks. I asked them to explain how they did those tasks and then I would explain how I did them. Hearing what they were doing seemed like a lot of work to me so I made suggestions on how to make the tasks easier. I also told them to get a back brace so they wouldn't hurt their back. Those suggestions fell on deaf ears because the next time I saw them I asked if they tried the different techniques. They answered, "No" and when I asked why they said, "We didn't want to try anything new." My first reaction was to say, "Why did you ask?" and then I caught myself and just said, "oh." I heard a few weeks ago that my cousin's wife hurt her back while trying to lift her mom, a back brace might have prevented this injury.

Throughout this book I have said over and over that everyones situation is different but I have also said that caregiving is an on going learning experience. I was the same way because I thought I was doing everything right but I always listened to when people gave me advice, especially when it was from one that actually had the experience of taking care of a parent. That type was few and far between so when I received it I would definitely listen. After I heard the advice I would see if I could use it and adapt to my parents situation. If I could that was great and if I couldn't that was also great because now I knew something I didn't know before. I didn't just shut down people but once again everyone is different.

I'm once again having a similar situation with another cousin who is starting to take care of his dad, my uncle. When his dad was sick he wanted my advice on everything he had to do and I told him. He listened and tried a lot of things I told him. Fortunately for him his dad got better and now he doesn't need any information from me. When I try to give him advice on what is coming it usually falls on deaf ears. His wife gets most of her information now from the internet and the mysterious "they." Whenever I say something or give advice she always says, "They say," and goes on with what she read somewhere on the internet. It is usually different from what I say and it also usually doesn't explain everything. Most of the time the information provided by the mysterious "they" doesn't work and causes complications. Hopefully my cousin will learn before something serious happens.

I don't give advice anymore unless I'm asked. Most of the time I know most people won't listen and to them I'm just talking. To them what I know happened a few years ago and it is not relevant to their situation. What they don't understand is that I took care of my parents for over twenty years. I did many tasks and had to deal with many situations. Someone that has had that much time being a caregiver is not easy to find. I wish I would have had someone with that much real experience that I could have gone to for advice. Most of the time the experience lasts five to ten years and it is very specific to one condition. It could have made my parents and my life a little easier.

Taste Of My Own Medicine

As I said earlier in this book I listened to advice from others and tried to adapt it to my situation. I also said that I got tired of getting advice from people that always thought their situation was the same as mine and they would tell me what I should or shouldn't be doing. Now that I am no longer taking care of my mother I am getting a taste of my own medicine.

I give advice when I am asked knowing that every situation is different. I usually say that if I was doing this or that this is how I would handle it. Most of the time no one listens and they don't try to adapt my recommendations or even try. This has happened a few times with a couple of cousins and I understand where they are coming from. My problem is if you are not interested in what I have to say or my experience, why ask in the first place? They don't have to try to be polite and ask my opinion if they're not interested in what that opinion is. I would rather they don't ask and just go along with their routines. I am not offended if someone doesn't ask my opinion and I won't offer any advice unless I am asked.

Like I have said many times in this book everyone situations different. Medical conditions vary and techniques are different for every person. What I did for my dad might not work for my uncle. How I cared for my mom won't work for someone else's mom. I understand this and people need to do what is best for them. I do have a lot of experience caring for my dad and mom because I did it for many years. I handled a lot of different situations both good and bad while I cared for my parents. If that experience is useful for them and they ask I have no problem letting them know how I handled those situations. All they have to do is ask if they really want to know.

People Can Take My Advice Or Not

Now that I am no longer a caregiver some people have asked my advice on how I took care of my parents. Most are family and friends and they are just starting to have to deal with the idea of taking care of their parents. I know some of their situations and I ask questions to get a feel of what they are dealing with. If I can give some advice I do but I always tell them, "Given the situation, this is what I would do." Or another answer is, "I had this happen and this is how I handled it." What I have noticed is most of the time they don't even try what I have done or suggested. They just say, "Thank you" and never give it another thought. I don't have a problem with that response because I don't know their complete situation. It might work for them or it might not. Only they know what their unique situation is and how they will handle it.

Even though I took care of my parents for over twenty years I am not an expert. I have had the experience but I do not have the education or certificate that says I am qualified. I learned through life experience and not from a book. When someone asks me how I know about a certain situation I can say that I actually did a certain task while I was taking care of my parents. I didn't read it, I just did it. I will still give my opinion or tell people how I did things in the past with my parents when I am asked. If they want to listen to what I say great, if they don't, that's fine too. I did what I had to do and if anyone is interested I will tell them how I did it.

I Don't Get Upset

I don't get upset when people don't listen to what I have to say about how I took care of my parents. Everyone has a different way of dealing with their unique situations. Some want to ask for help and others don't want or need any advice.

I spent years worrying about my parents health and their care that I no longer need to have to defend myself for any reason. I gave them the best care and I did the best job I possibly could. They had a good quality of life and my mom lasted longer than any of her siblings. I have to move on with my life and try to get my affairs back on track so I can go forward. I can't get upset if someone disagrees with me or doesn't want to hear my opinion about caregiving. If they ask my advice or opinion I will always give it. If they disagree or disregard what I say that's fine with me because I've already done it and I am moving on with my life.

I'm in my mid fifties and I do not need to get upset about something that I already have done because life is short and I have only a few years to get back on track. I have other things to worry about such as getting a decent job and a place of my own to live. I have to put my life back together after the twenty plus years I spent taking care of my parents. Over the last few years I have found out that this has become an enormous task because I lack a recent job history so it is making it harder to find employment. I have more important issues to concern myself than getting upset if someone doesn't listen to my opinion or advice on caregiving.

You Will Know And Learn How To Handle Unique Situations

Over time you will learn how to handle unique situations quicker because you will know almost everything about your parent. Challenges will become just bumps in the road because of all your previous experiences. Whenever you are thrown a curve you'll just take a deep breath and deal with it.

In the beginning I was nervous about taking care of my dad. When I was doing it part time it was easy because it was basically taking him to the doctors and listening to what was said. As his condition worsened I started doing more such as dispensing medication and giving him insulin shots. I worked my way slowly into a full time care situation. When I had to take care of him full time it was more of the cleaning and bathing that was a little different but I was able to handle it quickly.

When I started taking care of my mom it was the same situation with the exception I already had some experience with my dad's situation. It started off part time and then it became a full time job. With her we were always being thrown into unique situations because she required care that my dad never needed. I had to learn how to change diapers and incontinence pads. She had bed wounds that needed to be cleaned and dressed. She needed help in the shower and she needed to be lifted out of bed and the wheelchair several times a day. She needed constant help and it was even more difficult when we had to travel. Her illness also lasted a lot longer than my dad's so this was a long term caregiving assignment.

Every time a new challenge showed up I would step back and think how I could handle it with her condition. It might have taken a few minutes, hours or even a day or two, but I usually came up with a solution on how to handle it. I knew her so well that I was able to adapt to anything that she needed or required. When the end was near I knew this would my most unique situation. The last two weeks of her life when I knew she was fading I still adapted to make sure she was as comfortable as possible. That was the most challenging situation because I knew no matter what I did it wasn't going to change the outcome.

Chapter 59

OBSERVING OTHERS AFTER BEING A CAREGIVER

Some Know Everything

Some people think they know everything and therefore don't want any advice. I would always welcome advice as long as it was constructive and was not just criticism. It was fine to criticize my methods, procedures and the care I was giving my parents as long as you made a suggestion or offered a different solution. I would always listen and if I could use it in our situation or if it needed to be adapted so I could use it in the care of my parents I would be happy to try. It is impossible for one person to know everything because like I have said every situation is different.

Once again there are those that think they do know everything and shut the door on any type of advice. Some are just starting out and they have an idea that they know everything because a person at the hospital or medical facility told them what to do. That is great that they received this advice from a professional but day to day care requires adjustments and the only way you learn these adjustments is by trial and error or talk to someone that has been there and done that.

Today one of the biggest distractions is the internet because you can find information from a lot of "so-called experts." You have to be very careful with this type of advice because you don't know how it was tried and if it will work in your situation. I'm not saying not to listen to their advice or techniques but you need to be sure of the source. Anyone can post information but you need to make sure it is accurate and will help you and not cause any distress or problems for your parent.

I get tired of hearing, "They said," whenever you try to give someone advice from your experience. It seems that most of the time no one knows "who they" are. Even reading this book I have no problem with anyone questioning what I have written or done. Like I said before I am not an expert but what I have written is from my real world experience from taking care of my mom and dad for over twenty years. Please question my methods and experiences because they might help you or might mean absolutely nothing to you. It is your choice and responsibility to do what is right for your unique situation and your parent. I didn't know everything so I learned what I could and continued to learn because being a caregiver is an on going learning experience.

Some Want To Change Them

As a person gets older they are set in their ways and it is very hard to change them. I am in my mid fifties and I am definitely set in my ways and not open to much change. Some people think that they can change their parents to act and respond to a different way of life. This is easy to say but hard to do. One of the most difficult things for your parents to get use to is the fact that they need someone to take care of them. This is a major shock to their system and will take them a while to get use to. Trying to change other routines and practices could take a long time or longer depending on whether your parent wants to change.

My parents accepted the fact that I was going to take care of them very quickly. I knew they were set in their ways on a lot of other issues and routines. I did my best not to change those routines so they could have as close to a normal life as possible. My sisters would tell me that I would have to make them do this or that because it would make things easier for me and a lot of the times they were right. If my parents wanted to change their routines I would let them, if they wanted to leave them as they were that was fine with me also. Yes, most of the time it meant more work for me but it kept them in a familiar area and it made them feel like they were still in control because things were normal.

Being a caregiver requires a lot of give and take. For me it was more give because I decided I did not want to affect my parents life to the point where they no longer had any control. They were still in control of their mind and I didn't want to change them to where they gave up on life.

Others have to change their parents because there old routines could be considered dangerous or they don't remember the old routines. Once again that shows that everyone's situation is different and that a cookie cutter solution doesn't work for everyone.

Some Want To Control Them

Another thing some people try to do is that they want to control their parent. It depends on your situation and the condition of your parent if you need to control them. If they can hurt themselves or others it can be a point of concern otherwise it can lead to some difficulties as you try to care for your parents.

I never tried to control my parents, in fact they pretty much controlled me. Their condition and illnesses controlled every aspect of my life and the care that I gave them. I never had a problem with this because I was more interested in the care they received and their quality of life. I always had respect for my parents and in no way was I going to try to control them. Yes, I did have control of where they went and who came over but it was done with their cooperation. I never told them, "You have to do this," and I let them make their decisions. I would tell them what I thought and then they would decide what to do.

I remember when we would go into a doctors office or medical facility and I would hear other people talking down or scolding their parents. Once again I didn't know what their situation was but it just seemed so demeaning. I would see some get yelled at or criticized for everything they did. Sometimes my mom would comment to me after by saying, "Did you see that poor woman, the way they were treating her was so bad." I would agree with her and she would say, "I'm so lucky."

I hear my cousin and his wife talking about how his father, my uncle, is going to have to do this or that. He is going to have change and do what they want him to do. I keep telling them that probably won't happen and he is going to resist change or control. It will be interesting to see how it is handled and how the situation ends.

No Longer The Center Of Attention

Sometimes it is difficult for others to handle the idea of taking care of a parent because during that period they will no longer be the center of attention. Some can handle not being the center of attention and others have to be the focus all the time. This can be true in relationships because you have to dedicate so much time in taking care of your parent. This is why it is a must that you talk to your spouse or significant other before you decide you want to take care of a parent. This can prevent a lot of problems in the future.

I never had this problem because I never had a spouse or significant other. When I made the decision to take care of my parents it was just me. I didn't have to worry about their care competing with someone else and therefore I never had any problems. I have seen others who are caring for a parent and it causes all kinds of problems. I have seen when a wife gets upset because the parent takes to much time of their husband and they feel neglected. It can cause a lot of stress on a marriage or relationship. It also can cause stress on the parent and caregiver. One, the parent might feel in the way and try do more for themselves to the point where they can get hurt. The other is the caregiver is put in a no win situation because they have to choose between their spouse or the parent they are caring for.

This is why you need to discuss all the aspects of caregiving with your spouse or significant other. Everyone has a different personality and have unique tolerance levels. You need to know what your significant other expects of you and how much they can tolerate. You also need to see if they can accept the fact that taking care of your parent will take a lot of your time, meaning their might not be as much time left for them. Having this discussion brings everything out in the front so everyone knows what to expect. If not it can become a more stressful job than it needs to be.

Some Can't Handle It

Some can handle being a caregiver and some cannot. Some can handle their spouse or significant other caring for a parent and others can't. You need to know what category you, your spouse or significant other fall into.

This is part of the responsibility of being a caregiver. You need to know if you have what it takes to care for your parent. This usually evolves because at first you are apprehensive and then as you do more, it all becomes part of your normal routine. If you are having problems taking care of a parent or just can't do it, it is up to you to find an alternative. If you have the sense to realize this job is not for you then you should have the good sense to seek and alternative.

If you discuss the care of your parent with your spouse or significant other you need to know if they are on board with the situation. They might be left alone with your parent and might have to do some of the routines that you would normally do. If they are willing to help you that is a great benefit because it might give you a chance to step away for a few moments. If they are not willing to help or once again have a problem with the whole caregiving idea you need to step back and re-evaluate your decision. If you decide to still care for your parent by yourself you need to understand how much work it will be and that you probably will get little or no help. This decision could put a great strain on your marriage or relationship and cause a lot of stress on you while you are taking care of your parent. Being a caregiver is a stressful job and any added stress can only complicate the situation. Only you are the one that knows the answer to this question.

Some Call Them Useless

Some people call the elderly useless and want absolutely nothing to do with them. That is a disgusting attitude to have because you can learn so much from an elderly person. Some think that they have lived their life and times have changed so they have nothing left to contribute. That is so far off base and these people have no idea what they are talking about. You always learn from someone that has vast experience and has lived a long life. You might be surprised because they have probably done things that you would never do.

My parents were never useless and my sisters and I never even consider that term. Sure there were sometimes when we didn't want to hear what they had to say but that was because they were still our parents and they were telling us what to do as adults. That's a normal reaction and it doesn't mean that they were considered useless. They were concerned about us and wanted to give advice on how to handle our lives. We always listened to their advice and used it if we thought it could help us.

When I was caring for my dad and mom no matter how sick they were I never thought they were useless. No matter what I had to clean, change or dispense I was there to help them no matter what. People that say their parents are useless when they are old have to remember that people might think of them that way in a few years. Remember treat your parents how you would like to be treated if you were in their shoes. Just because someone is old and can't care for them self does not mean they're useless. We are the ones that make them useless because we try to push them out of our lives so we can go on with ours. Before you become a caregiver to your parent you have to ask yourself if you are ready for this responsibly. If you think they are useless you should consider other options because you might not give them the best care they can receive.

Only Thinking Of Themselves

Most people that call their parents useless are the ones that usually only think of themselves. They don't want the competition of an elderly parent around them interfering with their lives. They would rather push them aside and go on with their own life.

Thoughts like these never crossed my mind or even came into consideration. When my parents became ill I immediately jumped in and started caring for them. Whatever they needed I did, if they had to go somewhere I took them. I stopped what I was doing so they could get the care they needed to survive. I never considered my situation when I decided to care for my dad and mom. I probably should have put a little more thought into the process so I didn't end up the way I did but at the time I was not thinking about myself I was thinking about them. Their care became the most important thing in my life.

Some might say I'm strange or crazy but that is how I thought. I did not want them to be on their own and I definitely didn't want them to be forgotten. Many said I should have left them alone because they were responsible for their own lives and should take care of themselves. That they should hire someone and not expect me to take care of them. That's where they missed the most important point, my parents didn't expect me to take care of them, it was my decision. Over and over they would tell me that I should do something else and to forget about them. I should just let things happen and I could go on with my life. I told them they didn't raise me to be selfish and that they were stuck with me. After a while they dropped the subject because they knew that my mind was made up and I wasn't going to change it.

Selfish

Some people are so selfish that they can never take care of someone else. I didn't think these type of people existed but I finally noticed that they did when my mom was sick. The first time I was exposed to this idea was the last time she was in the hospital and the teacher for the college nursing program told me that most people think of themselves before they think of caring for a parent. She told me how lucky my mom was and how unusual it was for a son to take care of his mom. She said most would be too squeamish or vain to even consider the thought of taking care of their mom. She said daughters have a hard time and don't want to do all the work involved. She said one of the biggest problems is that caring for a parent interferes with their daily schedules and most people wont change to accommodate the needs of the parent. The bottom line of her conversation was when she said, "Most people are selfish and only think of themselves." I was floored because I couldn't fathom that reaction or condition.

It was an eye opening conversation but it was also an ego booster because she praised the care that my mom was receiving. Even the day my mom died and the police came to house, the officer was complimentary on my mom's condition and the order of the house. He told me, "Most people are too selfish to care for a parent." Once again this made no sense to me and showed that I was not in touch with the rest of the world. I also did not have any reason to notice what others were doing because I was too busy taking care of my mom.

After my mom died I started to notice how other were treating a parent they were caring for. Most of them always made sure the parent did things on their schedule and never considered what the parent wanted. They were saying, "No, you're doing things my way." I guess that sums it up and they gave no consideration to the parents wants or needs. I guess I was strange because that was something I never did or would ever do.

Chapter 60

DOCTORS AND BEING A CAREGIVER

Doctors

I was very fortunate to have doctors that would work with me. The family physician would do what I wanted for the care of my mom. I would tell him what I needed and if he agreed he would follow through with recommendations or a prescription for equipment.

When my mom needed spine surgery I was able to meet and discuss her condition and problems with all the doctors, surgeons, specialists and rehabilitation staff. Due to her age and health the spine surgery was a major concern because of how long the procedure would take. The hospital we chose had a Spine Center but some of our doctors were not members of the hospital staff. The doctors at the hospital had several phone conversations and meeting with our physicians and were alerted to all the problems and challenges. The surgery was a success in the fact that my mom survived. It was not a success because the damage to her spine was more severe than expected. Her spine was crushing so many nerves that the pain was being suppressed. When they did the spinal decompression the nerves that were crushed came back to life and instead of normal signals being transmitted it woke up the pain signals. She was in more pain after the surgery than she was before. The only possible solution was a spinal fusion surgery that would take up to seventeen hours to complete. All the physicians believed she would not survive that long of a surgery. This was the start of a long journey for my mom and myself.

When we moved from Lynwood, CA to Tehachapi, CA we found another wonderful doctor. He was a hometown physician and worked with us every way he could. He was my mom's treating physician all the way to the end. In fact he is still my doctor. He always spent time with my mom asking her the usual questions and was always surprised at her appetite and disposition. He made her feel good and important. That went a long way in her overall health.

Doctors Need To Work With You

The most important person you need when you are a caregiver is the doctor. They are there for your parent as well as you and can make life easier or harder for both of you. You need a doctor that will work with you instead of against you.

Now this might have change due to Obamacare, The Affordable Healthcare Act. When I was a caregiver Obamacare had not been implemented so I don't know if any changes have happened to the way doctors work with patients and caregivers. The other change that we experienced was HIPAA. This act took medical privacy to the extreme and it made it a little more difficult to deal with some healthcare professionals. It was not impossible but it meant a lot more paperwork and a little more effort on your part.

I made sure that all of our doctors knew what we expected and how we needed their help. Once we found a doctor we stayed with them for many years. We started with our family physician in 1970 and left him in 2008 when we moved out of the area. W found a new doctor and we stayed with him until my mom passed away. In fact I still go to this doctor and at the present time I am not living in the area. He worked with us and I find there is no reason to change. It's a drive for me but I make it a treat and go out for dinner.

The doctors or specialist that they recommend must also recognize your situation and have to work with you. Yes, diagnosis' are the same in many ways but personal situations are very different. I would make appointments for consultations with the doctors so I could make sure we were on the same page. Sometimes I had to pay a fee for the consultation when it was a specialist and that came out of our pocket because Medicare and insurance did not cover this service. It was well worth it because it made sure that we were working together. When she was in the hospital I would talk to the doctors in the hall and explain her situation and see how we could best handle her care.

Most doctors and healthcare professionals will work with you any way they legally can. In the long run it makes treatment easier for them because they have a better understanding of the patient. It also removes the problem of having to explain over and over the diagnosis and treatment plan. Most elderly people have a hard time hearing and have a problem deciphering the doctors explanation. When your there both of you hear what the doctor recommends and you are able to explain it to your parent.

Tell Doctors What You Need

A lot of people complain that doctors never listen to what they say. They have set answers and responses to all situations. There is a simple solution to this problem, tell the doctor what you need.

Over the years I have been involved with many doctors and some over time have become friends. One doctor was a pulmonary specialist who took care of my father. We worked closely together for many years and we became friends. One day we started talking about how arrogant some doctors were and he told me that a doctor was just like a plumber or electrician. He said they work for you, the only difference was that they went to school for a longer period of time. He said if you don't like what the doctor is doing or how they are acting, "Fire them."

We are of that age when you always showed respect for a doctor because they went to school for a long time. They were professionals and you never questioned what they said. Unfortunately this attitude contributed to a lot of doctors becoming extremely arrogant. They would become insulted if you questioned them or even asked for a second opinion. Their word was law and you had no right to dispute them. My doctor friend always told me that if a doctor was against a second opinion it was time to find another doctor. If they were afraid of a second opinion they weren't sure of their diagnosis. He said a good doctor would always welcome a second opinion because it would keep them in check. The second doctor most likely would agree with their assessment or they might find something they missed. He said it was always a good idea.

He also told me to talk to the doctor and tell them what you needed. It might be a prescription for medical equipment that would make your caregiving chore a little easier. It could be for recommendations on physical therapy or rehabilitations. It could be for support groups or titles of books that could help you take care of your parent. He said the doctor is not a mind reader and has no clue about what you need unless you tell them. If a doctor is too busy to listen to you, fire them and find one that will listen and help you.

I always thought this was great advice and it opened my eyes in a lot of situations that came along. Yes, I did fire some doctors but I ended up working with a lot of great ones. The bottom line, it was always for the best care of my father and mother.

Doctors Need To Earn Respect

My parents were raised to always show a doctor respect and this was due to the reason they were considered a professional and that they went to college. I was taught that a doctor was just like any other professional trade with the exception that they went to school for a very long time. In my parents day whatever the doctor said was law and you didn't question him for any reason. In my day it is perfectly normal and expected to ask the doctor questions and verify their diagnoses. Years ago second opinions were never considered and not a normal procedure. Times change, sometime for the better, and I think this is definitely a change for the better.

I always treat a doctor with respect when I first meet them. After I talk to them for a while and see how they treated my dad, mom or myself I decide if they keep that respect. Most of the time they did and we were patients for a very long time. Some of our doctors became personal friends over the years. Some after the first visit I lost any respect that I gave them with my first handshake. They were arrogant and talked down to you like you were bothering them and that they were more important than you. Those were the ones we never went back to for any reason.

I had great respect for all the doctors that treated my dad, mom and myself over the years. We stayed with them over the long haul because they were professional and very good at their specialty. They had great bedside manners and even a sense of humor. They showed a great interest in their patients and that made you feel good. They earned my respect and kept it.

A Doctor Is Like A Plumber

Over the course of my parent's illnesses I had to deal with a lot of doctors. I never had a problem with the one's we chose but I did have problems with some that were on staff at the various hospitals we visited. Fortunately our doctors were also on staff and were in senior positions so it made it easier to deal with those doctors that had an "attitude." One of our doctors told me once, "That a doctor is like a plumber or electrician, if you don't like what they are doing or how they are treating you, fire them." I always remembered this during my parents illnesses.

When my dad was in the hospital he would be visited by various treating physicians and residents. Most of them were very good and had great bedside manners. Once in a while you would encounter a treating physician or resident that would be an arrogant ass. Most of the time they had to try to show they knew more than the other doctors and would put my dad through hell with their examinations and procedures. We had one doctor that wanted my dad to do an exercise test to check his lung capacity. My dad was always short of breath and could barely walk a few steps before he became short of breath. This nut put him on an exercise bicycle to do a lung volume test. They started the test and my dad was having trouble from the very start. It was too much for my dad and he broke down, the doctor would not listen and told him he had to complete the test. The room was full of technicians and I put a stop to the test. I told the doctor, "He's done." She looked at me and said I couldn't stop the test because it was needed to check his condition. My dad had verifiable lung cancer and this nut wanted him to ride an exercise bicycle while they were taking lung volume measurements. I had one of the technicians call our doctor, who at the time was head of the pulmonary department. He came down right away and backed me up and put a stop to the test. I then looked at the doctor and told her she was fired and I never wanted to see her around my father again. Once again our doctor agreed and told her she was relieved. She said that I couldn't fire her from my dad's case and I told her that I could because her treatment was hurting him and placing him in danger. She walked out and she never treated my father again.

I had an incident when my mom was in the rehabilitation hospital after her spine surgery. One of the doctors told her that she was never going to go home unless she did all the rehabilitation exercises they required. My mom became hysterical, started to hyperventilate and cry. I applauded his idea because in the long run it would help her with her life but the guy had a personality like steel wool. He told her he would not allow her to be discharged unless she did what he said. I contacted our rehab doctor and he agreed that this was a good idea but the bedside manner was wrong and asked me what I wanted to do. I told him that I wanted a different doctor, one that would work with us instead of against us. The doctor with the steel wool personality came into my mom's room and once again told her that she was not going home until she did what he said. I asked him to step outside the room with me and I told him, "You are causing more harm by the way you are treating my mom, you are relieved and I do not want you to treat my mom anymore." He looked at me kind of puzzled and said, "Are you firing me?" I said, "Yes." He said, "Fine, but you're making a mistake, I will get you another doctor." I told him, "No thank you, I already had that covered." He was right in the fact that my mom needed to do the exercises but the way he handled the situation caused more harm than good. This put my mom into a tail spin where we could see that she was starting to fail. I knew it was going to be more work for me in the future but I needed to get her home so she could get well. Our doctor agreed and she was discharged. Within a few days she was better and was doing all the exercises that the home health physical therapist prescribed.

I was never trying to be difficult but my parents were my responsibility and I would not allow others to hurt them. I was fortunate that we had doctors that backed me up in these situations. I never got loud or showed anger but handled the situation in a normal business tone and it never became an issue where security to be called.

Firing A Doctor

Firing a doctor is never easy and in a lot of situations you can't do it. There are guidelines for autonomy of care that most hospitals follow which make it difficult for you to relieve a doctor from your care. You need to be able to explain your issues to have another doctor assigned to your treatment.

A personal physician is easy to fire because you just go to another doctor. No one forces you to go back to the same doctor. Even with HMO's, Health Maintenance Organizations, you can select different primary care doctor. You have a choice and you have a right to exercise that choice. Now under Obamacare I have no idea how this will change in the future.

I was lucky because I was able to dismiss doctors with ease because our primary physicians were the department heads in the hospital where my parents were admitted. I would talk to them first and tell them what I was going to do. Sometimes they talked me out of it but the times I needed to fire a doctor they backed me all the way.

It is not an easy task but it can be accomplished. Just remember to state your case, don't show any signs of anger and definitely don't become aggressive. If security has to be called you have caused more harm than good. You must always remember the main goal is the proper care of your parent. In these times it is always better to set up a meeting with the doctor to explain your situation and your concerns. This way everything can be discussed in a calm and cool manner.

Doctors Work For You

One thing you to remember about doctors is that they work for the patient. Yes, they are either self employed, work for a medical group or are on staff at a hospital but the patient is their customer. Some say the customer is Medicare, the insurance company or now the government but it is the patient's life. If you are responsible for the day to day care of your parent that means technically they also work for you. Medicare, insurance or the government might pay all or part of the bills but it is still your parent's life and that is your only concern.

If a doctor is not working with you, have a conversation with them so that you are all on the same page. If they are upsetting your parent and they don't want to work with you, go and find another physician. I know this is getting harder under the new Medicare rules and Obamacare but for now it still can be accomplished. You might have to spend more money or have more out of pocket expenses but it is about the quality care that your parent receives. After you spend all your time and energy taking care of your mom or dad you don't want to have some doctor reverse all your hard work. It is important to find a doctor that will work with you so the care your parents receive is always top notch.

I was lucky because all of our doctors worked with me every step of the way. Sometimes we had to have discussions because I was concerned about the direction of my dad or mom's treatment. We would sit down and they would explain their advice and I would do the same. We would then come up with a plan to address all issues discussed. In the beginning the doctor would charge for the consultation but as time went on these consultations became routine and no charges were involved.

Some family members would ask me if it was right for me to question the doctors diagnosis and treatment and one time they asked me in front of one of the physicians. His response was, "I have no problems when he has questions or doubts, the goal is the best possible treatment to get the best outcome for your father." We had a common goal and we just wanted to find a way to try to achieve it.

Doctors Talk Through Patient To You

A lot of doctors get frustrated when they are talking to an elderly person. These doctors are always busy and sometimes they talk soft and fast. A lot of elderly have a hard time hearing what the doctor is trying to tell them and they force the doctor to keep repeating himself. When your in the room with your parent the doctor will start talking to you and bypass talking to your parent. This can cause a problem because your parent wants the doctor to talk to them.

I had this problem with both my dad and mom. My dad would get frustrated because he had severe hearing loss and tinnitus so he could barely hear some of the physicians. He would tell them to speak up or to slow down. They would then look and me and proceed to tell me the situation. My dad would get mad and say, "Talk to me."

I solved this problem by alway sitting next to him so the doctor would be talking to both of us at the same time. I would hear everything he said and my dad felt that the doctor was talking directly to him. He was getting better at reading lips so it made him feel that he was hearing everything. Overtime as the doctors became more familiar with him they would speak louder and slower.

I had this same problem with my mom but for a different reason. She could hear fine but she couldn't understand some of the doctors because they used words she didn't understand. She would keep asking, "What's that?" or "What does that mean?" They would then start talking to me and bypass looking at her. Once again the solution was sitting next to her so the doctors had to talk to both of us. This was a little difficult at times because my mom was in a wheelchair and a lot of the exam rooms were small so I would have to crouch down next to the wheelchair. Once again over time they learned to use smaller words and explain things to my mom.

I can understand why it is so frustrating for them because it is their life and they want to know what's going on. The other fear when the doctor talks through them is that they are telling you something they don't want your parent to hear. This can cause anxiety because they feel something is wrong and you don't want them to know about it.

I always tried to make sure may parents knew about their condition and diagnosis. The doctors eventually learned to talk directly to them so they could understand. If my dad or mom didn't understand I would explain it to them. Once again this is an example of how you need to have a doctor that will work with you.

They Get Upset When Ignored By Doctor

Another thing that happens when a doctor ignores your parent is that they get upset. Sometimes they can get so nervous or excited that it can cause their blood pressure to escalate. It is their life and the doctor needs to discuss it with them.

Unfortunately todays doctors have to see many patients to sustain their practice or the medical group. With all the changes that are happening in the healthcare industry in only looks like it's going to get worse. Physicians spend less and less time with their patients because quantity has become a priority.

Most of our doctors had their own practice so they essentially were their own boss. They spent more time with their patients and did their best to explain their diagnosis and treatments. A few were part of small medical groups but our doctor was one of the major partners so they essentially could do what they wanted. They still spent a lot of time with us and explained their diagnosis.

My parents were rarely ignored by their doctors and if the physician started to talk through them they would immediately speak up and tell them, "Talk to me too." This started in the beginning with some but never happened again after they were reprimanded by my dad or mom. This was part of the vetting process we had for physicians, if they ignored my dad or mom, talked through them or made them upset and didn't correct themselves after they were told, we would not go back and would find another doctor. This only happened once to my dad and once with my mom. After seeing over fifty physicians with both their illnesses that was not bad.

Chapter 61

HOME HEALTH AND BEING A CAREGIVER

Social Workers

My only experience with social workers was with the ones that worked in the hospitals. They were more for what type of accessories do you need or do you require any special supplies. I never had any come to our home. I was lucky because there was no need for the county social workers to come to the house. We did not take any government assistance, except my mother was on Social Security and Medicare. When she went to the hospital she passed all the pre-admit inspections, and there were no signs of abuse, malnutrition or neglect.

The closest thing we had to an inspection was when we had home health nurses come to the house for wound care that was caused by a hospital stay. The supervising home health nurse came in for an interview and to check out the general condition of the home. We had this done at our Lynwood home and the nurse found no problems. After my mom's first hospital stay in Bakersfield, California, they asked if we wanted to have a home health nurse come to the house and give us some recommendations. I thought that they might be able to give me some new advice on taking care of my mom so we went ahead with the visit. When the nurse came to the Tehachapi house we learned that this was not to give us advice on my mom's care, it was a full inspection. The nurse came in and had no problem with the house condition. Her problem was with a wound on my mom's leg that was healing. This wound was under the care of a wound care physician at another facility. She was quite concerned and started to make a big deal of the situation. My mom started getting anxious and upset at the questions and the tone of the nurse. I was getting frustrated because she was there to check my mom after the surgery on her intestines and to make recommendations to possibly help with her care. As the interview went on, I called the treating wound physician and staff nurse. They both got on the phone and told the visiting nurse that they were treating my mom for her leg wound and that it was not her concern. They then called her supervisor and told her the situation. The supervisor called off the home health nurse. That same day I fired the home healthcare agency and kept driving my mom 150 miles to our normal wound care facility. It was worth the time and effort because she was comfortable with the doctor and staff. It was more work for me but I did not have to reinvent the wheel every time we visited the facility.

A few years ago you could speak out against certain types of healthcare and the providers. Today it might be different with new laws and Obamacare. You can challenge the home health nurse if you know what you are doing, have options and a doctor that works with you.

Home Nurses

During my mom's hospital stay after spine surgery in 2001 she received a huge wound on her backside because she was not turned enough while in bed. She was bed ridden and could not turn herself. When she was released she had a huge blister on her backside. The hospital dispatched home health to care for her wound.

The nurse supervisor made an appointment for the home health evaluation. Unfortunately when the nurse showed up for the visit we were not home and we were running late. I had to go to the pharmacy to pick up a prescriptions and as always I took my mom with me. When we turned the corner by our house we saw the nurse waiting. We were about fifteen minutes late. She came over to the car as I was lifting my mom out and putting her in the wheelchair. The nurse read me the riot act. She told me my mom was listed as bed ridden and Medicare would not allow her to be taken out of the house. I told her I was sorry but I could not leave her alone while I went out to get prescriptions. This relationship started off on a rocky foundation.

We went into the house and she actually started sniffing around the house. I asked why and she said she was smelling for urine. She said she could smell the smallest amount of pee. I was startled but I was not concerned. When I was in junior high school we would have to visit the local convalescent hospital as a project. Two things always stuck with me, one was how lonely these people were and the strong smell of urine when you walked into the front door. When I started taking care of my mom I made sure the house did not smell. Needless to say we passed the smell test with the home health nurse. As she checked out the house she kept asking me questions about the care of my mom. I answered as best I could and asked her questions on the best way to handle the wound.

After this sort of tense interview and filling out tons of paperwork she started working on my mom's wound. I stood to the side of her to watch what she was doing. Good thing I wasn't squeamish or afraid of blood. She cleaned the wound off and showed me what to do. She also showed me an easier way of changing the diaper on my mom.

She said she would come once a week and other LVN's would come during the week. We ended up having a good relationship with this home health agency. In fact we were told that the nurses would ask to come over because we treated them nice. The supervisor would come over once a week as she said and we got along very well. She started bringing over other nurses for training because she could show them the way things should be done. I would laugh because after the training session she would tell them that our situation was unique and most of the other calls would not be this easy, clean or polite.

With this agency I only had one nurse out of eight that was bad. This young lady came in with a chip on her shoulder. She was going to show me the proper way to take care of the wound. Unfortunately for her I was taught by the other seven that all did it the same way. Her treatment was completely different and in fact caused more pain and blood. As she was treating my mom I noticed that she was causing pain. I told her to stop and explained how the others cleaned the wound. She told me she was the nurse and knew what was best. I immediately called her office and spoke to the supervisor and explained the situation. I put her on the phone and they told her to leave immediately. They sent another nurse who corrected the situation. The supervisor apologized for the situation and said if it was someone else she would be concerned but because I knew the situation and had been taking care of the wound I knew what I was talking about. That nurse never came back or would I let her back.

I was responsible for my mom's care and watched how the other nurses worked. I was open to new treatments but if the seven other nurses did it one way that must be the proper procedure. If it also caused more pain, discomfort and blood there is a problem. A nurse should not be afraid of questions and should not get an attitude when they're asked why they are causing the patient pain. My mom was my responsibility and so I took charge of the situation because I knew I was right.

Chapter 62
DEALING WITH MEDICAL FACILITIES AND PROFESSIONALS
Hospitals

During the time that I was my mother's caregiver we visited four different hospitals. Each hospital was unique in their procedures and patient care. Some had a lot of outpatient facilities, some worked well with senior patients and all were accommodating to me as son and caregiver.

When we lived in Lynwood, California we went to a hospital in Whittier. After we moved to Tehachapi, California we used the hospital in town. This was more like a gateway to stabilize the patient then they would send you by ambulance to other hospitals forty-five miles away. The Tehachapi hospital sent us to two different hospitals in Bakersfield, California.

The Whittier hospital had a spine center, rehabilitation hospital, excellent wound center and a great home health group. This is the hospital were my mom's spine surgery was performed and this is also the hospital that my mom put the staff through hell. Through it all the staff performed very well and worked with me as caregiver every way possible.

When we moved to Tehachapi we were happy that there was a hospital in town. What I didn't know was that the hospital did not perform major treatment. They had a basic emergency room and did routine procedures but anything major they sent the patient to other hospitals in Bakersfield or Palmdale, California. These hospital were an hour away by ambulance depending on the weather. The three times we used the local hospital we went in around 10:00am, my mom was stabilized and was sent to two different hospitals in Bakersfield. We usually arrived at those hospitals around 9:00pm. Unfortunately that's life in a small city. The other problem with this arrangement was weather. Tehachapi was in the mountains above the California Central Valley. The highway from Bakersfield was an upward climb from the valley to the mountains. In the winter they would sometimes close this road due to snow and ice. One visit was around Christmas and the hospital made arrangements to discharge my mom early because it was starting to snow and they thought the road was going to be closed. They let us leave around 3:00pm and sure enough after we got home the road was closed about 5:00pm because of snow and ice.

I thought I did enough research into Tehachapi before we moved into the community. My mom and I made this decision together. We liked the area but this was one item that was overlooked. We adapted to the situation and in our case it was a lot more work when we went to the hospital. Looking back at the situation it did not affect the care that my mom received.

Rehabilitation

My mom had rehabilitation scheduled after she had her spine surgery. This situation did not go very well and if it continued could have cost my mom her life. She was not a good rehabilitation patient, she was stubborn and unwilling to go through with the treatment. This caused greater stress and work on her and me in later years.

At the time we thought her spinal surgery was a success but a few days later we found out it failed and caused more problems. When the surgery was completed she was placed in recovery and intensive care. The surgeon said all went well but it would take time to see if the surgery was a success. The next day while she was in the critical care unit she started to move her legs. This was something that she hadn't done in two years so it looked promising. She would react to touch and pressure so rehabilitation was scheduled. Her pain had subsided so we all thought that it was a successful procedure. The next day was a completely different story. She could still move her legs a little but she was in excruciating pain. On the scale of one to ten she yelled, "Twenty!" They gave her morphine for the pain and tried to get it under control. It didn't work and she started having spasms from the pain, her legs and body would shake almost to the point of her passing out. She would grab the bed rail so hard her knuckles would turn white. Many doctors came in and couldn't understand why there was so much pain and why they couldn't get it under control. They ordered x-rays and scans and then they found the answer. For so many years her spine compressed the nerves to the point where they were choked off. When they did the spinal decompression the nerves came back to life. This gave her the ability to move her legs but it also gave the pain signals a path to the brain. She was now in more pain than ever before. The only possible remedy was another spinal decompression and fusion of the lower back and spine. That could have been up to a seventeen hour surgery. All the doctors and I agreed that she would never survive that type of a surgery and the chances were fifty-fifty that it would be successful. We decided against the surgery so they came up with a plan for pain control and rehabilitation. That might have worked if my mom would have cooperated.

She refused to do the rehabilitation. She always had a fear of falling and every time the rehab specialist would come in and try to lift her up she was afraid she was going to fall so she would grab anything she could. It could be the trapeze, the bed rail or the bed and she would not let go. I would stand against the wall because they wanted me to watch so I could learn how to properly pick her up and do the rehab exercises. Nothing worked, once she grabbed something it was over and it actually got dangerous because it would affect the balance of the physical therapist to the point that they almost dropped her. I tried to reason with her and it fell on deaf years. She said no because she didn't want to fall, and then she would say, "I just want to go home." One of the rehab doctors tried everything to get her motivated and also they tried everything to get the pain under control. They could not find anyway to manage it and he told me they could not send her home until the pain was manageable. Another thing we both noticed was her health was deteriorating and she had no appetite.

We had many discussions but came up with no remedies. The doctors, physical therapists, psychologists and myself had no idea how to get her to do the rehabilitation. Some suggested putting her in a home and moving on, that is when I said no and she needed to be home. The rehab doctor agreed and said she needed to be home otherwise she wouldn't make it. He told me I was going to have a rough time and asked if I was ready for it? I said I was and, "I had to do what I have to do." He wanted to be clear that I knew what was coming. We stopped the rehab and concentrated on the pain control. The doctor tried a combination of a three day fentanyl patch and hydrocodone for break through pain. This seemed to control the pain for two of the three day and the hydrocodone would control most of it on the third day. They also prescribed morphine tablets if the pain became so severe that she would tense up and stiffen. They gave me all the instructions and also prescribed home physical therapy. I told her she was going home and it brightened her up. She finally really believed it when I got her ready and lifted her into the car.

When she got home she was a different person. She was alive again even though she had more pain. She had a bedsore and it needed to be nursed but she didn't care, she was home. Home health came and attended to the bed wound and taught me how to maintain the dressing. Home physical therapy came in and surprisingly she followed the instructions and did the therapy. They didn't try to lift her up or make her walk, they did the leg exercises and she followed them to the letter. We also kept the pain under control and she felt better. The one thing that showed that she was better was her appetite returned and she started eating full meals again. That's when I knew we were out of the woods.

The next week we had to go back to the rehab doctor and when he came into the room his faced dropped. He said, "I'm not looking at the same person I saw last week." She smiled and said, "I'm home and I feel better." He was amazed at the difference and prescribed a routine that we followed for many years. He called me that night to once again express his amazement and satisfaction. He said, "I knew I had to get her home otherwise she never would have survived." He and I were both pleased that we made the right call. They prescribed the morphine tablets for extreme pain and as a last resort. I never had to use those tablets.

Physical Therapy

The only time I had to deal with physical therapy was after my mom's spine surgery. She was going to have therapy in the hospital because the goal was to have her regain some use of her legs. Wishful thinking and hope but it never happened.

We knew a few days after my mom's spine surgery that things did not go as planned. She started to move her legs a great deal then the extreme pain started as well as the spasms and she was never able to move her legs again more than a few inches. The doctors still decided and rightly so, that some form of physical therapy was necessary to keep whatever movement she had from freezing up.

My mom was not a good patient with physical therapy. She always had a fear of falling and this just made her sick. Every time they would try to move her or have her try to put some weight on her legs she would panic. So much so that she would get sick and sometimes vomit. She would cry that she couldn't do it and she didn't want to fall. I would leave the room so I wouldn't be a crutch for her and then she would listen to the physical therapists. Every time after a few minutes they would come out and get me or even have me paged because they needed me to calm her down. Sometimes they would ask me to stay in the room so I could learn what they were doing and it still didn't make a difference. They tried to have her sit up and put some weight on her feet once she would stiffen up and it was all over. A neighbor who I grew up with was a physical therapist at that hospital so I requested that she come and help. I thought because my mom knew her for so many years she would try to work with her. I was wrong, the poor woman tried but she could not get my mom to cooperate. The only thing different was my mom would tell her, "I'm sorry I just can't do it." This was a change from, "No, no, no." During this time the rehabilitation doctor and I noticed that she was starting to fail and her health was deteriorating. That's when we decided it was best to take her home.

When I took her home they scheduled home physical therapy. She cooperated with that and did very well. The therapist that came to our house was impressed that she did what she was told and followed through with her exercises. She was warned about my mom's hospital experience. My mom finished the home therapy and continued to do it the rest of her life.

She never was able to put weight on her feet and over time she lost more feeling in her legs. Who knows if she would have done the therapy things may have been different. There is no way of knowing except for the experience of the therapist. If she would have done the therapy I think it would have helped us over the next few years. I don't blame the physical therapist and rehabilitation doctors for letting her go. She was not cooperating and they had many more patients that wanted to do physical therapy. They were right in leaving my mom alone. The only two my mom hurt was herself and me.

Hospitalization

During my dad's illness he only went to the hospital a few times and this was when he would spit up blood. As the cancer progressed he went to the hospital two more times because of his condition and finally a third time just before he passed away. The routine of taking him to the hospital was very easy, all I did was call his doctor, tell him of the situation and he would make arrangements to have him admitted to the hospital. I would take him to the hospital and take him to admitting, where they would start the process. I always had the paperwork with me that had his medication and medical history, insurance information and contact info. He would stay in the hospital a few days while they traced where the blood was coming from and then he would be discharged. The only time we had an ambulance take him to the hospital was the last visit two weeks before he died. He was spitting up blood, lethargic, weak and confused. We both knew what was happening and I asked him if he wanted to go to the hospital and he said, "Yes." I called the doctor and he told me to call 911 and he would make the arrangements for the hospital. The paramedics and ambulance came within a few minutes and we transported him to the hospital. When we got to the hospital they brought him to a room while I handled the admission process. He passed away two weeks later on Easter morning.

My mom's hospitalizations were similar but the process changed a little due to her condition. When she would vomit and it smelled like feces I knew I had to take her to the hospital to prevent dehydration. I called her doctor and he agreed and told me to take her to the emergency room. I would lift her into the car and take her to the local hospital. I would fill out all the paperwork and give them copies of her medication and medical list. I would also give them a copy of her Durable Power Of Attorney. This was a scary time for me because a hospital emergency room is the place where you can catch the flu or other problems. People would be crying, coughing and vomiting and I was always wondering what ailment my mom would catch. You can be so careful at home but when your in the emergency room everything is out of your control. We would wait about an hour and then she would be called in to see the triage nurse to see how serious her condition was and how soon she needed treatment. After the exam she would be put in an area of the emergency room to see the doctor. The doctor would come in about fifteen minutes later and I would explain the situation and they would put her on an IV and order x-rays and scans. After about five hours they would say she was impacted and they would have to send her to a larger hospital in Bakersfield. They would make the arrangements and an ambulance would take her from Tehachapi to Bakersfield, in which the trip took about an hour. When we arrived at the hospital in Bakersfield all the arrangements had been made but the process started all over again. The only difference was that we didn't have to wait in the waiting room, we waited in the emergency room treatment area. Two or three hours would go by and then she would be put in a room. By this time she had been inspected three times already and when she went to the room the admission nurse would give her body a full inspection while I was told to stay out of the room. This was to check to see if she was abused. After the body inspection they would call me in and ask questions about her condition. This would be around 11pm and we started the process about 10am. I was a long day for her and me. The next day they would do more tests and start her on her recovery path.

We did this three times after we moved to Tehachapi. When we lived in Southern California I never had to take her to the hospital for an emergency situation. The only time we went to the hospital was for planned procedures so everything was prepared ahead of time.

Bruises From Hospital

Whenever you take home your parent from the hospital you have to make sure they don't have any bruises, sores or marks. Make sure you check them out before you leave the hospital and have any unusual marks noted. Bruises can show up a few day later especially if they are thin skinned and their circulation is poor. Call your doctor to report any bruises that show up a few days later. These can be caused by laying in one position for a long period of time such as for diagnostic tests. Look for red marks on their backside because this is where bed sores usually start. Make notes of everything, just as the hospital checks them when they are admitted you need to check them when they are discharged.

There are new Medicare rules that hold the hospital responsible for bed sores and readmission because of the sores. If your parent is confined to the bed they have to be turned several times a day so they don't lie in one position. Because of their thin skin and reduced circulation sores can develop very quickly and can cause all kinds of problems. A lot of time the hospital will supply a foam egg crate under the sheets to help reduce bed sores. If sores are an issue and they have been documented you can ask the hospital to supply an air mattress. This is an expensive option and the hospital usually balks in providing this mattress so you have to prove that it is necessary. Your doctor can usually help with this situation.

I always checked my mom before we left the hospital. Any bruises or marks would be noted and told to the discharge nurse so they could be documented. The hospital protects themselves you need to protect yourself and your parent.

Bad Patient

During my mom's recovery after her spine surgery I realized she was not a good hospital patient. She was fine when I was there but when I left she became a different person and was afraid to be left alone. When she was in Intensive Care there was no problem and she cooperated with the nurses and staff. The problem started was when they moved her to the rehabilitation area of the hospital. In this unit she didn't cooperate with the nurses and staff unless I was present.

The first time she spent the night in the unit I stayed until about 9pm and told her I was going to go home and I would be back in the morning. She was drowsy and said, "Go home and get some rest, I'll be fine." I left and went home. The next morning I get a phone call around 4am from the nurses station to come to the hospital as soon as possible because my mom was causing problems. They told me to enter through the emergency room because that was the only entrance open at that time. It took about thirty minutes to get to the hospital and as I was walking down the hall I could hear her yelling, "Help me, Jim help me." I walked into the room and she yelled, "Get me out here and don't leave me again." I told her to calm down, everything was fine and I was going to see what had happened. I turned around and two nurses were behind me and told me they needed to talk to me. I told my mom I was going to talk to the nurses and she said, "Ok."

They informed me that she started yelling she wanted "to go home" as soon as I left the night before. She was disturbing the other patients by yelling, "Help me," and because she was so loud they had to close her door. I asked if there was anything wrong with her and they said she was fine but uncooperative. I told them I would take care of it and I went back into my mom's room.

I asked what was wrong and she said crying, "I just want to go home." I told her she couldn't go home until the doctors said it was ok and she needed to do the rehabilitation so she could get better. She calmed down and then asked if she could go home if she did it. I said, "Yes."

They started the rehabilitation that morning and I told her I was going to be outside the room and she said, "Ok." She gave the rehabilitation specialist a hard time and wouldn't listen to what he said. He called me back in the room and then she started to listen to his instructions. All was fine until he tried to get her to sit up and then she lost it. She kept crying, "I'm going to fall, I don't want to fall." He tried to lift her up and she grabbed the bed rail and he couldn't move her. He got a little nervous because he was in a bad position but he recovered and put her back on the bed. I didn't want to interfere because I didn't want to hurt him in the process or make it so she relied on me to do everything.

This happened several times that day and the rehabilitation team couldn't get her to cooperate because she was always afraid of falling. They finally stopped and told me they would teach me how to lift her with a lifting belt the next day. They thought if I did it she might be more cooperative.

That night I spent the night in a chair in her room and she never yelled or complained. One nurse came in and couldn't believe she was sleeping and was so quiet. She explained what happened the night before and all I could say was, "I'm sorry." It sounded horrible and I was surprised they didn't call me sooner to come in. She slept the night and I was stiff and sore in the morning.

The next day they tried once again to move her but this time I was there and they wanted me to do it. They showed me how to lift her with a lifting belt and it was not easy. She would move her arms and hold my arms, head, neck or whatever she could grab. I got her to sit up in bed but she was still afraid of falling. What we noticed was that fear went away when she held on to me or felt my arm and once I pulled away she was afraid she was going to fall. I was her crutch and she didn't trust anyone else. I had a big problem.

I stayed with her in the hospital for many days and nights so the other patients wouldn't be disturbed. The hospital brought in a cot so I was a little more comfortable than sleeping in the chair. I could leave during the day to go home and she would be fine as long as I told her I was coming back and I would only leave for about three hours and then return.

The rehabilitation staff threw in the towel with her therapy because she wouldn't cooperate. They apologized to me and I understood because they had many other patients that were happy to cooperate with them so they could get back to normal. Our new normal was I was going to have to lift her the rest of her life.

Another problem was that she was also failing while she was in the hospital. She didn't seem right and her appetite was small. Her doctor said she wasn't doing well and we needed to do something or she wouldn't make it. I told him the solution was to let her go home. He asked me, "Do you know how much work that's going to be for you?" I told him I did and that there was no other option. He agreed and discharged her in a few days. I brought her home and the first thing she wanted to do was eat. While she was eating her face was happy and she looked relaxed. She needed to be home and she was fine.

We had a similar problem in 2008 when she was admitted to a hospital in Bakersfield. I asked if she was okay to spend the night and she said, "Yes." I told her I was going to be back in the morning and she said, "Okay." I warned the nurses and staff of the earlier situation and told them to call me immediately and I would come back to help. I asked if I could stay in the room and they said, "It was against hospital policy." Sure enough she did it again but this time it was after she woke up around 4am. The nurses station called me and I went to the hospital. This trip took about an hour because we lived in the mountains and I had to drive down to the Central Valley of California. I could her yelling at a staff member from down the hall. I walked in the room and said, "Mom." She stopped yelling and then I told her I wasn't going to put up with her yelling at the staff and she needed to apologize right away. Without protest she told the staff member, "I'm sorry, I was wrong." That was it and she never did it again. That night the hospital allowed me to stay in the room to keep her under control but she was never a problem. One nurse came in and told me, "I don't believe I'm seeing the same lady from last night." Once again I apologized and told her I would do my best to not let it happen again and it didn't.

Those were painful and stressful times and I never found out why she was so afraid of hospitals and afraid of falling. The times following these incidents she never had a problem and she even stayed by herself in the hospital. The next time she was in the hospital she told me to, "Go home and get some rest." I told the nurses what to expect and to call me when they needed me. I went home and I couldn't sleep because I was expecting the phone to ring. It never did. I went to the hospital around 8am and when I walked into her room she was eating breakfast and the nurse told me she had a good night. I'm glad she got some sleep.

Jewelry And Personal Belongings

When you're taking care of your parent you need to be aware of how much jewelry they wear and personal belongings they carry. When they go in for diagnostic tests and procedures they can cause problems so it will have to be removed. Sometimes lockers are available to store their items but most of the time it is up to you to take possession and care of their personal belongings. When they are admitted to the hospital they can lose track of what they had on and what they were wearing. This is also true for a purse and other personal belongings.

My dad never wore any kind of jewelry except for his wedding band during his life. He was a pipe fitter so he had to braze and solder pipe so he would remove his wedding band so the hot solder could not fall on the ring and burn his finger. As he got older his fingers changed and he was no longer able to wear his wedding band. When he went in for diagnostic tests and procedures he never had any jewelry on his person so there was never a problem.

My mom liked to wear necklaces, bracelets and had a few rings on her fingers, including her wedding ring. Every time she had diagnostic tests or procedures I made sure she left all the jewelry at home except for her wedding ring. It was stuck on her finger and because of arthritis she couldn't remove it. It never caused a problem with any of her tests.

As time went on and her condition changed I no longer let her wear a necklace because I was afraid she would get them caught on something and hurt herself. She still wore a few rings and a bracelet when she went out. As her fingers kept changing because of the arthritis the rings would no longer stay on her fingers and they would fall off. Her wedding ring was still stuck behind a knuckle and would not come off. About a year later I made her stop wearing bracelets because she would catch them on the wheelchair handle and it could have caused bruising to her wrists. A few months later her fingers started to shrink and her wedding ring became loose. After a few months the ring could be removed and she was afraid she was going to lose it. She took it off and told me to put it in her jewelry box. That was the end of her wearing any jewelry. This was about a year before she passed away.

Whenever she was admitted to the hospital they would always ask if she was wearing any jewelry. When they took her for tests they always wanted to know if she had any jewelry on. It made things a lot easier when we left the jewelry at home or she no longer wore it.

Identification

You always need to make sure you have your parents identification available when you travel. You never know if you have to take them to a medical facility or if someone might question the prescription medications they are carrying. If the prescriptions are a controlled substance and/or narcotic you never know if you might have to show proof of who they belong to. When you are traveling to the local store or a long distance you always have to be prepared for any situation.

My dad always carried a wallet so he always had his drivers license and insurance card always available. When he was failing I would carry his wallet because the only time he would go out was with me. If I needed to rush him to the hospital I always had his identification and insurance cards with me.

Some carry a purse but my mom would carry a little bag that held her wallet that included her identification and insurance card. It wasn't a purse but one of those packs people wear around their waists. It was nice because I could wrap it around the arm of the wheelchair so she wouldn't drop it and she could hide it under the wrap she usually wore on her legs. We had that pouch with us every time we went out so I always had her information within reach. Near the end she no longer was able to hold the pouch so I ended carrying her wallet with her identification and insurance card. Once again it was always with me so we had it in case an emergency arose.

Every time you go to a new doctor, have test performed or are admitted to the hospital they always ask for your identification. In some instances when you go to the pharmacy they ask to see your identification. Even if you are stopped on the road because of a traffic violation or other situation you might have to show the identification of your passenger. You always need to have this document available otherwise it could cause a delay in medical tests, treatments or other routines.

Hospice

During my parents illnesses, hospice was a relatively new term. When my dad was sick we knew absolutely nothing about hospice care. In his situation it would not have made a difference. In my mother's situation it could have come into play.

When I made the decision to take care of my mom I knew it would be until the end. After her spine surgery she was not doing very well and one of the rehabilitation doctors said she might be a candidate for hospice care. The other rehab doctor said absolutely not and that she needed to be home in her normal environment so she could get better. We took the second option and she did recover. That was the first I heard of hospice care. I started to research it and learned that it was basically for the end when there was no hope.

I didn't think this was for us because my mom had the will to live and the only problem with her was she could not walk and was in a lot of pain. I asked our family physician about hospice and he said, "No." That was pretty much the end of our hospice discussion until she was in a Bakersfield hospital. The social worker at that facility mentioned it to us and said it might be a good alternative. Before I had a chance to say no, my mom said, "I'm not ready to die yet." I didn't realize she understood what hospice meant. I found out later that one of the hospital technicians asked her if she was on hospice? She wanted an explanation, so the tech told her, "It was for when your ready to die."

Needless to say we never discussed hospice again. When the end came she was fine till about one week before she died. She started to lose her appetite, became confused and stared through you. I knew the end was close and hospice would not have made a difference.

Chapter 63

WOUND CARE AND BEING A CAREGIVER

Wound Care

Wound care is a very important procedure in the care of an elderly person. Their skin is thin and since they tend to stay in positions for a long period of time in can turn into a dangerous situation. This is definitely a problem that needs to be addressed immediately or it can literally fester.

After my mom's spine surgery she received a bed sore on her backside because she wasn't turned enough while she was in the hospital. Part of this was because she was afraid of falling every time they turned her and they had no idea how to deal with her severe pain. When she was discharged the doctor, nurse and I noticed the bed sore and because of her condition it was recommended that home health take care of the situation.

When home health came in to care for my mom's bed wound it was small and didn't break the skin. I turned her every two hours in bed, had a foam egg crate under her sheets and used pillows to keep her comfortable. I tried not to put her in the same spot but her natural movement would always put her back on the sore when she was near that position. Within one week the sore broke the skin and increased in size. The home health nurse recommended that I take her to the wound care center at her hospital. She made the arrangements and I took her in for and examination.

This place was amazing, they dealt with all kinds of wounds from burns to diabetic conditions. From the first day we met and dealt with some incredible nurses, staff and one great doctor. The head nurse inspected my mom and asked me a lot of questions. I'm sure some of this was to see if I was the cause of the bed sore. I kept stressing that it was caused in the hospital and fortunately for us it was all documented. I lifted my mom from one exam table to a chair to a bed until they found something that was comfortable for her and also so they were able to work on her.

A few minutes later the doctor came in and introduced himself. He was a young guy and had a great personality. We started talking and he began asking a lot of questions. I explained the whole situation and my mom's condition. I was behind my mom and he asked me to roll her on her side. He went behind her and started examining the wound. By doing this he trapped me in the corner and I was able to watch everything he was doing. He started poking around the bed wound and then it ruptured and black goo, puss and blood gushed out. It smelt bad and he continued to "debreed" it.

Home health wound care stopped because Medicare and insurance would no longer cover it because they said, "Her son could take care of the wound." When I asked the home health nurse what about people that were squeamish or not able to properly take care of the wound she said, "Medicare and insurance don't care and they would have to learn to do it." She went on to say, "If they don't they could get in trouble for neglect." Fortunately for my mom I had no problems cleaning and changing the dressing on the wound.

The wound eventually healed and we no longer needed to visit the wound center. As the doctor and nurses predicted since my mom had a major bed sore she would be susceptible to wounds in the future, we had to return to the wound center on several occasions. It seemed that whenever my mom had a test, procedure where she had to lie on a hard table or a hospital stay she would get a wound on her backside. They were in different locations but in the same general area. I would notice the redness and when it started to get larger and darker red I knew it was time to go to the wound center. I would call and they would either give me instructions over the phone or make an appointment for a visit. Over the many visits they would always ask my mom about her appetite and eating habits. They were amazed at how much she ate and how she liked to eat. They would always ask what I was making for dinner. The doctor would come in and ask about some recipe I was making and always comment on how lucky she was to have a personal cook. One time we went in for an appointment and the doctor walked by the room and saw us getting ready. He turned to the nurse and said, "Oh good, the Colozzo's are here." A few minutes later he came in to chat and then left to see his other patients. He came in later to examine my mom and chatted some more while he went on with his task. He made her feel good and so did all the nurses and other providers. Whenever they had to clean out the wound and had to go in deep, that night the doctor would call to check on her condition. In fact when we moved from the area we always went back to this wound center for treatment. It was one hundred and fifty miles away and a two and half hour drive but it was worth it because of the care and the people.

We were very fortunate to find a wound care facility like this one. They were true professionals and made their patients feel important. Being in the examination area you could smell some of the wounds and the odors were terrible. You can only assume how bad these wounds looked and these professionals dealt with this on a daily basis. I never saw or heard any of them complain as they did their job. I really enjoyed working with them.

De-Breeding A Wound

De-Breeding a wound was one of the most disgusting and unusual procedures I had ever seen. There were huge amounts of blood and puss but the smell was awful. It is one of those experiences you want to forget but you never will.

I had this experience when my mom received a bed sore while she was in the hospital after her spinal surgery. I had to take her to the wound healing center that was part of the hospital where she had her surgery. We met some extraordinary people that worked at this center and I learned a lot.

After the nurses interviewed us and did a preliminary exam of my mom's wound it was time to see the doctor. My mom was laying on a bed and they asked her turn on her side. I moved her into position, the doctor and I had a perfect view of the sore on her backside. The doctor was next to me and trapped me against a wall in the corner. He gave her an injection to numb the area and then he started poking around the wound and then it exploded. A glob of blood and puss just oozed out of the bed sore. He kept poking kit with a surgical instrument as he cleaned it out. This thing was disgusting and it smelt horrible. He then turns to me and looked surprised and said, "I didn't see you there, I hope you're not afraid of blood, I wouldn't want you to pass out." I looked back at him and said, "No, but isn't it a little late to ask." He laughed and said, "Your right, and if you passed out I really couldn't do anything for you." I laughed and said, "Thanks for your concern." He just smiled as he continued to work on the bed sore. I was amazed at how much blood was in this wound. He started to explain what he was doing and I was fascinated by his treatment. He finished and told the nurses what to use to bandage it up. I watched as they applied medication and ointment and bandaged up the wound. This knowledge would come in very handy a few weeks later when I had to take over the wound care at home.

We would return once a week to the wound center for check ups on the wound. The first couple of times the doctor would look at me and say, "Good to see your still standing." I'd answer back, "You too," and he said, "I can't believe I did that." I told him, "I'm glad you did, I learned a lot." Over the course of treatment for my mom's bed wound this doctor never had a problem with the way I cleaned, applied the medication and bandaged the wound.

My mom's bed sore finally healed and we no longer had to go to the wound center. Although every time she was discharged from the hospital a small wound would show up and I would take her back just to make sure it didn't grow into something bigger. The last time they actually told me how to take care of the wound over the phone and we didn't have to drive down for a visit. We drove 150 miles each way to go to this wound center because of the wonderful staff and the care they gave their patients. It was well worth the time and effort.

Chapter 64
WHEN THE END COMES
The End

My dad was in the hospital for two weeks before he died. I stayed with him at night so he wouldn't be alone and my mom and sisters relieved me during the day so I could go home and freshen up. In the beginning he was in and out of consciousness but he was always confused. The cancer was attacking his brain and it was causing all his organs to shut down.

The hospital staff was very nice and accommodating and they even put us in a single bed room. We had privacy during the last few days of his life. He no longer could eat so they were feeding him through a tube in his nose. It was hard to see such a strong man go through this and how is body was just deteriorating. He had informed me and his doctors that he did not want any extraordinary procedures to keep him alive because he said he didn't want to prolong the situation. I also had it in writing so that there would no problems.

I would always talk to him and so did my mom and sisters. The medical technicians would come in and also talk to him. Sometimes we would get a response and other times there would be nothing. His doctors informed me that his body was shutting down and it was only a matter of time. A few days before he died he was having trouble during the breathing treatment. It was causing him a great amount of pain and anguish and you could see the heart monitor skyrocket when they tried to give him a treatment. Finally we decided to stop the treatments and let him go in peace. The technicians would still come in but we refused the treatment.

It was the Easter weekend of 1995 and he was no longer responding. His breathing was shallow and he would have long pauses between breaths. We knew the end was near. I stayed as usual during the night and that

Saturday his breathing was faint and there were extremely longer pauses. He was receiving oxygen through a cannula but it seems the air was just not going in. I talked to him all during the night. The pulmonary tech on duty came in to check on us and I told him that my dad's breathing was faint. Over the previous two weeks I struck up a good relationship with this man and the woman that worked during the day. He checked my dad's breathing with a stethoscope and looked at me and shook his head. That was about 1:55am and then his breathing stopped and he went cold. I was holding his hand and I could feel the life just go out of him.

I knew he was gone and even though I knew it was going to happen I teared up. I looked at the pulmonary tech and said, "He's gone." He looked at me and said, "Yes, I'm sorry." I was still holding my dad's hand and the pulmonary tech put his hand on my shoulder. He pressed the call button for the nurse and told her what had happened. He stayed for a few minutes and then he had to go to his other patients. This was Easter morning. My dad waited for the most important day of his faith to pass on.

The nurse came in along with several other people and they pronounced my dad deceased. They asked me if I needed anything and I told them that I needed to make some phone calls. I also asked if they could leave the body in the room because my mom would want to come in and see him again. I also asked that they remove all the tubes and wires from him. They obliged and cleaned up the body and bed.

I went to the nurses station and made the calls to my sisters. My mom was staying with my sister and her family a few miles away from the hospital. I called my sister that was watching my mom and as soon as she answered the phone I could her my mom crying and yelling, "Oh no," in the background. I told my sister what had happened and asked her if they were going to come to the hospital. She said yes and they would be there in about a half an hour. I then called my other sister that lived about sixty miles away and she said she wasn't going to come down but she would call the relatives.

I went back into the room and the nurses had cleaned my dad up like I asked. I sat by his bedside holding his hand and just remembered what a wonderful person he was. It was very hard for me to know he was gone. We had gone through so much together and he fought so hard but he finally tired and succumbed. About a half an hour later I could her some noise in the hall and I knew it was my mom and sister. My mom was still crying and she went to my dad and just hugged him. This was the woman that didn't attend her own parent's funerals because she was afraid and she was holding her husband's body. She kept crying and said, "I should have stayed, I knew it was going to happen." I told her she couldn't have stayed because they're was no place for her to rest and I was there so he wasn't alone. We stayed in the room for about two hours and then a nun came in to give him the last rites and then we were ready to leave. My sister went home by herself and my mom stayed with me.

We said our goodbyes and we left the hospital. This was the end of my dad's life and I knew it was the beginning of me taking care of my mom. It was time to keep my promise I made to my dad a few weeks before he died. I thought this chapter was over, the funeral would be the next week and then we could move on with our lives. I had no idea of the ordeal that was coming towards us and how long it would last. This was not the end it was just the beginning and I am still feeling some of those effects today. It has been a long journey and after twenty years it is still continuing.

No matter how much you see someone's health deteriorate you're never ready for the end to come. When you're a caregiver for a long period of time you know when the end is coming. This is what happened to me when my mom's health went downhill fast.

About six months before she died my mom became a lot more confused than she had ever been. My youngest nieces wedding was in October of 2012 and my mom was confused during most of the reception. We had to drive about one hundred miles to get to the wedding and reception. When we got to the church all was well and she conversed and knew everybody around her. During the church ceremony she was in the front, followed the Mass and answered all the prayers normally.

After the church ceremony we went to the reception, that's where things changed. We sat at the family table and she didn't recognize anybody. She dazed at people like she never saw them before. She thought she was at a restaurant and demanded her food. During the toast she yelled, "Where's the food. What kind of a joint is this?" My niece and her husband laughed and went along with the toast. We were amused and embarrassed at the same time. During the meal, my sisters and I were trying to help her and she wanted nothing to do with us. She looked at me and said, "Who are you?" When I told her who I was she started to settle down. The rest of the evening was uneventful and we left around 8pm to drive home. On the way home I asked her questions about the wedding. She remembered the people at the church and the ceremony but she was completely confused about the reception. She did remember that it took a long time for her to get her meal and that this guy kept bothering her. I told her that guy was "me" and she didn't believe it. I said I was prepping her meal so she could eat. She kept saying, "That was you?" We got home and I put her to bed without any problems.

Everything was somewhat normal after that but I noticed there were a lot of times she would have a blank stare on her face. You could be talking to her and she would have no response. She wouldn't acknowledge you and didn't respond. I would raise my voice and nothing would change. A few minutes later she would snap out of it and be normal. When we went to the doctor that month he said she was probably having micro strokes and it was starting to affect her. He also said there was not much we could do. We could have a brain scan but all it would do is confirm this condition and at her age it was pretty common. The doctor and I felt it would have put to much stress on her and decided not to have the scan done.

Thanksgiving and even Christmas were normal and we didn't see any extreme changes. One time I had a scare as we were driving down to Chino to see the great grandchildren. We were on the freeway about 40 miles from our destination and I looked over and she looked limp. I called her and there was no response. I yelled, "Mom" and still got no response. I felt her hand and it was normal but it did feel heavy. I started changing lanes to get off the freeway, hit a pothole and the jolt woke her up. She moved her hand and asked if we were there? I started asking her questions and she answered normally. She was fine the rest of the day.

Incidents like this started happening more frequently and the new thing that began were visions. When I would put her in bed some nights she would say there was a lady standing in the corner. One night she yelled for me and said, "There she is," as she pointed the corner of the room. There was no one there and she would get angry because I didn't see anybody. This also became more frequent as time went by.

In February of 2013 she had a bout with severe constipation. This time it was really bad and she couldn't keep anything down. When she vomited it smelled like feces and it looked bad. We went to the local hospital and as usual they stabilized her, started an IV to prevent dehydration and transferred her to the hospital in Bakersfield. At this hospital they used laxatives and enemas to clean her out. This worked in a few days and her digestive system was working again. During this hospital they also performed various x-rays and scans. Sure enough the scans showed she had many mini strokes as the doctor suspected a few month earlier. They also found several abnormalities on some of her organs. After talking to several doctors and specialists because of her age it was best to leave them alone. She would not survive the treatments or possible surgeries. This hospital visit lasted about a week and then I took her home.

When we got home I noticed a big change, she was not herself. Her motor skills were slower and she seemed more lethargic. Over the weeks after she came home I noticed another major difference was her appetite was starting to diminish. This was a woman that could eat half a chicken with all the sides and still have room for dessert, now she would only eat one piece. She still had room for dessert though.

This went on from February to the last week of March. The first week of April everything came apart and I knew the end was coming. She started having trouble finishing her meals and she didn't even want dessert. She had that lost look in her eyes and she was completely confused. She started talking gibberish and started acting like a toddler. She no longer recognized people and started talking about her mom and dad. She would move very little and when I would change her diaper she made no attempt to move or help. She was like a log and she seemed to be getting heavier.

My sister came up to visit and help. She stayed for a few days and saw how fast she was deteriorating. She gave her a shower and trimmed her hair. My sister had to leave on Saturday because she was on call for work the next day. That evening I made soup for dinner because it was easier for her to eat. She barely ate and was slow to respond. I put her in bed, kissed her on the forehead and she nodded.

I usually never slept through the night because I was always listening for her to make sounds that alerted me to a problem. That night I slept straight through. I got up around 6:15am and went into her room. She was in the same positions I left her the night before and her eyes were open and rolled up. She was stiff and was not breathing. Her skin was cold and she had no response or pulse. I called 911 and told them that she was non responsive and they wanted me to do CPR. I said it was not necessary and that she had a DNR, do not resuscitate order. They asked me if I was sure and I said, "Yes." I was taking the responsibility for the decision. The paramedics and police came right away. When they came into the house they made me stay in the front room as they checked my mom. They came out and pronounced her dead and said rigor was setting in. The police officer went in and checked the body and then came out and asked to see the DNR paperwork. I always took pride in being ready for everything so I went to my file cabinet and I couldn't find the DNR order. After fumbling through a bunch of files I noticed it fell out of the folder and onto the floor. I gave it to the officer and he read it. He told the paramedics that he would take it from there and make the arrangements. I was entering new territory.

Right After The End

After the paramedics left and the police and medical examiner were satisfied that my mom died a natural death one officer remained and asked if I had a funeral home in mind for the burial. Tehachapi was small and there was only one funeral home in town so I told him to contact them. This was early on a Sunday morning and he got in touch with a representative. After he made arrangements for the pick up of my mom's body I told him that he did not have to stay. He said that he would like to wait until the funeral home came and he had no problem staying with me for as long as I needed. I told him that I called the family while they were doing their investigation and they were on the way up. He said that was fine and he could stay with me until they arrived. I was amazed at the concern and professionalism of this officer and I will never forget it. We talked and he asked me about my mom and her condition. He wanted to know how long I had taken care of her and complimented me that she looked in great shape and told me that when he arrived he saw nothing that made him concerned or suspicious. He asked about my life and family. I made some coffee and he and I just talked. It was amazing and while we were talking I felt fortunate that I was living in a small town.

We talked for over an hour and it was nice just not to be alone for a while. Two men from the funeral home arrived and they came in and started prepping the body for transport back to the funeral home. I felt bad keeping the officer at the house for so long and I told him that I would be fine and it was okay for him to go back on call. He asked if I was sure and I said yes and he gave me his card and told me if I needed him to give him a call. He told me, "It was great talking to you sir and I'm deeply sorry for your loss. If you need me, please give me a call." He shook my hand and patted my shoulder as he left to go back on call. I enjoyed his company at a time I needed it.

The two men from the funeral home prepped my mom for transport and they wheeled her out into the living room. They had her in a body bag on a stretcher and it was open. They told me to take as much time as I needed to say good bye and then they went outside. I just stared at my mom while the tears started to roll down my face. I put my hand on her head, said good bye and zipped the bag closed. I called the men back in and they wheeled her to the station wagon and brought her to the funeral home.

As soon as they left the next door neighbor and his father, who lived across the street came over to give me their condolences. They knew something had happened when they saw the paramedics and police. They said they were saddened when they saw the funeral home arrive. They stayed for about an hour and kept asking what I needed and what they could do for me? They asked if I needed them to go to the store or if I needed them to call anybody? They were very nice and helpful. I told them that I was okay and if I needed them I would call or go over.

One sister arrived about an hour later with a cousin and the family slowly started coming up. My oldest sister was in Texas so she told me they were leaving to come back that afternoon. We ended up with about twelve people and it was nice to have the family around and my sister helped out a lot. We made a large meal and everyone sat around talking about our mom. They stayed till about 7pm and then they all left except for my sister. She stayed with me so we could make the funeral arrangements and plans.

Once again it was nice to have someone around that night. It was a long day and it was the end of a long journey. When I went to bed I could not sleep and it finally hit me that this was the first time in over twenty years that I wasn't taking care of my dad or mom. The only person I had to worry about and take care of was me. It was the beginning of a new chapter in my life.

We had the funeral the next weekend. It was a nice service that was attended by friends and family. We had it at the church next to the high school I attended and where my mom had a lot of fun when we use to do our fund raising events. Some of the teachers from the school attended because they remembered when she was around. The priest that said the service was a family friend and was my mom's favorite. She told me that when she went she wanted him to do the service. When I called him and told him what she said his answer was as he stated in his eulogy, "When I heard she asked for me, you don't say no."

Dad Died In The Hospital, Mom Died At Home

I had the experience of having one parent pass away in the hospital and the other at home. Each one was difficult in their own way and they both had challenges. Both parents wanted to stay at home but my dad went to the hospital because he didn't want to put my mom through to much stress.

My dad had a private room in the hospital and we were basically left alone because we all knew it was just a matter of time. The nursing staff and doctors made their rounds and kept him as comfortable as possible. The problem for me was that I was spending the night in the hospital so my dad would not be alone. Those hospital recliners are not very comfortable no matter how many pillows you bring. I would go home during the day and try to catch a nap as well as shower and change. My mom and sisters would be there during the day and stay with him all the time. My sisters would leave my mom, she was healthy then, so they could do errands and pick up their children from school. When my mom was by herself the staff took good care of her and constantly checked to see if she needed anything.

The only problem we had was when they were filming a movie at the hospital and they disturbed the access for visitors. I filed a complaint because they would limit access to the hospital while they were filming. I had an incident one day when I was taking my mom in to see my dad and they stopped us from walking into the door. I kept going and I guess I ruined the "shot." Some man started yelling at me and I answered back, "My dad is dying and you want me to worry about your movie?" One of the hospital security guards came and escorted us through the "shot" as he told me that they were driving him crazy and upsetting a lot of patients and families. He was glad that I told them off because it was a hospital not a movie set. A few days later I met with the hospital public relations representative and they told me that the hospital received a large donation for allowing the filming on the property. I told her that I thought it was disgraceful because they put the donation over the patients and their families. She said they had strict orders not to disrupt the patients but they overstepped their bounds. I told her she should have expected it because they "took over" and I hoped that the hospital was happy with the "donation." Leave it to a Catholic hospital to put a donation over patients and their families. As you can tell I was angry at this situation.

My dad died peacefully in the hospital and arrangements could have been easily made but Los Angeles County upset the entire situation. They took possession of my dad's body because he was on workers compensation and ran us through the ringer. They cost us thousands of dollars more than it should and could care less on how are lives were affected.

A few weeks later we finally had the funeral and laid my dad to rest but the situation was still not over because of the problems that Los Angeles County caused. Finally after nine months we were finally able to put the entire ordeal behind us and we were able to move on with our lives. I thought my died dying in the hospital would prevent a lot of problems, it didn't and it probably caused more.

My mom passed away at home and during the night. I didn't know what to expect but I figured it would be stressful. After I called 911 and the paramedics and police arrived I knew I was in unfamiliar territory. To my surprise Kern County was completely different from Los Angeles County. The police officer took control and after reviewing all the legal documents took care of the entire situation. I thought for sure since my mom died at home that an autopsy would be required but the police officer said probably not. He said, "There was no trauma to the body, your mom looked well taken car of and the house is well kept." He called the Medical Examiner's Office and he answered a lot of questions and he supplied them with the information I provided. They waived the autopsy and told us to call the mortuary for the funeral arrangements. I was expecting the worse and an enormous time delay and it was all handled in a couple of hours. I thought my mom dying at home would cause a lot of problems and it didn't happen. I was ready for anything because of my previous experience but fortunately it didn't materialize. I believe Kern County was much more professional and descent compared to Los Angeles County. That is my bias showing because of the unprofessional way they handled my dad's situation.

The only thing I had to do after my mom died was to disclose that she died at home when I sold the house. California has a rule that you must disclose if a person died in the home in the previous five years. I complied with the rules and I didn't have a problem with the sale of the house.

Both parents died in different locations and each one had its unique challenges. They both felt more comfortable at home and they never wanted to leave. My dad made the sacrifice to go to the hospital to save my mom from anxiety and stress. He was taking care of her all the way to the end.

Chapter 65
AFTER THE FUNERAL
The Aftermath

After my father died I pretty much went immediately to the part time care of my mom. A few years later it turned into a full time job and it lasted till the day she died. It has been over two years since she passed away and now I can see how much of a toll it took on my life.

The day she died I knew my life was going to be different from then on. I thought I would have a little of a rough patch for a few months but I never knew it would last over two years. I had depleted our funds in the care of my mom and we were living check to check. When she died the monthly income stopped and there was no money to pay the bills. All the money I put away for burial expenses was used for everyday living. I had purchased a family cemetery plot when my dad died so we had a place to bury my mom. Fortunately my sisters paid for the funeral expenses and we were able to put my mom to rest. After that there was no money for day to day living expenses. I filed the insurance claims and that took between one to three months to be completed. I cashed in my life insurance policies to cover day to day expenses. I had to borrow money from one sister to help with the expenses, she was also not in great financial shape but she sacrificed to help me out, even though she didn't know when she would get re-payed. I had garage sales to sell whatever I could to make ends meet. I sold items online to get a little extra cash. All during this time I was trying to find a job that would help me cover expenses. All the applications I completed online, none ever responded for any follow up or interview. The only response I received was the computer generated response, "Thank you for your application."I finally decided I had to sell my house because I could no longer afford the payments.

I put a $40,000.00 down payment on my house when I purchased it five years before but the housing market crashed and the house was worth about $40,000.00 less than I paid. I still had about $10,000.00 in equity because of my monthly payments. In order to save the realtor commission I decided to try to sell my house "by owner." I had a few showings and even a couple of offers but they were so low that I would have lost more money. I still could make my house payment but it was getting difficult so I took odd handyman jobs to help. This helped with the monthly expenses but I was getting farther and farther in debt. The good news was the house prices started to spike up and I decided to go with a realtor that previewed my home while I was trying to sell it. She was a go-getter and put the house back on the market. We got one cash offer that was extremely low and the house didn't sell in the six month term. Things were getting tight and the debts were mounting to where I no longer could pay the property taxes and I started being late and missing house payments. The phone was ringing off the hook because of past due payments and then one day the realtor called and wanted to show the house. I had caught a cold, felt horrible and could barely function so I asked if she could hold off for a few days. She said the person was in town for the day and really wanted to see the house. I told her okay and they came over to look at the house. I stayed away because I didn't want to make them sick so they viewed the home at their own pace. They came out of the bedroom and the prospective buyer said, "You're asking 209?" I said yes even though I was asking $219,000.00. He then said, "Deal, I'll take it." It was a cash offer with a 30 day escrow. They left and the next day I had a sale agreement and the house went into escrow. It closed in 30 days and all the past taxes and payments were taken out of the proceeds. I dodged a huge bullet because at least I didn't lose the house to foreclosure and I ended up with about $30,000.00 extra. I made $7,000.00 more than I paid so after commissions, closing costs, back taxes and payments I made a little money.

Moving was hectic and the weather didn't cooperate. It snowed on the day I had to be out of the house. Thank goodness I didn't catch pneumonia.

With the proceeds I paid back some of the debts and moved into a room at my cousin's house. I was homeless but at least I had a roof over my head. I continued to look for a job but the responses started coming back that I had no recent job history so they could not verify my application. This continued the entire time I was staying with my cousin.

One night I had my Suburban parked on the street and about 2:00am I heard a crash. It didn't sound close and I didn't hear my alarm so I started going back to sleep. The next thing I know was that someone was knocking on my door and said, "Jim, somebody just crashed into your car." I got up, dressed and sure enough someone totaled my Suburban. The entire left side of the vehicle was smashed and it looked like it was lifted on its side. It was a hit and run but fortunately for me the runaway driver left his front bumper with his license plate attached. The police were called and they ran the plate and found out he lived a few blocks away and they arrested him on suspicion of drunk driving.

I now had no home and no vehicle so I could try to do odd jobs. The insurance company finally settled and I was able to buy another vehicle. I had low milage on my Suburban so it retained some value. The new Jeep Patriot I bought held about a third of what I could put in a Suburban. The best news was it had great gas milage and there were no monthly payments.

I left that cousin's house because I didn't want to lose another car and moved in with another cousin about fifty miles away. His dad, my uncle, just moved across the street and he wanted me around him to help him take care of his dad. This is were I'm at now. My uncle is a retired business executive and he is helping me work on my resume to find employment. I have had no luck so far but I am still trying. In the meantime I supervised his home renovation out of state so he could put it up for sale.

I have no idea what is in store for the future. I have lost family, friends, my home and my vehicle because of this experience. When my mom died I thought it would take a few months to get back on my feet and I would easily get a job to get my life back. After two years it hasn't happened and I have realized what a large toll taking care of my parents has taken on my life. I still have no idea where I will end up or how this saga will end but I will keep trying until something happens and I can get my life back on track.

Life Moves On

After the funeral I filed for the insurance benefits and started closing accounts. This is when reality hit me like a brick and I found out there was no longer any income coming in and a huge amount of expenses going out. There was no money left and there was a huge debt load.

I applied for employment but I never received any call backs. The only information I received back was that I did not have a five year current job history so they could not consider me for employment. I am still in this situation over two years since my mom passed away. The situation has not changed and I have never been able to get a job interview. I am trying to sell handmade items online and I hope this will work till I can get back on my feet. Life moves on and I am hoping it will get better. Trying to rebuild your life after taking care of someone for so long is a challenge. It takes such a toll on your life that your future is uncertain and complicated. I thought I had a plan to deal with this situation, as usual I was wrong.

As long as you are taking care of your parent you never have time to think of what happens when they pass away. If you were taking care of them full time as I was, you were unable to earn a living. When they die you have no way to support yourself and you have to try to get back into the job market, sell property or use funds that you have put away. I had a plan to use money that I put into savings as we refinanced the house. I also planned to use the unused portion of my dad's civil service retirement. My mom was receiving a survivor benefit because my dad was on federal workers compensation and he died because of the result of an on the job injury. His civil service retirement was never used and was a back up in case the survivor benefit was revoked. When my mom died the retirement benefit was never used and the unused portion was to be distributed to the heirs. I was told back in 1996 that the estimated amount was about $35,000.00. Divided three ways, my sisters and I, this would give me the extra money and time to get my life in order and try to find a job. My alternate plan also included selling the house and using the proceeds to move on with my life. My mom and dad were very close and many thought my mom wouldn't survive too long after my father died. This happened in the family a few years earlier with one of my aunt's and uncle. She died in December and he lost the will to live and gave up on life and died three months later. None of the doctors thought my mom was a fighter and unknown to them she had a strong will to live. She lasted a lot longer than the doctors calculated. So the longer I took care of her the more we had to dig into savings for the uncovered expenses. That destroyed my plans and when she died all the money was gone. I applied for the retirement benefit and found out the rules changed in 1997 and the amount was reduced to $9,000.00. Divided three ways that was $3,000.00 a piece. I am still in the process of appealing this decision because it seems their numbers did not match the paperwork that was provided years earlier. Life insurance was very little and only covered two months worth of expenses. I had to go to the alternate plan and sell the house. Unfortunately the housing market collapsed and I did not get much money on the sale. I put a 20% down payment so I got some of that back. After I paid off some bills I had only $30,000.00 left over.

My expenses, covering previous bills and insurance was around $3,000.00 a month. Unable to find a job this amount didn't last long and caused me to do odd jobs. Most of these were small and were for just room and board. I also started selling some hand crafted items on the online sights just to scrape by.

My life changed and I had very little hope for the future because everything fell apart. The planning I had was useless and I had no more plans for the future. After all those years of being a caregiver I was now unemployed and broke.

Never Had A Chance To Grieve

I had an aunt, my dad's sister, that use to live in Rhode Island. Years ago when times were good I use to visit her to check on her because she was a widow and lived alone. She would tell me stories of the past and I learned a lot about the family. I learned that my dad took care of his mom, my grandmother, while my aunt was in school. My grandfather and dad took care of the family while my grandmother was in and out of the hospital. My dad and mom took care of his mother and father until she died. When my grandmother died my grandfather moved in with his youngest son, my uncle. They lived together until my uncle got married and my grandfather then moved in with my aunt and her husband. My aunt took care of her father until he died in 1965. My mom and dad were living in California at the time and had a family of their own.

Talking to my aunt I always noticed she was a hard and cold person. She didn't get emotional and was matter of fact and to the point. One time she told me that I was going to end up like her and I was going to take care of my mom and dad. She told me that I was going to have to do it because my sisters were married and had families of their own. At the time I didn't think she was right. During our conversations she told me how she took care of my grandfather and how hard it was but she had to do it.

She then told me how she took care of her husband when he became partially paralyzed after a stroke. She said it was difficult and she never had any help. She said that it took over her entire life and then it stopped all at once when he died. She had to plan the funeral then tried to get her life back together. She then told me something that I never forgot, she said, "I never had a chance to grieve. There was so much work and so much had to be done, I never cried." During the funeral and the aftermath she never had a chance to settle down and grieve. She told me it hit her about six months later when she was sitting at the kitchen table and she saw his empty coffee cup in the cupboard. She told me she broke down and just cried the whole day. It finally came out of her system and she had a chance to grieve. She told me it was a weight off her shoulder and she was then able to go on with her life.

I never thought about that conversation until after my mom died. When my dad was ill I took care of him until he died. I made all the arrangements for the funeral while I was trying to take care of my mom and help her grieve. I never stopped and I never had a chance to grieve. Life moved on and then my mom got sick and I started taking care of her full time. I did that all the way to the end. Once again I had to make all the arrangements and move on with my life. I never had a chance to grieve. The only time I had a few tears was when I saw her in the body bag.

Till this day I never had a chance to grieve. Looking back that has been over twenty years and it has never hit me. I'm sure someday when I see some remembrance of both of them or a small object that just had meaning to me and them it will finally get to me.

Your Future

In my case my future was uncertain and to this day I am still searching for a way to move ahead with my life. At fifty-four years old it is hard to rebuild your life, especially since you have been out of the workforce for almost twenty years. All the plans I made were useless and I had no clue how difficult it would be to move on with my life.

The job market is completely different to what I use to know. Everything is started online and there is very little face to face interaction. My video skills are twenty years old or older so I'm not exactly up to date. The technology I was familiar with in the video field no longer exists. I tried to keep updated on new equipment and technologies but it is not the same as hands on experience. Companies won't consider me because of my age because they can higher someone just out of college. People say that is age discrimination but all they have to say is that I was out of the workforce for a very long time. They can't take a chance on someone that has not had a verifiable job in over twenty years.

The other issue is health. I'm only fifty-four years old and I feel fine but the body can't do the same as it did years ago. Lifting is more strenuous, climbing is more difficult and learning new techniques takes a lot more time. Why would a company want to hire a border line senior citizen when they could hire a younger person just out of school?

Another issue is also experience. Even though my experience is from years ago is still shows that I know what I am doing and I have dealt with many situations. A prospected employer might consider that my salary requirement would be too high and would rather pay someone with no experience and train them on the job for lower pay. I worked for a supermarket chain years ago and when I left I was classified as full time. When I asked store managers in the area about applying they said I would not be considered because I would have to be hired at the full time rate. It was too expensive and they could hire three clerks for the cost of me. They also said that they could use those three clerks part time and not have to pay them benefits. If they hired me I would be considered a grandfather, they would have to pay me a higher rate, include benefits and guarantee me forty hours a week.

The job market has changed and there are many options for companies to exercise. My hope is to find a small company that will take a chance on an older person with experience and being out of the job market is not an issue. My future is still unfolding and I have no idea where I will end up. I am continuing to do odd jobs, selling items on online sites and I even wrote this book to hopefully make ends meet. It was never part of my plan but it is part of You Got To Do What You Got To Do.

Chapter 66

MY LIFE WAS CHANGED BEING A CAREGIVER
Your Life Changes

The one thing that is certain about being a caregiver is that your life changes and it will never be the same. As you take care of a parent you experience things that you never imagined you would have to do. I'm sure this keeps a lot of psychologists very busy.

When you become a caregiver you are deciding that you are going to take care of an elderly baby. You have to perform all the services that they can no longer perform themselves. This puts you in some unique situations and means you have to do some disgusting jobs. Cleaning up vomit from an adult is a lot different from cleaning up after a baby or child. Diaper changes are in no way similar to changing a baby. Washing them is not something a lot of us ever planned on doing.

A lot of people think it's like feeding them in a hospital after they have had surgery. You prep the meal tray, pour out the milk, juice, tea or coffee. Open the utensils and feed them the meal one spoon or forkful at a time. Being a caregiver just isn't for a few days, weeks or months, it could be for years. It might start off slow with just a few tasks you have to help with or do. Slowly they increase and you finally end up doing everything. In some cases it happens all at once because something catastrophic happens. You are washing, feeding and amusing them everyday. In my case with my mom that was over thirteen years.

This does change your life because you see things that you never expected to witness. At the same time your parents life has changed, they are in a situation that they never thought they would be in. Some can express this frustration or embarrassment and even if they can't I believe they know how hard it is for you and them.

Life Is Never The Same

Not only does your life change it will also never be the same. In the process of being a caregiver you are focused on one thing, taking care of your parent. Your routine is how to make them comfortable and their life as normal as possible. You worry more about them than you do about yourself because they are now your responsibility. Because of this you can lose touch with family and friends. Your routine changes because you don't have time to do what you did before you decided to become a caregiver.

When it's all over it is hard to get your life back to what was normal for you. It all depends how long you put your life on hold so you could take care of your parent. In my case twenty years was a long time and it was almost impossible to start again. I fact I am still in the process of rebuilding my life.

Loss Of Friends And Family

Being a caregiver takes up almost all of your time. In the process you don't have a lot of time to spend with family and friends. On the other hand some family and friends don't want to be around a sick or elderly person. If they come to visit you that's different but it is extremely hard to visit them when you have to lift your mom from chair to car, car to chair over and over.

We lost touch with several family member because we were unable to visit. They always wanted me to bring my mom to them even though they were younger, in better health and capable of traveling. Some would complain about their aches and pains but had no clue how serious my mom's condition was. Unfortunately they never asked or were interested.

I lost friends that I had since high school because I had no time to visit them. They stopped calling to see how things were going, they always expected me to call or visit. The only time we would see each other was at funerals. When my mom passed away I didn't even bother telling them. They weren't interested in us when she was alive why should I tell them when she died.

On the other hand I had some great friends that kept in touch and we would call each other often. When they called the first thing they would ask was how was my mom. They knew her from years ago when I volunteered at my old high school. When I would call them they would sound a little nervous when they heard my voice and ask, "How's your mom?" After we moved some even came to visit us even though it was a two and a half hour drive each way. It was a good excuse for me to make a big meal.

Like everything else in life, some people can handle being around sick and elderly people and some cannot. Some don't want anything negative to interfere with their lives and would rather withdraw than face reality until it affects them. Everyone is different so I can't blame them for what they did.

Chapter 67

WHAT YOU GIVE UP BEING A CAREGIVER

No Social Life

When you are a full time caregiver you have very little time for yourself. A lot of so-called experts say you need to get away and have a life outside of being a caregiver. This is easily said but very hard to do.

Trying to have a social life while being a caregiver is almost impossible unless you already have one. In my case running a business took the majority of my time and left very little room for a social life. I was married the business and it was an ordeal just to keep it afloat. It was not possible to try to juggle a social life at the same time. After I closed the business and became a full time caregiver there was even less time for a social life. It was hard to get together with friends and it was next to impossible to meet new ones.

I always had to bring my mom with me because she could not be left alone. We could not afford an outside person to watch her and my sisters had their own families to watch. So in my case there was no social life because it would have been awkward, "Hi, I'm Jim and this is my mom."

It was a personal decision and one I don't regret. There was no way any relationship could happen and it would not have been fair to anyone that might have been interested. Anything that would have started would have been doomed from the beginning because of my responsibilities and that would have not been fair.

Lost Almost Everything

After my mom passed away I realized that I had lost everything and I was by myself. For years I had to take care of her and she was my responsibility. Now I was on my own for the first time in over twenty years and I had no one to take care of except myself. It was a strange realization and feeling.

One thing that happened was I lost contact with some family members. They were not interested in me and were only interested in my mom so with her gone there was no reason to call or visit. It was like after my mom passed away my entire life disappeared and there was nothing left. I ended up getting rid of a lot of possessions so I could make ends meets and I also finally ended up selling my house and I knew it would be a long time before I would be able to buy another one if I could at all. When the house closed escrow there was a few days delay for the money to be wired into my bank account and I remember talking to my realtor and asking her why there was a problem. I told her, "I'm homeless and they didn't give me the money." She laughed and then got serious and later found out there was some delay at the escrow company. A few days later I finally received payment.

I had no assets left and I was trying to find a job. It was a shock that I was in this position but I had to move on and try to change the situation. I know I made the right decision to take care of my parents and I thought I had planned ahead but as it usually happens something changed and it ruined the plans. The only change I could think of was my mom lived a very long time and the expenses kept growing for her care. I'm not upset because I'm glad she lived a long life, I was mad at myself because I should have had a better plan. During this time is when I was told I made huge mistakes with my life and I should have paid someone to take care of her and gotten a job, even flipping burgers, so I could pay for her care. What those people didn't understand was hiring someone to care for my mom because of her condition would have cost a hell of a lot more than what I would make flipping burgers and her survivor benefit.

I am still in the process of trying to rebuild my life. I am still trying to sell items online and I have designed and am trying to sell hand made items such as quilt racks. I continue to look for a job and still trying to find an opportunity.

Lived On Survivor Benefit

Over the years of taking care of my mom we lived off her survivor benefit and whatever I could bring in from doing odd jobs and selling items online. We did this for all the years I took care of her and it worked very well until almost the end. It wasn't enough to cover all the expenses so I would have to dip into savings to cover the shortage. We made money on the sale of our Lynwood home and I put it in savings for an emergency. The emergency finally came and we had to use our savings to supplement our income. A few months before she died the savings ran out and we started going into debt. Taking care of her full time meant that I had no way to work a full time job. The area where we lived was also not a location where job's were plentiful and the one's that were available did not pay enough to support her care. I never told her of these problems because I never wanted to upset her. As far as she knew everything was fine and it was up to me to juggle the budget, handle the bills and take care of her. She never went without anything she needed and aways had her medication, supplies, accessories and food. It was after she passed away that everything collapsed and fell on me.

Refinanced House Many Times

When we lived in Lynwood and I was taking care of my mom we were starting to go in debt because of the cost of her twenty-four hour care. My folks had a modest house and it was paid off. This was the time when refinancing was popular and it was easy to qualify. We were in debt and it was getting hard to handle so I decided we needed to borrow on the house to cover the expenses. It was one of the biggest mistakes I ever made.

It started off small and I only borrowed a small amount only to cover the debts and pay them off. It worked but later and once again because of her expenses we needed more money. There was no option for me to go to work so I needed to do something else. Once again I borrowed on the house and this time I took a bigger chunk so we could pay off all our debts and have money available for the future and emergencies. Like a lot of people I was using the house for a credit card and I went deeper into debt. My mom agreed that this was a good idea and we went through with refinancing. I didn't borrow the full value of the house and made sure we still had a substantial amount of equity. We considered a reverse mortgage but were told this option was not available for our situation.

When we decided to move to Tehachapi I was able to sell the house, pay off the loan and have money for a down payment on a new house. I also was able to keep a little in savings in case of emergency so we could survive. I figured if the money ran out I would be able to run a business from home or get a part time job. My sister was going to live a few blocks away when she retired so I thought I had a good solution. We sold the Lynwood house and purchased the new home in Tehachapi and all went according to plan. We were doing fine and everything was going according to my budget.

As my mom started getting older and things started changing she started to require more supplies and accessories. I also had to spend more on heating and cooling because I had to keep her comfortable. The area was somewhat hot in the summer so we needed to run the air conditioning and we got snow in the winter so I had to run the heater higher. My mom got to that stage where she was always cold so I had to keep the house toasty to keep her comfortable. This went on for almost five years and then I realized the money was running out and it finally did just before she passed away.

When I had sometime to go over and see what went wrong with our finances I realized that the money ran out because she was enjoying her life and that's what should have been happening. I did make some mistakes on spending but nothing was obvious to where it made us go broke. It was just the cost to sustain her quality of life. I then ran the numbers from when I refinanced our house the first time and found something out that just made me angry. If I would have worked through the difficult times and not refinanced the house I never would have been in the situation I found myself in. I could have purchased our new home cash and would have had no outstanding debt. It would have been difficult but it could have been done. I would have had a house that was paid for and I would have been able to sell it and move on with my life. I can't go back and change the mistake I made. I took the easy way out and it cost me in the end. I still think I made the right decision at the time I just wish I would have thought it through a little better. I'll never know and you can't go back or change the past.

Unused Retirement

One of the things I always thought I had in our back pocket to survive after my parents passed away was my father's unused retirement. My dad worked for the Navy as a pipe fitter and he was diagnosed with asbestosis. He was placed on workers compensation and received a monthly benefit. If for some reason he no longer qualified for workers compensation he would have been able to collect his retirement from the civil service system. When he passed away, it was ruled that his death was due to his asbestosis and my mom received a survivor benefit from the Navy as long as she didn't remarry or go to work. If for some reason that benefit was terminated she could also collect from my dad's civil service retirement. If that retirement was never collected, the beneficiaries would collect the balance of the unused retirement. My two sisters and I were the beneficiaries.

My mom never collected any civil service retirement benefits so the balance was never used. I was told by one agency that the amount of retirement was substantial and that we would be able to collect it when my mom passed away. After she died I applied for the unused retirement benefit and waited over six month for any response. I had copies of all the documents my dad filed years before and I figured everything would be in order and the benefit would be paid.

Finally my sisters and I received a check for the payment of the benefit. It was in the amount of $9,000.00 which divided by three was $3,000.00 each. I was told back in 1996 that the unused retirement with interest was around $35,000.00 and if the benefit was not used it would be issued to my sisters and I along with accrued interest. My dad had used some of the retirement while he was waiting for his compensation benefit to be approved and when it was, he repaid the portion of the retirement that was disbursed. I even have a copy of the cancelled check that the government cashed. I called and did some research and found that the earlier numbers my dad and I had and the numbers I received in 2013 were completely different. I also learned that the rules had changed and interest on the balance was no longer paid after five years.

It seems that I was given bad information in 1996 or we received the wrong benefit in 2013. I filed an appeal and as of this date, September of 2015 I have never had any response. When I call the agency you have to wait for up to two hours on the phone, I am told that they are really backed up and they handle current retirees first and appeals are handled when they have time. I guess this is typical of bureaucracy, in the meantime I thought this benefit was going to help me get back on my feet and help rebuild my life. As with everything else of the aftermath of my mom passing away I find that it is just another challenge I have to deal with.

Refrigerator Bare

One of the scariest situations that happened to me after my mom died occurred almost a year later. Money was extremely tight to almost non existent and I opened the refrigerator and noticed it was almost empty. There was some milk and a few eggs but nothing else. That hit me like a brick because now I was seeing that my food supply was disappearing. The part that made it worse was that there was no money coming in and I had about ten dollars in my wallet.

I had some items online and I had hoped that they would sell. They did and that gave me enough money to buy food to get me by a little longer. I was always a penny pincher when I went shopping and I did use coupons to save money but as it always happens the items you need are usually not on sale. In our city we had one of those chain dollar stores and I found out that I could buy a lot of food items for a dollar. They were brands I knew but they were in smaller packages. It was great because I could usually buy about twenty dollars of food from the regular grocery store for about ten dollars at this dollar store. They sold bread, cold cuts, frozen dinners and canned goods and it kept me going for months. They even sold paper products and once again it was cheap. It was a little thin and course but it got the job done. I was by myself and I no longer had to make big meals because the family didn't come up to see me after my mom had died. Some people criticize these dollar stores because they say the food is poor quality and cheap. Yes, it is cheap because the package size is smaller than usual and the name brands are from other parts of the country but as long as it sealed and from the United States it wasn't a problem to me. These stores helped me get through difficult times because I was still able to buy food with the little money that was coming in. This was a scary time and it didn't end until I sold the house and was able to lower my overhead a little.

Don't Let Others Know

After my mom died one of the hardest things was to maintain my pride. I couldn't find employment and I felt like I was useless because I had no handle on the situation at hand. I was losing control of my life and it was drifting away without any plan. It was embarrassing and I didn't want others to know how bad it was.

Many years before when my business hit a rocky patch I had this dream that has haunted me ever since. I dreamt that I was exiting the freeway near a cousin's house. For years people would be at the exit holding signs that they would work for food. My dream was I looked at one of those people and saw myself, then I woke up.

After my mom died I still could see that dream and if felt like it was starting to come true. I wasn't standing at the corner but I was working for food. All the odd jobs I did went to pay for food. Now I know this is part of a normal economy and everyone technically works for food but that's all I was working for. I gave up my house and a large chunk of belongings just to survive and I didn't see much hope for a change very soon.

I kept it to myself because I was embarrassed and I didn't want my family and friends to know. When they would ask me, "How are things going?" I would always say, "Fine" or "I'm working on something." I wasn't fine and I was digging a deeper hole for myself. Most of the family has drifted away and they don't ask questions or care about what I'm doing anymore. They have their families and they should me more concerned with them. I'm sure they knew the situation I was in and felt it was better to walk away. That's fine because I need to take care of this situation myself and move on with my life.

Putting Up A Good Front

One thing I learned over the years was how to put up a good front. Over the years of taking care of my parents whenever someone asked , "How are you doing?" I would always say, "Great." It didn't matter how tired or exhausted I was I would always answer everything was fine. The reason was that most people really didn't care how I was and they didn't want to hear the real answer.

When they would ask about my parents condition the same answer always applied. They were not interested in what was wrong because it was not important to them. A lot of people are very shallow and they just go through the motions of caring and there is no concern what so ever. People would look at my mom and see her being lifted and placed in the car or wheelchair and ask, "What's wrong with her?" When I use to try to explain her condition most of them would cut me off and say, "My mom had that but she could walk," or "she got over it." It was as if they didn't believe how serious my mom's condition was and that she was faking it to get sympathy. Some would look at me like I was trying to milk her condition so people would have pity. Everyone knows better and no one wants to know the truth. I finally got to the point and just went along with what we needed to do. If someone asked what was wrong with my mom all I would say is, "She has a serious spinal condition." I would leave it at that and went on with what we were doing.

The same thing happened after she passed away and people saw me and asked what I was doing. When I would try to explain myself very few believed anything I said. This included family and friends and when I would tell them the difficult time I was having trying to find employment the response I would get is, "Everybody gets turned down once or twice." This is very true but I couldn't even get through the first door, the online application process. They looked at me like I was making things up and I didn't want to work. So finally when people asked me what I was doing or how I was doing I would say, "I'm getting by and I'm working on some leads." It is the truth but I just wish one would work out.

Delay In Benefits

The first time we had problems meeting expenses was when my dad passed away. I knew the end was coming and I had made some arrangements so we would be able to get along. My dad had lung cancer that was caused by asbestosis, a work related injury. He was receiving workers compensation from the U.S. Department Of Labor because he contracted the disease while working for the Navy at Quonset Point Naval Air Station in Rhode Island and the Long Beach Naval Shipyard in Long Beach, California.

If the disease caused his death my mom would be entitled to a survivor benefit from the workers compensation. An autopsy would have to be performed to insure that the cause of death was indeed from the asbestosis. I contacted the Office Of Workers Compensation and spoke to the supervising claim examiner that I had dealt with for many years. He informed me that an autopsy was not required in my dad's case because they had been paying the claim from 1979 and they knew from all the reports that my dad definitely had asbestosis and it was contributing to his death. He told me to, "Spend time with your dad and take care of your mom and don't worry, she will receive the survivor benefit." That was a relief and I stayed with my dad until he died.

After he passed away I made arrangements with a funeral home to pick him up from the hospital. When they arrived they were told the body was seized by the Los Angeles County Coroner because it was a workers compensation case and they had jurisdiction. The funeral home called me and I called the supervisor at the Department Of Labor. He assured me that the Office Of Workers Compensation did not seize the body or order the autopsy. He also informed me that Los Angeles County did not have jurisdiction because it was a federal workers compensation case that was decided years before. He told me he would investigate and get back to me. The funeral home was ordered to deliver my dad's body to the corners office and told me they had no choice under the law. The federal workers compensation office called back and said that Los Angeles County refused to listen and under a court decision from the 1920s said they had jurisdiction on all workers compensation cases. They were told to stay out of it or there would be problems. He told me that if the accident happened at the shipyard the county would have no jurisdiction unless they were called in by the federal authorities. He said technically the accident happened on federal property and your dad was technically a federal worker and that the county did not have jurisdiction. We were in a pissing match and we had absolutely no control because Los Angeles County had already seized the body.

Due to the inquiries made by the U. S. Department Of Labor, the Los Angeles County Coroner made us wait a week for the autopsy and then finally released the body. They informed us we could bury the body but we would not have a final death certificate for up to six months. We could not file for life insurance or the survivor benefit because we did not have a final death certificate. This put us in a serious bind because we had no income coming in and a lot of expenses going out, such as payment for the funeral. Los Angeles County played hardball because we had the nerve to challenge them because of technicality. It was a joke and the county could care less how our lives were being affected by their arrogance.

After about two months we finally received a conditional death certificate and to our shock it was for a different body. That was quickly rectified after we contacted the coroners office. They sent the proper death certificate but once again it wasn't complete. We had three amendments to the death certificate because Los Angeles County kept forgetting to attach the proper test results.

Finally after five months we received the proper death certificate with all the attachments. They were absolutely unprofessional and had no clue what they were doing. They were a prime example of incompetence in the public sector. They didn't care that they did the wrong job and didn't care how they were destroying lives. Talk about a broken system.

I was able to negotiate with the funeral home and make time payments on my dad's funeral. I also negotiated with the cemetery for the plots and was also able to make payments. Any savings we had, fortunately they were joint between my dad and mom, kept us going for those few months. I tried to continue with my business but I couldn't do it because of all the complications caused by Los Angeles County. After all the delays and incompetence they actually had the nerve to send my mom a bill for $10.00 for a document preparation fee. She refused to pay it and they said they were going to send it to collection. It was never paid because they cost us a lot more because of their delays and unprofessional work. We never heard about the unpaid amount ever again.

This always left me with a poor view of Los Angeles County and I couldn't wait to move out. The excuse is they're so big and busy that they will make mistakes. That means nothing to the people who's lives are affected by their incompetence and how people can be destroyed because the county doesn't care about their residents. Once again a prime example of why people have a poor view of government and their employees.

Went Through Savings

After my dad died and because of the delay caused by Los Angeles County we depleted the savings that my dad and mom had put away. It went for normal living expenses and it caused me to borrow on credit cards to make ends meet. After Los Angeles County corrected all the mistakes they made I was able to apply for my mom's survivor benefits and beneficiary benefits from my dad's life insurance.

This delay caused a major hit to our finances and one that took years to recover. Eventually we received the back pay from the survivor benefits and life insurance money and that all went to pay off credit cards, funeral and burial expenses. When all the money was disbursed we were still in a hole because monthly expenses continued even when no money was brought in.

I tried to keep my business running during this time but unfortunately I passed the point of no return and had to close. I started doing odd jobs to help bring in more money to cover current living expenses and previous bills. My mom and I were able to survive but we were never able to put money back into savings. There was always just enough or a little short so we were never able to build up an emergency fund.

During this time I was taking care of my mom part time. She was still able to walk and pretty much take care of herself with the exception of being alone. She could stay alone in the house during the day but did not like being alone in the evening or at night. Her condition steadily worsened and she was able to stand and walk less and less as time went on. She used a cane in the house and later started using a walker. She was always in pain and it kept increasing so our doctor tried various pain medication to get it under control. None of it worked and she suffered constantly. Every medication was a new expense and even though my mom had prescription coverage the copay was a percentage and it changed with each new medication. It seemed every time I thought we got our finances under control some new expense would come up and put us back in the hole. Like a lot of people, when that happened I used a credit card to get us back on track and as usual those expense kept growing. I knew sooner or later I would have to find a way to pay off those high interest rate credit cards.

Monthly Expenses Kept Growing

Monthly expenses never seemed to stop growing. Just the normal cost of living was always going up no matter what information the government put out. Gasoline and groceries seemed to never go down as well as the normal everyday items, like toilet paper. We searched the weekly sale papers for bargains and used coupons constantly. We followed a strict rule, "Do I want it or do I need it." If the answer was "I want it," then we didn't "need it." I made sure we always had the necessary items for my mom's health but that left little room for anything else.

I finally started taking care of my mom full time in 1999 when she could no longer stand or walk. As usual when your down you get hit with something big and we did. My Suburban had over 200,000 miles on it and the transmission failed. I was able to repair it myself but I knew it was only a matter of time. I needed a reliable car to take care of my mom. I saw the Saturn Vue and realized it would work with the care of my mom and it was somewhat affordable. I wanted another Suburban but they were way too expensive and there was no way we could afford the monthly payments. I contacted my credit union and they worked with me and I was able to get a car loan for the Saturn. They had huge rebates on the vehicles and I had a coupon from the manufacturer so I had to put no money down. We used my mom's social security monthly benefit to make the car payment. This put a squeeze on our monthly budget and we had to cut back on some other items. With better shopping techniques and lower insurance rates because of the car make and size we were able to just get by once again. A few months later I was driving the old Suburban and the transmission seized up and broke off the engine making the vehicle inoperable. I had it towed home and eventually taken to the junk yard. It was a good thing we made the sacrifice to purchase a new vehicle a few months before.

Another wild card expense that always went up every three to six months was my health insurance. At the time I was making quarterly payments and it seemed every time I got a new bill the price increased. These were not small increases they were as high as $50.00 a month or $150.00 per quarter. I needed my health insurance so I could remain healthy so I could take care of my mom. When you're on a tight budget every little increase hurts. People that never have to worry about monthly expenses or cash flow have no idea how hard it is to live month to month. My hardship was I had to make sure that the money was spent in the right place to make sure my mom was taken care of properly. I also had to make sure that I was okay so I could take care of her. It was a never ending struggle and battle. I thought I found a solution but it was only a quick fix and caused major problems down the road. The solution was borrowing on the house and I still say that was one of the biggest mistakes I ever made.

Trying To Make Ends Meet

One of the hardest challenges during the entire time I was taking care of my parents was trying to make ends meet. Their care took so much time and effort that I was never able to get my career back on track. This caused a problem because of all the expenses that we had to struggle with every month. This is a normal situation for most families but it causes more stress because you are afraid you will never get out of the hole. In my case it was true.

It seemed like the bills never stopped piling up and we could never get ahead. We needed a different medication and the co-payment was more than the previous one. We needed a different kind of supply that was more expensive than before. A new accessory was needed and it wasn't covered by Medicare or insurance. I needed a special ingredient to cook meals for a diabetic or sugar free protein drinks. There was always a new expenses or an increase on the old ones.

Technically we were on a fixed income because I was not able to bring in any extra money because I was not able to go out and spend time looking for or maintaining customers. If I was able to get an odd job I had to take my mom with me and it had to be close to home in case she "had to go." Her care put a limit on any job that I could try to get.

Every time I tried to do a job I made sure I could take my mom with me. Once in a while I was able to complete the job but most of the time, like clockwork, when I started, she would, "Have to go." After three or four tries I finally stopped because it was putting too much stress on her because she felt like she was letting me down. I had to try to find other ways the make ends meet.

Through the entire caregiving experience finances always took center stage just behind caring for my dad and mom. I tried not to let them worry about the situation but they always knew there was a problem and I was doing my best for us to get by. I always said I was hoping to get out of the situation but it never happened. I tried to make plans for when they passed away and once again those plans fell short. After my mom died I thought I had everything under control and once again the bottom was pulled out from under me. I am still in the situation of trying to make ends meet and there doesn't seem to be an end in sight.

Garage Sales

One of the ways I tried to make ends meet after my mom passed away was to have a garage or yard sale. I thought that I would be able to get a least one month of expenses paid by having one of these sales. I thought selling some of the medical equipment I purchased would have brought in enough money to help with the bills.

I thought it was a good idea but after three sales I only made $600.00 dollars. I did sell a lot of stuff from the garage but I had to practically give it away because I thought it was worth more than it was. I sold outdoor tables, chairs and yard equipment. I tried to sell old books, knick knacks and other so-called collectables we had around the house. I would say $5.00 and the counter offer was usually twenty-five to fifty cents. We would settle on a dollar or two but nothing more than that for the small items. The larger items went for a fraction of the cost but I had no choice because I needed the money.

I felt bad selling some of the things my mom liked but I once again I had no choice. I gave the family first choice and they took a few items they wanted but the rest went up for sale. As they say what you think is valuable is someone else's junk. What had value to my mom had no value to the rest of the family or strangers. It was hard to see people going through the items and then offering almost nothing for them. Life goes on and you have to do what you have to do so I had to sell the items to move forward. I just wish I could have sold a few more and made a few more dollars. The proceeds paid for food, utilities and some of the mortgage. It did help for the month but it also meant there was going to be a long road ahead.

Ruined Credit

When I started taking care of my parents I never considered how my financial situation would be affected. As time went on I knew that I was going to have a problem because the money I put away was starting to run out. After my mom passed away reality hit me in the face like a brick because I was unable to find a job because of my lack of a current job history.

At one time I had good credit and was able to finance anything I might need. When I purchased our new home in Tehachapi I had no trouble qualifying for a home loan. The mailbox was always full of credit card offers and I was happy not to accept them. I didn't believe in having many credit cards but I did feel that they were necessary for emergencies. I had gasoline company credit cards so it made it easier to travel. I had a home improvement store credit card as well as a few of the major bank cards. When times got tough these cards were maxed out very quickly and then even though they were being paid on time the companies got nervous and reduced the credit limits. The only one I never had a problem with was from my credit union and they always worked with me no matter what the problem. Finally I was late on a few payments on the bank cards and then everything tumbled. I kept the gasoline and store cards current in case of emergencies and so I could buy what I needed or get to a job interview if one ever came into play. Most credit cards for gasoline companies and stores are covered by the large banks so they reduced the limits on all the cards even if there were never any late payments. I kept making payments but as usual you get farther behind and in the process my credit was ruined. After I sold my house I brought the accounts current and am still in the process of paying off the debts. Once again my credit union was the only one that worked with me and did not dictate terms. They never cut me off or lowered my limit and allowed me to work out the situation. The other banks would only work with you as long as you followed their terms and would not budge if it was not their way. These are the companies that give big banks bad names. I know they are owed the money but they should want to work with you. I guess these are the new loan sharks and the only way is their way. The only difference is these new loan sharks are legal.

I am no longer interested in credit or credit scores because I need to be concerned on how I'm going to live and move forward. I know credit scores dictate our lives now days and I think it is a damn shame that we have given our lives over to the financial institutions. Because of their control of our lives we pay more for car insurance and they can restrict where you can live. I see people bending over backwards to kiss up to the big financial institutions and say how great they are because they have never had a problem. If these people ever have a problem they will learn real fast that these financial institutions have no concern if they were a good customer, all their concerned with is, "What are you doing to us now." Most of these companies were bailed out by the government using taxpayer money and in return for this taxpayer bailout they run their customers through a grinder. I refuse to be pushed around by these companies and my solution is to not use them anymore. My hope is to one day to make enough money to tell all of them to "go to hell," and move on with my life.

I Tried To Earn A Living, She Always Had To Go

Over the years I tried to earn a living while I was taking care of my dad and mom. I tried to do small jobs but it became harder as their illnesses progressed and they needed full time care. Once I started taking care of my mom full time there was no time to do small jobs and try to make a living.

I tried a few times doing some small handyman jobs as long as I could bring my mom with me. This was usually for friends and it never worked out. It seemed that every time I got to the location and I was ready to unload my tools my mom would have "to go." I wouldn't leave our house until she went to the bathroom and had a bowel movement. She would "go" so I thought I had the rest of the day to work without a problem. I don't know if it was the vibration of the car or just something in her mind but every time I would try to do a job she would have "to go." That meant that I would have to pack the car back up and race home because my car was too small for her to use a porta potty. She was embarrassed to go in her diaper at that time and she wanted to go home "to go." She never had an accident and messed in her diaper so she would "go" at home. When she was done she would always tell me, "We can go back now." My answer was also always the same, "Not today."

I had some friends that wanted me to do some small projects around their house. They were trying to help me out but I never could complete the job. I was able to change some door knobs and small things like that but I never could do the more time consuming projects. I finally told them that they needed to hire someone else because I could not do the job. The true friends that they were said it was no problem and I could take as long as I needed but I didn't feel comfortable in making them wait. That was the last time I tried to do some odd jobs when my mom was alive. This did put a crimp on our budget and caused me many sleepless nights. I was always looking for another way to bring in some extra money.

Nothing To Show For Your Work

All those years of taking care of my parents and I have nothing to show for it. I did gain a lot of experience in being a caregiver but what can I do with that knowledge? I am not a professional so I can't get a job with an agency or company because I do no have the educational background. I have actual experience but I do not have the book knowledge.

Listing that you were a caregiver on your resume does absolutely nothing to advance your career. I was in the video field what does taking care of you parents have with designing and building video systems. I had considerable construction experience, how does changing an adult diaper help with building or remodeling. I have worked on cars since I was ten years old, how does dispensing medication help in maintaining an automobile. I have always liked to cook but how does that help you get a job in a restaurant. What do you say, "I took care of my mom so I learned how to cut spaghetti and meatballs into pieces."

No one cares or will take a chance on that experience. All those years of doing almost everything while I was taking care of my parents means absolutely nothing in trying to gain employment. Some might say it shows dedication and then others might say I took family over a job. Most companies want your job to come first and the family to come after. I guess I failed in that task.

Total Cost-Personal And Financial

It can be easy to make the decision to take care of your parents in their senior years. What most people don't realize is that when you become a caregiver there is an enormous cost for that decision. It is not only a financial expense but is also causes an extreme personal cost. That personal cost can take a toll for the rest of your life.

In my situation the decision to take care of my parents took a huge financial and personal toll. When my father became ill I could no longer run my business and I had to close it. When I started taking care of my mom full time I was no longer able to get a job because she needed twenty-four hour care and could not be left alone. I made the sacrifice and decided that we could live off her survivor benefit so she could get the proper care with me being the caregiver. Looking back at the entire situation, I made the right decision.

When I started taking care of my parents I thought most of the medical costs would be covered by Medicare and supplement insurance. They did cover the medical expenses but the supplies and some of the accessories to help them survive were not covered. When my father was diagnosed with diabetes, Medicare would pay for the meter but they did not pay for the blood test strips. You can't use one without the other. After his bladder cancer surgery he had to wear an urostomy pouch. Medicare and insurance paid for the stoma flange and pouches but they would not pay for the powder and adhesive. Once again you can't use one without the other. All those necessary items were expensive and they came out of our pockets.

With my mom the same thing applied but to different items. When she had a bed wound, Medicare and insurance would cover all the wound supplies, medications and dressings. They would not cover the cleaning supplies, once again you can't use one without the other. She was susceptible to bed sores and Medicare agreed to rent an air mattress for a short time. When her doctor said it was a permanent condition Medicare and insurance pulled the plug on the air mattress. This time it was a life saving piece of equipment and they would not cover it. That was a huge expense and it came out of our pocket.

The other major expense is incontinence supplies and diapers. People think that babies and toddlers go through a lot of diapers, let me tell you and adult can go through much more. These items are not cheap and they were not covered by Medicare and insurance. Most packages contain eighteen to twenty-two diapers and you will go through at least two packages a week. They cost around $15.00 a package so that is at least $30.00 a week. There is also all the items to keep someone clean and fresh. Since they can't wash themselves you need to purchase items that can help you aid in washing them. The list goes on and on and so does the cost.

There is special food that you might have to purchase to help keep up their protein levels. Supplements and vitamins are also necessary to keep them healthy. Special clothes might be needed to help you to dress them or make it easier for them to dress themselves. Special gel chair pads to make them more comfortable when they are in the wheelchair or traveling. A different kind of shoe might be necessary for when their feet swell or to make them easier to fit on their feet.

There are so many items that it seems that you are always spending money on this or that to make them more comfortable. All these items cost money and will be paid for by you. They are costs that you will have to bear to take care of your parent.

The other cost is personal and it takes a greater toll on your life. When I made the decision to take care of my parents I never knew how much work it would be. I never realized that there would be no rest or break from the ordeal. I also never thought I would be going from taking care of my dad to immediately taking care of my mom. Life is not predictable and things happen so you have to deal with it.

I always thought I would get support from my family but I didn't expect it and always knew I would be on my own. Day after day I took care of them and catered to their needs without any regard to myself. The part that disappointed me was that I would be criticized for my decision and was given no alternatives. So I just passed it off and went ahead with my duties.

Looking back, taking care of my dad and mom took an enormous cost both financially and personally. After my mom died I realized that my life was changed forever. I was fifty-two when she died and I had no job or career. I lost most of my friends and my family distanced themselves from me. That when I knew I was finally alone and I had to start rebuilding my life. I am still in that process.

Chapter 68

WHAT YOU LOSE FINANCIALLY BEING A CAREGIVER
Work Suffers

I was self employed so my situation was unique, I could work from home. If I was employed by someone or company I might have made enough money to hire someone to help with the care of my mom. One thing is sure for both situations is that work suffers.

Being self employed you have to be disciplined enough to work without being motivated by a supervisor or co-workers. When you are a caregiver all your energy and motivation is going to your parent. When they need constant care and assistance this leaves very little time to run a business. In fact it leaves no time. After you get them ready in the morning you have a short time to do your work then you have to get them ready for lunch. The cycle starts again, you have a short time after lunch then you have to get ready for dinner. Then you have a short time after dinner then you have to get them ready for bed. After this you are exhausted.

If you work for someone else and have enough money you can hire someone for during the day. I'm sure that during the work day and especially at lunch you would be calling to check on your parent to see if all is well. When you come home from work you would make dinner and then start getting them ready for bed. Forget about getting a full nights sleep because in the back of your mind you're listening to see if they are sleeping properly. Then you start the routine all over. For both situations, you have take time off from work to take your parent to the doctors or for tests and procedures. Then you have the emergency situations such as when they have the flu or some other catastrophe.

Some say work is their escape from the day to day routine of being a part time caregiver. When you're a full time caregiver there is no escape. It is hard to focus on work when you know of your responsibilities with your parent. You can never get a complete day of work done. That might not go well with your boss and it certainly doesn't help when your self employed.

Unable To Gain Employment

During my mom's illness I was always wondering about the future. We were living month to month on her survivor benefit so we were able to barely make ends meet. Before I became a caregiver I was self employed and had a lot of experience in the video field. Since I had been out of the business for so long I figured I would not be able to find employment in that field again. I always thought I would be able to get a job in the retail field because I heard they liked older individuals because they were flexible on their schedule. I was wrong.

After my mom passed away I had to do some reflecting because I no longer had to be responsible for anyone but myself. I also did not have a steady job and selling items at garage sales and online was not going to pay the bills. The city we lived in had a very small job market, there were only ten thousand people in the city. Larger cities were at least forty-five miles away.

I was from the old school. You visited employers and left your resume with the employment office. You made phone calls and tried to get your foot in the door for an interview. Today everything is online. Companies don't accept resumes in person and they no longer have an employment office, it's called human resources now. You fill out an application online and hopefully you get a response. I filled out applications online for the local governments, corporations and retailers. To my surprise I didn't get any responses back. I talked to a former human resources manager for a retail company and I was told that I gave the companies a perfect excuse. Since I was older and had experience they would think I would require a higher salary and more hours. The excuse I gave them to pass me over was that I had no current job history. I hadn't worked for a company since before I started my business in 1984. I had no current verifiable job history so it was easy for them to dismiss my application. This was confirmed when I received and email from a company saying since I had no verifiable job history I could not be considered for employment. So much for trying to get back into the workforce.

To this day I have been unable to get employment. I've talked to workers at some retail establishments that are of similar age and they had no problem landing a job. All of them had worked for another company in the last five years. This has caused me to try other options like selling handmade items online and handyman services. That is even one of the reasons for writing this book, to make ends meet.

Out Of The Workforce

Taking care of my parents took its toll on my career. I made the decision back in 1983 to start my own video business. I left the comfort of a full time job at a major supermarket chain and go into business for myself. As my parents became sick being self employed gave me the freedom to help and take care of their needs.

As long as I had a business my income and job history could be verified. After I closed the business in 1996 and became a part time and then a full time caregiver I no longer had a verifiable job or business history. The longer I took care of my mother the longer I was out of the workforce. In fact my Social Security is affected because I have not paid into Social Security the last seven years because I have not made enough income. Not being in the workforce not only affects my job history it also affects my Social Security benefits. If I was to become disabled I could not collect Social Security Disability Benefits because I have not paid into Social Security for the last five years prior to the disability. So I'm screwed if I get hurt and can't do any work.

The longer you take care of your parent and don't work you are affecting your future. If you were fortunate to put money away, depending on your life style you will go through that in no time. If you have to pay for your own health insurance that is a huge expense, even in this day of subsidized health insurance. Your Social Security benefit could be affected as well as any retirement plan you set aside. If you don't keep contributing to them there is nothing there for the future.

When I started taking care of my dad and mom I knew that it was going to take a lot of time and effort. What I didn't know was how much I was going to lose in the process. I always thought when the end came and I was ready to move on with my life that I would be able to get right back into the workforce and once again start earning a descent living. This is one area where I was absolutely wrong and completely unprepared for the outcome. When my dad died I moved along and started taking care of my mom. When she died I had no job and a ton of bills that needed to be paid.

The entire job market and the way to apply for a job had changed and I was not prepared for this new system. I was taught you had a resume and you went door to door trying to sell yourself for the job that was available. This process doesn't exist anymore and everything is done online. In fact you can't even get in the front door and you have to apply online first. The amount of space available for you to present yourself varies from one employment website to another and some accept resumes and some do not. Of all the positions I applied for I never received a response back except for the occasional, "Thank you for applying." I did receive a few like, "Due to the lack of a recent employment history we are unable to consider you for this position."

Since I have been out of the workforce for so long I was unable to gain employment. I had over $30,000.00 in bills that were used for my mom's supplies and accessories. I still had a small mortgage of $1,000.00 a month plus other expenses. My monthly outlay was around $3,000.00 per month and I had nothing coming in. After life insurance paid, cashing in my life insurance policy, borrowing on another life insurance policy and borrowing from one sister I was able to survive for a few months. Trying to negotiate with credit card companies proved futile because the way they negotiate is, "It's our way or nothing." I finally had to sell the house and try to get out of debt. The housing market was slow in Tehachapi, California so I tried to sell the house myself to save on commissions. This didn't work out and in the process of trying to sell the house I met a realtor who was a professional, motivated and a go-getter so I listed the property with her. After eight months the property finally sold and I moved out. Selling the house meant I had no home.

I moved into a room at cousin's house and that proved to be a bigger disaster. While I was staying there a drunk driver totaled my Suburban while it was parked on the street at 2:00am in the morning. Now I had no home and no vehicle. Insurance paid for the loss and with the settlement I purchased a Jeep Patriot. Now I had a small SUV that could only carry one-third of what the Suburban could haul. This meant as I tried to do handyman jobs I couldn't carry all my tools or tow a trailer for my tools.

I left that cousin's home because I could not afford to lose another vehicle and I didn't want to leave my new Jeep on the street so another drunk could total it. The first claim I was fortunate to have a Suburban with low milage and it was still in great condition. So I didn't want to take that chance again so I moved into a room with another cousin where I could park my car in the driveway. His dad, my uncle, is eighty-seven years old and lives across the street and they wanted me to help with his care. I sort of became an advisor for his care and I also helped with handyman jobs at his two homes.

That's still where I'm at now, I am homeless but at least I have a roof over my head. I lost everything and the future for obtaining what I had seem's almost impossible. I am still trying to gain employment but the issue of no recent job history is still a problem.

Loss Of Health Insurance

Since my mom passed away I have been living day to day. I was living off whatever I could get from doing odd jobs and selling my belongings. In order to make ends meet I had to give up my health insurance because it was costing over $350.00 a month for a catastrophic medical policy. This savings helped me get along for a few months.

Unfortunately January 2014 was the start of Obamacare and this meant there was a fine for not having healthcare insurance. When I looked into medical plans the only thing Obamacare would do for me was put me on

Medicaid and this was something I didn't want. I always took care of myself and paid my own way therefore I didn't want a government handout. Progressive politicians don't understand that a lot of people like to take care of themselves and don't want the government to control their life. This is no longer an option and I went without health insurance until August of 2014. I sold the house in April of 2014 and because that was a major event and I moved to a different county I was able to obtain a medical policy with a $6,000.00 deductible for $350.00 a month.

In 2015 the policy increased to $375.00 a month and the deductible was raised to $6,500.00. So much for it being affordable. In September of 2015 I could no longer afford this health insurance coverage and I let the policy lapse. Once again my only option is Medicaid for insurance and once again that is something I will not consider.

Not being able to find a job has put me between a rock and a hard place so I don't break the law. Being able to take care of myself and make my own decision relating to healthcare is no longer an option. If I don't get a job the only health insurance I can get is Medicaid and if I find a job, health insurance might not be provided, once again it might not be affordable or Medicaid is the only option. In order to comply with the law I have to get a great job that pays very well, so far that hasn't happened or come even close. The other option is take a government handout and go on Medicaid. Leave it to the politicians to screw everything up and it's just something else to mess with my future.

Obamacare Fines

I'm sure I'm going to have to pay a fine on my 2014 taxes because I did not have health insurance for eight months unless I qualify for an exemption. I will also probably have to pay a fine for the four remaining months of 2015. I was told the fine in 2014 would be high because contrary to popular belief it was not around $95.00 a year it is approximately $95.00 a month for every month that you didn't have health insurance. In 2015 the fine increases to a higher number and once again it is per month without health insurance. I don't remember hearing that on the evening news or in any political speeches.

Once again because of progressive politicians, they destroy your dignity and kick you harder when you're down and there doesn't seem to be a way to get up without losing control of your life. These politicians always think they know what's best for you but as history has shown over and over they always mess things up. They always cause more harm than good and in the process destroy the lives of many people. Fortunately for them most of the time these same politicians are exempt from the laws they pass because they are special and privileged.

I don't want to get political but you get tired of people trying to run your life. I spent years taking care of my parents and because of that decision I suffered an enormous loss in a career and find no hope for the future. So while I am try to rebuild my life the government comes in and kicks me down as I'm trying to get up. I don't want public assistance I want to take care of myself!

Chapter 69

PUTTING YOUR LIFE BACK TOGETHER
Lots Of Sacrifice

Being a caregiver takes a lot of sacrifice and it also means a lot of work. You will lose sleep and won't be able to relax too often. Your always on call and ready if you are needed. Your life will change and a lot of things will go by without you, at least it did for me.

A lot of times I wanted to go to a family event and we were not able because my mom didn't feel well or was unable to go to the bathroom. Many times we were ready to leave and we had to cancel because she couldn't go to the bathroom or for some other reason. We both missed out at watching the grandchildren and great grandchildren grow and change. We missed weddings, birthdays and other events because we were not able to leave.

I lost friends because they would invite me to functions and I always had to decline. They just got tired of asking and hearing me say no. Now they never made an attempt to come up and see me so I didn't lose much sleep because they cut the ties. As far as I was concerned they were just looking for an excuse to walk away. If they were true friends they would have understood my situation. Fortunately I did have friends that knew my situation and never lost contact and are still friends today. They are true friends.

So many things changed and so many things had to be let go so I could take care of my dad and mom. One of the biggest sacrifices I made was not being able to go on with my career. I was in the video industry and even though my business eventually failed I still had contacts that I could have gone to for employment. Over time most of those contacts disappeared and I never could go back. After my mom passed away I tried looking up some of my former associates and I was stunned at how many had passed away and the rest retired or moved on to something else. I guess you can't go back.

I knew when I started taking care of my dad that I would have to make some sacrifices. I knew I wasn't going to be able to go out when I wanted or be able to travel. When I started taking care of my mom it was the same and I knew I had no life of my own. I guess that was the biggest sacrifice of all.

My Own Situation

I know a lot of people have taken care of their parents in the past and I'm sure many of them have documented their lives. There are a lot of books, articles and pamphlets available that also discuss the caregiving process for a parent. Most of these deal with the actual care process such as dispensing medication, changing, transporting , etc. They are very similar to what I have written with the exception that I'm telling the story of my situation. I am not only dealing with the caregiving process but I am also telling of the effects on the caregiver. I took care of both parents for a period of over twenty years both part and full time. Yes, it took its toll on my parents but I want people to understand how much of a toll it took on me and my life.

Because of the decision I made to become a caregiver it changed my life forever and has forced me into some predicaments that I would rather not be in. I'm sure others have been in a similar situation but no one ever wants to talk about it or make it a topic of discussion. This is the story of my own situation over the twenty years of being a caregiver to my parents. It was full of hard work, many choices, lots of expenses, tragedies, laughs, tears and too many challenges to remember. It was a life experience and I want others to know how their life can be changed by making the decision to take care of a parent. Mine changed forever and it is still evolving as I am trying to regroup, restart my life and move on. I think it will be a long process but I know I can deal with it and move on with my life.

Without Bad Luck I Would Have No Luck

I had a friend tell me about twenty-five years ago that if I didn't have bad luck, I wouldn't have any luck. I laughed then but looking back it almost seems true. All through your life you wait for things to slow down or to catch your breath, then all of a sudden something comes at you and turns everything upside down. That's the story of my life.

When my friend told me that statement my business was having its usual ups and downs and it was starting to become a struggle. My dad's illness was starting to take hold and he needed more and more attention. It started with more frequent doctors visits and then more diagnostic tests. It slowed down for a while and then my mom was diagnosed with breast cancer. We dealt with that situation and treatment and then a few months later my father was hit with bladder cancer. Once again we dealt with that diagnosis and treatment. That was the beginning and it was a roller coaster life ever since. My dad's health started to deteriorate more and then he was diagnosed with lung cancer and then that went throughout his body. He now needed full time care and my business was finished.

Within a few months he died and then there was the part time care of my mom as I tried to rebuild my business. No luck because it was hard to start over while I was taking care of her part time. She was still able to walk then and care for herself but she did not like being left alone. That put a damper on trying to drum up any new business so I tried to work from home. The internet was still new and I was just getting things started and once again something came right at me and hit. That was the morning she woke up and could not get out of bed. From then on there was no business and no chance of more income. That lasted until the day she died and is still going on today. I know success, failures, being lucky or unlucky is all part of life but I sure wish things would change in a good way.

Facing The Unknown

Since my mom died in 2013 I have been facing the unknown. All the plans I made failed and I have put myself in a difficult situation. I have tried to find employment and make ends meet but it is very difficult to get back on my feet.

When I sold my house in Tehachapi I new that it was going to be a long time before I would have my own home again, if ever. I knew that once that was sold the money would run out very quickly if I didn't get a job. I was right, the money is gone, I still owe debts for my mom's care and I am living off odd jobs.

I moved in with a cousin for a few months and did odd jobs around her house. When that didn't work out I moved in with another cousin who is just starting the journey of taking care of his father, who lives across the street. I am trying to give him advice and show him what he has to do and what is coming. He is still not aware of what is coming down the road and what it might do to his life.

I have always lived in a house and it is strange to now live in just a room. I am not complaining because at least I have a roof over my head and food in my stomach. I am still trying to find a job and my uncle is helping me with my resume and employment prospects. I never thought I would be in this position because I thought I had everything planned and my life would just move on. It just tells you that plans fall apart and life doesn't follow a straight path.

I started writing this book because I wanted people to know that taking care of a parent is not just about their health. It affects not only their life but it affects yours in ways that you might not ever imagine. I had no clue that I would be facing an unknown future when my time as a caregiver came to an end.

Not Bitter

I have been criticized and ridiculed by so many people that I don't care anymore. Family and friends have tried to shame me because I spent so many years of my life taking care of my parents. I am not bitter or mad at them because they have their opinions and have a right to speak them. I don't agree with those opinions and that is also my right. I had the ability and mindset to take care of my parents and they might not have that inclination. Taking on a huge responsibility like being a caregiver to a parent depends on the individual and if they are willing to make a long term commitment. I made that choice and commitment and in my opinion, did the best job possible. To me the only opinion that really mattered was that of my parents. My dad was always appreciative of all the work that I did for him and the responsibility I had taken on. My mom was the same way and even though somethings were embarrassing or difficult for the both of us we got through them. She was glad that I made the promise to take care of her all the way to the end.

That's why I am not mad or bitter about what others said or continue to say. I made my decision and I have to stand by it because I can't go back and change it. I did what I had to do and they can say whatever they want.

Trying Quick Fixes

Ever since I stopped working I have tried several ways to earn a living while I was taking care of my parents. Some worked for a while and others did not do as well as I hoped. Since I was unable to get a full or part time job while I was caring for my dad and mom I had to try other legal ways to try to supplement our income and cover all the expenses incurred.

One of the things I tried to do was keep my business running while I was taking care of my dad. I was a video system designer so I was still able to do a few small jobs and do a lot of the work at home and by phone. I could mail my designs to the customer and have a technician from one of the companies I dealt with do the installation. This was before the internet so there was no online alternative. This was okay for small jobs and it kept me going for a while. I had to pass on the larger jobs because they required a lot of field work which I was unable to do. When the care of my dad became a full time job it was impossible for me to do even the small jobs because his care took so much time.

After he passed away I tried to resume my old career and I found that my customers had moved on to other individuals and I was unable to get them back. I tried small video jobs and that worked for a while during the time I was taking care of my mom part time. Once again when her care became a full time job I was unable to take any job that required me to leave her at home or to hire someone to care for her while I was gone. There was not enough money to hire a stand in caregiver for me.

I was always interested in the stock market so I started investing with equities and was doing quite well. This helped supplement our income for quite a few years and I earned just enough to help us get by. The problem was that I had very little working capital so I was not able to invest enough to give me better profits. That was my problem all the time. I was descent at picking stocks that increased in value the problem was I could not buy enough shares to make enough profit to get us over the hill.

I did this during the time we lived in Lynwood and when we moved to Tehachapi. Then after my nephew died I lost my touch and I couldn't pick a good stock if I tried. His death really affected me and it took the wind right out of me. We were close and I just had a hard time getting over his death. He always wanted to learn my secret on how I invested and I never taught him. I didn't want him to lose his money and I didn't want him to take the risk. After he died for some reason all I could pick was losers.

As always with any kind of speculation I started losing working capital and finally it meant I was no longer making money. I stopped, took a break to tried to regroup and to regain my confidence and ability. During this time I started studying currency trading and it got my interest. I was fascinated by the way the forex market worked so I took an online course on trading currencies. I failed at this very fast and went back to the drawing board and to studying.

I finally regrouped and tried my hand at penny stocks and I started doing very well. I also started currency trading once again and also did very well. The problem, as before, was that I had very little working capital so the gains were small. Any profit I made I used immediately for living expenses. Once again I started to sputter and the trades started to fail and I was starting to lose money and I finally stopped before I lost too much. The money that was left in my brokerage accounts quickly went to monthly expenses and were completely drained.

I started selling my belongings and items I had left over from my business on the online auction websites. This worked well and brought in some very needed cash. I also started designing hand made items and selling them online and this has never completely taken off. I am still in the process of trying to find items that people will purchase and make a few dollars for me.

What I am trying to say is that when you are unable to work or find a job you try many quick fixes that you hope will get you out of a bind. That's exactly what I did and some actually worked for a while. Even writing this book is an attempt to bring in some extra money while I am telling the story of my experiences of taking care of my parents.

I Have No Life And No Future

Looking back as I'm writing this book I can see that if nothing changes I have no life and the future does not look promising. It has been over two years since my mom passed away and nothing has changed. I am still living day by day and I am unable to find employment. All the money from the sale of the house is gone and I am renting a room from a cousin. I have been able to do a few odd jobs just to get by but I am having an extremely difficult time trying to pay my bills and debts. I had health insurance but it was such a large expenses I had to cancel it in September of 2015.

I have submitted countless job applications online and I have received no responses. I am in my mid fifties and I can't find a job that will support me. Most of my family has walked away from me and basically I am alone.

When I made the decision to take care of my dad and mom I never thought that when they passed away my life would come to this. I always thought that I would be able to get a job and start rebuilding my life when the time came. I thought I had everything planned out and that I was sure that I would be able to take care of myself. Those plans failed to materialize and were very inadequate for my current situation and the future.

I know I made the right decision when I decided to take care of my parents. My problem was that I never realized how long it was going to take and that I would be out of the workforce for so long. My job history from twenty years ago means absolutely nothing in today's world. It is almost like I have never worked in my life. This reality has been hard to accept and it has hit me like a block of cement. I don't know how it's going to play out or what is going to happen to me in the near future.

When you are making the decision to take care of your parent make sure you look long into the future because you have no idea how long you will be a caregiver. You might have a good career today but if you have to put it on hold, there is no guarantee that you can go back. Think long and hard so you don't end up in a situation like mine.

It Took Its Toll

This whole ordeal has taken an extreme toll on my life. Not only the amount of work it took to take care of my parents but also the amount of time that was involved. The prime years of my life were used to take care of my parents and I sacrificed my career, life and future.

While I was caring for my parents I never considered what it was doing to my life because my entire focus was on them. They needed me and I was there to help them. I knew that one day I would be on my own but I always thought that I would have no problem getting back on my feet and taking care of myself.

I am now in my mid fifties and I can't do the things that I did back in my thirties. Employers are looking for younger individuals with college degrees and they are not interested in someone who is in their fifties and has experience. To them experience is expensive and they don't want to pay the price. They can't refuse to interview me because of my age but they can use the reason that I have no recent job history. Not working in the last twenty years wipes out all the experience I had and it is perfectly legal for them to refuse to interview me.

Some will say that I have to start at the bottom and work my way up and that is probably what is going to happen. Some fast food places like hiring older people because they are reliable but unfortunately that won't pay my bills and get me back on my feet. At the reduced schedules most employers are following I would have to work three jobs just to get me current with my bills and pay off the debts of my mom's care.

The amount of expenses to take care of a parent are considerable. Those costs seemed to rise on a monthly basis and if you don't have enough cash flow you use credit. Sooner or later you have to pay that credit back and that is now where I am.

Taking care of my dad and mom took its toll on my body and mind. It was a lot of hard and stressful work but I did it to make sure they received the best possible care. It also took an extreme financial toll on my life and that is one that I am still trying to overcome. It will be a long, bumpy and stressful road ahead.

It's A Different World And It Passed Me By

In the last twenty years the world has changed, morally, politically, economically and technically. Years ago when you wanted to apply for a job you checked the newspaper classified section or you walked door to door. You mailed or left your resume with a company and you were hoping to get a call for an interview. You talked to people you knew to see if they knew what company was hiring and then you called or paid them a visit in the hope of getting an interview. You could go to a location and fill out an application on the spot and hope you got a call back in a few days. Those days are gone and they are never coming back.

Today everything is done online and it is all interconnected. If you apply for a large company it is sent through all their divisions. You have a small area to tell about yourself and a lot of times you are limited to the size of your resume. Some say this is better because it gives you more exposure but they also say due to the fact they have so many applications they have to limit the amount of space available. You never talk or see anyone and you definitely never shake anyone's hand and try to present yourself. Some say this is a safety feature because of all the nuts who can't take rejection and try to cause violence.

Sometimes you get automated messages thanking you for your application and others you get no reply. Everything is done by email and there is almost no personal contact. If you are lucky to get an interview you have very little time to present yourself. They look into social media to see what type of person you are. I have no social media pages and because of this I couldn't fill out an online application once unless I provided a social media link. They look at your credit score to see if you are a good risk for employment. I have no idea why this is part of an application process unless you are trying to work for a bank, law enforcement or other financial institution. I know background checks are required for some jobs and that is understandable. The interesting thing is that information is spread to other divisions so if you fail at one you fail at all. It is almost like you have a personal employment score that companies use among themselves.

This is a whole new world to me and it has definitely passed me by. Years ago if you made a mistake you could always start over, today those mistakes follow you everywhere and are always available to anyone that wants to use the internet. This is a whole new world for me and I consider myself good with technology. The new attitude of job hunting is so different from I remember it is hard to adjust. I can't even get to the interview process because I have no recent job history so I have no idea what I would be in for if I got that far. This change has happened so fast or I was too busy taking care of my parents that I failed to notice. I'll keep trying because I have no choice if I want to survive I just hope it changes soon.

Never Thought I Would End Up This Way

In all my years I never thought I would end up this way. When you are young you have dreams of the future and as you get older you hope things will turn out for the best. As life goes on curves are thrown and you have to change your plans and adapt your future.

This has happened many times to me in the last fifty or so years. Every time I was thrown a curve I adapted and somehow managed to survive and move forward. The biggest challenge I had to tackle to date was to take care of my dad and mom. I jumped in with both feet so I could do the best possible job and care for them the best way I could. I did my job very well and they appreciated what I did for them. My mom survived for over thirteen years in a condition that a lot of people simply would have given up. She enjoyed her life and I feel that I was a major reason why she lived for a long time.

When her end was coming close I knew that I was going to have a problem but I thought it would be just a simple challenge that I would easily overcome. I couldn't have been more wrong because it was not a simple challenge it has become a huge mountain that I have just started climbing. I'm still near the bottom looking to the top and trying to figure out how I will get to the apex.

I never thought I would ever be in this type of a situation. One of the reasons I refinanced our house was so that this type of a situation wouldn't happen and that I could easily move on with my life. Once again another plan that failed. There is nothing left and it doesn't look like anything is going to happen soon. I am facing the unknown and I never thought I would have to.

I Am Very Direct, Like Me Or Hate Me, I Stand On Principle

I am a hard man and I don't get emotional so over the years I have grown a thick skin. People have been criticizing me for as long as I can remember so I don't let it get to me. If I let the criticism get to me that means my emotions are taking control and then I can't make good decisions. I needed this type of attitude when I was taking care of my parents because if I got emotional every time I was criticized I couldn't take care of my parents properly because I wouldn't be thinking straight.

I say things as they are and I don't care if you don't like to hear the truth. Somethings need to be said and it makes no sense not to say them directly and get them out in the open. When you speak the truth people tend to become defensive and try to deflect anything you say. I needed to be blunt and direct because I didn't have time to fool around when I was taking care of my parents. They needed my attention and therefore I didn't have time to play games. I came to the point and said what I meant so I could move forward.

Since I was so direct and blunt this made a lot of friends and family either like me or hate me which made them take sides. A few took my parents and my side but unfortunately a lot took a different side that liked to criticize everything that I did. Once again it made no difference to me because I was not interested in what they had to say. My only interest was the care of my parents and therefore I listened to what they said. I backed them up every step of the way and made sure I followed through with all their wishes. This attitude caused a lot of turmoil with some friends and family members but once again it was not important to me or my parents. Some sooner or later changed their attitudes when they saw how my mom was cared for and how well she was enjoying her life. Others came back and then left again after my mom passed away because for some reason they didn't want to be around me. I guess it is because I have a strong will and I don't put up with any of their crap or criticism.

I am a strong willed person who stands on principle and tries to do what is right. Some say I like to control the situation and that is true when it came to the care of my parents. I did what the doctors recommended as well as what my parents wanted. If that is controlling so be it because I did what I was told to do. I made promises to my parents and I did my best to keep them and if that meant some would become upset that was not my concern. I did what I was asked to do. I stood on principle, tried to do what was right and kept my promises. If that has torqued friends and family and is preventing them from accepting me today, that's just the way it will be and is part of life.

Friends Using You Until You Can No Longer Help Them

I lost some friends years ago because I was taking care of my mom. I did not have time to keep in contact with them and they just dropped me. One got upset because I didn't have time to spend with them and that I always had to pass whenever they wanted to go out. I lost another friend because I didn't call them and they just pushed me off to the side. The interesting thing with both of these friends was that they wanted me to call or contact them but they never contacted me. I told both of them once that it was a two way street, I contact you and you can contact me, but it fell on deaf years. It is almost like these friends wanted me around as long as I could help them out and I did help them out many times over the years of our friendship. Once I could no longer help them or be used by them they dropped me.

I am fortunate because I still have some wonderful friends that do contact me and I also contact them. They understood how much work it was to take care of my mom and they stood by me through all of it. They still keep in touch and check to see how I'm doing and I check in with them for the same reason. We don't get together as much as I would like because we live a distance apart but when we do visit it make it more enjoyable.

Once again a lot of people don't know how hard it is to be a caregiver. Some say they do but these are the one's that usually hire someone to take care of their parents or have them in a care facility. Their way of caring is visiting them once in a while or getting them something to eat or drink. They have no idea how hard it is to clean, change, lift and do everything that your parent needs. If you have friends and you are starting to care for a parent be prepared to lose some because they won't understand what you are trying to do and how you don't have time for them. This is when you find out who are your true friends.

I Had Plans And They Failed To Materialize

I never had a chance to think about what I was going to do after my mom passed away because I was always too busy. I thought that I would be secure and have enough money put away so I could get by until I was able to find a job. I had plans to move on with my life and try to rebuild my career.

After my mom died I realized that I had nothing to live on and that I was basically penniless. All the money was gone and there was no cash available for day to day living. I had assets but those would be hard and time consuming to turn into cash. I did not even have enough for the funeral service because all the money I had went for the care of my mom. My sisters paid for the funeral service and loaned me some money to get by but it was not enough to cover the bills. I put my house up for sale in the hope that I could get out of debt. It didn't sell and the bills kept piling up. I sold some belongings online and at garage sales but once again it was a drop in the bucket compared to the debts. I started doing odd jobs for family members and once again that helped but didn't cover the expenses. Finally the house sold and I was able to pay down some of the debt and try to move along with my life.

Any plans I had were shattered and I knew they would never materialize. I had no home and I was living in a ten by ten room at a cousin's house. It was almost like being in a cell and it was miserable. I lost control of my life and I couldn't see any way out of it. I kept trying to get a job but I could not get over the hurdle of not having a recent job history. I would have been happy to get a response, even if it was "no," but I didn't get any response. My only hope was to try selling hand made wood items on one of the online sites. I wanted to try to sell quilt racks but I had no place where I could make them. I had no home so I had no place to make the items.

I moved in with another cousin who was just staring to take care of his dad part time. He wanted me nearby so I could give him advice on taking care of his dad and help if necessary. His father had a house in another state and he wanted to get it ready to sell. I went and supervised the house renovation and dealt with the contractors and handymen. This gave me something to do but unfortunately it left me no time to make my quilt racks. The house project lasted from January to October of 2015.

When I had some down time in the evening I started writing this book in the hope that I could help others by describing my ordeal and experience. A lot of people think that taking care of a parent is just feeding them and turning on the television to give them something to watch. I am writing this book to tell you that there is a lot more to it and it will affect your life in ways you never imagined.

I am an example of someone who jumped in with both feet to take care of his parents. I never knew what it entailed or how it would affect my life and future. After I was done taking care of my parents I found out the hard way that my life would never be the same and it was extremely hard to get it back on track. I had plans and they failed to materialize and it became just another disappointment in my life.

I Have A Purpose, My Life Doesn't End This Way

I know that my life has a purpose and I don't believe that this is how I will end. I took care of my parents for over twenty years and I don't think that all that work was done just so I could fade away after they passed away. I know your life is what you make it and I am not ready to quit and give up.

I had a decent career as a video system designer and I tried my hand at many things. I have been called a "jack of all trades" and of course "expert of none" also comes along with that description. I did whatever I had to do because we could not afford to hire someone to do it. If a repair needed to be done, I did it. If I didn't know anything about it I would research it as much as I could. No matter how difficult it was I learned as much as I could before I actually did the repair. Most of the time I was successful and a few times I was not. Today with the internet you can look up anything and try to learn how to do it. Well, this was before the internet exploded so I had to learn things the old way, going to the library, asking others questions or trial and error.

I did what I had to do so I could take care of my parents and so we could move along with our lives. I had to do things that I thought I would never do and I ended up having to do them over and over. Washing my parents, dressing them, changing wound dressings and changing diapers was a small part of what I had to do.

I made enormous sacrifices in my life to take care of my parents. I wouldn't start a relationship because I felt I couldn't devout all my time to it. I let some very nice people get away and I never can get them back. I lost contact with some family and friends because I didn't have time to spend with them or keep in touch.

I lost a lot but I am not mad or bitter. I did what I had to do and I am proud of the decision I made to take care of my parents. I just don't think that my life is at its end and that I have nothing left to say or give. My life does have a purpose and it might be telling others my story. I'm sure that a lot of people are starting to go what I went through and have no idea what they are in for. Maybe by me telling my story I can help them avoid some of the pitfalls and challenges that I had to face. Hopefully in some situations their outcome can be better that what I had to deal with. If I can help others avoid some obstacles while they are caring for their parents means I still have something to give.

Chapter 70

MOVING ON

Still Fighting

Over two years after my mom passed away I am still fighting the past and criticism. It seems I still have to defend myself about the decision I made to take care of my parents. From the very beginning I never got any moral support when I started taking care of my dad. I did get physical support when I needed it but that only lasted for the visit. When I started caring for my mom the same thing happened and I never got any moral support for the task I had taken on. It was always you need to hire someone to help or take care of her. It didn't matter that was not what my mom wanted because it was what they wanted.

I still hear that I should have put her in a care facility so I could have gone on with my life. This is crazy talk because my mom wanted to stay at home and she never would have lasted in a care facility. For the amount of care she needed, I never could have afforded someone to do the day to day routines. That would have used what my mom received from her survivor benefit and what I would have been able to take home from a job. I still would be in the same position I find myself in now. There would be nothing left and I would have broken a promise to my dad.

Sure I might have a decent job today and my future could be normal but what toll would have been taken on my mom. Her quality of life could have been affected and she probably would have never had the chance to interact with her great grandchildren. There is no way to know what would have happened or what could have happened if I had made a different decision. There is no reason for me to have to keep defending my decision from over twenty years ago. When I made my decision I never knew or thought that there would be so much conflict and animosity. What's done is done and it is time to look toward the future and do my best to get my life back on track.

Finally Said Enough

After all the years of taking care of my parents and hearing about all I was doing wrong or what I should have done with my life I finally had enough. I finally told everybody that I made a decision and followed through with it to the end. Now that it is over I am only going to think about my future and how I am going to put my life back together. I don't care what they say about the past or what they want me to do for the future. It is my life and I am going to handle it in my own way.

This is the first time in my life that I have no one to worry about except myself. Anything I do affects only me and I won't be held responsible for anyone else. It's a strange feeling but that is where I am at and I need to deal with it.

I need to find a job that can pay off my debts, keep me healthy and allow me to try to get my own place. I need to be able to afford health insurance so I can follow the law and also protect myself. This is the path that I am on and I hope soon that the potholes will disappear.

Family and friends can continue to talk until they are blue in the face and it means absolutely nothing to me. I can't change the past or my decision just to make them happy. I still know I made the right decision when I decided to take care of my parents and whatever they say can't change that fact. I just need to move forward and rebuild my life.

A Failure

I have been called a failure by a few people because I took care of others instead of myself. They have also said that I was lazy and was too stubborn to work for others and could not be told what to do. Others have said that I was unemployable because I worked for myself for so long and I would have a hard time taking orders from someone else, especially from someone younger. Some even went so far as to say that I always want control and I could never work for anyone.

These comments have been from the same people that criticized me from the beginning because I chose to take care of my parents. What they don't understand is how much work was involved in caring for my parents and how many sacrifices I made in the process. Once again they have their opinions but to go as far as being called a failure I think that is a little harsh and uncalled for. They are looking at my current situation and feel if I had made a different decision I would not be in my current unemployed situation. There is no way to go back and there is also no way of knowing if I made a different decision if I would be in a different situation today.

Yes, I am nervous about working for someone else because I have been out of the workforce for so many years. Yes, I was self employed and I gave instructions to people that worked for me. It will be hard to take orders from someone else. Once again a lot of prospective bosses will be younger than me and have less experience so it could be difficult following instructions if I feel they are wrong. If I want to survive I have no choice but to swallow my pride, shut up and do what I am told if I find employment. The only other option is try to do something on my own and live off my own services, such as selling hand made products online. Going on government assistance is not an option and I would not feel comfortable because I am still able to work. I guess I like having control because I took care of my parents for so long and I controlled a lot of situations. But what of people don't know is that my parents controlled me all the way to just before they died. Yes, I helped them in their daily needs but they controlled every aspect of my life because they needed help with their everyday routines. My mom could not survive unless I was around and helped her with her daily life. I controlled the situations to make sure she was well cared for and safe but she decided what I did on a daily basis. If she wanted to go out or even stay in bed it was her choice and my job was to comply with her wishes.

People can call me anything because that might be their opinion and they have the right to voice it. I also have the right to voice my opinion and explanation because I have a right to defend myself. One thing is perfectly clear in the time I cared for my parents was that they were well taken care of and had a good quality of life all the way to the end. The only one who's life was destroyed was mine and now I am in the process of trying to rebuild it. If that is failure, so be it but I can't be concerned with any of those comments. I am too busy trying to rebuild my life so I can have a less stressful future and no longer have to face the unknown.

Some Say My Life Is Messed Up

Now that both of my parents are gone some say that I have messed up my life. They say that I should never have taken care of my parents and that I should have thought of myself. They also believe that is my fault and I should have hired someone to take care of my parents or put them into a care facility.

When I hear this reaction or statement I just pass it off because these people don't know what they are talking about. They don't know what it means to make and keep a promise because they are too shallow in their own lives. Some are embarrassed because they didn't have the courage to make this type of a decision so it is easier to criticize someone that has made the decision.

They can say whatever they want and it means nothing to me. I did what I set out to do and know I have to deal with the situation and the consequences. Trying to change the past will not help me with the future and constantly being told that I made the wrong decision will not change what has happened.

Is my life messed up? Yes, if you mean that I can't find a job and I am living in a small room at a cousins house. Is this a set back? Yes, but things will change and I will get my life back on track. Did I ever think I would be in this type of a situation? No, and it is new territory for me so I have to deal with it. Has family and friends left me because they think that I am a loser? Yes, some have and that is their choice and I am not going to try to explain my decisions over and over to them. Is my life over and this is the way it will be? No, because I am doing everything I can to try to get my life on track.

I don't listen when people say that I messed up my life because it is not true. I kept the promises I made to my dad and mom and it is about integrity and doing what was right. I am not giving up because I still have a lot to give and teach to anyone who wants to listen. I will find a way to move forward and get my life back and be self supporting once again. Just because I have hit a rough patch does not mean my life is messed up or over because I have a lot left and I can move forward and get back on track.

I Probably Hurt Myself More By Writing This Book

I have always been a private person and never opened up to anyone about my personal problems. In this day of social media where everybody tell others about what they ate or where they are going I always valued my privacy and am not interested in joining. On the other hand I do have a story to tell about how I cared for my parents and how it affected my life.

I experienced what a lot of people have done before and what a lot of others will do in the future. By telling my story I might be able to help someone avoid the problems that I experienced and help them with their future. If anything I can give them a little advice on what to avoid so they can plan ahead. In telling this story I have opened myself in a way that I never thought possible. In order to tell the story properly I had to write what the experience did to my parents and what it did to me. I had to talk about the past, present and future.

In doing so this has left me exposed and anyone reading this book will know a lot about me and my family. As in one of the job applications I tried to fill out it required a social media address. I'm sure they wanted this information so they could look at the applicants background. I don't have a social media address so I could not complete the application. Now if someone wants to find out about me all they have to do is read this book to see what type of person I am. This can hurt or help me depending on the situation. Some might think that I'm a loser because I waisted my life taking care of my parents and others might think it was a noble cause.

I didn't write this book to open my life to ridicule or praise. I wrote it to try to help others in the care of their parents so that they know how much work is involved and how much is at stake in their life. I didn't try to hurt myself or others in the telling of this story. In the process I have been able to open up and relive everything that I have done during this time. It was an eye opening experience for me because it made me remember, smile, laugh and cry. It was amazing to relive how much I had to do and how hard it was to take care of my parents. Then there are all the other influences that happened during this time that made me face many challenges. There was tragedy and some very difficult times that I had to deal with and was able to get through them. I just hope that I will be able to get thought one of the biggest challenges I am facing and that is getting along with the rest of my life.

Chapter 71

THANKLESS BUT REWARDING JOB

Somethings Are Different, Somethings Never Change

Looking back over the years I took care of my parents everyday was a learning experience. Caregiving is changing with the times and also with the advances in medicine. Comparing what I did over the years to what I see today all I can say is somethings are different and somethings never change.

One thing that never changes is that you are caring for your parent and you try to do the best job possible. Also you are responsible for their care and safety, which is something that will never change. Another item that will always be part of the caregiving experience is that you will always be learning.

There have been a lot of changes over the years since I started taking care of my parents. One of the biggest changes is the smartphone and the internet which can make a lot of tasks much easier. Just press a few buttons or swipe your finger and all kinds of information is instantly available. You can reorder prescriptions, make appointments and get test results at any time. You can use these smartphones to keep eyes on your parent or they can use them to summon you. They have cameras and recorders that you can use to record demonstrations so you can view over and over. Video's of different procedures are available whenever you need them. It is amazing how much information is now available. Gone are the days of waiting and wondering what you will have to do.

Another item that is changing is how Medicare and supplement insurance approves or denies procedures. Under Obamacare coverage options have changed and nobody knows how that will affect the healthcare system. Physicians are under new directives pertaining to care and its cost.

A lot of things that I had to deal with are no longer available and the way I handled certain situations could be considered interfering.

With all that is going on, once again you need doctors that are willing to work with you and be your partner while you are taking care of your parent. Together you can find out what is the best way to maneuver under the new healthcare system and rules. Even though somethings are changing, taking care of your parent the best you possibly can is not one of them.

Put Yourself In Their Shoes

One of the things you need to do while you are taking care of a parent is put yourself in their shoes. Ask yourself if you were in their situation what would you do, how would you feel and how would you want to be treated? This can go a long way in how you care for them and also make it a little easier for you.

If you put yourself in their shoes you pretty much know what to do. No one knows your parent better than you so you have an advantage of how they feel and what they want. You know all their quirks and wants and it can help you in the process of taking care of them.

I knew my dad and mom like a book. I knew their likes and dislikes. What they liked to eat, where they liked to go, what they like to watch, etc. So when they needed something I knew what to do without asking them. As time went on it was routine for me to do what they needed. I knew how they felt around people and who to avoid. I knew what made them uncomfortable and what they enjoyed.

My mom was immobile but it didn't stop her from enjoying herself. Just because she couldn't walk and get around by herself didn't mean she couldn't enjoy life. It was a lot of work for me but that is what it means to be a caregiver. She wanted to go to the store we went to the store. She wanted to visit the grandchildren we went for a drive and saw them. She wanted people over for dinner they came and had dinner. She wanted to go out for ice cream we went out for ice cream.

If it made her happy I did it because if I was in her shoes I would want to do the same. It required a lot of lifting, changing and driving but it gave her a better quality of life. No one wants to waste away and watch life pass them by, I know I don't.

When I'm Gone

Over the years many people told me that I was doing the right thing and that I cared very much for my parents. Others had no opinion and still some said I was making a big mistake. It was nice to get compliments and I really didn't listen to the criticism. The one thing I do know is that when I am gone no one will care about what I have done. All the sacrifices I made and how it affected my life will not mean a damn thing to any family or friends. I will be forgotten and all that I did will also be forgotten.

My father use to tell me that when he died I would have to go to the union hall to get pall bearers for his funeral. He said nobody would care and there would be nobody at his funeral. I told him many times that there would be a lot of people at his funeral and he always doubted me. He was wrong and when we had his funeral there were quite a few people in attendance. Some knew him and others knew my sisters and myself. In fact no one from the union came to the service. His pall bearers were nephews and his two grandsons. It was a very nice service and I kept a promise to him

When my mom died her funeral was also attended by family and friends. This time most of the people knew her because of the work I did at my old high school and she was always around the campus. There were also friends of my sisters and I and a lot of them also knew our mom. My niece, her granddaughter, made the eulogy along with her children as she remembered her grandmother and their great grandmother. It was very personal and it was wonderful. It was a nice service and a proper remembrance of my mom's life.

Both my parents had memorable funeral services that remembered their lives and consoled the family. I always told them that they would always be remembered after they were gone because they affected so many lives and had children, grandchildren and great grandchildren. The interesting thing is that making and keeping that promise to them left me with nobody. I never married or had children. I am alone. When I die there will be no one there because I have nobody. Whoever gets stuck making my funeral arrangements can't go to the union hall for pall bearers because I was not part of a union or any other group. I will be lucky if they can find a church and priest to do the service. I do have a cemetery plot but that's the last step. A lot has to be done before I can be put in the ground. I do have the arrangements made but I haven't contacted anyone about who will handle my final journey. I have two nieces and a nephew, soon one of them might get stuck with the job. Since the life insurance is gone, they will have to sell everything that I have left to pay for the funeral. That means I'll be in storage for quite a while before they can lay me to rest.

I spent all my time taking care of my dad and mom that I never thought of myself. When I'm gone no one will be there to remember me and I will be just a forgotten person. This is just the final fact in the decision to take care of my parents.

Love And Care

There are two things that are always at the center of caring for a parent. Love and care are the words that best describe what you are doing. You love them so much that you are willing to sacrifice to care for them. You are making a life changing commitment because you love your parent and you want to make sure they receive the care they need.

Looking back in my own situation I didn't realize this until I started taking care of my dad full time. At first it was nothing to take him to the doctors or medical facilities. Talking to his doctors and listening to their diagnosis and advice was all part of the normal routine and what a son or daughter would normally do for their elderly parent. It hit me when I started taking care of him full time and he relied on me for everything to survive. That was a great responsibility and I realized I did it because I loved him and I wanted him to stay around for a long time.

I had a good relationship with my father and he taught me almost everything I know. He was mechanical and he liked to make things. From an early age I can remember doing things with him when he would make something. I had my own toolbox when I was four years old and he encourage me to tinker. I remember he was building a brick barbecue in the backyard and I wanted to help. I was about five years old and he let me mix the cement with a hoe on the ground. I was so proud and I tried my best. It was a lot of work and I had a hard time pulling the hoe with the wet concrete. He stood there and encouraged me every step of the way. The next door neighbor was watching and he told my dad that I was learning and it was something I wouldn't forget. He was right and I still can see that day. I learned everything from my dad and he even taught me construction. He let me help him remodel the house and I was like a sponge and learned everything I could. Even the city building inspector was impressed with what I was learning and what I was doing. My dad told him, "I want him to know how to build a house not because he has to but so he can if he wants to." I never forgot that.

When I grew up I took all the knowledge I learned from him and put it to use with my business. Over my career I built some very unique video systems for companies and government agencies and they were all accomplished with the talents my dad taught me. I took him to some of the jobs I built and he was amazed at some the systems I put together and who the customers were that purchased them. It was nice to see his reaction because he was the reason I was able to build them.

I also had a great relationship with my mom. She was sports minded and I wasn't but she still tried to teach me baseball and I was absolutely horrible. She encouraged me through school but I never got above being an average student. My sisters on the other hand were "A" students and she tried to get me motivated by saying, "Your sister didn't get B's." I tried but not much stuck and I just got by in school. She never gave up and tried to make me a better student. My response was always, "I'm not smart but I can fix anything," and she was okay with that.

When I had my business she was always supportive of what I was doing and encouraged me on every project I worked on. I also brought her to some of the job sites and she was also amazed at how I put theses complicated systems together. I use to joke with her saying, "Not bad for someone who got B's, C's and D's in school." She would always laugh and say, "But you sisters still got A's" She just couldn't let that got and I loved her for it.

When they got sick I had no problem stepping in and taking care of them. I had no family of my own and therefore I had no responsibilities. I figured it was my job because my sisters were married and had families of their own. It was a simple decision to make and I don't regret it one bit. Yes, love and care was part of the decision. They loved and cared for me when I relied on them. Now it was my turn to show love and care when they needed me.

Quality Of Life

An important issue while being a caregiver is maintaining a certain quality of life for your parent. You want them to enjoy themselves and be happy even though they are ill and need someone to take care of them. You try to let them do as much as possible for themselves and let them have a purpose.

With my dad's illness he failed fast and his quality of life diminished within six months. He went from doing everything for himself to a short time of needing help to passing away. My mom went from taking care of herself to needing some help to needing full time care to living a long life to failing and then passing away. This took a period of eighteen years. During that time I tried to maintain her quality of life to the point that the only difference was she couldn't walk.

Once my mom could no longer walk and needed full time care I wanted her to still enjoy her life. That meant I became her arms and legs while she maintained her mind. She wanted to go somewhere, I took her and if she wanted to visit someone, she did. There was no reason to prevent her from doing her usual routines. The only time I would say no was if she had a cold or the person she wanted to visit was sick. We would wait until they recovered because I didn't want my mom to catch anything.

She ate well and enjoyed every bite, she wanted her favorite foods and I prepared them. She enjoyed her sweets and anything else that tasted good. She wanted to see the grandchildren and great grandchildren and they would visit often. She wanted to keep practicing her faith and she was able to do it. She wanted to play games and watch baseball and she did. I made her participate in her care and do a lot of things herself if she could. She helped with the care of the house and chores. She contributed to our daily lives and it helped her live longer because she was not treated as useless.

When her health had issues I made sure she would fight to live another day. Some would tell me that her quality of life wasn't much and I would get bitter and then I would tell them, "Look at her, she's enjoying herself." Sometimes they would disagree because she wasn't doing what they wanted. I didn't care what they wanted my mom was happy and that's all that mattered. She had hope and always looked forward to tomorrow, next week, next month and next year. This worked for over eighteen years and her quality of life never suffered because she was surrounded by people that loved her.

I've Done It

When I hear someone say that they could never take care of a parent because it is so much hard work I laugh and also get offended. They make it sound like it is a chore and that it is not worth the trouble because it will interfere with their lives. Yes, they are right and it does interfere with your life but it can be done and I know because I have done it.

My situation was not unique because a lot of people are taking care of a parent or parents. My parents didn't have conditions that affected their mind or that needed special medical equipment to keep them alive. My parents needed me to survive the everyday routine of life. I did do some strange procedures and I had to do a lot of things that I never thought I would ever have to do, like change an adult diaper. Unfortunately for me it was what was necessary to help my mom continue to live and to maintain her quality of life. In no time these procedures became routine and I never looked back or had a problem.

I never thought I was going to have to do things like this when I got older but things happen. We are all dealt different situations and conditions and we have to deal with them everyday of our life. To say you won't do it is not a good answer because you will not know how you will handle the situation until it is dropped in front of you. I know people can do things they never imagined because I have done it. Changing an adult diaper is easy and changing a bed wound dressing is challenging but I got through it and was able to do it over and over. Even the task of lifting my mom was hard at first but I got through it and adapted to make it easier for her and me. If someone would have told me when I was in my teens that I would become the caregiver of my parents I probably would have said, "Not me." Well it was me and I can proudly say, "I've done it."

Chapter 72
KEPT DIGNITY AND PROMISES
Do It All Over Again

It's been over two years since my mom passed away and over twenty years since my father died. With all that has happened in these years I started to reflect on how I handled both their situations. Looking back over all those years I wondered if I did the right thing.

The answer to that is a definite, "Yes." I have absolutely no regrets with how I handled their care under our circumstances. Sure somethings could have been done differently but in the end it would have made no difference in the care they received.

I made the decision to take care of them and I followed through on that promise. Yes, I did sacrifice a lot in the process but it was what was best for them to get the proper care. They did not have long term care insurance and they also did not have the money for any level of assisted care living. It was up to me and I did the best job that I could.

I never questioned if I made the right decision and I never looked back while I was taking care of them. I gave them the best care I could and made sure that the quality of their life was the best they could receive. I would definitely do it all over again because it was the right thing to do.

Conclusion

I started taking care of my dad in 1993 and it became a full time job in 1994. He passed away in 1995. After this I took care of my mom part time because she was still able to care for herself but did not drive and did not like to be left alone. She was always in an extreme amount of pain due to scoliosis and curvature of the spine. In 1999 she woke up one morning and could no longer stand or walk. From that day in September 1999 I became her caregiver and started taking care of her full time until she passed away in April of 2013.

The entire experience consumed my entire live and exhausted all my funds. I learned and had to do things I never dreamed I would have to do. I saw things that I never wanted to see but learned very fast because it was all part of life. I dealt with many medical professionals and facilities, some great and some just okay. I had to dispense all kinds of medication and had to make sure it was all done properly and did not cause any harm. It was all a great responsibility, a lot of work and caused a lot of stress.

I was criticized for my decisions by outsiders and family members for reasons to this day I have absolutely no idea. I lost touch with friends because I had a responsibility to take care of my parents. I have other friends that were supportive and understood what I was doing and are still around today. My sisters helped whenever they could even though they were not always available. I had nieces and nephews that gave us a lot of joy in visiting and making my dad and mom's day brighter.

I had to deal with tragedies and tell my mom one of the most horrible things a grandmother would ever hear, the loss of a grandson. I had to deal with sicknesses and death all while I was taking care of my mom and dad. I had to deal with my injuries and illnesses while I was caring for both of them.

My life changed forever when I became a caregiver. My entire world changed and I think for the better. I took responsibility for the care of my parents so others could go on with their lives. I wrote this book to let others know what they might be coming into when they decide to take care of a parent. There are all types of situations and anything can happen when you decide to take care of a parent. I made that decision, twice, and I would do it all over again in a heartbeat because I made the right one.

Final Thoughts

I started writing this book in 2014 because I felt that I had a good story to tell. I took care of my parents for over twenty years and I wanted people to understand how much work it was and how it affected my life. A lot of books have been written about caring for a parent but they usually cover only the care itself and never talk about the consequences of the decision to become a caregiver. My story talks about what needs to be done to care for a parent part and full time as well as how it affects your life and your future.

I have said throughout this book that every person is different and every situation is unique so it is necessary to gather as much information as you can. Deciding to care for a parent is a major decision that will affect their life as well as yours. In my case is changed my life and it will never be the same. I thought I planned everything out and I knew how I would be able to move forward with my life after my parents passed away. I cared for my parents for so many years that the world had changed and it basically passed me by. The career and skills that I once had were no longer needed when I tried to get back into the workforce. The entire employment process had changed with the advancement of the internet. I could not find employment because I no longer had a verifiable job history.

I had to sell my assets and went through all my money in the process of trying to survive. It has been over two years since my mom passed away and I am still looking for employment. The good news is that I am still standing and trying to rebuild my life. I haven't given up and I am trying to get back on track. This was a position I never thought I would be in and had no plans on how to rectify it. It happened and now I have to deal with it.

I hope that by reading this book you have learned from my successes and mistakes and try to plan your future when you decide to care for a parent. It is a major decision that you will be making and you need to know that there are some challenges and pitfalls ahead. I have only scratched the surface because you will encounter things that I never had to deal with and you will learn how to overcome them. It is all part of the caregiving experience.

I was lucky that my parents still had their memories for a long time and it made it easier to care for them. I was also fortunate that they backed me up in everything I did because they knew I was doing what was best for them. I knew from the start that caring for my parents was going to be a lot of work and that it would change my life. Even though things did not work out as I hoped after they passed away it was still the best decision I ever made because I kept my promises to my parents and I kept my dignity in the process.

Made in the USA
San Bernardino, CA
10 January 2017